San Diego Christian College
2100 Greenfield Drive
El Cajon, CA 92019

THE ANNALS OF
IMPERIAL ROME

TACITUS
THE ANNALS OF
IMPERIAL ROME

TRANSLATED
WITH AN INTRODUCTION BY
MICHAEL GRANT

Revised Edition

DORSET PRESS

This translation first published 1956
Reprinted with revisions 1959
Reprinted 1961, 1962, 1964, 1966, 1968
Revised edition 1971
Reprinted 1972
Reprinted with revisions 1973
Reprinted with revisions 1975
Reprinted 1975, 1976
Reprinted with revisions 1977
Reprinted 1978, 1979, 1980

———

———

1984, DORSET PRESS
This edition published by Dorset
Press, a division of Marboro Books Corp.,
by arrangement with Penguin Books, Ltd.

ISBN 0-88029-024-2

CONTENTS

*

LIST OF MAPS

TRANSLATOR'S INTRODUCTION

★

I. THE LIFE AND WORKS OF TACITUS

THE powerful personality of Cornelius Tacitus has survived in his writings, but we know extremely little of his life or his origin. Indeed, we are not even sure whether the first of his three names was Publius or Gaius. His family probably came from the south of France or from northern Italy (Cisalpine Gaul). If so, Tacitus – like other leading Latin writers – may not have been of wholly Italian ancestry. But we have no conclusive evidence. His father *may* have been an imperial agent at Trier or at Cologne, and paymaster-general for the armies on the Rhine; but again we are not certain.

At all events, Tacitus was born in about A.D. 56 or 57 (when Nero was emperor),[1] and was a member of the provincial upper class who found new prospects of careers open to them under the imperial regime. He lived and worked until the end of the emperor Trajan's reign (A.D. 98–117), and probably for some years into the reign of Hadrian (117–138). Much of the official career of Tacitus as a senator took place in a time of unhappiness and even terror for high officials, the black years of Domitian (A.D. 81–96). But Tacitus survived to enjoy the highest metropolitan post, the consulship, in A.D. 97 (during the short reign of Nerva, 96–8), and the governorship of the great province of western Anatolia ('Asia') – the climax of a senator's career – some fifteen years later.

He had received a careful Roman education. In his day that meant, particularly, an elaborate series of exercises in different kinds of public speaking, studied in the remarkable detail which we learn about from the treatises of Cicero and Quintilian; for advocacy in the courts was traditionally the most respected civil career. As a young man, Tacitus evidently studied at Rome with the leading orators of the day. He himself became one of the best known speakers of his time, and a life-

1. A list of Roman emperors will be found at the end of the book.

long interest in oratory emerges clearly from his writings.[1] Indeed, one of them – if, as is highly probable, Tacitus is its author – deals explicitly with the subject. This is the *Dialogue on Orators*, in which four historical characters, two lawyers and two literary men, very interestingly discuss the claims of oratory against those of literature, and the reasons why eloquence had declined during the century and more that had elapsed since Cicero's death. One reason of course – as is pointed out – was that this sort of impassioned disputation had much less part to play under emperors than amid the clashes of the outgoing Republic.

The *Dialogue* is dedicated to a consul of A.D. 102, and is likely to have been published then or soon after. Meanwhile, however, Tacitus had already begun to make it clear to the world that, even if oratory could never achieve its past glories again, the same was by no means true of history. The monographs with which he initiated his career as historian, the *Agricola* and *Germania*, were published within a short time of one another in *c.* A.D. 98. The *Agricola* to some extent recalls a familiar Greek tradition – that of the semi-biographical, moral eulogy of a personage;[2] here the personage is his own father-in-law. But Tacitus, giving the work an original structure of its own, inserts history and includes descriptive material about Britain. The *Germania* is an ethnographical study of Central Europe. Its purpose is not completely understood. But it does seem to contain recurrent moral contrasts, or implied contrasts, between the decadence of Rome and the crude vigour of the teeming, and potentially threatening, peoples beyond the Rhine. And indeed, eventually, these Germanic peoples played a large part in the eclipse of the Roman Empire in the West. But that was not until many years later.

Next followed Tacitus' two principal historical works. They told the story of the Roman emperors from A.D. 14 to 96. The *Histories*, which cover the later part of this epoch (from the death of Nero in A.D. 68), were written first. We have about a third of them, describing the terrible civil wars with which the period began.[3] Tacitus' last and

1. For the special relation between Roman oratory and history, see also below, p. 12.

2. This type of literature goes back at least as far as the *Evagoras* of Isocrates and the *Agesilaus* of Xenophon in the fourth century B.C.

3. For English translations of Tacitus' works see p. 437.

greatest creation was his *Annals*, translated in this book. The *Annals* tell of the Julio-Claudian emperors from just before the death of Augustus (A.D. 14) to the death of Nero. That is to say, they deal with the reigns of Tiberius, Gaius (Caligula), Claudius, and Nero. Not everything has survived; we lack more than two years of Tiberius, the whole of the short reign of Gaius, half of the reign of Claudius, and the last two years of Nero. We have lost some of the highlights. But we have kept forty years out of fifty-four; by far the greater part of the *Annals* has come down to us.

The period with which they deal is still of infinite significance. For the first and last time in world history, the entire Mediterranean region belonged to the same unit. The Roman Republic had begun to acquire overseas territories in the third century B.C. From its first two Punic Wars against Semitic Carthage (264–201) Rome had emerged as the strongest Mediterranean power; and it spent the next 150 years extending its dominion in Europe, Asia, and Africa. The other great empire of the world at this time, China of the Han dynasty, was too far away for any rivalry to occur. Besides, they were separated – and, later, for commercial reasons, jealously separated – by Parthia. That loose feudal empire, stretching from the Euphrates to the Hindu Kush, receives frequent attention in the pages of Tacitus. For its rulers were the only foreign monarchs with whom Rome had to compete on anything like equal terms; and Rome had received a shock when its armies were heavily defeated by Parthian cavalry at Carrhae (Haran) in 53 B.C.

But this was only one of many problems in the century preceding the period considered by Tacitus. It had already, in that last century before our era, become clear that in various ways Rome's small-town Republican constitution was – for all its famous 'balance' between the classes, stressed by the Greek historian Polybius – unfitted for imperial responsibilities. The solution which imposed itself was the autocracy of the dictators Sulla (81–79 B.C.) and Julius Caesar (48–44 B.C.). This autocracy was stabilized by Augustus, forcibly but with decorous façade, as the Principate; and his Roman peace and reorganization enormously increased the prosperity of his vast realms. The present book begins at the end of his long life, and tells us of the able and bizarre men who took on this immense task from him, and continued to lay the foundations of modern Europe.

Tacitus' story is the earliest account of this decisive period that has come down to us. Indeed it is almost the only Latin account. Our other main literary sources are the far less serious Latin biographies of his contemporary Suetonius, and the Greek history of Dio Cassius who wrote a whole century later. As an artistic and spiritual achievement his work eclipses theirs. Dio is pedestrian, and Suetonius, for all his vividness, accepts the traditional assumption that biography is a less important *genre* than history and falls infinitely short of the unique qualities of Tacitus. If we leave literature out of it and concentrate on that elusive commodity the historical 'fact', the situation is a little different. Suetonius was an imperial secretary and amassed much curious and irreplaceable material, and Dio lived close to the imperial court of his day and possessed more personal experience of exalted affairs than Tacitus. Yet Suetonius is often no sort of a critic of his material, and Dio lacks the imagination to grasp the affairs of the early empire. Tacitus is more dependable than either. He is the best literary source for the events of the early principate that we possess. There are, of course, other significant sources, provided by archaeology, and coins, and papyri, and art. But it is chiefly upon Tacitus that we have to rely for our knowledge of a critical epoch in the history of western civilization.

2. WHAT TACITUS INHERITED

What he attempted in this work is hard to follow without at least a brief glance at the historians who had gone before him. The world's first historians had been Greeks. Rome's cultural debt to Greece was incalculably great, and Tacitus cannot be wholly understood without bearing in mind certain peculiar, perhaps surprising, features of Greek historical writing. In the first place, the Greeks had begun by thinking of history as extremely close to epic poetry. Indeed, history owed its technique and its very existence to Homer and other Greek epic poets. Again, when Athenian tragic drama became great in the fifth century B.C., that also influenced Greek historical writing. These two facts emerge clearly from the works of Herodotus and Thucydides. And history never quite forgot its early links with poetry. As the great Roman educationalist Quintilian (an older contemporary of Tacitus) remarked, 'history is very near to poetry, and may be considered in some sense as poetry in prose'.

He may have been intending to make a point of style rather than content, yet the analogies went farther than that. Being so close to poetry, ancient history was often intended to arouse emotion. For one thing, it had habitually been read aloud to audiences, from the time of Herodotus onwards, and, even after silent or *sotto voce* reading gradually became more customary, the practice never ceased. Isocrates (436–338 B.C.) caused his pupils to see history as a branch of eloquence, and Greek historians after the time of Alexander the Great, such as Duris of Samos, carried the emotional, pathetic tendency to extreme lengths. This whole trend was sternly denounced by the great Polybius of Megalopolis (*c.* 203–120 B.C.), whose theme, although he too wrote in Greek, was nothing less than the universality of Rome. All historians of the age were influenced in one way or another by Aristotle (384–322 B.C.), who, even if his direct effect on historiography was not so extensive as has recently been supposed, enormously stimulated, through his own example and the work of his pupils, the development of a scientific attitude towards research.

Nevertheless, the emotional approach had come to stay, and particularly flourished in the Hellenistic age of later Greece when interest in biography became increasingly strong. As Roman history developed, patriotic emotion gained in importance as a factor in the situation. It is powerful, in a nostalgic way, in Sallust (86–*c.* 34 B.C.), who first gave the subject a magnificent Latin style, and its expression reached its zenith in Livy (59 B.C.–A.D. 17).

But patriotism is only one aspect of the moral tone that pervades Roman historians. This goes back to the very earliest of their Greek predecessors, since even Herodotus, for all his relaxed manner, had seen ethical lessons in the past. The task of edification seemed to become particularly imperative from the fourth century B.C. onwards, when philosophers had turned their main attention from speculations about the universe to the exploration of the soul of man. Decisive influences in this direction were Socrates' interest in the human personality, and the dialogues of Plato, and the *Ethics* of Aristotle. The schools of philosophy which descended from Aristotle all persisted with this moral emphasis, and none more than the Stoics whose doctrines were laid down in *c.* 300 B.C. by Zeno of Citium in Cyprus. He and his successors taught that Virtue is the Supreme Good; and this idea appealed to the Romans who, if often nasty, included, at their best, men of strong moral interests and preoccupations. Indeed, Stoicism of a sort, somewhat modified by Panaetius (*c.* 185–? 95 B.C.) to suit the practical requirements of society, came to pervade the general culture of the Greco-Roman world.[1] And so it affected most historians. Among them, too, there is a vigorous atmosphere of moralizing.

A moralist seeks to persuade, to teach, and to guide. 'The art of persuasion' is one of the definitions of the ancient Art – some called it a Science – of Rhetoric. This Art or Science continued to permeate ancient culture until, as has already been mentioned, it became the staple higher education of a Roman under the empire.

Greek educational theorists, trying to map out Rhetoric in systematic terms, had actually thought of history as part of it. We find this a strange idea, living as we do in an age when 'fine writing' and grand speaking are unfashionable, and when anything of the kind among historians is particularly suspect. Cicero, who was sympathetic to the rhetorical ideals of Isocrates (p. 11), regarded the two studies as mutually beneficial. Not only, he asserted, should orators be well versed in history, but history, in its turn, needs the sort of composition practised by public speakers.[2] Even if its first law is truth, it possesses an especially close relation to oratory[3] – by which he apparently means to convey, again, that it needs rhetorical techniques for its expression.

This has certain results which we find puzzling. For instance ancient historians are very much inclined to credit their personages with speeches which they clearly did not deliver, at least not in such a shape. These speeches provide background, in rhetorical form often accentuated by a *balance* between two opposing theses. 'I have put into each speaker's mouth', says Thucydides, 'sentiments proper to the occasion, expressed as I thought he would be likely to express them.'[4] Similar to these masterly but imaginative reconstructions of atmosphere are certain battle-scenes. Sometimes these are not realistic narratives so much as brilliant evocations of heroism, panic, reversals of fortune,

---

1. Stoic thought, as expanded by Seneca (c.5 B.C.–A.D. 65), can be read in a recent Penguin Classic (*Letters from a Stoic*).
2. Cicero, *De Oratore*, II, 62.   3. Cicero, *De Legibus*, I, 5. 3.
4. Thucydides, I, 22.

and the like. One can imagine how the battle-scenes of Tacitus were declaimed to an appreciative audience. With that in mind, a historian had to write effectively – that is, persuasively. In other words he had to write well. Cicero was convinced that a historian must not be only a scholar; he must be an artist too, and must endow his historical writing with every possible device of stylistic attractiveness.

Cicero also felt that Roman historians of earlier generations had failed to meet this requirement of a good style. For in his day (106–43 B.C.) history already had a fairly long, if not very distinguished, pedigree at Rome. As early as the third century B.C. the serious business of Roman politics – supremely important in the educated life of the Republic – had permitted and included the study and writing of history. The 'senatorial historians' combined varying amounts of Greek culture (the first of these writers even wrote in Greek) with a reverence for Roman traditions and institutions. This mixture must have been apparent in the lost work in which, in the second century B.C., Cato the Censor told the story of Rome from mythical times to his own day. In theory, he was opposed to the artificiality and stylistic self-consciousness of the Greeks, and he set out to demonstrate that Rome could do as well as them. In the process, he borrowed some of their stylistic devices – and indeed the very title of his book, the *Origins*, follows a Greek tradition.

Some generations before Cato, the Roman State had made a decisive contribution to history by instituting the publication of annual notices called the Records of the Priests. These were primarily concerned with the religious ritual which played such an immense part in Roman life. But this ritual involved references to political events – victories, declarations of war and peace, etc. So the Records began to summarize certain historical events. They left their mark on historians of Cato's century. Some of these, because they too followed an annual pattern, were called Annalists; and their influence on the annalistic arrangement of Tacitus' work is so clear that his book which is here translated was quite early known by its present title, the *Annals*.

Records of the sort that the Republican historians used were collected in an official publication of eighty volumes published in *c.* 123 B.C. Such records were sometimes authentic; but they were often legendary, for many myths had gathered round the origins of the great families. And next came a generation of Annalists who expanded this sort of material in the light of rhetorical ideas imbibed from Greece.

Despite such embellishments Cicero, as I have said, found them all inadequate as artists.

The stylistic shortcomings of Roman history were amply remedied by Julius Caesar (102/100–44 B.C.), Sallust (86–c. 34 B.C.), Livy (59 B.C.–A.D. 17),[1] and finally, in the most remarkable fashion of all, by Tacitus.

Caesar's 'Commentaries' include the *Gallic War* and the *Civil War*, with supplements by his staff officers. Caesar was a first-rate orator, and he wrote beautifully lucid Latin – which effectively clothed unremitting political justification. His work was far from being the unshaped raw material it might seem at first sight. It was, rather, a deliberate attempt to get away from the rhetorical history of Isocrates in favour of a tougher sort of history (reminiscent rather of Thucydides), written by someone who was not a professor but a leading actor in events. Yet because of his unadorned style he was less read by the ancients than his younger contemporary Sallust. Sallust's important *Histories* have only survived in relatively small portions, notably certain speeches. But we have his *Catiline*, about that fierce nobleman's conspiracy in the sixties B.C., and his *Jugurtha*, named after a North African king against whom Rome had fought fifty years earlier. These are the first important Roman historical monographs that have come down to us. The *genre* owed a good deal to Greece, but it was Sallust who attracted to it the attention of his compatriots.

Tacitus owes Sallust something of his vivid but careful abruptness, also his mask of austere impartiality, and his habit of digressions – often including speeches to clarify character. Echoes of Sallust, too, are apparent in Tacitus' pessimistic sketch of early civilization, and in other pieces of rhetorical moralizing; he is markedly Sallustian in his trenchant attitude. As a historian of events Sallust leaves a good deal to be desired, and it was said that he ought to be read not as a historian but as an orator.[2] Yet the wonderful vigour and dramatic power with which he presented action and discussion made men feel that at last

1. For their works in English, see p. 437.
2. Granius Licinianus, XXXVI.

Roman history was being treated with the eloquence and stylistic skill which Cicero had demanded of it.

So it was again in the next generation, when Livy spent forty years writing that superb history of Rome which, if it had all survived (less than a quarter of it has), would have filled thirty modern volumes. Livy possessed the true antiquarian spirit, but no taste for profound research. His first ten Books are a brilliant, mythical Virgilian evocation of Rome's past.

Although Tacitus is far removed from this romantic enthusiasm and rich florid style, Livy's power to stir the emotions left a legacy to him as well as to other historians. So did Livy's rhetoric – already beginning to become a potent force in Roman education. Like Tacitus after him, Livy's chief aim was to draw from the past its moral lessons. They were based on current ethical ideas; and, encouraged by the Stoic interpretation of the Roman Empire as the vehicle of human brotherhood,[1] these lessons were directed to the supreme purpose of Rome's greater glory. And with Rome was associated Italy. For Livy, like Virgil and perhaps like Tacitus, came from Italy's fringes and felt the emotional patriotism which people of the frontier so often feel. All three men – Virgil, Livy and Tacitus – possessed a metropolitan bias which was both aristocratic and conservative; and Virgil, like Livy, is deliberately echoed by Tacitus.

In the three-quarters of a century following the deaths of Augustus and Livy (A.D. 17) there were a number of historical writers. Most of their works, however, are lost, and this makes it difficult to assess their influence on Tacitus. But he must have owed much of his material to them, and notably to Pliny the elder (c. A.D. 23–79), whose *Natural History* we possess though his account of his own times is lost. Probably Tacitus' stylistic debts to this and other missing works were a good deal larger than has been realized. However, these first-century historians do not seem to have possessed talents comparable with those of Caesar, Sallust, and Livy. Besides, circumstances were less favourable to them. Certain of the emperors, as readers of Tacitus will find it easy to appreciate, were touchy. Their suspicions, as he suggests, may have prevented contemporary historians from doing themselves full justice.

But there may also have been quite different reasons for the appa-

1. By Panaetius (p. 12) and especially Posidonius of Apamea (c. 135–50 B.C.).

rent decline of historiography during this period. For one thing, there seems to have been an enlargement, a wider dispersal, of historical interest. To an increased extent, writers and thinkers now devoted themselves to subjects such as geography, science, and ethnography.

3. TACITUS ON EMPIRE AND EMPERORS

Such tendencies are apparent in the earliest historical writings of the greatest post-Augustan historian, Tacitus. In his later publications, and particularly in the work that I have translated here, he incorporates and blends in a single structure all the traditional features of historical writing. The manuscript heading reads only 'From the death of the divine Augustus', but the title soon given to the work, the *Annals*, recalls that Roman traditions are ever apparent. Here, too, are the interests of the later, Hellenistic, Greeks: ethnology, biography, psychology, rhetorical types and situations (his battle-scenes, for example, often create more factual problems than they solve), and emotional effects, aiming at pathetic stress and seeking to make events seem tragic and terrible.

Moral purpose, too, is never absent from Tacitus' mind. The sequence of events on which he chooses to focus his attention provoked the sternest moral reflections. To him, as to many others, decline and disaster seemed due to vice. Virtue and vice are continually emphasized and contrasted. As Tacitus himself says, 'It seems to me a historian's foremost duty to ensure that merit is recorded, and to confront evil words and deeds with the fear of posterity's denunciations.'[1]

That was the trend of Tacitus' mind; it was also the trend of ancient historiography as a whole, with its epic, tragic, and moralizing background. These influences combined to inspire Tacitus with an exalted conception of his task. To him, history is a conspicuously elevated theme. He deliberately concentrates on subjects which contribute to his dramatic, meaningful whole.

Now the highest and most significant drama appeared to be centred on the all-powerful, glamorous, sinister imperial court. So we hear much of the emperors and their *entourages*. The Roman imperial personages do not, in our own day, any longer play an integral part in

1. *Annals*, III, 65.

general culture, or exercise the fascination which once placed their lifesize marble busts in every mansion. True, the melodramatic novels of earlier days have not altogether ceased, and are now supplemented by even more spectacular burlesques in the cinema. But the Palace of the Caesars, like its picturesque evocations in Piranesi's eighteenth-century etchings, seems too outrageously remote from an age of quieter artistic tastes and economic aspirations. Or it may be that the even more formidable absolute rulers whom some countries have experienced in our lifetimes have made antique autocrats *vieux jeu*. Yet not only did the imperial tragedies give a permanently admirable historian his greatest opportunities, but the workings of a Roman emperor's power and influence, and his varying attitudes to problems of loyalty, have great relevance to the modern world.

The outlying territories are given a partial, tantalizing record; for example, Tacitus is interested in Asia, which he governed, and in Germany, which, again from personal experience, he saw as the source of the greatest future hazards.[1] Yet he remains the heir to the traditionally centripetal view of Roman history. The emperor into whose reign he may have lived, Hadrian (A.D. 117–38), was to develop the idea of a Roman Commonwealth in which the provinces had a proud role as constituent parts, anticipatory of the national states to come. But to Tacitus, perhaps implying a criticism of the new imperial ideas, Rome is all-important. It is towards Rome that the most lurid light is generally directed. When we read of the faults or fate of an occasional visitor or governor in the provinces, Rome is in mind. And Tacitus, thinking of Rome, thinks of its emperor. Indeed the provinces, too, chiefly figure as parts of the immense structure which conferred on its ruler the heaviest responsibility that man had ever had to bear.

He had once intended to cap his earlier major work, the *Histories*, with an account of his own happier times under Trajan and Hadrian. But he shelved this task provisionally – and as it turned out, permanently – in favour of the earlier period. For that contained the sources of recent evils; and on those evils, for all the improved conditions of his own day, he still brooded.

Tacitus claims that he is unmoved by indignation or partisanship, since in his case 'the customary incentives to these are lack-

---

1. His inadequate picture of other important areas, notably Spain, may have been partially remedied in the missing parts of his work.

ing'¹ – he has nothing to gain from them or to lose from their absence. Such protestations were conventional. Yet he was utterly sincere. So perhaps it must be said that to some extent (as we all do frequently) he deceived himself. For his famous character-study of Tiberius does not seem to us free from indignation or partisanship. The reign of Tiberius (A.D. 14–37) had ended nearly eighty years before Tacitus wrote about him. But the historian's hostile attitude reflects the fact that, when he wrote his major works, he had recently lived through the equally or even more sombre and – to senators – terrifying last years of Domitian (A.D. 81–96). The mental disturbance that this experience had caused was probably all the worse because Domitian was on Tacitus' conscience. For as a senator and high official he had been obliged or induced, as he hints in the *Agricola*, not merely to accept promotion but to acquiesce in purges undertaken by the emperor in circles close to the historian himself.

So Tacitus was obsessed by the real or imaginary Domitians of past history. Domitian had admired Tiberius. But there were many other reasons, too, why Tacitus decided that the evils which had proliferated under Domitian had their roots under Tiberius. Nowadays we believe that Tiberius was a gloomy but apparently honest ruler – a man who owed many of the tragedies of his reign to his inability to conduct personal and public relations. Augustus had conducted them excellently. Indeed Augustus' whole régime, with its elaborate constitutional fictions indicating that the autocracy was a restoration of the Republic, had depended not only on force but also on his delicate handling of people, individually and in the mass. The glum Tiberius did not handle them delicately. He does not seem to have been too keen to tackle the task at all. Perhaps he was too honest for it.

But Tacitus regards him as anything but honest. To him, Tiberius is the arch-hypocrite. Tacitus is always deeply preoccupied with the discrepancy between fact and impression, and he lays continual stress on the duplicity and concealment of Tiberius. In a series of terrible incidents and comments, he is depicted in the role of the stock tyrant of the ancient literatures, unjust, sensual, ruthless, and – above all – suspicious and cunning. His mother Livia, also, to the indignation of most modern historians, emerges as a fearsome intriguer and multiple murderess. To blacken her and Tiberius all the more effectively, their

1. *Annals*, I, 1.

young, attractive kinsman Germanicus is portrayed as a brilliant prince who can do no wrong; and his war in Germany is painted in glowing colours which almost conceal its expensive uselessness.

Tacitus suggests that Tiberius possessed a radically vicious nature which only became apparent by degrees. It is surmised, too, that the flaws might never have been apparent at all if he had not become all-powerful. The characters of other significant and powerful men are depicted by brief, passing, parenthetical observations: by this means a huge array of contemporary figures are isolated from the anonymous mass and vividly illuminated. They are of all degrees of power and significance. But they are mostly senators, and often leaders. Tacitus chiefly displays his art in the gradual, piece-by-piece presentation – or occasionally the full-length portrayal – of the dominant and mighty. And no one has ever equalled the might of a Roman emperor. Tacitus' study of Tiberius, with its ulterior preoccupations, is hardly a psychological study. But it is an indelible and unforgettable picture of a great man as another great man saw him.

Every resource of Tacitus' talent is devoted to painting this picture. One of his favourite devices, one of the touches by which he builds up a character, is the damning 'aside'. But he utilizes every possible sort of suggestion to imply the worst. For the facts do not always seem to confirm the sinister interpretations which he places upon them. Miss B. Walker[1] has invoked Jung's distinction between 'sensational' and 'intuitive' types – the former perceive things as they are, the latter pass details over carelessly, but are well able to appreciate the inner meaning of occurrences, and their potential relations and consequences. Tacitus, asserts this author, is of the latter, intuitive type; and that may help to explain his occasional distortion of the facts in arriving at his vivid impressions.

After Tiberius, his accounts of Claudius and Nero, viewed as character studies, can afford to be more straightforward. Though Claudius is now believed to have been a painstaking and bold administrator and reformer, his faults and those of his terrifying women Messalina and Agrippina, and the other evils of his court, spring readily to the eye. So do the tragedies and bad jokes of Nero's régime. It is true that Tacitus, with the old Roman love of aggressive glory, hardly refers to the Neronian Peace except in a sneering parenthesis – for aggression was

1. *The Annals of Tacitus* (1952, reprinted 1968), p. 189.

again fashionable in his own day, under Trajan – and we have learned from Sir Ronald Syme's *Tacitus* to be much more vigilant for contemporary references. Yet Nero himself was as 'vulgar, timid, and sanguinary' as Merivale called him. Merivale was following Tacitus. But Tacitus' accounts of these more straightforward reigns did not need to revive the techniques of damning suggestion lavished on Tiberius. Instead we can enjoy the writer's extraordinary, and very Roman, gift for pictorial description. We can read of the Great Fire, or of Agrippina's murder, or Tigellinus' party – those highlighted major descriptions at which Tacitus excels – without worrying whether he is playing fair. It is rather his account of Tiberius which seems to us to convict him of the hatred and partiality which he denies. But it is so enthralling that it carries conviction as a work of art – and very nearly carries conviction as history.

His interpretation of facts, then, whether unconsciously or through deliberate fervid intention, is often invidious, but the actual facts which he records are generally accurate – so accurate that they involuntarily contradict his sinister innuendoes. There is no doubt that he took a great deal of care in selecting his material. But where did he find it? Here we are lost. We often have no external check on what he says. And we still know very little about his sources. He himself does not greatly enlighten us. It must be granted that he mentions certain predecessors, for example the historian and literary historian Pliny the elder. But systematic, careful references are a modern invention. Ancient historians only specified their sources in a fragmentary and unsystematic fashion. Sometimes it seems as if pride impels them to mention only those on whom they have least relied – and this might almost be suspected of Tacitus. So when he claims judicious selection, this can, it is true, sometimes be taken at its face value, but often it proves to be another means towards a censorious hint, a damning delineation.

His attitude to the political structure of the State reveals, if not the split personality which some have identified, at least a very difficult and fundamental dilemma, which is as relevant to our world as to his. For Tacitus greatly admired, perhaps almost to the point of obsession, the traditional virtues of Rome and its antique Republic. Yet at the same time he fully understood that the Republic was a thing of the past and could never be revived. As the *Histories* are succeeded by the *Annals*, he even comes to regard political opposition to the autocrats, if it goes beyond passive, resigned disapproval, as theatrical and immoderate. Rome has declined so far, he seems to feel, that there is no room any longer for traditional valour. Passivity has become the only honourable course, and the decorous middle path followed by men like his father-in-law Agricola – as described in the biography Tacitus devoted to him – or by Marcus Lepidus or Seneca as they are summed up in the Annals,[1] is what now wins his admiration.

Again, when he is talking of post-Augustan tyrants, he appears, by way of contrast, to admire Augustus. Yet his introductory survey of Augustus' own reign (exceedingly valuable as a check on the official versions which had blared forth from the chancery) is one long list of sneers. He was writing under enlightened emperors, and, though some detect traces that he was disappointed even with Trajan,[2] he expresses grateful awareness of this relative good fortune. Yet it seems that he is not really able to believe that an autocrat can be good. For he constantly stresses the evils of rule by one man. Perhaps this conviction is the central point of his philosophy. No amount of experience, he infers, can stand up against the corrupting effects of autocratic authority. 'In spite of all his experience of public affairs,' he makes Arruntius say, 'Tiberius was transformed and deranged by absolute power'.[3] So it was under Tiberius that freedom suffered its most fatal losses. As these are remorselessly described we do not feel two thousand years distant.

Tacitus is deeply interested not only in the characters of individuals but in the whole range of group psychology, with all its cross-currents and irrationalities. A large proportion of the first book of the Annals, like a major part of the Histories, is concerned with the psychology of the army which was playing so sinister a role in this process of disintegration. And Tacitus is also fascinated, for the same reason, by the senate. His picture of this once mighty oligarchic body is intentionally a depressing one. Its powerlessness under the emperors is unsparingly described, for it illustrates the moral theme of degeneracy from the good old days of the past. Although Tacitus is a staunch senator, and a supporter of the traditional oligarchic view of society, he places no

---

1. Annals, IV, 20; XIII, 2; etc.
2. The circumstances in which Trajan came to the throne, after a brief threat of chaos under the weak Nerva, came as a shock.
3. Annals, VI, 48.

reliance on the senate of imperial times. For he knows that the senate is helpless against the ruler: it is he who, through his own direct and indirect means of influence, does everything that matters. That is why Tacitus examines the motives and morals of successive emperors so carefully. That also is why he examines those critical moments when one autocrat died and another began to rule. The *Histories*, with their detailed account of the Civil Wars of A.D. 68–70, had shown the disasters which could occur when the succession was disputed. This was another dilemma. For civil war, Tacitus felt, was even worse than any autocrat, because of the excesses it engendered and the temptation it offered to potential German and Parthian invaders.

Yet rule by one man was also utterly hazardous, for Tacitus' experience and temperament make him well aware that man is, and always has been, unreliable; so that, when the State is unified under an omnipotent ruler, human happiness hangs by a thread. When the emperor is a bad man, and rules badly, there is misery. Oppressive rule causes – as it is caused by – moral degeneracy. A series of themes continually reiterated by Tacitus illustrate the insidious increase of both. The idea of Progress was, in any case, alien to the mentality of the ancients, and here, already, is the Decline of the West which has so fascinated Spengler and Toynbee in our own day. Certainly, the emperors under whom Tacitus wrote were enlightened enough. But time had shown, he felt, that under an autocracy there was no certain safeguard against oppression. So he is embittered and pessimistic.

4. TACITUS AND THE WORLD

There are moments and whole epochs when everything seems, to Tacitus, to be at the mercy of a fate which is blind – and even malignant.

On such matters he is as inconsistent as most other ancient historians – and as most people are today. When specific causes for disasters are identifiable – such as moral degradation – he does not generally blame fate for them. Yet it sometimes appears to him that what has blighted events is anger from heaven: from the gods, as a Roman would put it (or he might also say, from God). Tacitus, spasmodically and with reserves, is a believer in prophecy and portents. At other times he is not certain whether there are any interested divine powers at all. And he is often afraid that mankind may be doomed. The existence of such an attitude suggests a reason why subsequent generations would increasingly turn to religion – why they withdrew into an other-worldliness which led to the prevalence of mystics, the victory of Christianity, and the proliferation of monks and nuns.

Human fate often looks black to Tacitus. So does human nature. Yet he is far from sceptical about the potentialities of the human spirit. Even in times of civil war and tyrannical government, he is able to point to human actions of extraordinary virtue, bravery, and pertinacity. Indeed he is a humanist, and one whose contribution to our western tradition of humanism has been immense and singularly inspiring.

Yet the *Annals* of Tacitus were almost unappreciated for nearly fourteen hundred years.[1] Indeed, they only survived by a narrow chance. Our knowledge of the work is based on a single medieval manuscript of the first half of the work and another of its second half – the two Medicean codices, now both at Florence. Boccaccio (1313–1375) seems to have known one of them. But certain aspects of their rediscovery in the fourteenth and fifteenth centuries are veiled in obscurity. The High Renaissance was less attentive to Tacitus than to Livy, who provided it with suitable heroes. However, before 1500, Tacitus – for the first time since his death – was beginning to exercise a rapidly growing influence. At that time ancient history was a favourite field for translation and study; and the fame of Tacitus reached sensational proportions.

The first complete edition of his surviving works was published at Rome in 1515. In the same century Machiavelli and Montaigne were greatly moved by him. Later, a committee of Venetian scholars was to blame Tacitus for the attitude of Machiavelli 'who would destroy public virtues'. This may seem an unfair judgement of Tacitus. But, if so, its unexpectedness illustrates a conspicuous feature of his reputation. He was so versatile, and his personality so complex, that he seemed to provide slogans for – and against – every section of political opinion. Everybody saw in him an adherent of something different. Thus, while the Venetians attacked him for political cynicism, a French royalist praised him as a supporter of autocratic law and order; and, in

1. For his attitude to the Christians and Jews, see below, p. 366.

reaction, he was attacked by John Milton as one who had despaired of the Republic. Towards the end of the seventeenth century Tacitus' reputation temporarily declined, because of two opposite factors: the impact of religious scruples, and the growth of rationalism, neither of which phenomena was in harmony with the historian's attitude. After 1700, however, he found new followers. They were particularly numerous in England, where, ever since Francis Bacon, he had been admired as the enemy of despots. In France, too, he exercised a profound influence on thinkers of the Revolutionary age. 'The utterance of his name,' declared André Chénier, 'turns tyrants pale.' Madame Roland was reading him in prison before her execution, and the echoes of Tacitus in *Le Vieux Cordelier*, the journal of Camille Desmoulins, caused Robespierre to have the paper burned. And the Founding Fathers of the United States of America studied him with equal care – deeply concerned with his warning against a constitution of mixed type,[1] which was what they hoped to establish.

Such impassioned discussion, during the last four hundred years, affords a striking contrast to the neglect of Tacitus in the Middle Ages, when all references to him are of the most tenuous character; and in the latter part of antiquity itself, to which he left no school. Why, for much more than a millennium after his death, was he so little regarded?

5. THE STYLE OF TACITUS: TRANSLATOR'S NOTE

The principal cause of this neglect was unquestionably the unusual and difficult Latin in which he wrote. The outstanding quality of Tacitus is his brilliance as a literary artist. Racine called him 'the greatest painter of antiquity'. Others have compared his work not so much to a series of pictures as to a continuous frieze. But of his supreme artistic genius there can be no doubt. A large part of this artistry resides in his style – the aspect of his talent which a translator has least hope of reproducing. Now ancient readers usually recognized stylistic talent, and by no means found that it interfered with their enjoyment when history contained a strong infusion of rhetoric. But the style of Tacitus, as it had developed to its culminating point in these *Annals*, was indeed

1. Tacitus, *Annals*, IV, 33, 1.

extraordinary. It displays a sharp, astringent and certainly deliberate contrast to the rotund periods of Cicero and to the flowing, 'milky' diction of Livy (p. 15).

For one thing, since Livy's day rhetoric had gained mightily in strength as the basis of Roman education and taste. Under the influence of rhetorical declamations in school and society, the rounded fluency of classical style had been superseded by the pointed brevity of Silver Latin writers, such as Seneca (p. 12), who was not only one of the chief political figures of the age described in the *Annals* but a very clever moralizing epigrammatist – and the son of a leading professor of rhetoric. But the mature prose of Tacitus, besides undergoing all the influences of Silver Latin, has added to them his own formidable individuality.

The colour of his prose differs greatly in accordance with the varied intensity of his feeling. Sometimes, to give us a rest, there is a pedestrian factual passage. His style is at its most idiosyncratic when the subject-matter is not factual but emotional. When Tacitus ponders on oppression or moral decline, he writes in short, abrupt sentences, in staccato phrases, in trenchant, surprising epigrams far removed from our Ciceronian grammar-books. The vividness of his words and phrases often has a semi-poetical quality. If he borrowed much (p. 15), he made it his own; though the traditional and original elements in his style are notoriously hard to disengage, there is no doubt about its peculiarity. Much Latin literature is remote from the spoken tongue, but never had it been as remote as this. Tacitus is known to have become a fine orator (p. 7). In his writings, and especially in these *Annals*, he has transformed the rhetoric and 'point' of the Silver Age from the second-rate quality of all too many of its exponents into an unequalled brilliance.

But what a problem this brilliant style sets to the translator! The task has been attempted many times. But the more prudent translators have prefaced their efforts by apologetic reminders that 'Tacitus has never been translated, and probably never will be' – that he is 'the despair of the translator'; it is 'une œuvre impossible'.

To begin with, textual ambiguities quite often make it hard even to decide what Tacitus *wrote*. Since the text of each half of the work depends entirely on a single medieval manuscript, there is ample room for suspicions that error may have crept in. However, let us now assume, optimistically, that the meaning is understood. The next problem is to convey, in such minute degree as is practicable, the heart of the matter – that is to say, to reproduce the meaning in English; to convey, as faithfully as possible, the essential thought and significance of what Tacitus wrote. But ought one not also to attempt to reproduce his *expression*? In theory a translator, as opposed to a mere paraphraser, ought to do so. In practice, too, he ought to attempt to do so – at least to a limited extent. For example, a translation of Tacitus must aim at conciseness. It will be too far from his spirit altogether if it succumbs to our national inclination 'that the writer shall set out his ideas with some space between them'. But any attempt to render Tacitus' peculiar Latin into peculiar English would mean abysmal failure in another most peremptory requirement. For, in our mid-twentieth century, it would not be *readable* – and, except as a mere crib, an unreadable translation of a great master has obviously not done its job.

In translating in this series the fantastic Apuleius, Robert Graves remarked: 'Paradoxically, the effect of oddness is best achieved in convulsed times like the present by writing in as easy and sedate an English as possible.' 'Sedate' is surely not an ambitious enough epithet for a good rendering of Apuleius, or of Tacitus; but his reminder that twentieth-century English has to be plain is still relevant. No amount of colourful or fanciful language will make the strange personality of Tacitus understandable to contemporary readers, who find rhetoric and the grand style unnatural and unreadable. Today the only faint hope of rendering his complexity lies in as pungent a simplicity as the translator can achieve.

Unlike Tacitus, I have sought to avoid confusion by giving names in full, and also by placing (I), (II), etc., after them when more than one person of the same name is mentioned in the course of the book. I have only withheld these numerals in the case of the two Agrippinas:[1] in Part 1 'Agrippina' means Agrippina the elder, in Part 2 her daughter. 'Gaius' is the emperor (Caligula), 'Gaius Caesar' is Augustus' grandson. 'Nero Drusus' is Tiberius' brother, 'Drusus' his son, 'Drusus Caesar' his grandnephew. Yet in spite of all these pre-

1. And for the various kings called Cotys and Mithridates, unless they belong to a numbered sequence of monarchs in their own kingdoms; but most of those mentioned belong to different kingdoms along Rome's *cordon sanitaire*.

cautions the Imperial House can only be disentangled by employing the genealogical tables which are at the back of the book.

Wherever possible I have avoided or translated technical phraseology. For example, I have tried to Anglicize words relating to the Roman army – most of which are wholly incomprehensible without an effort at modernization. I am very grateful to Mr Eric Birley for supplying me with equivalents for Roman military terms which he, with his great experience of this subject, regards as close enough to be serviceable. Some may miss a few familiar words, military and otherwise; I preferred not to keep them, in the interests of throwing off the more misleading parts of the traditional apparatus.

Thus I have revolted against the outworn 'freedman' and 'colony'. 'Freedman' means nothing in modern English, so I have preferred 'ex-slave', 'freed slave', or 'former slave'. 'Colony' is misleading (partly because Roman colonies were towns, not countries), so I have used the word 'settlement'.¹ Also included are those few basic Roman official terms for which even the broadest or vaguest equivalent in English does not exist, such as 'consul' and 'praetor' – and 'sestertius' or sesterce, on which my note owes part of its information to the late Professor A. H. M. Jones.

I have translated the names of rivers and mountains (when these are identifiable), but it has not seemed possible to do so in the case of towns, of which the modern designations are sometimes Christian or Moslem and would sound anachronistic. Instead I have marshalled the ancient and modern names alongside each other in a list at the end. Almost every place-name mentioned by Tacitus is included (in its ancient form) in one of the maps.

Throughout the centuries it has been disputed whether translators ought, or ought not, to borrow felicitous words or phrases from their forerunners. There have been so many versions of Tacitus that strict avoidance of precedent would have added a further and almost insuperable difficulty to my task. Indeed, it would sometimes have meant that the only possible happy rendering would have to be avoided – too high a price to pay for the illusory advantage of complete independence. I owe a debt of gratitude to those translators into English whose thoughts I have, on occasion, consciously or unconsciously appropriated.

1. See List of Technical Terms at end of book (EX-SLAVE, SETTLEMENT).

I owe an acknowledgement to the Cambridge University Press for allowing me to include in this Introduction certain passages from my book *Roman Literature*. Amendments incorporated in reprints are owed to Professor M. I. Finley, Professor E. N. Lane, Professor Sir Ronald Syme, Mr K. Wellesley and Professor E. C. Woodcock. I am also very grateful to Dr E. V. Rieu and Mrs Betty Radice, successive editors of Penguin Classics, for their help.

Gattaiola, 1971   M. G.

THE ANNALS OF
IMPERIAL ROME

★

PART ONE

TIBERIUS

CHAPTER I

From Augustus to Tiberius

*

WHEN Rome was first a city, its rulers were kings. Then Lucius Junius Brutus created the consulate and free Republican institutions in general. Dictatorships were assumed in emergencies. A Council of Ten did not last more than two years; and then there was a short-lived arrangement by which senior army officers – the commanders of contingents provided by the tribes[1] – possessed consular authority. Subsequently Cinna and Sulla set up autocracies, but they too were brief. Soon Pompey and Crassus acquired predominant positions, but rapidly lost them to Caesar. Next, the military strength which Lepidus and Antony had built up was absorbed by Augustus. He found the whole state exhausted by internal dissensions, and established over it a personal régime known as the Principate.[2]

Famous writers have recorded Rome's early glories and disasters. The Augustan Age, too, had its distinguished historians. But then the rising tide of flattery exercised a deterrent effect. The reigns of Tiberius, Gaius, Claudius, and Nero were described during their lifetimes in fictitious terms, for fear of the consequences; whereas the accounts written after their deaths were influenced by still raging animosities.

1. See Key to Technical Terms (TRIBES).
2. Tacitus refers to the following events: 753 B.C. legendary date of the foundation of Rome, 510 kings supposedly expelled by Lucius Junius Brutus, 451–49 constitution suspended in favour of two successive annual Councils of Ten to prepare codes of laws, 444–367 (at intervals) commanders of tribal contingents granted consular powers, 87–4 four consulates of Lucius Cornelius Cinna, 82–79 Sulla's dictatorship, 60/59–3 informal 'First Triumvirate' of Pompey, Marcus Licinius Crassus, and Julius Caesar, 49–4 Julius Caesar's dictatorships, 43 'Second Triumvirate' of Antony, Octavian (the future Augustus), and Marcus Aemilius Lepidus (III), 43 deaths of Brutus and Cassius, 36 Sextus Pompeius defeated and Lepidus dropped, 30 suicide of Antony.

So I have decided to say a little about Augustus, with special attention
to his last period, and then go on to the reign of Tiberius and what
followed. I shall write without indignation or partisanship: in my case
the customary incentives to these are lacking.

The violent deaths of Brutus and Cassius left no Republican forces
in the field. Defeat came to Sextus Pompeius in Sicily, Lepidus was
dropped, Antony killed. So even the Caesarian party had no leader
left except the 'Caesar' himself, Octavian. He gave up the title of
Triumvir, emphasizing instead his position as consul; and the powers
of a tribune, he proclaimed, were good enough for him – powers for
the protection of ordinary people.

He seduced the army with bonuses, and his cheap food policy was
successful bait for civilians. Indeed, he attracted everybody's goodwill
by the enjoyable gift of peace. Then he gradually pushed ahead and
absorbed the functions of the senate, the officials, and even the law.
Opposition did not exist. War or judicial murder had disposed of all
men of spirit. Upper-class survivors found that slavish obedience was
the way to succeed, both politically and financially. They had profited from the revolution, and so now they liked the security of the
existing arrangement better than the dangerous uncertainties of the
old régime. Besides, the new order was popular in the provinces.
There, government by Senate and People was looked upon sceptically
as a matter of sparring dignitaries and extortionate officials. The
legal system had provided no remedy against these, since it was wholly
incapacitated by violence, favouritism, and – most of all – bribery.

To safeguard his domination Augustus made his sister's son Marcellus a priest and a curule aedile – in spite of his extreme youth – and
singled out Marcus Agrippa, a commoner but a first-rate soldier who
had helped to win his victories, by the award of two consecutive consulships; after the death of Marcellus, Agrippa was chosen by Augustus
as his son-in-law. Next the emperor had his stepsons Tiberius and
Nero Drusus hailed publicly as victorious generals. When he did this,
however, there was no lack of heirs of his own blood: there were
Agrippa's sons Gaius Caesar and Lucius Caesar. Augustus had adopted
them into the imperial family. He had also, despite pretended reluctance, been passionately eager that, even as minors, they should be entitled Princes of Youth and have consulships reserved for them. After
Agrippa had died, first Lucius Caesar and then Gaius Caesar met with

premature natural deaths – unless their stepmother Livia had a secret hand in them. Lucius died on his way to the armies in Spain, Gaius while returning from Armenia incapacitated by a wound.

Nero Drusus was long dead. Tiberius was the only surviving stepson; and everything pointed in his direction. He was adopted as the emperor's son and as partner in his powers (with civil and military authority and the powers of a tribune) and displayed to all the armies. No longer was this due to his mother's secret machinations, as previously. This time she requested it openly. Livia had the aged Augustus firmly under control – so much so that he exiled his only surviving grandson to the island of Planasia. That was the young, physically tough, indeed brutish, Agrippa Postumus. Though devoid of every good quality, he had been involved in no scandal. Nevertheless, it was not he but Germanicus, the son of Nero Drusus, whom the emperor placed in command of the eight divisions on the Rhine – and, although Tiberius had a grown son of his own, he ordered him to adopt Germanicus. For Augustus wanted to have another iron in the fire.

At this time there was no longer any fighting – except a war against the Germans; and that was designed less to extend the empire's frontiers, or achieve any lucrative purpose, than to avenge the disgrace of the army lost with Publius Quinctilius Varus. In the capital the situation was calm. The titles of officials remained the same. Actium had been won before the younger men were born. Even most of the older generation had come into a world of civil wars. Practically no one had ever seen truly Republican government. The country had been transformed, and there was nothing left of the fine old Roman character. Political equality was a thing of the past; all eyes watched for imperial commands.

Nobody had any immediate worries as long as Augustus retained his physical powers, and kept himself going, and his House, and the peace of the empire. But when old age incapacitated him, his approaching end brought hopes of change. A few people started idly talking of the blessings of freedom. Some, more numerous, feared civil war; others wanted it. The great majority, however, exchanged critical gossip about candidates for the succession. First, Agrippa Postumus – a savage without either the years or the training needed for imperial responsibilities. Tiberius, on the other hand, had the seniority and the military reputation. But he also possessed the ancient, ingrained arrogance of the Claudian family; and signs of a cruel disposition kept breaking out, repress them as he might. Besides, it was argued, he had been brought up from earliest youth in an imperial household, had accumulated early consulships and Triumphs, and even during the years at Rhodes[1] – which looked like banishment but were called retirement – his thoughts had been solely occupied with resentment, deception, and secret sensuality. And then there was that feminine bully, his mother. 'So we have got to be slaves to a woman', people were saying, 'and to the two half-grown boys Germanicus and Drusus. First they will be a burden to the State – then they will tear it in two!'

Amid this sort of conversation the health of Augustus deteriorated. Some suspected his wife of foul play. For rumour had it that a few months earlier, with the knowledge of his immediate circle but accompanied only by Paullus Fabius Maximus, he had gone to Planasia to visit Agrippa Postumus; and that there had been such a tearful display of affection on both sides that the young man seemed very likely to be received back into the home of his grandfather. Maximus, it was further said, had told his wife, Marcia, of this, and she had warned Livia – but the emperor had discovered the leakage, and when Maximus died shortly afterwards (perhaps by his own hand) his widow had been heard at the funeral moaning and blaming herself for her husband's death. Whatever the true facts about this, Tiberius was recalled from his post in Illyricum (immediately after his arrival there) by an urgent letter from his mother. When he arrived at Nola, it is unknown whether he found Augustus alive or dead. For the house and neighbouring streets were carefully sealed by Livia's guards. At intervals, hopeful reports were published – until the steps demanded by the situation had been taken. Then two pieces of news became known simultaneously: Augustus was dead, and Tiberius was in control.

The new reign's first crime was the assassination of Agrippa Postumus. He was killed by a staff-officer – who found it a hard task, though he was a persevering murderer and the victim taken by surprise unarmed. Tiberius said nothing about the matter in the senate. He pretended that the orders came from Augustus, who was alleged to have instructed the colonel in charge to kill Agrippa Postumus as soon as

1. Tiberius spent the years 6 B.C.–A.D. 2 on the island of Rhodes.

Augustus himself was dead. It is true that Augustus' scathing criticisms of the young man's behaviour were undoubtedly what had prompted the senate to decree his banishment. But the emperor had never been callous enough to kill any of his relations, and that he should murder his own grandchild to remove the worries of a stepson seemed incredible. It would be nearer the truth to suppose that Tiberius because he was afraid, and Livia through stepmotherly malevolence, loathed and distrusted the young Agrippa Postumus and got rid of him at the first opportunity. But when the staff-officer reported in military fashion that he had carried out his orders, Tiberius answered that he had given no orders and that what had been done would have to be accounted for in the senate.

This came to the notice of Tiberius' confidant, Gaius Sallustius Crispus. It was he who had sent instructions to the colonel, and he was afraid that the responsibility might be shifted to himself – in which case either telling the truth or lying would be equally risky. So he warned Livia that palace secrets, and the advice of friends, and services performed by the army, were best undivulged; and Tiberius must not weaken the throne by referring everything to the senate. The whole point of autocracy, Crispus observed, is that the accounts will not come right unless the ruler is their only auditor.

Meanwhile at Rome consuls, senate, knights, precipitately became servile. The more distinguished men were, the greater their urgency and insincerity. They must show neither satisfaction at the death of one emperor, nor gloom at the accession of another: so their features were carefully arranged in a blend of tears and smiles, mourning and flattery. The first to swear allegiance to Tiberius Caesar were the consuls Sextus Pompeius (II) and Sextus Appuleius; then in their presence the commander of the Guard, Lucius Seius Strabo, and the controller of the corn-supply, Gaius Turranius; next the senate, army, and public. For Tiberius made a habit of always allowing the consuls the initiative, as though the Republic still existed and he himself were uncertain whether to take charge or not. Even the edict with which he summoned the senate to its House was merely issued by virtue of the tribune's power which he had received under Augustus. His edict was brief, and very unpretentious. In it he proposed to arrange his father's last honours, and stay by the side of his body. This, he said, was the only State business which he was assuming.

Nevertheless, when Augustus died Tiberius had given the watch-word to the Guard as its commander. He already had the trappings of a court, too, such as personal bodyguards and men-at-arms. When he went to the Forum, or into the senate, he had soldiers to escort him. He sent letters to the armies as though he were already emperor. He only showed signs of hesitation when he addressed the senate. This was chiefly because of Germanicus, who was extremely popular and disposed of a large Roman force and hordes of auxiliary troops. Tiberius was afraid Germanicus might prefer the throne to the prospect of it. Besides, in deference to public opinion, Tiberius wanted to seem the person chosen and called by the State – instead of one who had wormed his way in by an old man's adoption, and intrigues of the old man's wife. Afterwards it was understood that Tiberius had pre-tended to be hesitant for another reason too, in order to detect what leading men were thinking. Every word, every look he twisted into some criminal significance – and stored them up in his memory.

At the senate's first meeting he allowed no business to be discussed except the funeral of Augustus. But first the emperor's will was brought in by the priestesses of Vesta. Tiberius and Livia were his heirs, and Livia was adopted into the Julian family with the name of 'Augusta'. Grandchildren and great-grandchildren had been named as heirs in the second degree. In the third degree came the most prominent men in the State; Augustus had detested a good many of them, but their inclusion bragged to posterity that he had been their friend. His legacies were in keeping with the standards of ordinary citizens, except that he left 43,500,000 sesterces to the nation and people of Rome, a thousand to every Guardsman, five hundred each to the troops of the capital, three hundred to every citizen soldier, whether he belonged to a regular brigade or to an auxiliary battalion.

A discussion of the funeral followed. The proposals regarded as most noteworthy were those of Gaius Asinius Gallus and Lucius Arruntius. What Gallus wanted was that the procession should pass through a triumphal arch. Arruntius proposed that the body should be preceded by placards showing the titles of every law Augustus had passed and the names of every people he had conquered. Marcus Valerius Messalla Messallinus (I) also suggested that the oath of alle-giance to Tiberius should be repeated every year. When Tiberius asked him to confirm that he, Tiberius, had not prompted t his proposal, Messalla answered that it was his own idea – and that in matters of public importance he intended to use his own judgement and no one else's, even at the risk of causing offence. This show of independence was the only sort of flattery left.

Members clamoured that the body of Augustus should be carried to the pyre on the shoulders of senators. Tiberius, with condescending leniency, excused them. He also published an edict requesting the populace not to repeat the disturbances – due to over-enthusiasm – at the funeral of Julius Caesar, by pressing for Augustus to be cremated in the Forum instead of the Field of Mars, his appointed place of rest. On the day of the funeral the troops were out, apparently for protective purposes. This caused much jeering from people who had witnessed, or heard from their parents, about that day (when the nation's enslavement was still rudimentary) of the ill-starred attempt to recover Republican freedom by murdering the dictator Caesar – a fearful crime? or a conspicuously glorious achievement? Now, they said, this aged autocrat Augustus seems to need a military guard to ensure his undisturbed burial, in spite of his lengthy domination and the foresight with which his heirs, too, have been allocated resources for the suppression of the old order.

Then there was much discussion of Augustus himself. Most people were struck by meaningless points such as the coincidence between the dates of his first public office and his death, and the fact that he died in the same house and room at Nola as his father, Gaius Octavius. There was also talk about his numerous consulships – which equalled the combined totals of Marcus Valerius Corvus and Gaius Marius – of his tribune's power continuous for thirty-seven years, of the twenty-one times he was hailed as victor, and of his other honours, traditional or novel, single or repeated. Intelligent people praised or criticized him in varying terms. One opinion was as follows. Filial duty and a national emergency, in which there was no place for law-abiding conduct, had driven him to civil war – and this can be neither initiated nor maintained by decent methods. He had made many concessions to Antony and to Lepidus for the sake of vengeance on his father's murderers. When Lepidus grew old and lazy, and Antony's self-indulgence got the better of him, the only possible cure for the distracted country had been government by one man. However, Augustus had put the State in order not by making himself king or dictator but by creating the Principate. The empire's frontiers were on the ocean, or distant rivers. Armies, provinces, fleets, the whole system was interrelated. Roman citizens were protected by the law. Provincials were decently treated. Rome itself had been lavishly beautified. Force had been sparingly used – merely to preserve peace for the majority.

The opposite view went like this. Filial duty and national crisis had been merely pretexts. In actual fact, the motive of Octavian, the future Augustus, was lust for power. Inspired by that, he had mobilized ex-army settlers by gifts of money, raised an army – while he was only a half-grown boy without any official status – won over a consul's brigades by bribery, pretended to support Sextus Pompeius (I), and by senatorial decree usurped the status and rank of a praetor. Soon both consuls, Gaius Vibius Pansa and Aulus Hirtius, had met their deaths – by enemy action; or perhaps in the one case by the deliberate poisoning of his wound, and in the other at the hand of his own troops, instigated by Octavian. In any case it was he who took over both their armies. Then he had forced the reluctant senate to make him consul. But the forces given him to deal with Antony he used against the State. His judicial murders and land distributions were distasteful even to those who carried them out. True, Cassius and Brutus died because he had inherited a feud against them; nevertheless, personal enmities ought to be sacrificed to the public interest. Next he had cheated Sextus Pompeius by a spurious peace treaty, Lepidus by spurious friendship. Then Antony, enticed by the treaties of Tarentum and Brundusium and his marriage with Octavian's sister, had paid the penalty of that delusive relationship with his life. After that, there had certainly been peace, but it was a bloodstained peace. For there followed the disasters of Marcus Lollius (I) and Publius Quinctilius Varus; and there were the assassinations, for example, of Aulus Terentius Varro Murena, Marcus Egnatius Rufus and Iullus Antonius.[1]

And gossip did not spare his personal affairs – how he had abducted the wife of Tiberius Claudius Nero, and asked the priests the farcical

1. Tacitus refers to the following events: 23 execution of Aulus Terentius Varro Murena for alleged conspiracy, 19 execution of Marcus Egnatius Rufus for alleged conspiracy, 16 defeat of Marcus Lollius in Germany, 2 Antony's son Iullus Antonius forced to suicide, A.D. 4 Augustus adopts Tiberius, 9 Publius Quinctilius Varus defeated and killed by Arminius in Germany.

question whether it was in order for her to marry while pregnant. Then there was the debauchery of his friend Publius Vedius Pollio. But Livia was a real catastrophe, to the nation, as a mother and to the house of the Caesars as a stepmother.

Besides, critics continued, Augustus seemed to have superseded the worship of the gods when he wanted to have himself venerated in temples, with god-like images, by priests and ministers. His appointment of Tiberius as his successor was due neither to personal affection nor to regard for the national interests. Thoroughly aware of Tiberius' cruelty and arrogance, he intended to heighten his own glory by the contrast with one so inferior. For a few years earlier, when Augustus had been asking the senate to re-award tribune's powers to Tiberius, the emperor had actually let drop in a complimentary oration certain remarks about Tiberius' deportment, style of dressing, and habits. Ostensibly these were excuses; in fact they were criticisms.

After an appropriate funeral, Augustus was declared a god and decreed a temple. But the target of every prayer was Tiberius. Addressing the senate, he offered a variety of comments on the greatness of the empire and his own unpretentiousness. Only the divine Augustus, he suggested, had possessed a personality equal to such responsibilities – he himself, when invited by Augustus to share his labours, had found by experience what hard hazardous work it was to rule the empire. Besides, he said, a State which could rely on so many distinguished personages ought not to concentrate the supreme power in the hands of one man – the task of government would be more easily carried out by the combined efforts of a greater number.

But grand sentiments of this kind sounded unconvincing. Besides, what Tiberius said, even when he did not aim at concealment, was – by habit or nature – always hesitant, always cryptic. And now that he was determined to show no sign of his real feelings, his words became more and more equivocal and obscure. But the chief fear of the senators was that they should be seen to understand him only too well. So they poured forth a flood of tearful lamentations and prayers, gesticulating to heaven and to the statue of Augustus, and making reverent gestures before Tiberius himself.

At this juncture he gave instructions for a document to be produced and read. It was a list of the national resources. It gave the numbers of regular and auxiliary troops serving in the army; the strength of the navy; statistics concerning the provinces and dependent kingdoms; direct and indirect taxation; recurrent expenditure and gifts. Augustus had written all this out in his own hand. Furthermore, he had added a clause advising that the empire should not be extended beyond its present frontiers. Either he feared dangers ahead, or he was jealous.

The senate now wallowed in the most abject appeals. Tiberius remarked incidentally that, although he did not feel himself capable of the whole burden of government, he was nevertheless prepared to take on any branch of it that might be entrusted to him. 'Then I must ask, Caesar,' called out Gaius Asinius Gallus, 'which branch you desire to have handed over to you.' This unexpected question threw Tiberius off his stride. For some moments he said nothing. Then, recovering his balance, he replied that, since he would prefer to be excused from the responsibility altogether, he felt much too diffident to choose or reject this or that part of it. Gallus, however, who had guessed from Tiberius' looks that he had taken offence, protested that the purpose of his question had not been to parcel out functions which were inseparable; it had been to obtain from the lips of Tiberius himself the admission that the State was a single organic whole needing the control of a single mind. Gallus went on to praise Augustus and remind Tiberius of his own victories, and his long and splendid achievements as a civilian. All the same he failed to appease the indignation he had caused. Tiberius had hated him for years, feeling that Gallus' marriage to his own former wife, Marcus Agrippa's daughter Vipsania, was a sign that Gallus had the arrogance of his father Gaius Asinius Pollio (I) – and was over-ambitious.

Next Lucius Arruntius spoke in rather the same vein as Gallus. He too gave offence. Tiberius, in his case, had no longstanding hostility. But he was suspicious of Arruntius, whose wealth, activity, and talents were celebrated. Augustus, in one of his last conversations, had gone over the names of men who would be fit and willing to become emperor, or unfit and unwilling, or fit but unwilling. He had described Marcus Aemilius Lepidus (IV) as suitable but disdainful, Gaius Asinius Gallus as eager but unsuitable, and Lucius Arruntius as both fit and capable of making the venture, if the chance arose. (There is agreement about the first two names; but in some versions Arruntius is replaced by Cnaeus Calpurnius Piso.) All those mentioned, apart from Lepidus, were soon struck down on one charge or another, at the instigation of

Tiberius. Others who chafed his suspicious temperament were Quintus Haterius and Mamercus Aemilius Scaurus. What Haterius did was to ask: 'How long, Caesar, will you allow the State to have no head?' The fault of Scaurus was to say that, since Tiberius had not vetoed the consuls' motion by his tribune's power, there was hope that the senate's prayers would not be unrewarded. Tiberius lost no time in abusing Haterius. But the intervention of Scaurus, against whom his anger was more implacable, he passed over in silence.

Finally, exhausted by the general outcry and individual entreaties, he gradually gave way– not to the extent of admitting that he had accepted the throne, but at least to the point of ceasing to be urged and refuse. There is a well-known story about Haterius. He went into the palace to apologize, and, as Tiberius walked by, grovelled at his feet. Thereupon Tiberius crashed to the ground, either by accident or because he was brought down by the grip of Haterius – who was then all but killed by the guards. However, the emperor's feelings were not softened by the dangerous predicament of the senator, until Haterius appealed to the Augusta – as Livia was now called – and, at her urgent entreaty, was saved.

She, too, was flattered a great deal by the senate. It was variously proposed that she should be called 'parent' and 'mother' of her country; and a large body of opinion held that the words 'son of Julia' ought to form part of the emperor's name. He, however, repeatedly asserted that only reasonable honours must be paid to women – and that, in regard to compliments paid to himself, he would observe a comparable moderation. In reality, however, he was jealous and nervous, and regarded this elevation of a woman as derogatory to his own person. He would not even allow her to be allotted an official attendant, and forbade an Altar of Adoption and other honours of the kind. For Germanicus, however, he requested a special command. A mission was sent to confer it and at the same time to console Germanicus' sorrow at the death of Augustus. The same request was not made for Drusus because he was consul elect and in Rome.

The elections were now transferred from the Assembly to the senate. With regard to the number of praetors Tiberius adhered to the precedent established by Augustus and nominated twelve candidates. The senate asked him to increase the number, but he declared on oath that he would never do so.

Up to this time, although the most important elections were settled by the emperor, some had been left to the inclinations of the national Assembly drawn up by 'tribes'.[1] The public, except in trivial talk, made no objection to their deprival of this right. The senate acquiesced gladly, since it relieved them from the necessity of undignified canvassing and outlay. Tiberius guaranteed that he himself would not recommend more than four candidates, who would have to be appointed without competition or rejection.

At the same time the tribunes petitioned to offer, at their own expense, an annual display which would take its name from the late emperor and be added to the calendar as the Games of Augustus. But it was decided to pay for them from public funds, and to allow the tribunes to wear triumphal robes in the Circus Maximus (they were not, however, to be permitted the use of chariots). It was not long before the organization of this show was transferred to the praetor who is concerned with lawsuits between citizens and non-citizens.

1. See Key to Technical Terms (TRIBES).

CHAPTER 2

Mutiny on the Frontiers

★

WHILE these events were taking place at Rome, mutiny broke out in the regular army in Pannonia. There were no fresh motives for this, except that the change of emperors offered hopes of rioting with impunity and collecting the profits afforded by civil wars. Three brigades were stationed together in a summer camp with Quintus Junius Blaesus in command. When he heard of the death of Augustus and accession of Tiberius, he suspended normal duty for public mourning (or rejoicing). This was when insubordination and altercation began.

Before long, easy living and idleness were all the troops wanted; the idea of work and discipline became distasteful. There was a man called Percennius in the camp. Having become a private soldier after being a professional applause-leader in the theatre, he was insolent of tongue, and experienced in exciting crowds to cheer actors. The soldiers, simple men, were worried – now that Augustus was dead – about their future terms of service. Percennius gradually worked on them. After dark or in the evening twilight, when the better elements had dispersed to their tents and the riff-raff collected, they talked with him.

Finally Percennius had acquired a team of helpers ready for mutiny. Then he made something like a public speech. 'Why', he asked, 'obey, like slaves, a few commanders of companies, fewer still of battalions? You will never be brave enough to demand better conditions if you are not prepared to petition – or threaten – an emperor who is new and still faltering. Inactivity has done quite enough harm in all these years. Old men, mutilated by wounds, are serving their thirtieth or fortieth year. And even after your official discharge your service is not finished; for you stay on with the colours as a reserve, still under canvas – the same drudgery under another name! And if you manage to survive all these hazards, even then you are dragged off to a remote country and "settled" in some waterlogged swamp or untilled mountainside. Truly the army is a harsh, unrewarding profession! Body and soul are reckoned at two and a half sesterces a day[1] – and with this you have to find clothes, weapons, tents, and bribes for brutal company-commanders if you want to avoid chores.

'Heaven knows, lashes and wounds are always with us! So are hard winters and hardworking summers, grim war and unprofitable peace. There will never be improvement until service is based on a contract – pay, four sesterces a day; duration of service, sixteen years with no subsequent recall; a gratuity to be paid in cash before leaving the camp. Guardsmen receive eight sesterces a day, and after sixteen years they go home. Yet obviously their service is no more dangerous than yours. I am not saying a word against sentry-duty in the capital. Still, here are we among tribes of savages, with the enemy actually visible from our quarters!'

Percennius had an enthusiastic reception. As one point or another struck home, his hearers indignantly showed their lash-marks, their white hair, their clothes so tattered that their bodies showed through. Finally, in frenzied excitement, they clamoured that the three brigades should be merged into one. But jealousy wrecked this suggestion, because everyone wanted it to take his own brigade's name. So the proposal was altered, and instead the three Eagles, and the standards of the battalions, were put side by side. Turf was piled up, and a platform erected so as to make the place as conspicuous as possible. As they were hurrying ahead with this, Blaesus came up and began to revile them. Seizing hold of one man after another, he cried: 'Dye your hands in my blood instead! It would be less criminal to kill your general than to rebel against the emperor. As long as I live I shall keep my troops loyal – if I die, my death will help to bring them to their senses.'

Nevertheless, the mound of turf kept rising. But when it was already breast-high, the stubborn perseverance of Blaesus won the day and they gave up the project. Then he made a tactful appeal to them. Rioting and mutiny were not, he said, the best ways of bringing grievances to the emperor's notice. The army had never in former days put such unheard-of-proposals to its commanders. Nor had they

1. See Key to Technical Terms (SESTERCE).

themselves ever put them to the divine Augustus. Besides, at this early stage of the reign it was untimely to add to the emperor's burdens. If, however (Blaesus continued) it was their firm intention to claim, in peacetime, what even the winners of civil wars had never claimed, then they must not plan violent, undisciplined, insubordinate measures – they must appoint delegates and brief them, in his presence. There was a clamorous reply that Blaesus' own son (a colonel) should be the delegate and should request the sixteen-year term of service, his further instructions to follow when the first had produced results. The colonel left for Rome. Then things became fairly peaceful. But the men were pleased with themselves, since the fact that the general's son had gone to speak in the common cause showed clearly that force had secured more than correct behaviour could ever have.

Before the disturbances began, detachments had been sent to Nauportus for various tasks such as road-making and bridge-building. When these men heard of the troubles in camp, they tore down their colours and looted the villages nearby and even Nauportus itself, a community large enough to rank as a town. Company-commanders who tried to restrain them were jeered at and abused, and finally beaten. The principal object of their anger was the corps chief-of-staff, Aufidienus Rufus. They pulled him out of his carriage, piled baggage on his back and drove him along at the head of the column, with frequent mocking inquiries whether he enjoyed these heavy burdens and protracted marches. For Rufus, promoted to company-commander and then to his present post after long service in the ranks, was all for reviving strict old-fashioned service conditions. He had won free from drudgery himself – but what he had endured made him all the more ruthless.

The arrival of the men from Nauportus revived the mutiny. Now marauders began to roam about ransacking the whole district. A few who had looted more than the rest were ordered by Blaesus to be flogged and confined to cells, in order to frighten the others; for he was still obeyed by the company-commanders and the steadier ordinary soldiers. As they were dragged away they offered resistance and grabbed at the legs of bystanders. Shouting out the names of their friends, and of their companies, battalions, and brigades, they cried that the same fate was in store for everybody – all this with repeated insults against the general and invocations of the gods. In fact, they did everything possible to arouse sympathy, indignation, ill-feeling, and panic. Everyone surged to their rescue. The cells were forced open, and deserters and condemned murderers were released and joined them.

Now the mutiny gained momentum. More and more leaders came forward. A private soldier called Vibulenus was hoisted on the shoulders of the men standing round the general's dais. The excited crowd, watching to see what he would do, heard him speak:

'I know you have brought these poor innocent men back to life and daylight. But you can't give my brother back to me, or me to him! The army in Germany sent him to talk to you about our common interests – and the general had him murdered last night by the gladiators whom he keeps armed to butcher us soldiers. Answer, Blaesus – where have you put his corpse? Even enemies don't refuse a grave. Later, when I have embraced his corpse and mourned my fill, you can tell them to murder me as well. But they mustn't grudge us burial. We are not dying because of any crime. We are dying because we worked for the army's good!'

To add to the inflammatory effect, Vibulenus wept and struck his face and beat his chest. Then he pushed aside those who were holding him on their shoulders, and hurled himself flat in front of one man after another, appealing to them. They went frantic with impassioned hostility. One group arrested the gladiators who were slaves in the service of Blaesus while others captured the rest of Blaesus' household, and a further band rushed off in search of the body. Indeed if it had not rapidly come to light that there was no body to be found, that the slaves denied the murder even under torture, and that Vibulenus had never had a brother, they were not far from killing the general himself.

As it was, they turned out the other senior officers, including the chief-of-staff – looting their luggage as they fled. The company-commander Lucilius lost his life. In joking army talk his nickname was 'Another-please', because every time he broke a stick over a soldier's back he used to shout loudly for another and then another. His fellow-officers found safe hiding-places, except only Julius Clemens, who was kept because his intelligence was thought to qualify him for presenting the mutineers' demands. The eighth and fifteenth brigades nearly came to blows when one shouted for the death of a company-commander, Sirpicus by name, and the other protected him. Finally, the men of the ninth brigade intervened with appeals – and with threats of violence against those who ignored them.

The natural inscrutability of Tiberius was always particularly impenetrable in a crisis. However, this news impelled him to send to the scene his son Drusus with a distinguished staff and two battalions of the Guard. Drusus was given no definite instructions – he was to act as the circumstances required. The Guard battalions were strengthened beyond their usual numbers by picked drafts, and were further augmented by a substantial part of the horse Guards and also by the best of the Germans who at that time guarded the emperor's person. With them went a man whose influence over Tiberius was very great, Lucius Aelius Sejanus, joint commander of the Guard with his father, Lucius Seius Strabo. He was to be the prince's adviser, and not to let the rest of the party forget what they stood to gain – or lose.

As Drusus approached, the soldiers met him. Ostensibly this was a mark of respect. But there were none of the customary demonstrations of pleasure and glittering full-dress decorations. The men were disgustingly dirty, and their expressions, intended merely to display dejection, looked virtually treasonable. As soon as Drusus had passed inside the outworks, they picketed the gates, and set armed detachments at key points of the camp. Everyone else crowded round the dais in a gigantic mob. Drusus mounted it with a gesture calling for silence. The mutineers, looking round at the great crowd, set up a truculent roar. But the next instant, as they caught sight of the Caesar, their nerve faltered. Violent yells alternated with confused mutterings, and then silence. They were terrifying and terrified in turn, as their feelings shifted. When Drusus finally got the better of the noise, he read out a letter from his father. It stated that the heroic Roman soldiers, his comrades in so many campaigns, were particularly near his heart, and that as soon as the shock of his bereavement was over, he would refer their claims to the senate. Meanwhile he had sent his son to grant without delay any concessions that could be awarded immediately. The remaining points must be saved up for the senate, which was as capable, they must understand, of generosity as of severity.

The answer came from the crowd that the company-commander Julius Clemens was briefed to put forward their demands. He started by proposing a sixteen-year term of service, with gratuities at its com-

pletion, pay of four sesterces a day, and no recalls after release. Drusus
urged that the senate and emperor must have their say. This caused
uproar. 'Why have you come', they shouted, 'if you are not going
to raise salaries, improve terms of service, or help us at all? Anyone,
on the other hand, is allowed to murder and flog! It used to be Tiberius
who blocked the regular army's grievances by citing Augustus. Now
Drusus has revived the same old trick. It looks as though our visitors
will always be young men with fathers. How curious it is that the only
army matters which the emperor refers to the senate are reforms in
service conditions! If he does this, he ought also to consult them when
death penalties or battles are in store. Clearly when rewards are concerned, he is not his own master – whereas no one controls punishments.'

At last they left the dais. But if they came upon any Guardsmen on
Drusus' staff, they made menacing gestures, to create ill-feeling and
give a pretext for open hostilities. They were particularly bitter against
Gnaeus Cornelius Lentulus (II), whose seniority and military distinction made them think that, being more disgusted than anyone with
the scandalous conduct of the army, he was stiffening Drusus' attitude.
Shortly afterwards they caught him leaving, escorted to the gate by
Drusus. Lentulus had seen danger ahead and was withdrawing to the
winter camp. The men gathered round him and asked him where he
was going. Was he on his way to the emperor, or to the senate – to
oppose army reforms there too? Then they closed in on him and began
throwing large stones. One hit him and drew blood. He was convinced that his end had come. But the hasty arrival of Drusus' main
force saved him.

The night looked like ending in a disastrous criminal outbreak. But
this was averted by a stroke of luck. Suddenly, in a clear sky, the light
of the moon was seen to decline. The soldiers did not know why this
was, and detected an omen of their own situation. The waning moon
seemed to provide an analogy to their own efforts: success would only
crown the measures they were adopting if the moon-goddess shone
brightly again. To produce this result they made a clattering of brass
instruments and blew blasts on every sort of trumpet. The light
seemed stronger, and they were happy. Then it looked dimmer, and
they were mournful. Finally clouds hid it from view altogether. Men's
minds, once unbalanced, are ready to believe anything; and now they

howled that heaven was sickened by their crimes, and endless hardships were in store for them.

Drusus felt that advantage must be taken of this turn of events; a lucky chance could be exploited in the interests of good sense. Summoning Julius Clemens and any other officers whose kind natures had made them popular, he ordered them to go round the tents. Insinuating themselves among the watches and pickets and sentries they worked on the men's hopes and fears. Was it desirable, they questioned, to go on besieging the emperor's son? Where would these disputes end? Were they going to swear loyalty to Percennius and Vibulenus? Percennius and Vibulenus were not going to replace Neros and Drususes as lords of the Roman world. They were not going to pay the army and give ex-soldiers land. 'We were the last to give offence,' the officers suggested, 'so let us be the first to be sorry. Reform by collective agitation is slow in coming: individuals can earn goodwill and win its rewards straightaway.' This made a profound impression. Mutual suspicions began to undermine the solidarity between one brigade and another, between young and old. A sense of obedience gradually came back. The gates were left unguarded, and the Eagles and standards set up side by side at the beginning of the mutiny were returned to where they belonged.

At daybreak Drusus called a meeting. Though not a practised orator, he spoke with natural dignity. He censured their former behaviour, and expressed approval of their new attitude. Intimidation and menaces, he said, made no impression on him. If, however, he found that discipline had prevailed and they were pleading for pardon, he would write to his father recommending a merciful hearing for their pleas. They begged him to do this. So the younger Blaesus was again sent to Tiberius, accompanied by a Roman knight on Drusus' staff, Lucius Aponius, and a senior company-commander, Catonius Justus. There was now a division of opinion. One proposal was that the return of this delegation should be awaited, and that meanwhile the soldiers should be treated gently and humoured. Others favoured a more forceful solution, arguing that the masses only dealt in extremes and would terrorize unless they were terrorized – once intimidated, they could be disregarded with impunity: now, when superstition had a hold of them, was the time for the general to intensify their panic by striking down the leaders of the mutiny. Drusus had a natural preference for severe measures. Summoning Vibulenus and Percennius, he ordered them to be executed. Report has it that they were buried inside the general's tent. According to another account, however, the bodies were thrown outside the lines to be exhibited. Then all the chief instigators of the mutiny were hunted up. Some were killed by company-commanders or Guardsmen as they wandered blindly about outside the camp. Others were given up by their own units as a proof of loyalty.

The hardships of the soldiers were made worse by an early winter with unceasing rain. It rained so hard that they could hardly leave their tents to confer. They could only barely save the standards from being carried away by hurricane and flood. Besides, they were still afraid of divine wrath – extinguished planets and torrential downpours seemed directly connected with their criminal actions. The only cure for their misfortunes appeared to be the evacuation of this sinister, defiled camp and their return, purged of guilt, to their various winter quarters. First the eighth brigade left, then the fifteenth. The men of the ninth had loudly favoured waiting for a reply from Tiberius. But the withdrawal of the rest left them stranded, and they did voluntarily what they would soon have been forced to do anyway.

Drusus felt that the situation had become reasonably calm. So, without awaiting the delegation's return, he left for Rome.

At just about this time, and for the same reasons, the regular brigades in Germany mutinied too. They were more numerous, and the outbreak was proportionately graver. Moreover they were in high hopes that Germanicus, unable to tolerate another man as emperor, would put himself at the disposal of the forces, which would then sweep all before them. There were two armies on the Rhine bank. The army of Upper Germany was under the command of Gaius Silius (I), the army of Lower Germany under Aulus Caecina Severus. Their supreme commander was Germanicus, but he was occupied at this time in assessing the property-tax in the Gallic provinces.

The forces of Silius did not regard the mutiny as their own concern and watched it with mixed feelings. But the army of Lower Germany lost its senses. The two brigades which took the initiative, the twenty-first and fifth, brought in the first and twentieth, which shared their summer camp upon the borders of the Ubii and were occupied on light duty, or none at all. When the death of Augustus became known, the simple minds of the majority came under the influence of the masses of town-slaves who had recently been conscripted in the capital. Naturally insolent and lazy, they now argued that the moment had come for old soldiers to demand long-overdue demobilization, and for the younger men to demand an increase in pay. Everyone should insist on relief from their hardships, and retaliate against the savagery of their company-commanders. Here it was not just a matter of one Percennius, as in the army of Pannonia, or of soldiers nervously thinking of other and more powerful armies. This was a massive outbreak. There was a universal cry that they had won Rome's victories, her fate rested with them, and army commanders used a surname (Germanicus) derived from them.

The general, Caecina, took no counter-measures. The scale of the disturbances broke his nerve. Suddenly, in a passionate frenzy, swords drawn, the men attacked their company-commanders – the customary targets of the army's ill-will, and the first victims of any outbreak. They were hurled to the ground and given the lash, sixty strokes each, one for each of them in the brigade. Then, broken and mutilated, they were cast outside the lines or thrown into the Rhine, more dead than alive. One, Septimius, took refuge on the general's dais and fell at Caecina's feet. But he was shouted for so violently that he had to be given up to his fate. Gaius Cassius Chaerea, who later went down to history as the murderer of the emperor Gaius and was at this time young and fiery, fought his way through the armed mob which held him up. Colonels, corps chiefs-of-staff had no control any longer. Patrols and sentries, and whatever else circumstances demanded, were organized by the men themselves. Students of army psychology could see the momentous and implacable character of the revolt from the fact that its instigators were not few and far between, but there was universal, silent fury, as resolute and unanimous as if they were acting on orders.

At this time Germanicus, as I have said, was engaged upon assessments in Gaul. There he learnt that Augustus was dead. Germanicus was married to his granddaughter Agrippina (I) and had several children by her; and since he was the son of Tiberius' brother Nero Drusus, one of his grandparents was the Augusta. Yet Germanicus suffered from the fact that his grandmother and uncle hated him, for reasons which were unfair but all the more potent. For Nero Drusus still lived on in Roman memories. It was believed that if he had obtained control of the empire he would have brought back the free Republic. The hopes and goodwill thus engendered passed to his son, Germanicus. For this young man's unassuming personality and popular manner were very different from the haughty, ambiguous looks and words of Tiberius. Ill-feeling among the women made things worse. The Augusta had a stepmother's aversion to Agrippina. Agrippina herself was determined, and rather excitable. But she turned this to good account by her devoted faithfulness to her husband.

At all events Germanicus' proximity to the summit of ambition only made him work more enthusiastically on behalf of Tiberius. After taking the oath of loyalty himself, he administered it to his immediate subordinates and to the Belgic communities. Then came the news that the army was rioting. He set out for it hurriedly.

The men met him outside the camp. They kept their eyes fixed on the ground, ostensibly remorseful. As soon as he entered their lines, however, they assailed him with all manner of complaints. Some grasped his hand as though to kiss it, but instead thrust his fingers into their mouths to make him touch their toothless gums. Others showed how old age had deformed them. They crowded round him to listen – in no sort of order. Germanicus told them to divide into their units. But they shouted back that they would hear better where they were. He said that they must at least bring their standards to the front so that it could be seen which battalion was which. Slowly they obeyed. Then Germanicus, after paying a reverent tribute to Augustus' memory, praised the victories and triumphs of Tiberius and, by way of climax, his glorious achievements in German lands with those very brigades. He spoke appreciatively of Italy's unanimous support for the government, and of the loyalty of the Gauls – of the perfect harmony and order prevailing everywhere.

This was received in silence or with indistinct muttering. But then Germanicus passed on to the mutiny. What on earth had happened, he asked, to their famous, traditional military discipline, and where had they driven their colonels and company-commanders? The soldiers' reply was to tear off their clothes one after another, and point abusively to the scars left by their wounds and floggings. There was a confused roar about their wretched pay, the high cost of exemptions from duty, and the hardness of the work. Specific references were made to earthworks, excavations, foraging, collecting timber and fire-wood, and every other camp task that is either necessary or invented to occupy spare time. The most violent outcry came from the old soldiers, who pointed to their thirty years' service and more, and appealed for relief from their exhaustion before death overtook them in the same old drudgery. 'End this crushing service!' they begged. 'Give us rest – before we are utterly destitute!'

Some asked Germanicus for the legacies which the divine Augustus had left them – adding expressions of personal support for Germanicus. If he wanted the throne, they showed they were for him. At this point he leapt off the dais as if their criminal intentions were polluting him, and moved away. But they blocked his path and menaced him until he went back. Then, however, shouting that death was better than disloyalty, he pulled the sword from his belt and lifted it as though to plunge it into his chest. The men round him clutched his arm and stopped him by force. But the close-packed masses at the back of the crowd, and even, remarkably enough, certain individuals who had pushed themselves into prominent positions, encouraged him to strike. A soldier called Calusidius even drew his own sword and offered it, remarking that it was sharper. But even in their de-mented frame of mind the men found this a brutal and repellent gesture. There was a pause; and Germanicus' friends had time to hurry him into his tent.

There they considered what was to be done. The soldiers were reported to be organizing a deputation to bring over the army of Upper Germany. They were also, it was said, planning to destroy the capital of the Ubii, and after that taste of looting to burst into the Gallic pro-vinces and plunder them too. The situation was all the more alarming because the Germans knew of the mutiny in the Roman army: the abandonment of the Rhine bank would mean invasion. Yet to arm auxiliaries and loyal tribesmen against the rebellious regulars would be civil war. Severity appeared dangerous. But large concessions would be criminal. It would be just as desperately risky for Rome to give way about everything or about nothing. When all the arguments had been weighed and compared, it was decided to make a statement in the emperor's name. In this, demobilization was promised after twenty years' service. Men who had served sixteen years were to be released but kept with the colours with no duties except to help beat off enemy attacks. Moreover, the legacies which they had requested were to be paid – twice over.

The soldiers saw that these concessions were hastily improvised and demanded their immediate implementation. The discharges were speedily arranged by the senior officers. The cash payments, however, were held up until the troops reached winter camps. Two brigades, the fifth and the twenty-first, refused to move from their summer quarters until, there and then, the whole sum was paid. It had to be scraped together from the travelling funds of Germanicus himself and his staff. The general Caecina took the remaining two brigades, the first and the twentieth, back to the Ubian capital. It was a scandalous march – Eagle, standards, and the cash stolen from the commander, all were carried along together.

Then Germanicus moved on to the army of Upper Germany. He had no difficulty in inducing the second, thirteenth and sixteenth brigades to take the oath; the fourteenth only took it after hesitation. Though there were no demands for discharges and money payments, both were conceded. In the territory of the Chauci, however, a fresh outbreak occurred, among a garrison consisting of detachments from the insubordinate brigades. The trouble was soon stamped out by two prompt executions. This illegal but salutary measure was carried out on the orders of the corps chief-of-staff Manius Ennius. Then, as the mutiny began to swell, he got away. But he was discovered. Relying on a bold course for the safety which his hiding-place had failed to provide, he cried out that their offence was not just against an officer, it was against Germanicus their commander – against Tiberius their emperor! At the same time, intimidating all opposition, he seized the standard and pointed it towards the Rhine. Then, shouting that everyone who fell out would be treated as a deserter, he conducted his men back to their winter camp – still rebellious, but frustrated.

Meanwhile the senate's mission to Germanicus found him back at the Ubian altar[1] and capital. The first and the twentieth brigades were in winter quarters there, and also the soldiers who had recently been released but not yet demobilized. Mad with anxiety and bad conscience, these men were also terrified that the concessions which they had won

1. The altar of Augustus at the Ubian capital (the later Cologne) was the centre of his cult in the provinces of Germany.

by mutinous methods would be cancelled by the senatorial delegation. Crowds habitually find scapegoats, however unjustifiably, and now they attacked the chief envoy, the former consul Lucius Munatius Plancus, charging him with instigating sanctions against them in the senate. Early in the night they began to clamour for their standard, which was kept in Germanicus' residence. They rushed the door and forced him to get up and – under threat of death – to hand it over. Then, roaming the streets, they encountered the members of the delegation, who had heard the uproar and were on their way to Germanicus. The soldiers heaped abuse on them. Indeed they had it in mind to kill them, and especially Plancus. His high rank made it impossible for him to run away; and in his extreme danger the only available refuge was the camp of the first brigade. There he found sanctuary, grasping the Eagle and standards. But if a colour-sergeant named Calpurnius had not protected him from his fate, then, without precedent even between enemies, the altars of the gods would have been stained with the blood of an emissary of the Roman people, in a Roman camp.

At last morning arrived; and commanders and private soldiers, and the night's doings, were seen for what they were. Germanicus came into the camp and ordered Plancus to be brought to him. Escorting him on to the dais, he assailed this disastrous, maniacal revival of violence. 'It shows how angry the gods are', he said, 'rather than the soldiers!' Then he explained why the delegation had come, and spoke with gloomy eloquence about the rights of envoys, and the deplorable and unfair treatment of Plancus himself – a disgrace to the brigade. The gathering was hardly pacified, but it was cowed; and Germanicus sent the delegates away under the protection of auxiliary cavalry.

In this alarming situation Germanicus was generally criticized for not proceeding to the upper army, which obeyed orders and would help against the rebels. Enough and more than enough mistakes had been made, it was felt, by releases and payments and mild measures. And even if he did not value his own life, people asked why, among these madmen who had broken every law, he kept with him his baby son and his pregnant wife. Surely he owed it to the nation and their imperial grandfather to send them back! Germanicus was long hesitant. His wife scorned the proposal, reminding him that she was of the blood of the divine Augustus and would live up to it, whatever the danger. Then he burst into tears – and clasping to him the expectant mother and their child, persuaded her to go. It was a pitiable feminine company that set out. The supreme commander's own wife, a refugee, clutched his infant son to her breast. Her escorts, his friends' wives – forced to leave with her – were in tears. Those who remained were equally mournful. The scene suggested a captured city rather than a highly successful Caesar in his own camp.

The women's sobbing and lamentation attracted the attention of the soldiers, who came out of their tents and asked why they were crying and what was wrong. Here were these distinguished ladies with no staff-officers or soldiers to look after them, none of the usual escort or other honours due to the supreme commander's wife. And they were off to the Treviri, to be looked after by foreigners! The men felt sorry for them, and ashamed, when they thought of her ancestry – her father was Agrippa, her grandfather Augustus, her father-in-law Nero Drusus – and of her impressive record as wife and mother. Besides, there was her baby son, Gaius, born in the camp and brought up with the regular troops as his comrades. In their army fashion they had nicknamed him 'little Boots' (Caligula), because as a popular gesture he was often dressed in miniature army boots. But their jealousy of the Treviri was what affected them most.

So now they wanted to prevent Agrippina's departure, and appealed that she should stop and come back. Some ran to intercept her, the majority returned to Germanicus. He stood among them, still smarting with grief and anger. 'My wife and son', he told them, 'are not more dear to me than my father and my country. But my father has his august dignity to protect him, and the Roman empire has its other armies. I would willingly see my wife and children die for your greater glory. Now, however, I am taking them out of your demented reach. Whatever atrocities are impending, my life alone must atone for them. Do not make your guilt worse by murdering the great-grandson of Augustus, the daughter-in-law of Tiberius!

'In these last days you have committed every possible crime and horror. I do not know what to call this gathering! You men who have used your fortifications and weapons to blockade your emperor's son can hardly be called soldiers. And "citizens" is not the name for people who cast aside the authority of the senate. The international code too, rights due even to enemies, the sanctity of ambassadors – you have outraged them. The divine Julius Caesar suppressed a mutiny by one word: when his men would not take the oath he called them "civilians". The divine Augustus put fear into his troops at Actium by a look. I cannot yet compete with them. But I am their descendant; and if the soldiers even in Spain or Syria – where I am not known – were disrespectful to me, it would be surprising and scandalous enough. And here we have you, the first brigade, which received its colours from Tiberius, and you, the twentieth, his comrades in many battles. He rewarded you amply. How splendidly you are repaying your old commander! This, it seems, is the report I must make to my father – amid the good news that he has from every other province – that his own old soldiers, his own recruits, they and they alone, not content with releases and gratuities, are slaughtering their company-commanders, ejecting their colonels, arresting their generals, until the camp and the river are soaked in blood, and I myself, surrounded by hatred, live only on sufferance!

'When, at that first day's meeting, you pulled away the sword I was preparing to plunge into my body, your friendly solicitude was inconsiderate. A better, truer friend was the man who offered me his own sword. At any rate I should have died with my conscience spared all my army's crimes! The leader whom you would then have chosen need not have avenged my death. Instead he could have avenged Publius Quinctilius Varus and his three brigades. For heaven forbid that the distinction and glory of having helped Rome, and suppressed the peoples of Germany, should go to the Belgae – Gauls and foreigners – for all their offers. Divine Augustus, I call upon your spirit now in heaven! Nero Drusus my father, I invoke your image that is in our memories! Come to these soldiers of yours (into whose hearts shame and pride are making their way); wash clean this stain! Direct these revolutionary passions against enemy lives instead. And you men: I see your looks and hearts have changed. Will you give the senate back its delegates, be obedient to the emperor again – and return me my wife and son? Then shake off the contagion. Single out the culprits! That will show you are sorry, and prove you are loyal.'

At this they petitioned for mercy. Admitting the justice of his rebuke, they begged him to punish the guilty, and forgive those who had slipped. He must lead them against the enemy, they urged. And first his wife must be summoned back – the boy they bred must also return, and not be given to Gauls as a hostage. Germanicus agreed that his son should return, but excused his wife since her confinement was at hand, and so was winter. The rest, he said, was up to them. Changed men, they hastened round arresting the leading rebels and dragging them before the commander of the first brigade, Gaius Caetronius. Each ringleader in turn was tried and punished by him in the following fashion. The men, with drawn swords, stood in a mass. One after another the prisoners were paraded on the platform by a colonel. If they shouted 'Guilty', he was thrown down and butchered. The soldiers revelled in the massacre as though it purged them of their offences. And Germanicus, though the orders had not been his, did not intervene. For the disgust caused by this savagery would be directed against its perpetrators, and not against him.

The discharged men acted similarly. Soon afterwards, they were sent to Raetia. The pretext was defence against a threat from the Suebi; but the real intention was to remove them from a camp with hateful memories of crimes and of their equally appalling retribution. Then Germanicus revised the roll of company-commanders. Each in turn came before him and reported his name, company, birth-place, length of service, and any battle distinctions and decorations. If the colonels and men spoke favourably of his work and character, then the company-commander kept his job. If, however, he was unanimously described as grasping and brutal, he was dismissed from the service.

This relieved the immediate crisis. But there was still equally serious trouble from the truculent attitude of the fifth and twenty-first brigades wintering sixty miles away at Vetera. It was they who had started the mutiny and committed the worst atrocities. Now they were as angry as ever, undeterred by the punishment and contrition of their fellow-soldiers. So Germanicus, ready to use force if his authority were set aside, prepared to transport auxiliary troops and arms down the Rhine.

When Rome heard of the rebellion in Germany – before the final developments in Illyricum were known – the whole population rounded panic-striken on Tiberius. Here was he with his insincere hesitation, making fools of the helpless, unarmed senate and Assembly; while the soldiers mutinied! Two half-grown boys, they felt, could not control these rebellions. Tiberius ought to have gone himself, and confronted them with his imperial dignity: they would have given

way when they saw their experienced emperor, with sovereign powers
of retribution and reward. It was recalled that Augustus had made
several visits to the Germanies in later life – yet here was Tiberius, in
his prime, sitting in the senate quibbling at members' speeches! The
enslavement of Rome, men said, was well in hand. Now something
must be done to calm the troops and make peace.

Such talk made no impression on Tiberius. He was determined not
to jeopardize the nation and himself by leaving the capital. His worries
were various. Germany had the stronger army, Pannonia the nearer.
The former had Gaul's resources behind it, the latter threatened Italy.
So which should he visit first? And what if the one placed second
should take serious offence? Whereas, through his sons, he could deal
with both simultaneously and keep intact his imperial dignity – which
was, indeed, more awe-inspiring at a distance. Besides, it was excus-
able for the young Germanicus and Drusus to refer some points to
their father, and resistance offered to them could be conciliated or
broken by himself. If, on the other hand, the emperor were treated
contemptuously, no expedient was left.

All the same, as though he were going to start at any moment, he
chose his staff, collected equipment, and prepared ships. Then, however, he offered various excuses about the weather, and pressure of
business. The deception worked – on intelligent people for a little, on
most people for some time, and on those in the provinces for longest
of all.

Germanicus had brought his troops together and was ready for
counter-measures against the mutineers. But he decided to give them
more time in case they might profit by the example of the other brigades. So he sent word to Caecina saying that he was coming with a
strong force and that, unless they first punished the agitators, he would
execute them indiscriminately. Caecina read the letter privately to the
colour-sergeants and sergeant-majors and other reliable elements in
the camp, and appealed to them to save the army's honour, and their
own lives. 'In peace-time', he said, 'backgrounds and justifications
are considered; but when war comes, the innocent fall with the
guilty.' Sounding the men whom they thought reliable, they found
that the greater part of the two brigades was loyal. So in consultation
with the general, they fixed a time at which the grossest offenders were
to be struck down. At a given signal, they burst into the tents, and

surprised and killed their victims. Only those in the secret knew how the massacre had begun – or where it would end.

This was unlike any other civil war. It was not a battle between opposing forces. Men in the same quarters, who had eaten together by day and rested together by night, took sides and fought each other. The shrieks, wounds, and blood were unmistakable. But motives were mysterious, fates unpredictable. There were casualties among the loyalists, too; for the culprits also had seized weapons when they realized who were being attacked. Generals, colonels, offered no restraining hand. Mass vengeance was indulged and glutted.

Soon afterwards Germanicus arrived in the camp. Bursting into tears, he cried: 'This is no cure; it is a catastrophe!' Then he ordered the bodies to be cremated.

CHAPTER 3

War with the Germans

*

THERE was still a savage feeling among the troops – and a desire to make up for their lunacy by attacking the enemy. Honourable wounds, they felt, on their guilty breasts, were the only means of appeasing the ghosts of their fellow-soldiers. Germanicus encouraged these ambitions, and built a bridge across the Rhine.

Across it he transported twelve thousand regular troops, twenty-six auxiliary battalions, and eight cavalry regiments, of which the loyalty had not been affected during the rising. While we were immobilized, first by the mourning for Augustus and then by the mutinies, the Germans were in high spirits – and not far off. But a rapid march through the Caesian forest brought the Roman army across the line begun by Tiberius. Germanicus pitched camp on the line with earthworks to his front and rear, and palisades on his flanks. Ahead were dark forests and two paths – one the short, usual route, and the other so hard and unfamiliar that the enemy left it unwatched. After a conference the Romans chose the longer way. Their advance was rapid, since according to intelligence reports there was a German festival that night with ceremonial banquets and performances. Caecina was instructed to go on ahead with light-armed auxiliary battalions to clear a passage through the forests, the regular brigades to follow not far behind. A starry night helped. Each village they came to in the country of the Marsi found itself surrounded by a ring of Roman pickets. The Germans were lying in bed or beside their tables, unafraid, with no sentries posted. There was careless disorganization everywhere. Of war there was not a thought. Their condition was one of peace – in this case, an uncontrolled, drunken prostration.

To increase the scope of the raid, Germanicus divided his enthusiastic troops into four columns. These ravaged and burnt the country for fifty miles around. No pity was shown to age or sex. Religious as well as secular centres were utterly destroyed – among them the temple of Tanfana, the most revered holy place of those tribes. There were no Roman casualties, since their victims were scattered, unarmed and half-asleep. But neighbouring tribes, the Bructeri, Tubantes, and Usipetes, disturbed by the massacre, occupied the woods on their way back. Germanicus discovered this and took the road in readiness either to march or fight. A cavalry force and auxiliary battalions went ahead, followed by the first brigade in the centre, the twenty-first and the fifth on the left and right flanks respectively, and the twentieth in the rear. Behind came the remaining auxiliaries.

The enemy did not budge until the whole column was strung out in the wood. Then, feinting against the vanguard and flanks, they directed their full force against the rear. The massed German attacks disorganized the light-armed auxiliary battalions. Germanicus rode up to the twenty-first brigade and shouted that now was the time to wipe out the mutiny – by one rapid stroke, their disgrace could be turned into glory. Then the brigade by a single, passionate attack broke through the German army and drove it with heavy losses into open country. Simultaneously the vanguard emerged from the woods and established a fortified camp. From then on, the journey was without incident. The troops settled into winter quarters, their morale improved and the past forgotten.

Tiberius' reaction to German developments included worry as well as relief. He was glad the mutiny had been put down. But he was not pleased that Germanicus had courted the army's goodwill by money payments and accelerated discharges – not to speak of his military success. Tiberius reported the achievements of Germanicus to the senate. But what he said, though complimentary, was so ostentatiously elaborate that it did not ring true. The few words with which he praised Drusus for ending the mutiny in Illyricum sounded more heartfelt and sincere; and he extended to the regular troops in Pannonia the concessions which Germanicus had granted to those on the Rhine.

This was the year when Julia (III) died. Her father Augustus had imprisoned her – for immorality – first on the island of Pandateria and then in the town of Rhegium on the straits opposite Sicily. While Gaius

Caesar and Lucius Caesar were still alive, she had been married to
Tiberius, but had looked down on him as an inferior. That had been
the fundamental reason for his retirement to Rhodes. When he became
emperor, he eliminated her last hope by the removal of Agrippa Postumus. Then he let her waste away to death, exiled and disgraced, by
slow starvation. He calculated that she had been banished for so long
that her death would pass unnoticed.

There were similar motives behind his harsh treatment of Sempronius Gracchus. This shrewd, misguidedly eloquent aristocrat
had seduced Julia while she was Marcus Agrippa's wife. Nor was that
the end of the affair, for when she was transferred to Tiberius this
persistent adulterer made her defiant and unfriendly to her new husband. A letter abusing Tiberius, which Julia wrote to her father
Augustus, was believed to have been Gracchus' work. So he had been
dismissed to the African island of Cercina, where he endured fourteen
years of exile. Now soldiers were sent to kill him. They found him
standing on a promontory, fearing the worst. When they landed, he
asked for a few moments so that he could write his wife Alliaria certain
last requests. Then he offered his neck to the assassins. His life had fallen
short of the prestige of the Sempronii. His brave death, however, was
worthy of them. According to another account the soldiers did not
come from Rome, but were sent by the governor of Africa, Lucius
Nonius Asprenas. This version, however, originated from Tiberius –
who hoped (unsuccessfully) to blame the murder on the governor.

In the same year, there was a religious innovation: a new Brotherhood of Augustus was created, on the analogy of the ancient Titian
Brotherhood founded by King Titus Tatius for the maintenance of
Sabine ritual. Twenty-one members were appointed by lot from the
leading men of the State; and Tiberius, Drusus, Claudius, and Germanicus were added. The annual Games established in honour of
Augustus were also begun. But their inauguration was troubled by disorders due to rivalry between ballet-dancers. Augustus had tolerated
such performances out of indulgence to Maecenas, who was passionately fond of a contemporary star, Bathyllus. Besides, Augustus
himself liked this sort of entertainment, and thought it looked democratic to join in the people's amusements. Tiberius' character took a
different course. But he did not yet venture to introduce the long-pampered Romans to austerity.

In the next year, when the consuls were Drusus and Gaius Norbanus, a Triumph was decreed to Germanicus. The war, however, was not over. Its next stage was a sudden raid on the Chatti in early spring. But he was planning a large-scale summer campaign against the major enemy, the Cherusci. It was hoped that their allegiance was split between Arminius and Segestes. These two leaders stood respectively for treachery and goodwill to Rome. Arminius was Germany's trouble-maker. Segestes had often warned Publius Quinctilius Varus that rebellion was planned. At the feast which immediately preceded the rising Segestes had advised Varus to arrest Arminius and the other chiefs, and also himself, on the grounds that their removal would immobilize their accomplices and Varus could then take his time in sorting out the guilty from the innocent. However, Varus was destined to fall to Arminius. Segestes had been forced into the war by the unanimous feeling of the Cherusci. But relations between the two Germans were still bad. Domestic ill-feeling contributed because Segestes' daughter, engaged to another man, was stolen by Arminius. The girl's father and husband detested each other. The marriage relationship, which brings friends closer, increased the bitterness of these two enemies.

For the operation against the Chatti, Germanicus transferred to Aulus Caecina Severus four brigades with 5,000 auxiliaries, also some German emergency levies from this side of the Rhine. He himself retained the same number of brigades with twice as many auxiliary troops. He built a fort on Mount Taunus – on the remains of a construction of his father's – and proceeded with rapid, lightly equipped forces against the Chatti. He left a force under Lucius Apronius to put roads and bridges in order, since rain and floods were feared on the return journey; but now a drought, rare in those parts, had emptied the rivers, and gave him an uninterrupted advance.

Germanicus completely surprised the Chatti. Helpless women, children, and old people were at once slaughtered or captured. The younger men swam across the river Eder and tried to prevent the Romans from building a bridge. But they were driven back by missiles and arrows. An unsuccessful attempt was made by the tribesmen to come to terms. Then there were some desertions to the Roman side. But the majority evacuated their towns and villages, dispersed and took to the woods. Germanicus burnt their capital, Mattium, and, ravaging the open country, started back for the Rhine. The enemy did not dare to harass the rearguard, as they are fond of doing when they have retreated for strategic purposes rather than in a panic.

The Cherusci had been inclined to help the Chatti; but a series of swift manoeuvres by Caecina deterred them. He also defeated the Marsi who had ventured to engage him. Soon afterwards a deputation arrived appealing for the rescue of Segestes, besieged by his hostile compatriots. Arminius was in power. He was leader of the war-party – in disturbed times uncivilized communities trust and prefer leaders who take risks. Segestes had included his own son Segimundus in the deputation. The latter, reflecting on his record, had hesitated. For in the year of the German rebellion he had taken off the insignia of his Roman priesthood at the Ubian altar, and had run away to the rebels. However, he was persuaded to hope for Roman indulgence, and served as his father's envoy. He was well received, and escorted across to the left bank of the river.

Germanicus thought it worth his while to wheel round, engage the besieging force, and rescue Segestes and many of his relations and dependants. These included women of high rank, among whom was Segestes' daughter, the wife of Arminius. She was temperamentally closer to her husband than to her father. From her came no appeals, no submissive tears; she stood still, her hands clasped inside her robe, staring down at her pregnant body. The party brought with them trophies from Varus' disaster, many of them distributed on that occasion as loot to those who were now surrendering.

And then there was Segestes himself, a huge figure, fearlessly aware he had been a good ally. 'This is not the first day I have been a true friend to Rome,' he cried. 'Ever since the divine Augustus made me a Roman citizen, my choice of friends and enemies has been guided by your advantage. My motive has not been hatred of my people – for traitors are distasteful even to the side they join – but the belief that Roman and German interests are the same, and that peace is better than war. That is why I denounced to your former commander Varus the man who broke the treaty with you – Arminius, the robber of my daughter!

'But Varus indolently put me off. I lost faith in due processes of law, and begged him to arrest Arminius, and his partisans – and myself. May that night confirm my story – I wish I had not survived it!

What followed is matter for mourning rather than excuses. But I did imprison Arminius; and his supporters have imprisoned me. And now, at my first meeting with you, I tell you I favour the old not the new – peace, not trouble. I am not after rewards; I want to clear myself of double-dealing. And if the Germans prefer remorse to suicide, I am a fitting agent. For my son's youthful misdeeds I ask pardon. My daughter, I admit, was brought here by force. It is for you to say which shall count the more, the son she is bearing to Arminius, or the fact that I am her father.'

Germanicus answered kindly, promising safety to Segestes' children and relations, and a home in Gaul for himself. Then Germanicus withdrew his forces, allowing himself to be hailed as victor on Tiberius' initiative. A son was born to Arminius' wife; he was brought up at Ravenna. I shall write elsewhere of the ironical fate in store for him.

The news of Segestes' submission and good reception pleased those who did not want fighting, distressed those who did. Arminius' violent nature was maddened by his wife's abduction and the prospect of servitude for their unborn child. He made a rapid tour of the Cherusci, demanding war against Segestes and Germanicus. These were some of his savage taunts: 'What a fine father! What a glorious commander of a valiant army, whose united strength has kidnapped one helpless woman! I, on the other hand, have annihilated three divisions and their commanders. My fighting has been open, not treacherous – and it has been against armed men and not pregnant women. The groves of Germany still display the Roman Eagles and standards which I hung there in honour of the gods of our fathers.

'Let Segestes live on the conquered bank, and make his son a Roman priest again – with a human being to worship! But Germany will never tolerate Roman rods, axes, and robes between Rhine and Elbe. Other countries, unacquainted with Roman rule, have not known its impositions or its punishments. We have known them – and got rid of them! Augustus, now deified, and his "chosen" Tiberius have gone away frustrated. There is nothing to fear in an inexperienced youth and a mutinous army. If you prefer your country, your parents, and the old ways to settlement under tyrants abroad, then do not follow Segestes to shameful slavery – follow Arminius to glory and freedom!'

Besides the Cherusci, the tribes around responded to his call. It also won over Arminius' uncle, Inguiomerus, long respected by the Romans. This increased Germanicus' alarm. To create a diversion, and break the force of the expected blow, he sent Caecina with forty regular battalions through the territory of the Bructeri to the river Ems, while cavalry under Pedo Albinovanus crossed the Frisian borderland. Germanicus himself sailed with four brigades across the lakes. Then infantry, horse, and fleet effected a junction on the Ems, and a contingent offered by the Chauci was incorporated. A flying column under Lucius Stertinius, sent by Germanicus against the Bructeri when they started burning their possessions, went killing and looting, and found the Eagle of the nineteenth brigade, lost with Varus. Then the army ravaged all the country between the Ems and the Lippe, marching to the extremity of Bructeran territory.

Now they were near the Teutoburgian Wood, in which the remains of Varus and his three divisions were said to be lying unburied. Germanicus conceived a desire to pay his last respects to these men and their general. Every soldier with him was overcome with pity when he thought of his relations and friends and reflected on the hazards of war and of human life. Caecina was sent ahead to reconnoitre the dark woods and build bridges and causeways on the treacherous surface of the sodden marshland. Then the army made its way over the tragic sites. The scene lived up to its horrible associations. Varus' extensive first camp, with its broad extent and headquarters marked out, testified to the whole army's labours. Then a half-ruined breastwork and shallow ditch showed where the last pathetic remnant had gathered. On the open ground were whitening bones, scattered where men had fled, heaped up where they had stood and fought back. Fragments of spears and of horses' limbs lay there – also human heads, fastened to tree-trunks. In groves nearby were the outlandish altars at which the Germans had massacred the Roman colonels and senior company-commanders.

Survivors of the catastrophe, who had escaped from the battle or from captivity, pointed out where the generals had fallen, and where the Eagles were captured. They showed where Varus received his first wound, and where he died by his own unhappy hand. And they told of the platform from which Arminius had spoken, and of his arrogant insults to the Eagles and standards – and of all the gibbets and pits for the prisoners.

So, six years after the slaughter, a living Roman army had come to bury the dead men's bones of three whole divisions. No one knew if the remains he was burying belonged to a stranger or a comrade. But in their bitter distress, and rising fury against the enemy, they looked on them all as friends and blood-brothers. Germanicus shared in the general grief, and laid the first turf of the funeral-mound as a heartfelt tribute to the dead. Thereby he earned Tiberius' disapproval. Perhaps this was because the emperor interpreted every action of Germanicus unfavourably. Or he may have felt that the sight of the unburied dead would make the army too respectful of its enemies, and reluctant to fight – nor should a commander belonging to the antique priesthood of the Augurs have handled objects belonging to the dead.

Arminius retreated into pathless country. Germanicus followed. When opportunity arose, he instructed the cavalry to move forward and rush the flat ground where the enemy were stationed. Arminius first ordered his men to fall back on the woods in close order. Then he suddenly wheeled them round, and a force he had secretly posted in the forest was given the signal to charge. The Roman cavalry were disorganized by this new front. Reserve battalions were sent up. But, battered by the retreating mass, they only added to the panic, and were almost forced on to marshy ground, well known to their victorious opponents but perilous for strangers. Then, however, Germanicus brought up his regular brigades in battle formation. This intimidated the enemy, and gave the Romans heart. The battle was broken off without a decision.

Germanicus now withdrew his forces to the Ems. The regular troops which had come by ship returned by the same means. Part of the cavalry were instructed to return to the Rhine along the sea-coast. Caecina took back his own force. His route was familiar, but he was told to proceed as quickly as possible across the Long Bridges. This was the name of a narrow causeway built some years back through a vast swamp by Lucius Domitius Ahenobarbus (I). All round was slimy, treacherous bog, clinging mud intersected by streams. Beyond lay gently sloping woods. These were now occupied by Arminius, who by forced marches, using short-cuts, had outstripped the baggage-laden, heavily armed Roman column. Caecina was not sure how he could repair the old, broken causeway and at the same time keep the enemy off. So that repairs and fighting could proceed simultaneously, he decided to pitch his camp on the spot.

The Germans, by fierce pressure on front and flanks, tried to break through the outposts and attack the working party. Workers and combatants combined made a terrible din. Everything was against the Romans. The waterlogged ground was too soft for a firm stand and too slippery for movement. Besides, they wore heavy armour and could not throw their javelins standing in the water. The Cherusci, on the other hand, were used to fighting in marshes. They were big men, too, whose thrusts with their great lances had a formidable range. The Roman brigades were wavering when night rescued them from defeat.

Made tireless by success, the Germans did not rest even now. They started to divert towards the low ground streams rising in the surrounding hills. Floods overwhelmed what work the Romans had done, and the soldiers' task was doubled. However, Caecina remained unperturbed. In his forty years of service as soldier and commander, he had known crisis as well as success. Looking ahead he could see nothing for it but to keep the enemy in the woods until his wounded and the heavier part of his force had passed on. Between the hills and the swamp there was enough flat ground for a slender line of battle. The fifth brigade was chosen for the right flank and the twenty-first for the left; the first was to be vanguard, and the twentieth to hold off pursuers.

The night brought no rest. And there was a contrast between the echoes resounding in the low-lying valleys and the forests, as the natives feasted with their savage shouting and triumphant songs, and the occasional murmuring of the Romans round their smouldering fires, as they lay here and there by the breastwork or wandered around the tents, dazed but sleepless. The general had a horrible dream – Varus, covered with blood, seemed to rise out of the morass, and call him: but he would not obey; and when Varus held out his hand he pushed it back. When dawn came, the Roman brigades on the flanks, frightened or disobedient, withdrew from their positions, hastily occupying a level space beyond the swampy ground. This gave Arminius a clear approach. At first he did not attack, until he saw the Romans' heavy equipment stuck in the mud and the ditches. The men round it became disorganized. Units overlapped, and as usual in such circumstances everyone was hurrying about his own interests, deaf to orders.

Then Arminius ordered the Germans to attack. At the head of a picked force, crying that here was another Varus and his army caught in the same trap again, he broke through the Roman column. His chief targets were the horses, which slipped in their own blood and the slimy bog and threw their riders, scattering everyone in their way and trampling on those who had fallen. The Eagles caused particular difficulty, as the rain of missiles held the colour-sergeants back, and they could not plant them in the mud. While Caecina was struggling to maintain the line, his horse was killed under him. As he fell he was nearly surrounded; but the first brigade rescued him. Fortunately, the greedy Germans stopped killing and went after loot. So towards evening the Romans forced their way out on to firm, open ground. But their hardships were not yet ended. Earthworks had to be constructed, and their material collected; and most of the equipment for moving soil and cutting turf had been lost.

Units had no tents, the wounded no dressings. As the muddy, bloodstained rations were handed round, men spoke miserably of the deathly darkness, and the end which tomorrow would bring to thousands. A horse broke loose and cantered around, frightened of the shouting. It struggled when men tried to stop it, and caused a panic-stricken belief that the Germans had broken in. There was a stampede for the gates, especially the main gate – farthest from the enemy and so best for escape. Caecina discovered that there was no cause for fear. But his authority and appeals, and even force, did not suffice to hold the men back. Then he blocked the gate by throwing himself down across it. The men were not hard-hearted enough to go over the general's body. Then colonels and company-commanders explained that it was a false alarm.

Caecina collected the men at his headquarters, and called for silence. He described the critical situation. The only way out was to fight, he said. But the fighting must be planned. They must stay inside the defences until the enemy approached to storm them. Then the entire force must break out – and so to the Rhine! Running away would only mean more forests, worse swamps, savage attacks; but success would be glorious. Caecina spoke of their dear ones at home, of their victorious battles. Of setbacks nothing was said. Then, without respect of persons, he distributed the horses of the generals and colonels – starting with his own – to the best fighters in the army. They were to charge first, the infantry to follow.

On the German side, too, there were commotions – because of clashes of opinion among the greedy, optimistic chiefs. Arminius' plan was to let the Romans come out, and then trap them again on difficult swampy ground. Inguiomerus was for the more sensational measures which natives enjoy – surround the camp, he said, and you can easily storm it; that is the way to win more prisoners, and collect loot undamaged. Following his advice, at daybreak they filled in the ditches, constructed bridges, and poured across them.

When they grasped the top of the parapet they saw only a few Roman soldiers, apparently paralysed with fright. But as they went clambering over, the battalions received their signals, and the horns and bugles sounded. Shouting, the Romans fell upon the German rear. 'Here there are no woods or swamps,' they jeered. 'It's a fair field, and a fair chance!' The enemy had been imagining the easy slaughter of a few badly armed men. The blare of trumpets, the glitter of weapons, was all the more effective because it was totally unexpected. The Germans went down – as defenceless in defeat as success had made them impetuous. Arminius got away unhurt, Inguiomerus badly wounded. The massacre of rank and file went on as long as fury and daylight lasted. Finally, at night-fall, the Romans re-entered their camp. They were as hungry as ever, and their wounds were worse. But they had their cure, nourishment, restorative, everything in one – victory.

Meanwhile behind the Rhine a rumour had spread that the army was cut off and a German force was on the way to invade Gaul. Some, in panic, envisaged the disgraceful idea of demolishing the bridge.[1] But Agrippina put a stop to it. In those days this great-hearted woman acted as commander. She herself dispensed clothes to needy soldiers, and dressed the wounded. Pliny the elder, the historian of the German campaigns,[2] writes that she stood at the bridge-head to thank and congratulate the returning column. This made a profound impression on Tiberius. There was something behind these careful attentions

1. The Rhine bridge was at Vetera (near Birten).
2. Pliny, whose *Natural History* has survived, also wrote *German Wars*, now lost.

to the army, he felt; they were not simply because of the foreign enemy. 'The commanding officer's job', he reflected, 'is a sinecure when a woman inspects units and exhibits herself before the standards with plans for money-distributions.' As though it were not pretentious enough to parade the commander's son around in private soldier's uniform and propose to have him called 'little Boots' Caesar! Agrippina's position in the army already seemed to outshine generals and commanding officers; and she, a woman, had suppressed a mutiny which the emperor's own signature had failed to check. Lucius Aelius Sejanus aggravated and intensified his suspicions. He knew how Tiberius' mind worked. Inside it, for the eventual future, he sowed hatreds. They would lie low, but one day bear fruit abundantly.

Meanwhile Germanicus handed over the second and fourteenth brigades, which he had brought by ship, to Publius Vitellius, who was to take them back by land. This was designed to lighten the fleet, in case of shallow water and grounding at low tide. At first Vitellius had an easy journey. The ground was dry or only slightly waterlogged. But then at the autumnal equinox, when the North Sea is always at its roughest, his column was harassed and confused by a northerly gale. The country was deluged. Sea, land, and shore all looked the same. There was no way to distinguish solid from treacherous ground, shallow water from deep. Men were knocked down by waves and dragged under. Pack-animals, baggage, dead bodies floated about and struck against each other. Units lost their identity. Men stood up to the chest or even the neck in water. Then they lost their footing, and were carried away or went under. Their shouts to encourage one another were unavailing against the floods. Brave men or cowards, good sense or bad, planning or the lack of it, were all one, in the grip of the raging elements.

Finally Publius Vitellius and his column struggled out on to higher ground. They spent the night without fire or other necessities. Many men were naked or hurt – as badly off as a besieged army, indeed worse, since for such an army death is at least glorious, not squalid as it was here. With daybreak land reappeared, and they got through to a river, where they found Germanicus' fleet and embarked. Reports that they had been drowned persisted until Germanicus and his army were back and on view.

By now Segestes' brother Segimerus, whose submission Lucius Stertinius had been sent ahead to accept, had been escorted back to the Ubian capital with his son. Both were amnestied. Segimerus' case was simple, but his son caused more hesitation since he was alleged to have treated Varus' corpse insultingly.

The Gallic and Spanish provinces and Italy competed to make good the army's losses, offering weapons, horses, or gold, as their resources permitted. Germanicus commended their public spirit, but only accepted arms and horses for the war. He assisted his men from his private means, and tried to distract them from thoughts of their past hardships by personal kindness – inspecting the wounded and their injuries, praising individual feats, playing on their pride or ambition. By these attentions and conversations all round, he intensified their fighting spirit and their loyalty to himself.

In this year honorary Triumphs were awarded to Aulus Caecina Severus, Lucius Apronius, and Gaius Silius (I) for their service with Germanicus.

In spite of repeated popular pressure, Tiberius refused the title 'Father of his Country'. He also declined the senate's proposal that obedience should be sworn to his enactments. All human affairs were uncertain, he protested, and the higher his position the more slippery it was.

Nevertheless, he did not convince people of his Republicanism. For he revived the treason law. The ancients had employed the same name, but had applied it to other offences – to official misconduct damaging the Roman State, such as betrayal of an army or incitement to sedition. Action had been taken against deeds, words went unpunished. The first who employed this law to investigate written libel was Augustus, provoked by Cassius Severus, an immoderate slanderer of eminent men and women. Then Tiberius, asked by a praetor, Quintus Pompeius Macer, whether cases under the treason law were to receive attention, replied: *the laws must take their course*. Like Augustus he had been annoyed by anonymous verses. These had criticized his cruelty, arrogance, and bad relations with his mother.

The tentative charges against Falanius and Rubrius, members of the order of knights, are worth recording. For they illustrate the beginnings of this disastrous institution – which Tiberius so cunningly insinuated, first under control, then bursting into an all-engulfing blaze. Falanius was charged, first, with admitting among the worshippers of Augustus, in the cult maintained by households on the analogy of priestly orders, an actor in musical comedies named Cassius who was a male prostitute, and, secondly, with disposing of a statue of Augustus when selling some garden property. Rubrius was charged with perjury by the divinity of Augustus.

When Tiberius heard of these accusations, he wrote to the consuls saying that Augustus had not been voted divine honours in order to ruin Roman citizens. The actor, he observed, together with others, had regularly taken part in the Games which his mother the Augusta had instituted in Augustus' honour – and to include the latter's statues (like those of other gods) in sales of houses or gardens was not sacrilegious. As regards the perjury, it was parallel to a false oath in Jupiter's name: the gods must see to their own wrongs.

Shortly afterwards Marcus Granius Marcellus, governor of Bithynia, was accused of treason by his own assistant, Aulus Caepio Crispinus. But it was the latter's partner Romanius Hispo who created a career which was to be made notorious by the villainous products of subsequent gloomy years. Needy, obscure, and restless, he wormed his way by secret reports into the grim emperor's confidence. Then everyone of any eminence was in danger from him. Over one man he enjoyed an ascendancy; all others loathed him. His was the precedent which enabled imitators to exchange beggary for wealth, to inspire dread instead of contempt, to destroy their fellow-citizens – and finally themselves.

He alleged that Marcus Granius Marcellus had told scandalous stories about Tiberius. The charge was damning. The descriptions the accuser imputed to him recounted the most repulsive features in the emperor's character. Since these were not fictitious it seemed plausible that Marcellus should have described them. Hispo added that Marcellus had placed his own effigy above those of the Caesars, and that on one statue he had cut off the head of Augustus and replaced it by Tiberius.

The emperor lost his temper and, voluble for once, exclaimed that he personally would vote, openly and on oath. This would have compelled other senators to do the same. But, since there still remained some traces of declining freedom, Cnaeus Calpurnius Piso asked a question; 'Caesar, will you vote first or last? If first, I shall have your

lead to follow; if last, I am afraid of inadvertently voting against you.'
This struck home, and Tiberius, regretting his impetuous outburst,
meekly voted for acquittal on the treason counts. Charges of embezzlement were referred to the proper court.

However, investigations in the senate were not enough for Tiberius.
He also began to sit in the law courts – at the side of the platform, so
as not to oust the praetor from his official chair. His presence successfully induced many verdicts disregarding influential pressure and
intrigue. Nevertheless, it also infringed on the independence of judges.

At about this time also, a junior senator named Aurelius Pius protested that his house had been undermined by the government's
construction of a road and aqueduct. He appealed to the senate. The
praetors in charge of the Treasury resisted the claim, but Tiberius
came to his help and paid him the value of his house. For the emperor
was prepared to spend in a good cause, and kept this good quality
long after his others were gone. When an ex-praetor, Propertius
Celer, asked to resign from the senate on grounds of poverty,
Tiberius, finding that his lack of means was inherited, presented him
with one million sesterces. Others then applied. But he requested
them to prove their case to the senate. Even when he acted fairly his
austerity made a harsh impression; and the applicants preferred silent
impoverishment to publicized subsidy.

In the same year the Tiber, swollen by persistent rain, flooded low-
lying parts of the city. When it receded, much loss of life and buildings was apparent. Gaius Asinius Gallus proposed consultation of the
Sibylline Books. Tiberius, with his preference for secrecy – in heavenly
as in earthly matters – demurred. Instead, Gaius Ateius Capito and
Lucius Arruntius were instructed to control the water-level. Achaea
and Macedonia begged for relief from their tax burdens, and it was
decided, for the present, to transfer them from senatorial to imperial
government.

A gladiator-show was given in the names of Germanicus and Drusus.
The latter was abnormally fond of bloodshed. Admittedly it was
worthless blood, but the public were shocked and his father was
reported to have reprimanded him. Tiberius himself kept away.
Various reasons were given – his dislike of crowds, or his natural glum-
ness, or unwillingness to be compared with Augustus, who had cheerfully attended. It was also suggested, though I would scarcely believe

it, that he deliberately gave his son a chance to show his forbidding character – and win unpopularity.

Disorders connected with the stage had started in the previous year, and now their violence increased. There were civilian casualties. Soldiers, too, and a company-commander were killed, and a colonel of the Guard injured, in keeping order and protecting officials from disrespect. The senate discussed the disturbance, and it was moved that the praetors should be empowered to have ballet-dancers flogged. When the tribune Decimus Haterius Agrippa vetoed the proposal, he was attacked by Gaius Asinius Gallus. Tiberius, who allowed the senate such pretences of freedom, did not speak. But the veto stood, for the divine Augustus had once ruled that these people were exempt from corporal punishment – and to Tiberius his decisions were sacred. However, numerous measures were passed to limit the salaries of this profession and check the violence of their partisans. In particular, senators were debarred from entering the houses of ballet-dancers, and knights from escorting them when they appeared in public. Moreover, performances outside the theatre were forbidden. The praetors were also empowered to exile spectators who misbehaved.

A Spanish application to build a Temple of Augustus at the settlement of Tarraco was granted, thus providing a precedent for every province. There was public discontent with the 1 per cent auction tax instituted after the Civil Wars. But Tiberius pointed out that the Military Treasury needed these funds, and added that the national resources were still insufficient unless the troops served for a full twenty years. So the misguided concession of a sixteen-year term, extorted in the recent mutinies, was cancelled. The next question discussed was whether the Tiber floods should be checked by diverting the streams and lakes which nourished it. The discussion was led by Lucius Arruntius and Gaius Ateius Capito. Deputations from the country towns were heard. The Florentines begged that the river Chiana should not be moved from its natural bed into the Arno, with disastrous effect on themselves. Interamna's case was similar: acceptance of the plan to spread the waters of the Nera far and wide in small channels would ruin the best land in Italy. The people of Reate protested equally vigorously against the damming of the Veline Lake (at its outlet into the Nera), since it would burst its banks into the surrounding country. Nature, they said, had done best for humanity by allotting to each river its appropriate mouth, course, and limits too; and respect must be paid to the religious susceptibilities of the inhabitants, who had honoured the rivers by their homes with rites, and groves, and altars – and indeed Tiber himself would scarcely be glad to flow less majestically, deprived of his associate tributaries. Because of the pleas from towns, or superstitious scruples, or engineering difficulties, the senate carried a proposal by Cnaeus Calpurnius Piso that nothing should be changed.

In his imperial governorship of Moesia, with which Achaia and Macedonia were merged, Gaius Poppaeus Sabinus was kept on. It was one of Tiberius' customs to prolong the tenures of these posts; both military and other governors were often left unchanged until their dying day. Different explanations of this practice have been offered. According to one account Tiberius found recurrent problems tedious, and preferred making a single permanent decision. Others attribute his policy to a jealous desire that not too many people should benefit. An alternative suggestion is that his natural subtlety placed him in a dilemma: he disliked bad characters, but did not search out exceptional ability. Misconduct he deplored, as likely to cause public scandal – but outstanding merits would be a threat to himself. In the end his indecisiveness became so pronounced that he gave governorships to men whom he was never going to allow outside Rome.

About the elections to consulships, from this first year of Tiberius until his death, I hardly venture to make any definite statement. The evidence in historical accounts, and indeed in his own speeches, is conflicting. Sometimes he suppressed candidates' names, but described their social positions, antecedents, and service records – in terms revealing their identity. On other occasions he suppressed even these clues, but merely warned candidates not to invalidate the elections by bribery – promising his own assistance to the same end. He usually stated that those whose names he had passed to the consuls were the only applicants for nomination. But others, he would say, were still entitled to apply, if their popularity or record encouraged them to do so. Such pronouncements sounded plausible. Yet in relation to the facts they were meaningless, if not disingenuous. The impressiveness of the Republican façade only meant that the slave-state, which was to grow out of them, would be all the more loathsome.

Next year the consuls were Sisenna Statilius Taurus and Lucius Scribonius Libo. Trouble broke out among the dependent kingdoms and provinces of the East. The Parthians were the originators. They had requested and received a king from Rome; and though he was a member of their Arsacid royal house, they despised him as a foreigner. This was Vonones I. He had been given to Augustus as a hostage by King Phraates IV, who, for all his expulsions of Roman armies and generals, had shown the emperor conspicuous respect. As a bond of friendship he had sent Augustus several of his children – not so much from fear of Rome as from doubts of his own people's loyalty.

When domestic disputes removed Phraates and his successors, a deputation from the Parthian leaders had visited Rome to invite Vonones, his eldest child, to the throne. Augustus regarded this as a compliment and presented Vonones with valuable gifts on his departure. The Parthians gave him the good reception that they habitually give new kings. But this was soon replaced by an ashamed feeling of national humiliation at having accepted, from another world, a king tainted with enemy customs. A monarch was being imposed on the Parthian throne, they told themselves. It was being allocated like a Roman province. If their ruler was to be a man who for years had been Augustus' slave, then the glory of Crassus' slayers[1] and Antony's conquerors was dead.

Their scorn was intensified because their national habits were alien to Vonones. He rarely hunted and had little interest in horses. When passing through a city he rode in a litter. The traditional banquets disgusted him. Moreover, he was laughed at because his entourage was Greek, and because he kept even ordinary household objects locked up. The Parthians, unfamiliar with his good qualities – accessibility and affable manners – took them for unusual vices. His good and bad points alike were alien and hateful.

So another royalty, Artabanus III, was produced. He had been brought up among the Dahae. Now, after an initial defeat he rallied and seized the throne. The defeated Vonones took refuge in Armenia. This buffer-state between the Roman and Parthian empires was at the time without a ruler. Armenia was no friend of ours because Antony, pretending friendship, had treacherously trapped its king Artavasdes

1. The Parthians had defeated and killed Marcus Licinius Crassus at Carrhae in Mesopotamia in 53 B.C.

I, only to arrest and kill him. The latter's son Artaxias II, remembering his father, hated us, and called in the Parthian monarchy to protect himself and his throne. When Artaxias II fell by the treachery of his own relations, Augustus made Tigranes II king of Armenia and Tiberius settled him on the throne. But his reign was brief and so was that of his two children, though according to foreign custom they were husband and wife as well as joint rulers. Next Artavasdes II had been made king, by imperial order. His deposition, which followed, was a setback to us; and Gaius Caesar was appointed by Augustus to solve the Armenian problem. Gaius' nominee Ariobarzanes, a Mede by origin, had a fine character and splendid appearance which endeared him to the Armenians. But when he died a natural death they would not have his child. Instead they tried feminine government, under Erato. However, she was soon deposed. Drifting into chaos, anarchic rather than free, its people accepted the fugitive Vonones as king. But they could do little against Artabanus' threats, and if Rome gave them armed support it would mean war with Parthia. So the imperial governor of Syria, Quintus Caecilius Metellus Creticus Silanus, extricated him, allowing him royal state and rank, but keeping him under guard. Vonones' effort to escape from this undignified situation will be described at the appropriate place.

Tiberius was not sorry that the Eastern situation was disturbed. For this provided a pretext for separating Germanicus from his familiar army and subjecting him to the intrigues and hazards of a new provincial command. Germanicus, however, as his troops (in contrast to the emperor) became increasingly enthusiastic about him, grew all the more ambitious for a quick victory in Germany. Reflecting on invasion routes in the light of his successes and failures during the past two campaigns, he saw that, though in open battle and fair country the Germans were beaten, their forests, swamps, short summers, and early winters favoured them. His own men had suffered less from wounds than from protracted marches and shortages of arms. The supply of horses from Gaul was exhausted. Besides, long baggage-trains were vulnerable to surprise, with the odds against their defenders.

The sea, he felt, provided a better route. It was easily controlled – and inaccessible to enemy intelligence. Besides, arrival by sea would mean an earlier start to the campaign and simultaneous transportation of Roman infantry and supplies; while cavalry, horses, and men alike could be taken up-river from the coast and landed intact in mid-Germany. So Germanicus decided accordingly. Two generals, Publius Vitellius and Gaius Antius, were sent to assess Gaul for taxation; Gaius Silius (I), Anteius, and Aulus Caecina Severus were entrusted with the building of a fleet. A thousand ships were calculated to be enough. They were constructed quickly. Some were short and broad – with little prow or stern – to stand a rough sea. Some were flat-bottomed, so as to run aground undamaged. Others, more numerous, had rudders at each end, so that the oarsmen could suddenly reverse direction and land them on either side of a river. Many had decks for catapults and also served to carry horses and supplies. The fleet was well adapted for rapid sailing or rowing. It was formidable and impressive, the more so because of the soldiers' high morale. The rendezvous decided upon was the Batavian island. Its good landing places made it well-suited for receiving troops and carrying the war into Germany. The Rhine, which has until this point flowed in a single channel – broken only by unimportant islands – divides into two main streams at the Batavian frontier. The branch bordering Germany keeps its name: it goes on flowing swiftly down to the sea. The broader, slower stream on the Gallic side is called the Waal in this region, and then, lower down, the Meuse; it discharges into the same sea, in the great estuary of the latter river.

While the fleet was assembling, Gaius Silius was instructed to take a light force and raid the Chatti, but owing to sudden rains achieved nothing except a little loot and the capture of the wife and daughter of Arpus their chief. Germanicus himself heard that a fort upon the river Lippe was besieged, and proceeded towards it with six divisions. But the besieging force gave him no opportunity at all for a battle since it melted away at news of his approach. First, however, it destroyed the funeral mound recently raised to commemorate Varus' army, and an earlier altar in honour of Nero Drusus. Germanicus reconstructed the altar and himself headed a procession of his force in honour of his father. It was decided not to erect the mound again. The whole region between Fort Aliso and the Rhine was heavily fortified by new highways and embankments.

The fleet had now collected. Supplies were sent ahead, and the regular brigades and auxiliaries allotted their ships. Germanicus himself, entering the channel[1] called Drusiana after his father, called on the memory and example of his words and deeds to give generous and auspicious aid to this enterprise modelled on his achievements. Then, setting sail through lakes[2] and sea, he reached the Ems without incident. The troops disembarked in the more easterly arm of the Ems. But a mistake was made in not transporting the troops upstream or landing them farther south, nearer to their destination. As it was, days were wasted in bridge-building. The cavalry and regular infantry made a well-disciplined crossing of the first tidal marshes, before the tide rose. But then the auxiliaries in the rear, including Batavians, jumped into the water – to show off their swimming – and there was confusion and loss of life. While Germanicus was laying out his camp, it was reported that a tribe, the Angrivarii, had revolted in his rear, and auxiliary cavalry and light infantry were at once sent under Lucius Stertinius to burn and kill in revenge for this treachery.

Now the Weser separated the Romans from the Cherusci. On its bank stood Arminius and the other chieftains. He inquired whether Germanicus had come, and, hearing that he had, asked to be allowed to speak to his brother Flavus in the Roman army. Flavus was very loyal; he had lost an eye some years earlier, fighting under Tiberius. Permission was granted, and Flavus came forward to the river-bank. Arminius greeted him and, dismissing his own attendants, asked that the bowmen stationed along our bank should likewise withdraw. When they had gone he asked his brother to explain his face-wound. The place and the battle were told him. Then he asked what reward Flavus had got. Flavus mentioned his higher pay, chain, and wreath of honour and other military decorations. 'The wages of slavery are low,' sneered Arminius.

Then they argued their opposing cases. Flavus spoke of Rome's greatness, the emperor's wealth, the terrible punishment attending defeat, the mercy earned by submission – even Arminius' own wife and son were not treated like enemies. His brother dwelt on patriotism, long-established freedom, the national gods of Germany – and their mother, who joined him in imploring that Flavus should not choose

1. Nero Drusus had built a canal linking the northern branch of the Rhine (the Waal), near Arnhem, with the Ijssel (down which Germanicus next proceeded).
2. The Zuiderzee (Flevum).

to be the deserter and betrayer, rather than the liberator, of his relatives and his country. The discussion soon became abusive: blows would have followed – in spite of the river barrier – if Lucius Stertinius had not hastened up and restrained Flavus, who was angrily calling for his horse and weapons. Across the river Arminius was to be seen, shouting threats and challenges to fight – a good many of them in Latin, since he had formerly commanded a Cheruscan force in the Roman army.

On the next day, the German army drew up beyond the Weser. Germanicus believed it would be bad strategy to risk the regular infantry without properly guarded bridges. So he first sent over the cavalry under Lucius Stertinius with a senior staff officer, Aemilius. They crossed by fords at different points so as to divide the enemy. The Batavians under their leader Chariovalda plunged through where the current was strongest. The Cherusci pretended to give way and drew them on to a level space with wooded hills around. There they made an enveloping attack, and drove in the Batavians' front. The latter, falling back hard-pressed, formed a circle, but suffered severe casualties both at close quarters and from missiles. Chariovalda resisted this savage assault steadfastly. Finally, commanding his men to force a way through the attackers in mass formation, he plunged into the thick of the battle and fell beneath a rain of javelins, with his horse killed under him. Many of his chieftains fell with him. The rest of the force was preserved partly by its own exertions and partly by the arrival of the cavalry to relieve them.

When Germanicus crossed the Weser, a deserter gave him information. Arminius had chosen his battle-ground. Other tribes too had collected, in a wood sacred to Hercules. And a night attack on the camp was planned. The informant was believed. Indeed, German fires were visible and a reconnaissance party which went near reported the neighing of horses and the noise of a vast, undisciplined advance. So now the critical moment was at hand.

Germanicus decided he must test his troops' morale. He considered how this could be done authentically – reflecting that the reports of colonels and company-commanders are cheerful rather than reliable, ex-slaves remain slaves at heart, friends are flatterers. If he called a meeting, initiative would be shown by a handful, the majority would applaud them. Mess-time, he decided, was the time to discover what they really thought, as the men talked intimately, unsupervised, of their hopes and fears. So after dark, dressed in an animal-skin, he left the general's tent by an exit unknown to the sentries, with one attendant. As he walked the camp lines and stood near the tents, he basked in his own popularity, as he heard admiring remarks about his great origins and splendid looks. There was general praise of his endurance, his friendliness, his equability in serious and relaxed moments alike. All agreed that they must show their gratitude by fighting well: the treacherous treaty-breakers must be offered up to vengeance and glory.

An enemy who knew Latin now rode up to the stockade. In Arminius' name he called out, promising every deserter a wife, some land, and a hundred sesterces a day for the rest of the war. This insulting suggestion infuriated the Roman soldiers. 'Wait until tomorrow and the battle,' they shouted. 'We will help ourselves to German lands and wives. This is a good omen! Their women and their wealth are going to come to us as loot.'

At about midnight an attempt was made on the Roman camp. But not a spear was thrown. The attackers found vigilance everywhere, the fortifications lined with men. During the same night, Germanicus had a pleasant dream. He dreamt that he was sacrificing, and, as his robe was spattered with the victim's blood, his grandmother the Augusta handed him another, finer robe. The omen encouraged him. The auspices, too, proved favourable. So, parading his army, he announced the steps his experience had dictated together with such remarks as seemed called for on the eve of battle.

'Open ground is not the only battle-field favourable to a Roman,' he said. 'Woods, wooded hills, are good too, if he acts sensibly. The natives' great shields and huge spears are not so manageable among tree-trunks and scrub as Roman swords and javelins and tight-fitting armour. You must strike repeatedly, and aim your points at their faces. The Germans wear no breastplates or helmets. Even their shields are not reinforced with iron or leather, but are merely plaited wicker-work or flimsy painted boards. Spears, of a sort, are limited to their front rank. The rest only have clubs burnt at the end, or with short metal points. Physically, they look formidable and are good for a short rush. But they cannot stand being hurt. They quit and run unashamedly, regardless of their commanders. In victory they respect no law, human or divine; in defeat they panic. If you are tired of marching and sailing,' went on Germanicus, 'this is the battle to relieve you of them! Already we are nearer the Elbe than the Rhine. Once you give me victory where my father and uncle have trodden before me, the fighting will be over!' The speech was enthusiastically received; and the signal for battle rang out.

Arminius and the other German chiefs also each addressed their men, reminding them that these Romans were Varus' runaways – men who had mutinied to escape battle. Some had backs covered with wounds, others were crippled by storm and sea; and now, hopeless, deserted by the gods, they were again pitted against a relentless enemy. They had taken to ships and remotest waters to evade attack – and escape pursuit after disaster. 'But once battle comes', cried Arminius, 'winds and oars cannot prevent their defeat!' He urged his troops to remember how greedy, arrogant, and brutal Rome was. The only alternatives, he insisted, were continued freedom or – in preference to slavery – death.

Excited by this appeal, the Germans clamoured to fight. They were marched to a level area called Idistaviso, which curves irregularly between the Weser and the hills; at one point an outward bend of the river gives it breadth, at another it is narrowed by projecting high ground. Behind rose the forest, with lofty branches but clear ground between the tree-trunks. The Germans occupied the plain and the outskirts of the forest. The Cherusci alone occupied the heights, waiting to charge down when the battle started. The Roman army moved forward in the following order: first, Gallic and German auxiliaries followed by unmounted bowmen; next, four Roman brigades, and Germanicus with two battalions of the Guard and picked cavalry; then four more brigades, each brought by light infantry and mounted bowmen to divisional strength; and the remaining auxiliary battalions. The troops were alert and ready to deploy from column of march into battle order.

Units of the Cherusci charged impetuously. Seeing this, Germanicus ordered his best cavalry to attack their flank, while the rest of the cavalry, under Lucius Stertinius, was to ride round and attack them in the rear: and he himself would be there at the right moment. He saw a splendid omen – eight eagles flying towards and into the forest. 'Forward,' he cried, 'follow the birds of Rome, the Roman army's protecting spirits!' The infantry attacked, and the cavalry, which had been sent ahead, charged the enemy's flanks and rear. It was a strange sight. Two enemy forces were fleeing in opposite directions, those from the woods into the open, those from the open into the woods.

The Cherusci between began to be dislodged from the slopes: among them Arminius, striking, shouting, wounded, trying to keep the battle going. His full force was thrown against the bowmen, and it would have broken through if the standards of the Raetian, Vindelician, and Gallic auxiliary battalions had not barred the way. Even so, by sheer physical strength aided by the impetus of his horse, he got through. To avoid recognition he had smeared his face with his own blood. One story is that Chauci among the Roman auxiliaries recognized him and let him go. Inguiomerus was likewise saved, by his own bravery or by treachery. The rest were massacred. Many tried to swim the Weser. They were battered by javelins, or carried away by the current, or finally overwhelmed by the mass of fugitives and collapse of the river banks. Some ignominiously tried to escape by climbing trees. As they cowered among the branches, bowmen amused themselves by shooting them down. Others were brought to the ground by felling the trees.

It was a great victory, and it cost us little. The slaughter of the enemy continued from midday until dusk. Their bodies and weapons were scattered for ten miles round. Among the spoils were found chains which they had brought for the Romans in confident expectation of the result. The troops hailed Tiberius as victor[1] on the battle-field, and erected a mound on which, like a trophy, they set arms with the names of the defeated tribes. The sight of this upset and enraged the Germans more than all their wounds and losses and destruction. Men who had just been planning emigration across the Elbe now wanted to fight instead, and rushed to arms.

Germans of every rank and age launched sudden and damaging attacks against the Romans on the march. Finally they selected a narrow swampy open space enclosed between a river and the forest – which in its turn was surrounded by a deep morass (except on one side where a wide earthwork had been constructed by the Angrivarii

1. Salutations as victor (*imperator*) were now reserved for members of the imperial family. The emperor himself was hailed because Germanicus was fighting under his 'auspices', i.e. his supreme command.

to mark the Cheruscan frontier). Here the Germans stationed their infantry. The cavalry took cover in the woods nearby, so as to take the Romans in the rear when they came into the forest. Germanicus was aware of all this. He knew their plans, positions, their secret as well as their visible arrangements; and he planned to use their strategy for their own ruin. His cavalry, under the command of Lucius Seius Tubero, was allotted the open ground. The infantry were divided. Part were to proceed along the level ground to the wood, the rest were to scale the earthwork. He undertook this more difficult project himself, leaving the remaining tasks to his generals.

Those allocated the level ground broke into the wood easily. But the men scaling the earthwork were virtually climbing a wall, and received severe damage from above. Seeing that fighting conditions were unfavourable at close quarters, Germanicus withdrew his brigades a short way, and ordered his slingers into action to drive off the enemy. Simultaneously, spears were launched from machines. Exposure cost the defenders heavy casualties; they were beaten back, the earthwork was captured, and Germanicus personally led the Guard battalions in a charge into the woods. There, hand-to-hand fighting began. The enemy were hemmed in by the marsh behind them, the Romans by the river or hills. Both sides had to fight it out on the spot. Bravery was their only hope, victory their only way out.

The Germans were as brave as our men, but their tactics and weapons proved their downfall. With their vast numbers crammed into a narrow space they could neither thrust nor pull back their great pikes. They were compelled to fight as they stood, unable to exploit their natural speed by charging. The Romans on the other hand, with shields close to their chests and sword-hilts firmly grasped, rained blows on the enemy's huge forms and exposed faces, and forced a murderous passage.

Either Arminius had been through too many crises, or his recent wound was troubling him: he did not show his usual vigour. Inguiomerus, however, was in every part of the battle at once. His courage did not fail him – but he had bad luck. Germanicus, who had torn off his helmet so as to be recognized, ordered his men to kill and kill. No prisoners were wanted. Only the total destruction of the tribe would end the war. Finally, late in the day, he withdrew one brigade from the battle to make a camp. Apart from the cavalry, whose battle was indecisive, the rest sated themselves with enemy blood until nightfall.

Germanicus congratulated the victorious troops and piled up a heap of arms with this proud inscription: DEDICATED TO MARS AND THE DIVINE AUGUSTUS BY THE ARMY OF TIBERIUS CAESAR AFTER ITS CONQUEST OF THE NATIONS BETWEEN THE RHINE AND THE ELBE. Of himself he said nothing. He may have feared jealousy; or perhaps he felt that the knowledge of what he had done was enough. Shortly afterwards he sent Lucius Stertinius to fight the Angrivarii unless they rapidly surrendered. They begged for mercy unconditionally and received an unqualified pardon. Next, summer being already at its height, part of the army were sent back to winter quarters overland, while the majority embarked on the Ems and sailed with Germanicus down to the sea.

At first only the sound of a thousand ships' sails, and the motion of their oars, disturbed the calm. But then, from dense black clouds, descended a hailstorm. Squalls blew up from every side, and the rising waves destroyed visibility and upset steering. The troops, terrified and unfamiliar with the perils of the sea, impeded the professional sailors by getting in the way and offering unwanted help. Soon sea and sky were swept by a southerly gale – nourished by waterlogged Germany and its deep rivers and mighty clouds, and aggravated by the savage North Sea just beyond. The gale caught the ships and scattered them over the open sea or on to islands with sharp cliffs and treacherous sunken shoals. Scarcely had these hazards been avoided when the tide turned and ran in the same direction as the gale.

Now the anchors held no longer, and no bailing could keep the torrential waters out. Horses, baggage, animals, even arms were jettisoned to lighten the ships as they leaked at the joints and were deluged by waves. The North Sea is the roughest in the world, and the German climate the worst. The disaster was proportionately terrible – indeed it was unprecedented. On one side were enemy coasts, on the other a sea so huge and deep that it is held to be the uttermost, with no land beyond. Some ships went down. Others, more numerous, were cast on to remote islands, where the men were obliged to eat the horses washed up with them or starve to death. Germanicus' warship landed alone in the realm of the Chauci. He spent days and nights on the rocky headlands – cursing himself for the catastrophe. His friends could scarcely prevent him from drowning himself in the same sea.

At last, when the tide turned and a favourable wind blew, the crippled ships came back with most of their oars lost, or with clothes for sails, or towed by less damaged craft. Rapidly repaired, they were sent by Germanicus to search the islands, and in this way many men were recovered. Many more were ransomed from remoter tribes. The Angrivarii, who had recently submitted, acted as intermediaries. Others had been carried to Britain, and were sent back by its chieftains. Men coming from these remote regions told strange stories – of hurricanes, unknown birds, sea-monsters, and shapes half-human and half-animal, which they had seen or in their terror had imagined.

Rumours that the fleet was lost raised the Germans' military hopes and led Germanicus to take repressive measures. Gaius Silius (I) was ordered to attack the Chatti with a force of 30,000 infantry and 3,000 horse. Germanicus himself, with the larger of the two forces, proceeded against the Marsi, whose chief, Mallovendus, had recently submitted and now reported that the Eagle of one of Varus' brigades lay buried in a neighbouring grove, protected by only a small guard. A detachment was at once sent to provide a frontal diversion, while another went round behind and dug. Both achieved success. This encouraged Germanicus to penetrate further into the interior, plundering and exterminating an enemy who either did not dare to encounter him or was routed wherever he attempted a stand. Prisoners reported unprecedented demoralization. The Romans were said to be invincible and proof against every misfortune – their fleet and their arms were lost, the shores heaped with bodies of men and horses, and yet they had returned to the attack with undiminished courage and ferocity, apparently more numerous than ever.

Then the army returned to its winter-camps, gratified to have compensated the disasters at sea by this successful expedition. Germanicus treated them generously, satisfying every claim for losses. It was felt certain that the enemy were collapsing and about to sue for peace – one more summer's campaign would end the war. But repeated letters from Tiberius instructed Germanicus to return for the Triumph that had been voted to him. 'There have been enough successes,' wrote the emperor, 'and enough misfortunes. You have won great victories. But you must also remember the terrible, crippling losses inflicted by wind and wave – through no fault of the commander. I was sent into Germany nine times by the divine Augustus, and I achieved less by force than by diplomacy; thereby the Sugambri were forced to submit, and the Suebi and their King Maroboduus compelled to keep the peace. Similarly the Cherusci and other rebellious tribes, now that we have duly punished them, can be left to their own internal disturbances.'

When Germanicus asked for another year to complete the job, Tiberius subjected his unpretentious adoptive son to even stronger pressure by offering him the prize of a second consulship – to be occupied personally at Rome. The emperor added that, if the war must continue, Germanicus should leave his brother, Drusus, some chance of distinction; for, in the absence of enemies elsewhere, Germany was the only place in which Drusus could earn a salutation as victor and the triumphal laurels. Germanicus knew that this was hypocritical, and that jealousy was the reason why Tiberius denied him a victory that was already won. But he acquiesced without further delay.

CHAPTER 4

The First Treason Trials

*

IT was about now that Marcus Scribonius Libo Drusus was accused of subversive plotting. Since this case initiated an evil which for many years corroded public life, I will give details of its beginnings, progress, and conclusion. Libo was a fatuous young man with a taste for absurdities. One of his closest friends, a junior senator named Firmius Catus, interested him in astrologers' predictions, magicians' rites, and readers of dreams. Catus reminded Libo that the Caesars were his cousins – besides being a great-grandson of Pompey, he was grandnephew of Scribonia, at one time the wife of Augustus – and that his own house, too, was full of ancestral statues.

By encouraging Libo's extravagances and debts and sharing his dissipations and embarrassments, Catus accumulated damning evidence. When he had collected enough witnesses – including slaves to corroborate the account – he requested an interview with the emperor. Tiberius already knew who was accused, and why, through a knight, Vescularius Flaccus, who was more intimate with the emperor than Catus was. Tiberius did not refuse the information of Catus but declined personal contact, indicating that they could continue to communicate through the knight as intermediary. Meanwhile he made Libo praetor and invited him to dinner. No unfriendliness was apparent in Tiberius' expression or talk. His malevolence was completely concealed. He could have stopped all Libo's actions and words. Instead, he preferred to note them.

Finally, however, a certain Junius whom Libo had approached to practise necromancy reported him to Lucius Fulcinius Trio, a man known for his talents as a prosecutor – and eager for notoriety. Trio immediately pounced on Libo, applied to the consuls, and demanded an inquiry by the senate: which was summoned, to discuss (it was added) a grave and terrible matter. Meanwhile Libo put on mourning and, with an escort of aristocratic ladies, went from house to house appealing to his wife's relatives and seeking for an advocate in his perilous position. Everyone refused. Their excuses were different, but they were all afraid. On the day of the meeting he was prostrate with fear and ill-health (possibly, as some said, assumed), and had to be carried in a litter to the senate-house door. Leaning on his brother's arm he stretched out his hand to Tiberius and cried for mercy. The emperor, without altering his expression, read out the accusation and its signatures in a toneless voice calculated neither to aggravate nor to extenuate the charges.

Trio and Catus had now been joined by further accusers, Fonteius Agrippa and Gaius Vibius Serenus (I). They all competed for the principal speech. Finally, as none of them would give way and Libo was undefended, Vibius announced that he would take the charges one by one; and he produced the documents. They were preposterous. In one, Libo asked a fortune-teller if he would become rich enough to pave the Via Appia with money as far as Brundisium. Other stupidities were equally pointless – indeed, if indulgently regarded, pitiable. But in one paper, mysterious or sinister marks against the names of imperial personages and senators were alleged by the prosecutor to be in Libo's handwriting. Libo denied this. But slaves identified his hand; and it was decided to interrogate them under torture. Since, however, there was an ancient senatorial decree forbidding such investigations of slaves in capital charges against their masters, Tiberius – by an astute legal innovation – ordered the slaves to be sold individually to the Treasury Agent. And all this in order to use slaves' evidence against a man of Libo's position, without infringing a senatorial decree!

The defendant thereupon requested an adjournment until the following day, and left for his home. He entrusted his relative Publius Sulpicius Quirinius with a final appeal to Tiberius. The emperor's answer was that Libo should apply to the senate. Meanwhile his house was surrounded by Guardsmen. The sound and sight of them, clanking about in front of the door, plagued the dinner-party which Libo had arranged as his last pleasure on earth. Gripping his slaves' hands and thrusting his sword into their grasp, he cried out for someone to kill him. The slaves shrank away in terror, and knocked over the table-lamp. For Libo it was the darkness of death. He stabbed himself twice in the stomach, and fell moaning. Ex-slaves ran up. The soldiers saw he was dead, and left.

In the senate, however, the prosecution continued with undiminished earnestness. Tiberius pronounced on oath that, whatever Libo's guilt, he himself would have interceded for his life if he had not so hastily killed himself. Libo's property was divided among the accusers, and those of them who were senators received supernumerary praetorships. Then Marcus Aurelius Cotta Maximus Messallinus proposed that Libo's statue should be excluded from his descendants' funeral-parades, and Cnaeus Cornelius Lentulus (II) that no Scribonius should ever again bear the name of Drusus. On the motion of Lucius Pomponius Flaccus, days were appointed for public thanksgiving. Lucius Munatius Plancus, Gaius Asinius Gallus, Marcus Papius Mutilus, and Lucius Apronius voted thank-offerings to Jupiter, Mars, and Concord, and a resolution that 13 September – the day of Libo's suicide – should become a public holiday. I have listed these distinguished proposers and their servilities to show how long ago this national disgrace started. The senate also ordered the expulsion of astrologers and magicians from Italy. One, Lucius Pituanius, was thrown from the Tarpeian Rock, another, Publius Marcius, executed by the consuls in traditional fashion to the sound of the bugle, outside the Esquiline Gate.

At the senate's next meeting Quintus Haterius and Octavius Fronto, a former consul and praetor respectively, denounced current extravagance. The use of gold plate for private entertainments was prohibited, and so were the silk clothes into which male costume had degenerated. Fronto went further and demanded restrictions on silver plate, furniture, and slaves. (It was still a usual practice for senators, when their turn came to speak, to put forward any matter that they believed to be in the public interest.) Gaius Asinius Gallus spoke in opposition. 'The extension of the empire', he argued, 'has meant the growth of private fortunes. This is nothing new; indeed it is in keeping with the most ancient history. Wealth meant one thing to the Fabricii, another to the Scipios. It must be judged in relation to the country. When the nation was poor, people's houses were small. In its present grandeur individuals, too, expand.

'In slaves, plate, or any other article for use, the only criterion of moderation or excess is the owner's means. Senators and knights have special property qualifications, not because they are intrinsically different, but because their precedence in station, rank, and honours warrants special provision for their mental and physical well-being. Otherwise leading men would have all the worries and dangers, and none of their compensations.' This euphemistic admission of debauchery readily won his audience, since extravagance was widespread. Moreover, Tiberius had observed that this was not the time for a censorship: but if morality deteriorated, he said, his services as reformer would be available.

At this meeting Lucius Calpurnius Piso (II) denounced official sharp practices - corruption in the courts, and bullying by advocates, with their continual threats of prosecution. He himself was going to leave Rome, he said, and retire to some remote, inaccessible country place. Then he proceeded to walk out of the senate-house. Tiberius was upset and made every effort to mollify Piso, besides requesting his relations to use their influence and entreat him to stay.

Soon afterwards Lucius Piso gave another, equally remarkable display of outspoken indignation. For he summoned to court Urgulania, whose friendship with the Augusta had placed her above the law. Urgulania defied Lucius Piso, refused to obey, and drove to the palace. Thereupon the Augusta complained that it was an insult to her dignity. However, Lucius Piso persisted. Tiberius decided that, without acting autocratically, he could back his mother up to the point of promising to appear before the praetor and support Urgulania. Ordering his military escort to follow at a distance, he left the palace, and was seen by the crowd walking composedly and discussing various matters to pass the time. But Lucius Piso's relatives could not induce him to desist - and the Augusta gave instructions that the sum demanded should be paid. Thus ended an incident which did Lucius Piso credit and increased the emperor's popularity. However, Urgulania's influence remained so excessive that on one occasion, when she was summoned to the senate as witness in a case, she refused to attend. A praetor was dispatched to interrogate her at her home - though even priestesses of Vesta traditionally attend legal proceedings in the Forum to give evidence.

The senate's adjournment this year is only noteworthy because of the dispute regarding it between Gaius Asinius Gallus and Cnaeus Calpurnius Piso. Tiberius had said he would be away. But Cnaeus Piso considered this an additional reason for business to continue, it being in the public interest that senate and knights should be able to undertake their proper duties in the emperor's absence. Gallus, forestalled by Piso in the display of independence, protested that to conduct business without the emperor's presence and supervision was incompatible with the national dignity; so the numerous Italian and provincial visitors ought to await his presence. Tiberius listened in silence as the argument raged. Finally, the adjournment was carried.

A dispute next arose between Gallus and the emperor. Gallus moved that officials should be elected five years in advance, and praetorships should immediately be earmarked for major-generals who had not yet held them, the emperor nominating twelve candidates a year. This proposal obviously had profound implications attacking the whole unspoken premises of autocracy. But Tiberius replied as if the suggestion actually envisaged an enlargement of his powers. He could not presume, he said, to make so many selections and postponements – even the annual system easily caused offence, but its rebuffs were mitigated by hopes of an early reversal. Rejection for five years would indeed cause ill-feeling. 'So far ahead', protested Tiberius, 'a man's attitude, family connections, and resources are unpredictable. Even when nomination is one year before office, men become haughty in the interval – what if they had five years of putting on airs? The proposal invalidates the laws establishing time-tables for canvassing, and seeking or holding office. It also virtually multiplies officials fivefold.' This speech had a popular ring. But its effect was to safeguard Tiberrius' dominant position.

He also gave certain senators financial assistance. So it was curious that he dealt high-handedly with the appeal of Marcus Hortensius Hortalus, a young nobleman who was obviously poor. Hortalus was a grandson of the orator Quintus Hortensius, and had been persuaded by a grant of a million sesterces from Augustus to marry and have children, thus preventing the extinction of his famous family. When Hortalus' affairs were debated in the senate and his turn came to speak, his four sons were posted at the door of the hall. Hortalus turned towards the statue of Augustus, and also to that of Hortensius among the orators (for they were meeting on the Palatine). 'Senators,' he cried, 'these boys – you see how numerous they are – have been brought up at the emperor's wish, not mine. And he was right; for my ancestors deserved to have descendants! In these changed days, I myself have not been able to inherit or acquire money, or popularity, or even our family characteristic – eloquence. If my small resources neither disgraced me nor encumbered others, I was content. Then I married, because the emperor told me to. Behold the descendants of all those consuls and dictators! I say this in no competitive spirit but to arouse your compassion. Under your glorious rule, Caesar, they will win whatever honours you choose to give. Meanwhile I beg you to save from destitution the great-grandsons of Quintus Hortensius, the protégés of the deified Augustus.'

The senate received this so favourably that the emperor lost no time in objecting. 'If every poor man is to come here', he said in effect, 'and start requesting money for his children, the applicants will never be satisfied and the nation's finances will collapse. When our ancestors authorized senators to digress sometimes from their subject-matter and raise matters of public importance when it was their turn to speak, this was not to enable us to promote our private interests and personal finances. Such attempts are invidious for senate and emperors alike, whether they grant the subsidies or refuse.

'Besides, this is not an appeal but an ultimatum – and an unforeseen and untimely one. A member interrupts a session – convened for other purposes – by rising and embarrassing the senate with a list of his children and their ages! I am involved, and a determined attempt is made on the Treasury. But if we empty it by favouritism, we shall need criminal methods to fill it. Hortalus: the divine Augustus gave you money, but he did so spontaneously – and with no guarantee of a permanent supply. For permanent concessions would mean an end of all effort and all enterprise, because their incentives, fear and ambition, would be gone. Everyone would look irresponsibly elsewhere for relief, without lifting a finger for himself – a dead weight on the community.'

This sort of argument was applauded by those who habitually applaud emperors, right or wrong. But the majority received it in silence or with suppressed mutters. Tiberius perceived this. After a pause, he announced that, though he had given the applicant his answer, he would, if the senate approved, bestow two hundred thousand sesterces

on each of Hortalus' male children. There were grateful acknowledge-
ments. But Hortalus said nothing. Perhaps he was frightened. Or perhaps, even in his reduced circumstances, he preserved some inherited
dignity. The house of the Hortensii continued to sink into abject
destitution. But Tiberius showed it no further pity.

In the same year, the country was nearly plunged into the horrors
of civil war by the daring of a single slave – only prompt measures
prevented disaster. He was called Clemens. He had belonged to
Agrippa Postumus, and when he heard of Augustus' death he had
formed the very un-slave-like scheme of proceeding to the island of
Planasia, rescuing Agrippa Postumus by force or a trick, and conducting him to the armies in Germany. The slowness of a cargo-boat upset
his plans: when he arrived his master had already been assassinated.
Then Clemens fell back on a more ambitious and desperate project.
He stole Agrippa's ashes, and proceeded to Cosa on a promontory of
Etruria, where he hid himself until his hair and beard had grown. For
in age and appearance he resembled his master.

Then selected companions from his hiding-place spread the rumour
that Agrippa Postumus was alive. It was first whispered secretly, as
forbidden stories are. Then the news spread to every fool with cocked
ears, every subversive malcontent. Clemens himself would appear in
a town after dark. He never showed himself openly or stayed in one
place; no sooner was he heard of than he was gone, to spread the
rumour in a new place. Publicity and immobility bring out the truth
too clearly – impostures need mystery and movement.

So the story that, by heaven's intervention, Agrippa Postumus was
safe, spread throughout Italy. It had believers at Rome. Great crowds
welcomed Clemens at Ostia – and met him secretly in the capital.
Tiberius was in two minds whether to use the army to suppress his
own slave or to let time eliminate the naïve public credulity. At one
moment he was alarmed, and felt that no measure should be omitted.
At another, he would reflect ashamedly that all things were not terrifying.

Finally he entrusted the matter to Gaius Sallustius Crispus. The
latter selected two of his own dependants – soldiers according to some
accounts – and instructed them to approach Clemens and, pretending
complicity, to offer him money and support, come what might. They
carried out their instructions. Then, awaiting a night when Clemens

was unguarded, they took an adequate detachment, bound and gagged him, and brought him to the palace. When Tiberius asked how he had made himself into Agrippa Postumus, Clemens is reported to have answered: 'As you made yourself into a Caesar.' He could not be compelled to reveal his associates. Tiberius dared not execute him publicly, but ordered him to be killed in a secluded part of the palace, and his body to be removed secretly. Many members of the emperor's household, and also senators and knights, were alleged to have advised and subsidized Clemens. But no inquiries followed.

At the end of this year an arch was dedicated near the temple of Saturn celebrating the recapture, under the leadership of Germanicus and the auspices of Tiberius, of the Eagles lost with Varus. Other dedications included a temple of Fors Fortuna near the Tiber – in the gardens which the dictator Caesar had left to the nation – and a shrine to the Julian house and statue of the divine Augustus at Bovillae.[1]

In the following year the consuls were Gaius Caelius Rufus and Lucius Pomponius Flaccus. On 26 May Germanicus celebrated a triumph over the Cherusci, Chatti, Angrivarii, and all other German tribes this side of the Elbe. The procession included spoils, prisoners, and pictures of mountains, rivers, and battles. The war, which he had not been allowed to complete, was regarded as terminated. Attention was riveted on the splendid figure of the commander, accompanied by five children in his chariot. And yet there were unspoken misgivings. Men recalled that popularity had not helped his father Nero Drusus. And that great favourite his uncle, Marcellus, had been carried off at an early age. The loves of the Romans seemed brief and ill-omened.

In the name of Germanicus, the emperor distributed three hundred sesterces a head to the population, and proposed to serve personally as his fellow-consul. But people did not believe his affection was sincere. Next he decided to find honourable excuses for the young man's elimination. Some pretexts were invented, others happened to be available. Archelaus had been king of Cappadocia for fifty years. He was hated by Tiberius, to whom, during the latter's residence at Rhodes, he had shown no attention. This omission had not been intended insultingly, but was prompted by associates of Augustus,

1. Legend ascribed the foundation of Bovillae to Alba Longa, which itself claimed to have been established by the 'founder of the Julian House', Aeneas' son Iulus (Ascanius).

because while Gaius Caesar was in the ascendant and on a mission to the East it had been considered inadvisable to be Tiberius' friend.

However, the house of the Caesars became extinct, and Tiberius reigned. He now made his mother write luring Archelaus to Rome. She did not conceal her son's resentment but held out hopes of indulgence if he came to beg for it. He came without delay, being either unsuspicious of treachery or afraid of suffering violence if he showed he anticipated it. The emperor's reception of Archelaus was unrelenting, and before long he was prosecuted before the senate. He was worn out, not by the charges – which were fictitious – but by distress and old age. Kings are not used even to equality, much less to subordination. So Archelaus died, by his own hand or the course of nature. His kingdom was turned into a province; and the emperor announced that its revenue enabled him to reduce the 1 per cent auction tax, which was fixed at ½ per cent for the future.

At about the same time Commagene and Amanus were unsettled by the deaths of their dependent kings, Antiochus Epiphanes III and Philopator II respectively. Royal rule still had some supporters, but most of the inhabitants wanted annexation by Rome. Other problems had arisen in Syria and Judaea, where the provincials were finding their financial burdens oppressive and petitioning for a reduction of direct taxation.

These developments, and the Armenian situation mentioned above, were brought before the senate by Tiberius. The eastern troubles, he said, could only be put right by the wisdom of Germanicus. For he himself, he said, was of advancing years, whereas Drusus was not yet sufficiently mature. So the senate entrusted the overseas provinces to Germanicus, with powers superior (wherever he might go) to those of all governors of imperial and senatorial provinces alike. But Tiberius had removed Syria's imperial governor Quintus Caecilius Metellus Creticus Silanus (who had betrothed his daughter to Germanicus' eldest son, Nero Caesar), replacing him by Cnaeus Calpurnius Piso. This ferocious, insubordinate man inherited his violent character from his father (of the same name), who during the civil war had vigorously helped the revived Republican party in Africa against Julius Caesar, and then supported Brutus and Cassius. Nevertheless he had been allowed to return to Rome; at first he had not sought office, but finally, when Augustus personally solicited him to take the consulship, he accepted it. In addition to his father's spirit, Piso had his wife Plancina's lineage and wealth to spur him on. He grudgingly allowed Tiberius first place, but looked down on Tiberius' children as far beneath him.

Piso was certain that the purpose of his Syrian appointment was the repression of Germanicus' ambitions. According to one view, he received secret instructions from Tiberius to that effect. Plancina certainly received advice from the Augusta, whose feminine jealousy was set on persecuting Agrippina. For the court was disunited, split by unspoken partisanships for Drusus or Germanicus. Tiberius supported Drusus, as the son of his own blood. But the popularity of Germanicus had increased, partly owing to his uncle's hostility, and partly because his mother's family gave him precedence. He could point to Augustus as great-uncle and Antony as grandfather, whereas Drusus was great-grandson of a knight, Titus Pomponius Atticus,[1] who hardly added lustre to the Claudian genealogy. Besides, Germanicus' wife Agrippina was more distinguished than Drusus' wife Livilla – and had more children. However, the brothers were good friends, unperturbed by the rivalries around them.

Drusus was now sent to Illyricum, to be introduced to army life – and win favour among the troops. Tiberius also considered that the camp would be better for him than his present frivolous life of juvenile extravagance in Rome. Besides, he himself would feel safer with both his sons commanding armies.

But the pretext for Drusus' departure was an appeal by the Suebi for help against the Cherusci. For now that the Romans had gone and there was no external threat, national custom and rivalry had turned the Germans against one another. The two nations were well matched in strength, and their leaders equally capable. But the Suebi did not like the royal title of their leader Maroboduus, whereas Arminius was popular as champion of freedom. So in addition to his old soldiers – the Cherusci and their allies – two Suebian tribes, the Semnones and Langobardi, from the kingdom of Maroboduus also entered the war on Arminius' side. These additions looked like turning

---

1. Cicero's friend and correspondent. Atticus' daughter Pomponia or Caecilia Attica, the first wife of Agrippa, was the mother of Drusus' mother Vipsania. (Agrippa's second wife was Marcella I and his third Julia III.) See Table 3.

the scale. However, Inguiomerus and a group of his followers deserted to the Suebi, merely because the old man was too proud to serve under his young nephew.

Each army had high hopes as it drew up for battle. The old German unsystematic battle-order and chaotic charges were things of the past. Their long wars against Rome had taught them to follow the standards, keep troops in reserve, and obey commands. Arminius rode round inspecting his whole army. He reminded each unit, as he came to it, that freedom was back again, that they had annihilated Roman armies – that many of his men were actually carrying Roman spoils and spears. He denounced Maroboduus as a runaway who, lurking in the Hercynian forest without a single fight, had begged Rome for peace with presents and deputations. 'He is a traitor, an imperial agent!' cried Arminius. 'Eject him as fiercely as you killed Varus. Remember all those battles and their result – the expulsion of the Romans. That shows who won!'

Maroboduus too spoke, praising himself and reviling the enemy. Grasping Inguiomerus by the hand, he credited him with all the glory of the Cherusci – the brain behind their successes. Arminius, he said, was a senseless inexperienced man who took the credit due to others because he had treacherously trapped three straggling divisions and an unsuspecting commander, an action disastrous to Germany and dishonourable to Arminius himself, since his wife and son were still in slavery. 'But I myself', he continued, 'when attacked by twelve divisions under Tiberius, maintained German honour unblemished. We parted on equal terms!¹ As regards Rome we have the choice, I am proud to say, between war with our resources intact, and peace without oppression.'

Besides these speeches, the armies had motives of their own to excite them. The Cherusci had the glorious past to fight for, and their new allies, the Langobardi, their freshly acquired freedom from the Suebi. Their enemy's aim was expansion. Never had a result been so unpredictable. Both right wings were routed. However, instead of renewing the battle, as was expected, Maroboduus transferred his camp to the hills. This showed he was beaten. Then, weakened by a

1. Maroboduus had survived a full-scale Roman invasion in A.D. 6 because the Roman armies, under Tiberius, had to withdraw to deal with a grave revolt in Pannonia and Dalmatia.

series of desertions, he retreated to the territory of the Marcomanni and sent a delegation to Tiberius requesting help. The answer was that, since he had not helped Rome against the Cherusci, he was not justified in claiming Roman support against them. However Drusus, as I have said, was sent to establish peaceful conditions.

In the same year twelve famous cities in the province of Asia were overwhelmed by an earthquake. Its occurrence at night increased the surprise and destruction. Open ground – the usual refuge on such occasions – afforded no escape, because the earth parted and swallowed the fugitives. There are stories of big mountains subsiding, of flat ground rising high in the air, of conflagrations bursting out among the debris. Sardis suffered worst and attracted most sympathy. Tiberius promised it ten million sesterces and remitted all taxation by the Treasury or its imperially controlled branches for five years. Magnesia-by-Sipylus came next, in damage and compensation. Exemptions from direct taxation were also authorized for Temnus, Philadelphia, Aegeae, Apollonis, Mostene (the Macedonian Hyrcanians), Hierocaesarea, Myrina, Cyme, and Tmolus. It was decided to send a senatorial inspector to rehabilitate the sufferers. The choice fell on an ex-praetor, Marcus Aletius. The governor of Asia was a former consul, so the embarrassments of rivalry between equals were avoided.

Tiberius supplemented this impressive official generosity by an equally welcome private benefaction. The wealthy Aemilia Musa died intestate, and her property was claimed for the emperor. But he transferred it to Marcus Aemilius Lepidus (IV), with whose house she was apparently connected. Again, when a rich member of the order of knights named Pantuleius died, Tiberius was named as one of the legatees; but he handed over the whole property on finding that an earlier and evidently authentic will had named Marcus Servilius Nonianus (I) sole heir. Moreover, he refused to accept any bequests which he had not earned by friendship. He had no truck with strangers, or with people who named the emperor their heir because they had quarrelled with others.

While relieving honourable and unoffending poverty, he removed from the senate (or allowed to resign) persons whose means had vanished through extravagance or misbehaviour, namely Vibidius

Virro, Marius Nepos, Appius Appianus, Cornelius Sulla, and Quintus Vitellius.

In this period, too, he dedicated certain temples which Augustus had begun to restore when they had decayed or been burnt down. These were the temples of Liber, Libera, and Ceres near the Circus Maximus (vowed by Aulus Postumius Tubertus and Marcus Poblicius Malleolus when they were aediles); and of Janus (built in the vegetable market by Gaius Duilius, who gained the first Roman naval victory – over the Carthaginians – and won a Triumph for it). The temple of Hope, which Aulus Atilius Calatinus had vowed in the same war, was consecrated by Germanicus.[1]

Meanwhile, the treason law was maturing. Appuleia Varilla[2] was charged under it for speaking insultingly about the divine Augustus (whose sister was her aunt), as well as about Tiberius and his mother, and for committing adultery. The latter offence was ruled to be a matter for the Julian adultery law.[3] As regards the treason, Tiberius insisted on a distinction between disrespectful remarks about Augustus – for which she should be condemned – and about himself, on which he desired no inquiry to be held. Asked by the consul what his ruling was about Appuleia's alleged slanders against his mother, he did not reply. But at the next meeting of the senate he requested in his mother's name also that no words uttered against her should in any circumstances be made the subject of a charge. He released Appuleia from liability under the treason law. For her adultery he deprecated the severer penalty, but recommended that according to traditional practice her relatives should remove her two hundred miles from Rome. Her lover, Manlius by name, was banned from Italy and Africa.

When the praetor Vipstanus Gallus died, the appointment of his substitute was disputed. Germanicus and Drusus, who were still both at Rome, supported Decimus Haterius Agrippa, who was related to Germanicus. However, it was strongly urged – and was legally correct – that the number of the candidates' children should be the decisive

1. According to tradition the temples mentioned were founded in c. 493 B.C. c. 240, c. 260, and some time during the first Punic War (264–41 B.C.) respectively.
2. The daughter of Sextus Appuleius and Marcella I, whose mother was Augustus' sister Octavia (see Table I).
3. This Julian law was a measure of Augustus in 18 B.C. directed against adultery.

factor. Tiberius enjoyed seeing the senate divided between his sons and the law. Naturally the law lost, but it took time and the majority was small; and after all, that is how laws had been overruled even when they still meant something.

In the same year war broke out in the province of Africa, under a Numidian leader called Tacfarinas. He had deserted from service as a Roman auxiliary. His first followers were vagabonds and marauders who came for loot. Then he organized them into army units and formations, and was finally recognized as the chief, no longer of an undisciplined gang, but of the Musulamian people – a powerful nomad tribe on the edge of the African desert. Taking up arms, they brought in the neighbouring Mauretanians, under their leader Mazippa. Their army was in two parts. Tacfarinas retained in camp an élite force equipped in Roman fashion, which he instructed in discipline and obedience; while Mazippa's light-armed troops burnt, killed, and intimidated. The substantial tribe of the Cinithii came over to the rebels.

At this stage Marcus Furius Camillus, governor of Africa, confronted Tacfarinas with his Roman brigade and its auxiliaries. Though this was a small army compared to the masses of Numidians and Mauretanians, his chief concern was to prevent the enemy from cautiously evading battle. Actually, the Africans were optimistic – and this lured them into an unsuccessful engagement. The Roman brigade was posted in the centre, the auxiliary infantry battalions and two cavalry regiments on the wings. Tacfarinas accepted the challenge, and the Numidians were routed. After centuries the Furian family had won military glory again. For ever since the great Marcus[1] to whom Rome had owed its revival, and his son Lucius, success in the field had passed to other families; and the present commander was believed to be no general. So Tiberius was all the readier to praise his victory in the senate. Camillus was voted an honorary Triumph – and lived so unassumingly that he survived it.

1. Traditional 'liberator' from the Gauls in 387 B.C. and refounder of Rome afterwards. His son and grandson were both called Lucius (the latter usually plays the greater part in tradition).

CHAPTER 5

The Death of Germanicus

*

IN the following year Tiberius was consul for the third time, Germanicus for the second. The latter assumed office at Nicopolis in the province of Achaia, which he had reached along the Adriatic coast after visiting his brother Drusus, then stationed in Dalmatia. Since both the Adriatic and the Ionian seas had been stormy, he spent a few days at Nicopolis overhauling the fleet. He employed this opportunity to visit the gulf famous for the victory of Actium, and its spoils dedicated by Augustus, and Antony's camp. The place brought memories of his ancestors, for (as I have pointed out) he was the grand-nephew of Augustus, and the grandson of Antony. Here his imagination could re-enact mighty triumphs and mighty tragedies.

Then he visited Athens, contenting himself with one official attendant, out of regard for our treaty of alliance with that ancient city. The Greeks received him with highly elaborate compliments, and flattery all the more impressive for their emphasis on the bygone deeds and words of their own compatriots. Next, after crossing by way of Euboea to Lesbos (where Agrippina gave birth to her last child Julia Livilla), he skirted the coast of the Asian province, and after calling at the Thracian ports of Perinthus and Byzantium passed into the Bosphorus and the Black Sea. He visited famous historical sites enthusiastically. He also worked to rehabilitate these provinces, exhausted as they were from internal disputes and misgovernment. On the way back, he tried to visit the religious centre of Samothrace,[1] but northerly winds drove him off. However, he inspected Troy's venerable reminders of fortune's vicissitudes and Rome's origins. Then, coasting again along the Asian province, he put in at Colophon, to

1. The gods worshipped at the Mysteries of Samothrace were the Cabiri.

consult the oracle of Apollo at Clarus. Here there is no priestess, as at
Delphi, but a male priest, chosen from certain families (usually from
Miletus). He is told the number and names (only) of his consultants,
and then descends into a cave, drinks water from a sacred spring, and
– though generally illiterate and ignorant of metre – produces a set
of verses on whatever subject the visitor has in mind. Rumour had it
that the oracle of Clarus (in the cryptic fashion of oracles) foretold
Germanicus' early death.

Cnaeus Calpurnius Piso was in a hurry to execute his designs. His
impact on the Athenians was alarmingly violent. In a speech savagely
attacking them, he criticized Germanicus (without naming him) for
excessive compliments, incompatible with Roman dignity, to a people
whom he called Athenians no longer (since successive catastrophes
had exterminated them), but the dregs of the earth: allies of Mithridates VI of Pontus against Sulla,[1] of Antony against the divine Augustus. And he even brought up ancient accusations – their failures against
Macedonia and oppression of their own countrymen. He had personal reasons also for his hostility. For they had refused to release a
certain Theophilus whom the Athenian High Court had condemned
for forgery.

Then a quick sea-journey by a short cut through the Cyclades
brought him to Germanicus at the island of Rhodes. Though aware of
Piso's attacks on him, Germanicus behaved so forgivingly that when
a storm was driving Piso on to the rocks – so that his death could have
been put down to accident – Germanicus sent warships to rescue his
enemy. However, Piso was not mollified. Grudging even a single
day's delay, he left Germanicus and went on.

On reaching the army in Syria he was lavish with gifts, bribes, and
favours even to the humblest soldiers. He replaced company-commanders of long service, and the stricter among the colonels, by his
own dependants and bad characters. He allowed the camp to become
slack, the towns disorderly, and the men to wander in undisciplined
fashion round the countryside. The demoralization was so bad that he
was popularly called 'father of the army'. And Plancina went beyond
feminine respectability by attending cavalry exercises – and insulting
Agrippina and Germanicus. Yet some even of the better soldiers were

---

1. Sulla had conducted the first of several wars against King Mithridates VI
of Pontus (N. Anatolia) in 87–5 B.C.

misguided enough to support her, because of secret rumours that the emperor's approval was not lacking.

Germanicus knew what was happening. But his more urgent concern was to reach Armenia first. The national character and geographical position of that country have long been equally equivocal. It shares an extensive frontier with Roman provinces. It also stretches as far as Media Atropatene. So it is between the two great empires of Rome and Parthia – and often opposed to them, since the Armenians hate Rome and are jealous of Parthia. At this moment they were kingless, Vonones having been turned out. Popular feeling – among high and low alike – favoured Zeno, the son of King Polemo I of Pontus, because he had copied Armenian customs and clothes since earliest childhood: he loved hunting and feasting and other barbarian pastimes. So at a great gathering in the city of Artaxata, with the agreement of the aristocracy, Germanicus crowned him king. The Armenians paid him homage and acclaimed him as King Artaxias III, after the city. Cappadocia, on the other hand, was converted into an imperial province with Quintus Veranius (I) as governor. To make Roman rule seem the preferable alternative, certain of its royal taxes were diminished. Commagene was annexed to the province of Syria, and put under Quintus Servaeus. So Germanicus had solved every eastern question.

Yet his satisfaction was ruined by Piso's arrogance. Germanicus had ordered him to conduct part of the Roman army to Armenia, or send it with his son. Piso had done neither. Finally, at the winter quarters of the tenth brigade at Cyrrhus, they met. Their features were carefully composed, Piso's to show no fear, Germanicus' not to seem menacing. He was, as I have said, a kind-hearted man. But his friends knew how to work up ill-feeling, and piled up a variety of exaggerated facts and hostile fictions against Piso, Plancina, and their sons. A few friends were present at their meeting. Germanicus spoke first, with ill-concealed indignation. Piso apologized – insolently. They parted in undeclared enmity. Subsequently, Piso rarely sat on Germanicus' dais, and, when he did, he looked sullen and critical. At a banquet given by the dependent king of the Nabataei,[1] when heavy gold crowns were presented to Germanicus and Agrippina and lighter ones to Piso and the others, Piso was heard to say that the guest of

1. In Jordan, Sinai and N. W. Arabia.

honour was son of a Roman emperor, not of a Parthian king. He pushed his own crown aside, with a prolonged denunciation of extravagance. This was irritating for Germanicus. But he endured it.

A deputation now came to him from the Parthian king Artabanus III. Its mission was to recall the friendship and alliance between the two empires, and to request a renewal of pledges. The king would pay Germanicus the compliment of coming to the bank of the Euphrates. But meanwhile he asked that Vonones should not be kept in Syria, from which, at short range, his agents were inciting tribal chieftains to disloyalty. Germanicus answered with courtesy about the alliance between Rome and Parthia, and with becoming modesty as regards the king's visit and politeness to himself. Vonones was moved to the Cilician coastal town of Pompeiopolis. This was not just because of Artabanus' request. It was also a rebuff to Piso, whose friend Vonones had made himself by numerous attentions and gifts to Plancina.

While Germanicus was spending the summer in various provinces, Drusus distinguished himself by inducing the Germans to fight among themselves; and he thereby put an end to the already broken Maroboduus. Among the Gotones there was a young German nobleman called Catualda who had been expelled by Maroboduus, and now, seeing him in difficulties, was eager for revenge. Invading Marcomannic territory with a strong force, Catualda bribed the leading men to co-operate, and broke into the palace and adjoining fort. There he found old Suebian loot. There, too, were business-men and camp-followers from the Roman provinces. They had been induced first by a trade agreement, then by hopes of making more money, to migrate from their various homes to enemy territory. Finally they had forgotten their own country.

Maroboduus, completely deserted, was obliged to appeal to the emperor's mercy. Crossing the Danube – at the point where it borders on the province of Noricum – he wrote to Tiberius. His tone was not that of a refugee or petitioner, but reminiscent of his former greatness. When he had been a powerful monarch, he said, and many nations had made approaches to him, he had preferred the friendship of Rome. The emperor answered that he should have a secure and honourable home in Italy as long as he stayed there, and if it became advantageous for him to leave Italy he could go as freely as he had come. In the senate, however, he asserted that Maroboduus had been more dangerous than Philip had been to Athens, or Pyrrhus and Antiochus III to Rome. The speech has survived. It emphasizes the king's power, the ferocity of his subject peoples, Italy's peril from so near an enemy – and the emperor's skill in eliminating him.

Maroboduus was kept at Ravenna, and whenever the Suebi became disorderly they were threatened with his restoration. But for eighteen years he never left Italy, growing old, his reputation dimmed by excessive fondness for life. Catualda's fate and refuge were similar. Overthrown shortly afterwards by the Hermunduri under Vibilius, he was admitted inside the empire and lodged at Forum Julii, a Roman settlement in Narbonese Gaul. The native followers of the two princes were not allowed to inhabit and disturb peaceful provinces: they were settled beyond the Danube between the rivers Morava and Váh and a king, Vannius from the Quadi, was provided for them.

News now arrived of Germanicus' coronation of Artaxias III. The senate voted that Germanicus and Drusus should receive ovations on entering the city. Moreover, arches bearing their statues were erected on either side of the temple of Mars the Avenger.

Tiberius was happier to have secured peace by prudent negotiation than if he had fought a victorious war. So now he used the same diplomatic methods with Rhescuporis, king of Thrace. On the death of the previous king, Rhoemetalces I, who had controlled the whole country, Augustus had divided it between his brother Rhescuporis and his son Cotys IV. The partition gave Cotys the cultivated parts, the towns, and the vicinity of the Greek cities, while Rhescuporis got a wild, savage land with hostile neighbours. The kings' characters were similarly contrasted, the former being attractive and civilized, and the latter grim, ambitious, and an unwilling partner. At first, however, there was ostensible harmony. But soon Rhescuporis began to encroach and annex territory allotted to Cotys, meeting resistance with force. He proceeded tentatively during the lifetime of Augustus, who had created the two kingdoms and might (Rhescuporis feared) punish disrespect. But when he heard of the change of ruler he provoked war, by infiltrating bandit groups and demolishing forts.

Tiberius, whose greatest horror was an upset arrangement, sent a staff-officer to tell the kings to keep the peace. Cotys at once dismissed the force which he had mobilized. Rhescuporis, pretending to be reasonable, requested a conference at which disputed matters could be settled verbally. Place and time were soon fixed, and agreement was reached. Concessions were readily made, for Cotys was good-natured – and Rhescuporis treacherous. He gave a banquet, ostensibly to ratify the treaty; and when the festivities and drinking had continued far into the night, Cotys, off his guard, was imprisoned.

As soon as Cotys realized the trick, he appealed to the sacred right of kings, to the gods their family shared, to the laws of hospitality. But Rhescuporis now possessed all Thrace. He wrote to Tiberius alleging that there had been a plot against himself, but that he had forestalled its instigator. Meanwhile, on the excuse of a tribal campaign against the Bastarnae and Scythians, he reinforced his infantry and cavalry. Tiberius replied gently that, if he had acted in good faith, he need not worry since he was not culpable; but neither he himself nor the senate would judge the rights and wrongs of the case until they heard it. So Rhescuporis must give up Cotys, come to Rome, and relinquish to others the unpopular task of criminal investigation.

The emperor's letter was sent to Thrace by Latinius Pandusa, imperial governor of Moesia, together with a force to take over Cotys. Rage and fear battled in Rhescuporis' mind. Finally he thought it better to be charged with a crime committed than a crime attempted, and ordered Cotys to be killed, alleging suicide. Tiberius' policy however, once fixed, remained unmodified. Pandusa (whom Rhescuporis had accused of hostile bias) died, and his successor in Moesia was Lucius Pomponius Flaccus, an old soldier whose close friendship with the king made it easy to trap him. Flaccus crossed into Thrace, and by large promises induced Rhescuporis (who had hesitated, when he considered his offences) to enter the Roman lines.

A strong guard was attached to him, ostensibly as a courtesy. Its colonels and company-commanders advised and coaxed him. As Thrace receded, their surveillance became increasingly apparent, until at last he saw, as they conducted him into Rome, that there was no choice. He was accused in the senate by the widow of Cotys, and exiled from his kingdom. Thrace was divided between his son Rhoemetalces II, who was known to have opposed his father's policy, and the children of Cotys. Since, however, these last were not of age, a former praetor, Titus Trebellenus Rufus, was to act as their regent. (In the same way, at an earlier epoch, Marcus Aemilius Lepidus (I) had been sent to Egypt to look after the children of Ptolemy IV Philopator.) Rhescuporis was deported to Alexandria, where he was killed while attempting (so it was said) to escape.

In the following year (the consuls were Marcus Junius Silanus Torquatus and Lucius Norbanus Balbus) Germanicus went to Egypt to look at the antiquities. His ostensible object, however, was the country's welfare; by opening the public granaries he lowered the price of corn. His behaviour was generally popular. He walked about without guards, in sandalled feet and Greek clothes, imitating Scipio Africanus, who is said to have done likewise in Sicily though the Second Punic War was still raging.

Tiberius criticized Germanicus mildly for his clothes and deportment, but reprimanded him severely for infringing a ruling of Augustus by entering Alexandria without the emperor's permission. For one of the unspoken principles of Augustus' domination had been the exclusion of senators and knights from Egypt without his leave. He had thereby isolated Egypt, to minimize the threat from any hostile power which, however weak itself and however powerful its opponents, might by holding that country – with its key-positions[1] by land and sea – starve Italy.

Germanicus, still unaware that his expedition was frowned upon, visited the nearest of the Nile mouths, which is sacred to Hercules; the inhabitants say that others of comparable prowess later took his name, but that its original bearer came from their country. Germanicus then proceeded upstream, starting from Canopus, founded by the Spartans to commemorate the burial there of the steersman Canopus when Menelaus, returning to Greece, had been driven off his course on to the Libyan coast. Next Germanicus inspected the imposing remains of ancient Thebes. On its massive masonry, in Egyptian writing, are testimonies to ancient splendour. One of the older priests, requested to interpret the native tongue, told how the country had once possessed 700,000 men of military age, with whom King Rameses II had made his conquests. The tribute-list of the subject lands (they were Libya, Ethiopia, Media, Persia, Bactria, and Scythia; his empire had

1. Pharos island, with its lighthouse, and Pelusium.

also included Syria, Armenia, and its neighbour Cappadocia, and had extended to the Bithynian and Lycian coasts) could be read – the weight of gold and silver was recorded, and the numbers of weapons and horses, the temple-offerings of ivory and spices, the quantities of corn and other materials contributed by every country: revenues as impressive as those exacted nowadays by Parthian compulsion or Roman imperial organization.

Germanicus was interested in other remarkable sights, too, particularly the stone statue of Memnon which gives out the sound of a voice when the sun's rays strike it; the pyramids, mountainous monuments of royal competition and wealth, erected on drifting and almost pathless sands; artificial lakes to receive the Nile's overflow;[1] and elsewhere gorges and depths unplumbed. He came to Elephantine and Syene, once the frontier-posts of the Roman Empire, which now, however, extends to the Red Sea.[2]

At about this time Vonones, whose deportation to Cilicia has been mentioned, bribed his guards with a view to escaping, via Armenia, to the lands of the Albani and Heniochi and to a Scythian tribal chieftain who was related to him. Under the pretence that he was going hunting, he moved inland, aiming for the trackless woods. With a fast horse he made quick time to the river Ceyhan. But on the news of his escape the local inhabitants had destroyed its bridges, and the river was unfordable. So he was arrested on the bank, by a cavalry colonel, Vibius Fronto. Soon afterwards a reservist called Remmius stabbed him to death – ostensibly in a fit of anger, but the man's former position as the king's chief guard increased suspicions that he had connived at the escape and had murdered Vonones to avoid detection.

On leaving Egypt Germanicus learnt that all his orders to divisional commanders and cities had been cancelled or reversed. Between him and Piso there were violent reciprocal denunciations. Then Piso decided to leave Syria. But Germanicus fell ill, and so Piso stayed on. When news came that the prince was better and vows offered for his

1. One lake which 'receives the Nile's overflow' is the Birket-al-Qurûn in the Fayyum.
2. What Tacitus here calls the 'red sea' has been variously interpreted as the Red Sea and the Persian Gulf (which Trajan reached in A.D. 115 and Hadrian evacuated in 117).

recovery were being paid, Piso sent his attendants to disperse the rejoicing crowds of Antioch, with their sacrificial victims and apparatus. Then he left for Seleucia Pieria, to await the outcome of Germanicus' illness. He had a relapse – aggravated by his belief that Piso had poisoned him. Examination of the floor and walls of his bedroom revealed the remains of human bodies, spells, curses, lead tablets inscribed with the patient's name, charred and bloody ashes, and other malignant objects which are supposed to consign souls to the powers of the tomb. At the same time agents of Piso were accused of spying on the sickbed.

Germanicus, alarmed and angry, reflected that if his own house was besieged and his enemies were actually watching as he died, the prospects of his unhappy wife and babies were gloomy. Apparently poisoning was too slow; Piso was evidently impatient to monopolize the province and its garrison. But Germanicus felt he was not so feeble as all that – the murderer should not have his reward. He wrote to Piso renouncing his friendship, and it is usually believed that he ordered him out of the province. Piso now delayed no longer, and sailed. But he went slowly, so as to reduce the return journey in case Germanicus died and Syria became accessible again.

For a time Germanicus' condition was encouraging. But then he lost strength, and death became imminent. As his friends stood round him, he spoke to them. 'Even if I were dying a natural death', he said, 'I should have a legitimate grudge against the gods for prematurely parting me, at this young age, from my parents, children, and country. But it is the wickedness of Piso and Plancina that have cut me off. I ask you to take my last requests to your heart. Tell my father and brother of the harrowing afflictions and ruinous conspiracies which have brought my wretched life to this miserable close. My relatives, those who shared my prospects, even those who envied me in my life, will lament that the once flourishing survivor of many campaigns has fallen to a woman's treachery!

'You will have the opportunity to protest to the senate and to invoke the law. The chief duty of a friend is not to walk behind the corpse pointlessly grieving, but to remember his desires and carry out his instructions. Even strangers will mourn Germanicus. But if it was I that you loved, and not my rank, you must avenge me! Show Rome my wife – the divine Augustus' granddaughter. Call the roll of our six children. Sympathy will go to the accusers. Any tale of criminal instructions given to Piso will seem unbelievable or, if believed, unforgivable.'

His friends touched the dying man's right hand, and swore to perish rather than leave him unavenged. Turning to his wife, Germanicus begged her – by her memories of himself and by their children – to forget her pride, submit to cruel fortune, and, back in Rome, to avoid provoking those stronger than herself by competing for their power. That was his public utterance. Privately he said more – warning her of danger (so it was said) from Tiberius. Soon afterwards he died.

The province and surrounding peoples grieved greatly. Foreign countries and kings mourned his friendliness to allies and forgiveness to enemies. Both his looks and his words had inspired respect. Yet this dignity and grandeur, befitting his lofty rank, had been unaccompanied by any arrogance or jealousy. At his funeral there was no procession of statues. But there were abundant eulogies and reminiscences of his fine character. Some felt that his appearance, short life, and manner of death (like its locality) recalled Alexander the Great. Both were handsome, both died soon after thirty, both succumbed to the treachery of compatriots in a foreign land. But Germanicus, it was added, was kind to his friends, modest in his pleasures, a man with one wife and legitimate children. Though not so rash as Alexander, he was no less of a warrior. Only, after defeating the Germans many times, he had not been allowed to complete their subjection. If he had been in sole control, with royal power and title, he would have equalled Alexander in military renown as easily as he outdid him in clemency, self-control, and every other good quality.

Before cremation the body of Germanicus was exposed in the main square of Antioch, which was to be its resting-place. It is uncertain if the body showed signs of poisoning. People came to opposite conclusions according to their preconceived suspicions, inspired by sympathy for Germanicus or support for Piso.

The other senior officials, generals and senators present now discussed who should govern Syria. The only two who pressed their claims were Gaius Vibius Marsus and Cnaeus Sentius Saturninus. Between them, competition was prolonged. Finally, as Sentius was the older and more insistent, Vibius withdrew. Publius Vitellius,

Quintus Veranius (I) and others began preparing charges and indict-ments against Piso and Plancina as though the trial was already on. At their demand, Sentius dispatched to Rome a woman called Martina who was notorious in the province as a poisoner: Plancina was very fond of her.

Agrippina, exhausted by grief and unwell, but impatient of any-thing that postponed revenge, took ship with Germanicus' ashes and her children. Everyone was sorry for this very great lady, splendidly married hitherto, accustomed to attracting the gaze of respectful and admiring crowds. Now, she clasped to her bosom the remains of the dead. The prospects of vengeance were dubious, her own future peri-lous, her fertility accursed – for it only multiplied hostages to fortune.

Meanwhile Piso heard at Cos that Germanicus was dead. Temples were visited, victims sacrificed, in an orgy of celebration. His own extravagant pleasure was eclipsed by that of Plancina, who chose this moment to exchange her mourning (for the death of a sister) for fes-tive clothes. Company-commanders flocked in from Syria, urging that the Roman garrison was for Piso and that he should reoccupy the province, improperly taken from him and now masterless. He took counsel what to do. His son Marcus recommended a speedy return to Rome, since so far he had done nothing irremediable – unconfirmed suspicions òr empty rumours were nothing to be frightened of. 'Your quarrel with Germanicus', said Marcus, 'may earn you unpopularity, but not punishment. Besides, your enemies have satisfied themselves, by annexing your province. Return to Syria, on the other hand, means civil war, if Sentius resists. And you can expect no lasting sup-port from company-commanders and soldiers. They still vividly re-member their commanding officer, and their dominant emotion is a profound attachment to the Caesars.'

But one of Piso's closest friends, Domitius Celer, opposed this advice. 'Use your opportunity', he said. 'You, not Sentius, were made imperial governor of Syria, with its insignia, its jurisdiction, and its garrison. In event of opposition, the man with the post of governor (not to speak of private instructions) is pre-eminently entitled to take up arms. Besides, it is advisable to give rumours time to fade; when indignation is fresh it often overwhelms even the innocent. But if you keep and strengthen the army, chance might take an unforeseen favourable turn. Why hasten to reach Rome at the same instant as

Germanicus' ashes? If you do, the weeping Agrippina and the witless crowd will bring you down at once on hearsay, your defence unheard. You have the Augusta's complicity, the emperor's sympathy – secretly. No one is so delighted by Germanicus' death as its most ostentatious mourners.'

Piso, naturally impetuous, was easily converted to this course. He wrote to Tiberius accusing Germanicus of extravagance and haughtiness, and asserting that he himself had been expelled to leave the way clear for a rebellion, and that he had now resumed his command as loyally as he had held it before. He put Domitius Celer on board a warship with instructions to proceed to Syria across the open sea, avoiding the coasts and islands. Deserters, streaming in, were organized in units; and weapons were distributed to camp-followers.

Piso crossed to the mainland and intercepted a force of recruits on its way to Syria. He also wrote requesting the Cilician princelings to send him reinforcements. His son Marcus, though he had advised against war, helped actively in its preparations. As they coasted along Lycia and Pamphylia they met the ships taking Agrippina to Italy. The meeting was hostile, and both squadrons prepared to fight. But mutual fears limited them to recriminations. A message from Gaius Vibius Marsus urged Piso to return home to plead his cause. Piso sarcastically replied that he would attend when the praetor in charge of poisoning cases notified accused and accusers of a date.

Meanwhile Domitius had landed at the Syrian city of Laodicea. He made for the winter camp of the sixth brigade which seemed to him the likeliest for his rebellious designs. But he was forestalled by its commander Pacuvius. Sentius wrote informing Piso of this and warning him to keep subversive agents away from the army, and war away from the province. Then, collecting together all whom he knew to cherish Germanicus' memory or dislike his enemies, and emphasizing that this was a forcible attack on the emperor's majesty, he took personal command of a strong force, ready for battle.

Piso's project had started badly. However, he took the safest course in the circumstances by seizing a fortified Cilician town, Celenderis. The Cilician chiefs had sent troops. By adding deserters, the recently intercepted recruits, and his and Plancina's slaves, Piso had brought them to the strength of a division. He insisted to them that he, the emperor's governor, was kept out of the province the emperor had given him – not by the army (he was returning at its invitation), but by Sentius, whose slanders were a cloak for personal ill-will. 'Stand in line', he said, 'and the soldiers will not fight, when they see Piso whom they themselves formerly called "Father"! If right is what matters, my cause will prevail – and if it comes to force, too, it is not a weak one!'

Then Piso drew up his troops in front of the city's fortifications, at the top of a precipitous hill bounded on the other sides by the sea. Against him were old soldiers in regular units, backed by reserves. Piso's position was favourable; but his men, unlike the good troops on the other side, were dispirited and unhopeful, with rustic or make-shift weapons. When the battle started, suspense only lasted while the Roman battalions were clambering up to level ground. Then the Cilicians fled and shut themselves into the fortress. Meanwhile Piso tried to attack the fleet which was lying close by – but without success. Returning, he stood on the walls and beat his breast, calling on individuals by name with offers of reward. These incitements to mutiny had the effect of bringing over the colour-sergeant of the sixth brigade with his Eagle.

But then Sentius ordered the trumpets and bugles to sound. At his command a mound was thrown up, ladders planted and mounted by chosen men supported by a rain of spears, stones, and firebrands from the engines. Finally Piso's stubbornness gave way. He pleaded to be allowed to stay in the fortress if he gave up his arms, while the verdict on the Syrian governorship was referred to the emperor. These terms were refused. All that was granted to him was a naval escort and safe conduct home.

At Rome, when the news of Germanicus' illness spread, with all the sinister exaggerations customary for distant events, there was grief and indignation. So this then, it was angrily said, was why he had been dismissed to a remote country, and Piso given the governorship. This had been the purpose of the Augusta's private talks with Plancina. So it was true what older men said about Nero Drusus, that rulers do not like affability in their sons! Germanicus and Nero Drusus had been struck down precisely because they had planned to give Romans back their freedom, with equal rights for everyone.

This sort of talk was greatly aggravated by the news of Germanicus' death. Without awaiting an official edict or senatorial decree, all business was suspended, the courts emptied, houses shut. There was universal silence and sorrow – no organized display or outward tokens of mourning, but profound, heartfelt grief. Some business-men who had left Syria while Germanicus was still alive happened to come with a more hopeful report of his progress. It was immediately believed and repeated at every chance encounter, and the uncritical hearers spread it again, with joyful embellishments. Crowds ran through the city and broke open temple doors. Night encouraged credulity, and assertions waxed readier in the dark. Tiberius left the false rumours uncontradicted, for time to dispose of. Then, disillusioned, the people were all the more sorrowful – as though they had lost Germanicus a second time.

He was decreed every honour which love or ingenuity could devise. His name was introduced into the Salian hymn: curule chairs, crowned by oak-wreaths, were to be placed in his honour among the seats of the Brotherhood of Augustus; his statue in ivory was to head the processions at the Circus Games; his posts of priest of Augustus and augur were to be filled by members of the Julian family only. The knights of Rome gave the name 'Germanicus' to the block of seats, in the theatre, which had been called the 'junior block'; and they laid down that on 15th July every year his likeness should head their parade.[1] There were to be arches at Rome, on the Rhine bank, and on Mount Amanus in Syria, with inscriptions recording his deeds and his death for his country. Antioch, where he had been cremated, was to have a sepulchre: Epidaphne, where he died, a funeral monument. His statues and cult-centres were almost innumerable. It was also proposed to place a huge golden medallion-portrait among the busts of the great orators. But Tiberius announced that he himself would dedicate one of the usual sort – like the rest – since opulence was no criterion of eloquence and it was compliment enough to be ranked with the classic writers. A good many of these honours are still paid, but some were discontinued, at once or in course of time.

While the mourning was still fresh, Germanicus' sister Livilla – the wife of Drusus – gave birth to twin sons. This happy event, rare even in ordinary homes, gratified the emperor so much that he could not resist boasting to the senate that twins had never been born to so dis-

1. Augustus revived the traditional review of knights (see Key to Technical Terms, KNIGHTS) on 15 July every year.

tinguished a Roman father before. He extracted material for self-congratulation from everything – even accidents! But among the people even this, at such a time, was unwelcome. The increase in Drusus' family seemed a further blow to that of Germanicus.

In the same year the senate passed stringent decrees against female immorality. The granddaughters, daughters, and wives of Roman gentlemen were debarred from prostitution. A woman called Vistilia, belonging to a family that had held the praetorship, had advertised her availability to the aediles, in accordance with the custom of our ancestors who believed that an immoral woman would be sufficiently punished by this shameful declaration. Her husband Titidius Labeo was also requested to state why, when his wife was obviously guilty, he had refrained from enforcing the statutory penalty. He alleged, however, that the sixty days allowed him for consultation had not expired. It was therefore decided to take action regarding the woman only, and she was deported to the island of Seriphos.

Another discussion concerned the expulsion of Egyptian and Jewish rites. The senate decreed that four thousand adult ex-slaves tainted with those superstitions should be transported to Sardinia to suppress banditry there. If the unhealthy climate killed them, the loss would be small. The rest, unless they repudiated their unholy practices by a given date, must leave Italy.

The emperor reported that a priestess of Vesta had to be chosen in place of Occia, whose saintly priesthood had lasted fifty-seven years. He thanked Fonteius Agrippa and Comicius Pollio for the patriotic rivalry with which they had offered their daughters. The choice fell on Pollio's child, the reputation of Agrippa's family having suffered from his divorce. However, Tiberius consoled the rejected girl by a dowry of a million sesterces.

There was popular agitation against the terrible expense of corn. Tiberius fixed the sale price and promised a subsidy of two sesterces a bushel for dealers. But he still rejected the title 'Father of his Country', which was not offered him again because of this. He also severely reproved people who spoke of his occupations as 'divine' and himself as 'master'. So the paths of speech were narrow and slippery. For though the emperor dreaded freedom, he detested flattery.

I find from the writings of contemporary senators that a letter was read in the senate from a chieftain of the Chatti named Adgandestrius, offering to kill Arminius if poison were sent him for the job. The reported answer was that Romans take vengeance on their enemies, not by underhand tricks, but by open force of arms. By this elevated sentiment Tiberius invited comparison with generals of old who had forbidden, and disclosed, the plan to poison King Pyrrhus. However, the Roman evacuation of Germany and the fall of Maroboduus had induced Arminius to aim at kingship. But his freedom-loving compatriots forcibly resisted. The fortunes of the fight fluctuated, but finally Arminius succumbed to treachery from his relations.

He was unmistakably the liberator of Germany. Challenger of Rome – not in its infancy, like kings and commanders before him, but at the height of its power – he had fought undecided battles, and never lost a war. He had ruled for twelve of his thirty-seven years. To this day the tribes sing of him. Yet Greek historians ignore him, reserving their admiration for Greece. We Romans, too, underestimate him, since in our devotion to antiquity we neglect modern history.

Agrippina pressed on with her journey over the wintry sea. When she reached the island of Corcyra, opposite the Calabrian coast, she paused for a few days to calm herself. Her misery was unendurable. Meanwhile, at the news of her approach, people flocked to Brundusium, the nearest and safest port of disembarkation. Close friends came, and many officers who had served under Germanicus; also many strangers from towns nearby, some to pay duty to the emperor, others (more numerous) imitating them. As soon as her squadron was seen out to sea, huge sorrowing crowds filled the harbours and shallows, walls, house-tops – every vantage point.

They wondered whether they ought to receive her landing in silence or with some utterance. As they still hesitated about the appropriate course, the fleet gradually came nearer. There was none of the usual brisk rowing, but every deliberate sign of grief. Agrippina, with her two children, stepped off the ship, her eyes lowered, the urn of death in her hands. Her companions were worn out by prolonged grieving; so the sorrow of the fresh mourners who now met her was more demonstrative. Otherwise everyone's feelings were indistinguishable; the cries of men and women, relatives and strangers, blended in a single universal groan.

Tiberius had sent two battalions of the Guard, and had ordered the officials of Calabria, Apulia and Campania to pay their last respects to his adoptive son. So, as his ashes were borne on the shoulders of colonels and company-commanders, preceded by unadorned standards and reversed axes, at each successive settlement – in proportion to its wealth – the populace clothed in black and the knights in purple-striped tunics burnt garments, spices, and other funeral offerings. Even people from towns far away came to meet the procession, offering sacrifices and erecting altars to the dead man's soul, and showing their grief by tears and lamentations.

Drusus came out to Tarracina with Germanicus' brother Claudius and those of his children who had been at Rome. The consuls Marcus Valerius Messalla Messallinus (II) and Marcus Aurelius Cotta Maximus Messallinus had now begun their term of office, and they, the senate, and a great part of the population thronged the roadside in scattered groups, weeping as their hearts moved them. There was no flattery of the emperor in this. Indeed everyone knew that Tiberius could scarcely conceal his delight at the death of Germanicus.

He and the Augusta made no public appearance. Either they considered open mourning beneath their dignity, or they feared that the public gaze would detect insincerity on their faces. I cannot discover in histories or official journals[1] that Germanicus' mother Antonia (II) played a prominent part in these happenings, although the names not only of Agrippina, Drusus and Claudius, but of all his other blood-relations as well are recorded. Ill-health may have prevented her. Or perhaps she was too overcome by grief to endure visible evidence of her bereavement. But it seems to me more plausible that Tiberius and the Augusta, who remained at home, kept her there too, so that the dead man's grandmother and uncle might seem, by staying indoors, only to be following the mother's example, and grieving no less than she.

On the day when the remains were conducted to the Mausoleum of Augustus there was a desolate silence – rent only by wailing. The streets were full, the Field of Mars ablaze with torches. Everyone – armed soldiers, officials without their insignia, the people organized in their tribes – reiterated that Rome was done for, all hope gone. In the readiness and openness of their talk, they seemed to forget their rulers. But what upset Tiberius most was the popular enthusiasm for

1. These *acta diurna* dated from Julius Caesar's first consulship (59 B.C.).

Agrippina. The glory of her country, they called her – the only true descendant of Augustus, the unmatched model of traditional behaviour. Gazing to heaven, they prayed that her children might live to survive their enemies.

Some people missed the pageantry of a state funeral. How different, they said, had been the magnificent rites devoted by Augustus to Germanicus' father, Nero Drusus! In deepest winter the emperor had gone to Ticinum, and had not left the body until it entered Rome. Statues of Claudii and Livii had surrounded the bier. Nero Drusus had been mourned in the Roman Forum, praised from its dais – every honour ever thought of, ancient or modern, had been his. Yet Germanicus had not even received the honours due to any nobleman. Certainly, he had died so far from Rome that his body had to be cremated unceremoniously in a foreign land. 'But if due marks of respect were thus at first fortuitously denied him, they should be all the more numerous later. His brother[1] went only one day's journey to meet him. Even the gate was too far for his uncle! What had happened to the traditional customs? The image at the head of the bier, the formal poems of eulogy, the panegyrics – the tears, which at least simulated sorrow?'

Tiberius heard of all this. Then, to silence the widespread talk, he issued the following statement. 'Many famous Romans have died for their country. But none has ever been so ardently lamented before. That seems admirable to all, myself included – provided that moderation is observed. For the conduct of ordinary households or communities is not appropriate for rulers or an imperial people. Tearful mourning was a proper consolation in the first throes of grief. But now be calm again. Remember how Julius Caesar, when he lost his only daughter, and Augustus, when he lost his grandsons, hid their sorrow – not to mention Rome's courageous endurance (on earlier occasions) of the loss of armies, the deaths of generals, the total destruction of great families. Rulers die; the country lives for ever. So return to your ordinary occupations – and since the Megalesian Games[2] are nearly due, to your pleasures.'

So business started again. People went back to work; and Drusus

---

1. Germanicus' 'brother' here is presumably Drusus, his adoptive brother (since Drusus' father Tiberius had adopted Germanicus as his son).
2. In honour of the Anatolian Great Mother, the goddess Cybele.

left for the armies of Illyricum. Everyone looked forward to retribution for Piso. It was widely complained that he was insolently and treasonably loitering in pleasure trips round Asia and Achaia, and meanwhile suppressing the proofs of his crimes. For it had become known that the notorious poisoner Martina (sent to Rome, as I have mentioned, by Cnaeus Sentius Saturninus) had suddenly died at Brundusium; and that, although her body bore no signs of suicide, poison had been found hidden in a knot of her hair.

Meanwhile Piso sent his son Marcus ahead to Rome with soothing messages for the emperor. He himself visited Drusus, from whom he hoped to find gratitude for the removal of a rival rather than estrangement because of a brother's death. Tiberius, to show his open mind, received Piso's son courteously, with the presents customarily given to young noblemen. Drusus said to Piso that, if the rumours were accurate, his own fury would be greater than anybody's – but that he prayed they were false and baseless, and that Germanicus' death would ruin no one. This was said openly; Drusus avoided a private interview. It was generally believed that his answer, which displayed an old man's diplomacy foreign to his youthful affability and directness, was prompted by Tiberius.

Piso crossed the Adriatic, left his ships at Ancona, and caught up a brigade marching from Pannonia to Rome on its way to join the army in Africa. Gossip stressed that he persistently brought himself to the troops' attention during the march from Narnia. But then, to avoid suspicion – or perhaps because frightened men change their plans – he embarked on the Nera, and subsequently the Tiber, and increased his unpopularity by landing beside the imperial Mausoleum. It was a busy time of day and the river-bank was crowded. But Piso with a large escort of dependants, and Plancina surrounded by women, went on their way with cheerful expressions. Moreover, his house, which overlooked the Forum, was festively decorated; and a dinner-party followed. In that crowded area nothing was private – and indignation mounted.

On the next day Lucius Fulcinius Trio applied to the consuls for leave to accuse Piso.[1] Germanicus' staff, led by Publius Vitellius and

1. Lucius Fulcinius Trio had asked for the case to be heard by the senate. The emperor heard it briefly first. In important cases these two new procedures superseded the normal machinery of the law-courts.

Quintus Veranius (I), objected that Trio had nothing to do with the matter, but that they themselves were available – not as accusers, but as witnesses to the facts, and bearers of Germanicus' instructions. Trio waived his proposal to prosecute on this charge, but obtained authority to attack Piso's previous career. The emperor was then asked to take over the inquiry. The accused was not sorry. He anticipated malevolence among senators and others, but believed that Tiberius had the strength to ignore gossip and was also immobilized by his mother's complicity. Besides, he argued, it was easier for a single judge to distinguish truth from defamation: numbers encourage prejudice and hostile emotion.

Tiberius was fully aware of the problems of the investigation and of the malignant rumours about himself. So, after listening – with the help of a few close friends – to the accusations and pleas of defence, he referred the whole case to the senate. (At this stage Drusus returned from Illyricum and entered the city, postponing the ovation decreed him by the senate for the suppression of Maroboduus and his other achievements in the summer before last.) Men asked by Piso to defend him – Lucius Arruntius, Publius Vinicius, Gaius Asinius Gallus, Marcus Claudius Marcellus Aeserninus, and Sextus Pompeius (II) – declined on various pretexts. But he received support from Marcus Aemilius Lepidus (IV), Lucius Calpurnius Piso (I), and Livineius Regulus (I). The whole of Rome was excitedly asking: would Germanicus' friends keep their word? What was Piso's defence? Would Tiberius succeed in repressing his feelings? Never had there been so much intense public interest, and so much private criticism and unspoken suspicion of the emperor.

On the day of the senate's meeting the emperor spoke with studied moderation. 'Cnaeus Piso', he said, 'was my father's friend and governor, and I myself, with the senate's approval, made him Germanicus' helper in his eastern duties. It must be decided objectively whether, having upset the prince by disobedience and quarrelsomeness, he rejoiced at his death, or whether he murdered him. For if he has exceeded his position, failed in respect to his senior, and exulted in his death – and my sorrow – then I will renounce his friendship and close my doors against him, but not use a ruler's power to avenge personal wrongs. If, however, there is proof of murder, a crime which would require vengeance whatever the victim's rank, it will be your duty to give proper satisfaction to the children of Germanicus and to us his parents.

'You must also consider these questions. Did Piso incite his troops to mutiny and rebellion? Did he bribe them to support him? Did he make war to recover the province? Or are these lies spread and elaborated by the accusers? Their excessive vigour has given me cause for irritation. For to strip the body and expose it to the stares of the public, thus encouraging – among foreigners – the report that he was poisoned, served no good purpose since this question is still undecided, and the subject of inquiry.

'I grieve for my son, and always shall. But I offer the accused every opportunity of producing evidence which may establish his innocence or Germanicus' unfairness, if there was any. And I implore you not to regard charges as proofs because my personal grief is involved. Those whose blood-relationship or loyalty to Piso have made them his defenders should help him in his peril with all the eloquence and industry they possess; and I urge the accusers to be no less industrious and determined. I propose that Germanicus should be placed outside the law in one respect only: the investigation of his death is being conducted by the senate in its House and not by judges in a law court. Let similar restraint mark the rest of the case, regardless of the tears of Drusus or my own sorrow – or slanders invented against us.'

It was decided to allow the prosecution two days and then – after an interval of six days – the defence three. Lucius Fulcinius Trio opened with an ancient, pointless story of corruption and extortion during Piso's Spanish governorship. Proofs of this would not damage the accused if he refuted the recent charges, and likewise its disproof would not exonerate him if he were convicted of the graver offences. Then Quintus Servaeus, Quintus Veranius, and Publius Vitellius spoke, all earnestly and Vitellius brilliantly. They alleged that Piso, hating Germanicus and hankering after rebellion, had allowed the troops to become undisciplined and overbearing to the provincials, corrupting them into calling him, as the riff-raff did, 'father of the army'. Against every good man, on the other hand, he had borne malice – and particularly against the staff and friends of Germanicus. Finally, they continued, he had killed Germanicus by spells and poison. Then, after his and Plancina's evil rites and sacrifices, he had made war on the State, and had to be defeated before he could be prosecuted.

Under every head except one the defence faltered. Bribery of the troops, abandonment of the province to every rascal, and insults against the commander, was undeniable. The poisoning charge alone was refuted. No conviction was carried by the story of the accusers that, at a party of Germanicus, Piso, his neighbour at dinner, had himself put poison into his food. It seemed fantastic that he should have attempted this, with many people looking on – including another man's slaves – and under Germanicus' own eyes. Piso offered his own slaves for torture and demanded that the waiters should be tortured too.

But for various reasons the judges were implacable – Tiberius because he had made war on the province, the senate because it remained unconvinced that Germanicus had died naturally.[1] Both the emperor and Piso refused to produce private correspondence. Outside the senate-house the crowd were shouting that, if the senate spared him, they would lynch him. They dragged statues of him to the Gemonian Steps[2] and began to destroy them; but on the emperor's orders they were saved and put back. Piso was set in a litter and escorted home by a colonel of the Guard, whose role was variously interpreted as protector of his life or supervisor of his execution.

Plancina was equally loathed, but she had more influence. So it was doubted how far Tiberius could act against her. As long as Piso's fate was uncertain, she swore she would share whatever happened to him, and if necessary die with him. But the Augusta's private appeals secured her pardon. Thereafter she gradually dissociated herself from her husband, and treated her defence separately.

Piso saw that this was a fatal sign, and hesitated whether to continue the struggle. Finally, pressed by his sons, he steeled himself to enter the senate again. Renewed charges, hostile cries from senators, relentless enmity everywhere, he endured. But what horrified him most was the sight of Tiberius, pitiless, passionless, adamantly closed to any human feeling. Piso was carried home. He wrote a brief note – ostensibly preparation for the next day's defence – and handed it, sealed, to an ex-slave. Then he performed his usual toilet. Late at night, when his wife had left the bedroom, he ordered the door to be

1. There is a gap in the text here.
2. The Gemonian Steps, descending from the Capitol to the Forum, were used for the exposure of the bodies of executed criminals.

shut. At dawn he was found with his throat cut. A sword lay on the floor.

I remember hearing older men speak of a document often seen in Piso's hands. He never made it known. But his friends insisted that it contained a letter from Tiberius with instructions relating to Germanicus. If, they alleged, Piso had not been deceived by insincere promises from Sejanus, he had intended to disclose this to the senate – thereby convicting the emperor. Moreover, his death, according to this story, was not by his own hand, but by an assassin's. I cannot vouch for either version. But I have felt bound to repeat this account given by people who were still alive when I was young.

In the senate Tiberius wore a sad expression. The manner of Piso's death, he complained, was calculated to discredit him. He repeatedly interrogated Marcus Piso concerning his father's behaviour during that last day and night. Apart from a few indiscretions, the young man answered prudently. Tiberius then read aloud a memorandum written by Piso, of which this was the gist:

'Conspiracy among my enemies, and the odium caused by a lying charge, have ruined me. There is no place for my guiltless honesty. But I call heaven to witness, Caesar, that I have always been loyal to you, and dutiful to your mother. I beg you both to protect my children. Cnaeus has not shared my doings, good or bad, since he has been in Rome all this time. Marcus urged me not to return to Syria. How I wish I had given way to my young son, rather than he to his old father! I pray, therefore, all the more earnestly that he, who is innocent, should not be punished for my mistakes. By my forty-five years of loyalty, by our joint consulship, I, whom your parent the divine Augustus favoured, whom you yourself befriended, beg you to spare my unlucky son. It is the last thing I shall ask.' Of Plancina nothing was said.

Tiberius exonerated Marcus from the charge of civil war, pointing out that the son could not have disobeyed his father's orders. He also expressed pity for this great family and for the terrible end, merited or otherwise, of Piso himself. On behalf of Plancina he made a deplorable and embarrassed appeal, pleading his mother's entreaties. All decent people were, in private, increasingly violent critics of the Augusta – a grandmother who was apparently entitled to see and talk to her grandson's murderess, and rescue her from the senate. The feeling was that Germanicus alone had been refused the rights which every citizen possesses by law. 'His mourners were Publius Vitellius and Quintus Veranius', people said, 'and meanwhile the Augusta and the emperor were protecting Plancina. Now, no doubt, it is Agrippina's turn, and her children's, to suffer from Plancina's wiles and poisons, so satisfactorily tested! And so this fine grandmother and uncle will have their fill of the unhappy family's blood.'

Two days were spent on the sham investigation of Plancina. Tiberius encouraged Piso's sons to defend their mother. But accusers and witnesses competed in their attacks, and no one answered. People felt sorry for her rather than hostile. The consul Marcus Aurelius Cotta Maximus Messallinus was asked to speak first (for when the emperor presided, it was his custom to include officials among those called upon for their views). The consul's proposal was that Piso's name could be deleted from the calendar; that half his property should be confiscated and the other half allowed to his son Cnaeus, who should change his first name; that Marcus Piso should be deprived of his rank and sent away for ten years, with a subsidy of five million sesterces; and that owing to the Augusta's pleas Plancina should be pardoned.

The emperor reduced the proposed penalties in various respects. He would not have Piso's name removed from the calendar, when it still contained the names of Antony, who had made war on his country, and his son Iullus Antonius, who had outraged Augustus' family. Tiberius excused Marcus from degradation and allowed him his father's property. For, as I have often mentioned, he was no miser, and now his shame at Plancina's acquittal increased his leniency. Similarly, he rejected proposals by Marcus Valerius Messalla Messallinus (I) and Aulus Caecina Severus for a golden statue in the temple of Mars the Avenger, and an Altar of Vengeance, on the grounds that such monuments were appropriate for foreign victories but that domestic disasters were occasions for silent mourning.

The former of these proposals had added that Tiberius, the Augusta, Antonia (II), Agrippina, and Drusus should be thanked for avenging Germanicus. Claudius was left out; and it was only when Lucius Nonius Asprenas publicly asked whether the omission was deliberate that his name was included. The more I think about history, ancient or modern, the more ironical all human affairs seem. In public opinion, expectation, and esteem no one appeared a less likely candidate for the throne than the man for whom destiny was secretly reserving it.

Some days later, Tiberius recommended the senate to admit Publius Vitellius, Quintus Veranius, and Quintus Servaeus to the Pontifical Order. He also promised to back Lucius Fulcinius Trio for office, but warned him not to ruin his eloquence by excessive forcefulness. So the avenging of Germanicus ended. Contradictory rumours have raged around it among contemporaries and later generations alike. Important events are obscure. Some believe all manner of hearsay evidence; others twist truth into fiction; and both sorts of error are magnified by time.

CHAPTER 6

Tiberius and the Senate

*

DRUSUS left the city to resume his command, and returned soon afterwards to receive a formal ovation. A few days later his mother Vipsania died. Of Agrippa's children, she alone died peacefully. The rest were either killed in battle or allegedly poisoned or starved to death.

In the same year Tacfarinas, whose defeat in the previous summer by Marcus Furius Camillus I have recorded, resumed hostilities. After nomad raids – too swift for reprisals – he began destroying villages and looting extensively. Finally, he encircled a Roman regular battalion near the river Pagyda. The energetic and experienced commander of the fort, Decrius, considered the siege a disgrace, and ordered his men to fight in the open, forming line in front of the camp. The battalion succumbed to the first attack, but Decrius hurled himself into the rain of missiles to bar its flight, cursing the sergeant-majors for letting Roman soldiers run away from irregulars and deserters. He turned towards the enemy, wounded in body and face (one eye was pierced), and went on fighting until he fell. His men abandoned him.

When Lucius Apronius, the successor of Camillus, heard of this, he was less worried by the enemy's success than by the Roman disgrace. Adopting an ancient procedure, now rare, he drew lots in the discredited battalion and had every tenth man flogged to death. The severity was effective. When the same force of Tacfarinas attacked the fort of Mala, a detachment of only five hundred old soldiers routed it. In the battle a private soldier, Helvius Rufus, won the honour of saving a citizen's life. Apronius decorated him with the honorific chain and spear, and the Citizen's Oak-wreath was added by Tiberius. The emperor pretended to deplore that Apronius, as governor and commander-in-chief, had not made this award, like the others, on his own initiative.

Since the Numidians were demoralized and impatient of siege warfare, Tacfarinas conducted a guerrilla campaign, giving way under pressure and then attacking from the rear. The tired Romans, frustrated and ridiculed by these tactics, could not retaliate. But finally Tacfarinas turned aside to the coast and, immobilized by all the plunder he had collected, kept close to a stationary base; and then the Roman governor's son, Lucius Apronius Caesianus, sent against him with cavalry, auxiliary infantry, and the most mobile Roman regulars, won a victory and drove the Numidians into the desert.

Aemilia Lepida (II) was now indicted. In addition to her glorious Aemilian lineage, she was great-granddaughter of both Sulla and Pompey. She was accused of falsely claiming to bear a son to the rich and childless Publius Sulpicius Quirinius. There were additional charges of adultery, poisoning, and consultation of astrologers regarding the imperial house. She was defended by her brother Manius Aemilius Lepidus. Though disreputable and guilty, she attracted compassion since Quirinius, even after their divorce, had treated her vindictively.

The emperor's attitude during the trial is not easy to reconstruct. Alternately, or simultaneously, both anger and indulgence were perceptible. First he asked the senate not to consider the charges of treason. Then he enticed from a former consul, Marcus Servilius Nonianus (I) and other witnesses precisely the evidence which he had ostensibly wanted to exclude. He also handed over to the consuls Lepida's slaves (who were under army guard); but he forbade their interrogation under torture on any question concerning their own household. Again, he exempted Drusus, the consul-elect, from speaking first in the matter. This was variously interpreted as a non-autocratic step, relieving other speakers from the obligation to agree with Drusus, or as an ominous sign, since only a vote of condemnation would need such a postponement.

The trial was interrupted by Games. While they were on, Aemilia Lepida, accompanied by other distinguished ladies, entered the theatre and with loud lamentations called upon her ancestors, including Pompey himself whose memorials and statues stood before everyone's eyes. The crowd was sympathetic and tearful, and howled savage curses upon Quirinius as a childless, low-class old man to whom a woman once destined to be Augustus' daughter-in-law (for she had been engaged to Lucius Caesar) was being sacrificed. But then the torture of her slaves disclosed her misconduct. On the proposal of Gaius Rubellius Blandus she was condemned as an outlaw; and, though others had favoured greater leniency, Drusus supported the penalty. However, at the appeal of a senator, Mamercus Aemilius Scaurus, to whom she had given a son, confiscation of her property was waived. It was only now that Tiberius revealed his discovery from Quirinius' slaves that Lepida had tried to poison their master.

So within a short time the Calpurnii had lost Piso, and the Aemilii had lost Lepida. Among these catastrophes to great families the return of Decimus Silanus to the Junii was consoling. His history was briefly this. For all the divine Augustus' good fortune in public affairs, his home life had been unhappy owing to the immorality of his daughter and granddaughter. He expelled them from the city, and executed or banished their lovers. For he used the solemn names of sacrilege and treason for the common offence of misconduct between the sexes. This was inconsistent with traditional tolerance and even with his own legislation. The fates of the other victims I hope to record as part of a general history of the period, if I fulfil my present aim and live to undertake further labours. As for Decimus Junius Silanus, his adultery with Augustus' granddaughter had only been punished by the withdrawal of the emperor's friendship. But he had realized that this meant exile.

It was not until Tiberius became emperor that Decimus Junius Silanus ventured to appeal to him and the senate. He employed as intermediary his powerful brother Marcus Silanus (I), conspicuous nobleman and speaker. Marcus was thanking the senate for its indulgence when Tiberius intervened. He too, he intimated, was glad that Marcus' brother had returned from his distant travels, as he was entitled to since he had not been banished by the senate or by law; he himself however still felt, unabated, his father's aversion to Decimus – his return had not annulled the wishes of Augustus. Subsequently Decimus lived in Rome, without office.

It was next proposed to mitigate the Papian-Poppaean law.[1] This

---

1. The Lex Papia Poppaea of A.D. 9 had supplemented a Julian law of 18 B.C. regulating matrimonial matters.

had been authorized by Augustus in his later years, as a supplement to the Julian legislation, to tighten the sanctions against celibacy, and to increase revenue. It had failed, however, to popularize marriage and the raising of families – childlessness was too attractive. But increasingly many people were liable to penalties, since every household was exposed to informers' technicalities. The danger was now not so much misbehaviour as the law itself.

This prompts me to go into some detail about the origins of law, and the ways in which it developed into our endless and complicated statute-list. Primitive man had no evil desires. Being blameless and innocent, his life was free of compulsions or penalities. He also needed no rewards; for he was naturally good. Likewise, where no wrong desires existed, fear imposed no prohibitions. But when men ceased to be equal, egotism replaced fellow-feeling and decency succumbed to violence. The result was despotism – in many countries, permanently. Some communities, however, either immediately or when autocratic government palled, preferred the rule of law. Laws were at first the simple inventions of simple men. The most famous laws are those designed for Crete by Minos, for Sparta by Lycurgus, and then the more extensive and sophisticated code which Solon gave Athens.

We ourselves, when Romulus' autocratic régime ended, were subordinated by Numa to a religious code, to which Tullus Hostilius and Ancus Marcius introduced adjustments. But our outstanding maker of laws – binding even on kings – was Servius Tullius. After Tarquin's expulsion the community took many measures against the ruling class in the interests of freedom and unity. A new Council of Ten, by incorporating the finest elements from all sources, drew up the Twelve Tables. That was the last equitable legislation. For subsequent laws, other than those directed against specific current offences, were forcible creations of class-warfare, designed to grant unconstitutional powers, or banish leading citizens, or fulfil some other deplorable purpose.

Hence arose demagogues like the Gracchi and Lucius Appuleius Saturninus – and the senate's partisans such as Marcus Livius Drusus with their equally comprehensive offers. By these, Italian hopes were raised, only to be dashed by tribunes' vetoes. Even during the Social and Civil Wars, contradictory legislation continued. Then the dictator

Sulla repealed or altered earlier laws, and passed more himself. A pause followed; but not for long, since disorder quickly returned owing to the legislation of Marcus Aemilius Lepidus (II), and the tribunes soon regained their power of unlimited popular agitation. Thenceforward measures were concerned with personal instead of national issues. Corruption reached its climax, and legislation abounded.

Pompey, in his third consulship, was chosen to reform public life. But his cures were worse than the abuses; and he broke his own laws. Force was the means of his control, and by force he lost it. During the twenty years of strife that followed, morality and law were non-existent, criminality went unpunished, decency was often fatal. Finally Caesar Augustus, when consul for the sixth time, felt sure enough of his position to cancel all that he had decreed as Triumvir, in favour of a new order: peace and the Principate.[1]

From then onwards restraints were stricter. There were spies, encouraged by inducements from the Papian-Poppaean law, under which failure to earn the advantages of parenthood meant loss of property to the State as universal parent. The spreading encroachments of these informers grievously affected all citizens, whether in Rome, Italy, or elsewhere, and caused widespread ruin and universal panic. To rectify the situation, Tiberius appointed a Commission consisting of five former consuls, five former praetors, and five other senators, chosen by lot. It disentangled numerous legal complexities, and temporarily produced a slight alleviation.

At about the same time the emperor commended to the senate Germanicus' son Nero Caesar, now approaching manhood. Mirth was caused by Tiberius' proposal that Nero Caesar be permitted to stand for the quaestorship five years ahead of the legal age, with exemption from service on the Board of Twenty. The emperor argued that at Augustus' request he himself and his brother had obtained the same concessions. But even at that time, I feel, such applications must have

1. Tacitus refers to the following events: 451–49 B.C. Twelve Tables drawn up by Councils of Ten, 133 and 123-2 attempted 'democratic' reforms of the two Gracchi, 100 agitation of Lucius Appuleius Saturninus, 91 proposals and murder of Marcus Livius Drusus, 91–88 the Social (Marsian) War, 88-2 Civil Wars between Marians and Sulla, 82 dictatorship of Sulla, whose constitution is reversed by Marcus Aemilius Lepidus (II) (consul 78) and Pompey and Crassus (70), 52 Pompey's third consulship, 28 Octavian's sixth consulship.

earned secret ridicule. And yet those had been the earliest days of imperial power, when ancient custom had counted for more: besides, Tiberius as grandfather of his candidate, Nero, was a closer connection than Augustus as stepfather of his.

Nero Caesar was also admitted to the Pontifical Order, and on the occasion of his official début there was a free distribution to the public. Their delight to see a son of Germanicus already growing up was increased by his marriage with Drusus' daughter Livia Julia. But that good news was counterbalanced by their dissatisfaction at the betrothal of Claudius' son to the daughter of Sejanus. This was felt to depreciate the nobility of the imperial house, while exalting Sejanus even beyond the excessive hopes which suspicion attributed to him.

At the end of the year two notable Romans died, Lucius Volusius Saturninus (I) and Gaius Sallustius Crispus. Volusius' family, though ancient, had previously never risen above the praetorship, but he contributed a consulship and held censorial functions for the selection of knights as members of the judicature. He was also the first to amass the wealth for which his family became so greatly conspicuous. Crispus was a knight by birth. He took his name from his grandmother's brother, the eminent historian Sallust, who had adopted him. So he had easy access to an official career. But he followed the example of Maecenas and, without senatorial rank, exceeded in power many ex-consuls and winners of Triumphs. Elegant and refined – the antithesis of traditional simplicity – he carried elaborate opulence almost to the point of decadence. Yet underneath was a vigorous mind fit for great affairs, all the keener for its indolent, sleepy mask. So, as a repository of imperial secrets, he was second only to Maecenas during the latter's lifetime, and thereafter second to none. Sallustius was privy to the murder of Agrippa Postumus. But in his later years his friendship with Tiberius was impressive rather than active. It had been the same with Maecenas. Influence is rarely lasting. Such is its fate. Or perhaps both parties become satiated, when the ruler has nothing more to give, the collaborator nothing more to ask.

The following year witnessed the fourth consulship of Tiberius and the second of Drusus – a noteworthy partnership of father and son. Three years earlier, Germanicus had shared the same position with Tiberius. But they had not been such close relatives, and the association had brought the emperor no pleasure. Now, at the beginning of the year, he withdrew to Campania, ostensibly for his health. Perhaps he was, by degrees, rehearsing for a prolonged, unbroken absence. Or he may have wished by his retirement to leave Drusus as sole consul. Indeed, a small matter which turned into a serious dispute happened to give the prince a chance of popularity. A former praetor Cnaeus Domitius Corbulo (I) complained to the senate that a young nobleman, Lucius Cornelius Sulla, had refused to give up his seat to him at a gladiatorial display. Corbulo had on his side age, traditional custom, and the sympathies of the older men. Sulla was supported by his connections, including Mamercus Aemilius Scaurus and Lucius Arruntius. There was a vigorous exchange, and much talk of our ancestors' strict decrees censuring youthful disrespect. Finally Drusus uttered some conciliatory words, which were transmitted to Corbulo by Mamercus Scaurus, Sulla's uncle and stepfather and the most fluent speaker of the day. So Corbulo received satisfaction. However, he then complained about another matter. Many Italian roads, he said, were breached and impassable owing to contractors' dishonesty and slackness among officials. He expressed willingness to initiate prosecutions. But the resulting convictions and compulsory sales destroyed many reputations and fortunes, without corresponding benefit to the public.

A little later, Tiberius wrote to the senate reporting that an incursion by Tacfarinas had again broken the peace in Africa. He requested them to choose a governor who was an experienced commander and physically fit for active service. Sextus Pompeius (II) seized the opportunity of ventilating his dislike of Manius Aemilius Lepidus, whom he described as a lazy degenerate pauper who ought to be excluded from the ballot both for Africa and for Asia.[1] The senate objected, since it regarded Lepidus as mild rather than lazy, and his irreproachable bearing of an illustrious name – despite inherited poverty – as praiseworthy rather than discreditable. So Lepidus was appointed to Asia. With regard to Africa it was decided to let the emperor choose.

During the debate Aulus Caecina Severus proposed that no one appointed to a governorship should be allowed to take his wife. 'My wife and I are good friends', he said, 'and have produced six children. But I have practised what I preach, by keeping her at home in Italy

---

1. Africa and Asia were the greatest 'senatorial' governorships, reserved for former consuls (see Key to Technical Terms, GOVERNORS).

during all my forty years of service in various provinces! The rule
which forbade women to be taken to provinces or foreign countries
was salutary. A female entourage stimulates extravagance in peace-
time and timidity in war. It makes a Roman army resemble an oriental
progress. Women are not only frail and easily tired. Relax control,
and they become ferocious, ambitious schemers, circulating among
the soldiers, ordering company-commanders about. Recently a
woman conducted battalion parades and brigade exercises! Remember
that whenever officials are tried for extortion most of the charges
are against their wives. The wives attract every rascal in a province. It
is they who initiate and transact business. Two escorts are necessary,
two centres of government – and the women give the more wilful
and despotic orders. They have burst through the old legal restrictions
of the Oppian[1] and other laws, and are rulers everywhere – at home,
in the courts, and now in the army.'

This speech pleased only a few people. There was a chorus of inter-
ruptions, questioning both its relevance to the current discussion and
Caecina's fitness to be censor in so important a matter. He was
answered by Marcus Valerius Messalla Messallinus (I), who possessed
some shadow of the eloquence of his father, Marcus Valerius Messalla
Corvinus (I). 'Old-fashioned austerity has been satisfactorily mitigated
in many ways,' he declared. 'For the city is no longer beleaguered, the
provinces no longer hostile. So we make, nowadays, a few concessions
to women's requirements – but not the sort to upset their husbands'
households, much less the provincials. In all else wives fare like their
husbands. And why not, in peace-time? Certainly men must travel
light in war. But when they return from their labours they are surely
entitled to relax with their wives. Some women, we hear, are schemers
or money-grubbers. But officials themselves often show every sort of
imperfection: yet governorships are filled. Granted that husbands are
often corrupted by bad wives – is bachelorhood the ideal, then?

'The Oppian laws were once accepted because the national situation then required them. Later, they were relaxed and alleviated as
expediency suggested. Let us avoid euphemisms for our own slackness. If a woman misbehaves, it is her husband's fault. Besides, the
weakness of one or two husbands is no reason to deprive all of them

1. The short-lived sumptuary Lex Oppia was passed during the Second Punic
War (215 B.C.).

of their wives' partnership in good times and bad. Moreover, that would mean abandoning and exposing the weaker sex to its own temptations and to masculine sensuality. Marriages scarcely survive with the keeper on the spot – whatever would happen with some years of virtual divorce to efface them? When reforming abuses elsewhere, remember the immorality of the capital.'

Drusus added a short speech about his own marriage, pointing out that the imperial family often had to visit remote provinces. The divine Augustus, he recalled, had frequently travelled with his wife, to east and west – and he himself had been to Illyricum and if need be would go elsewhere, but not always happily if severed from his beloved wife and all their children. So Caecina's proposal was evaded.

At its next meeting, the senate heard a letter from Tiberius blaming them (by implication) for referring all their difficulties to him, and nominating two men from whom they were to choose the governor of Africa – Marcus Aemilius Lepidus (IV) and Quintus Junius Blaesus. Both then addressed the senate. Lepidus emphatically asked to be excused, pleading ill-health, young children, and a marriageable daughter. He did not mention what was in their thoughts – that Blaesus was beyond competition, being Sejanus' uncle. Blaesus, too, pretended to decline – but less convincingly, and with many flatterers to contradict him.

Next a practice causing widespread secret discontent was made public. Bad characters were increasingly slandering and insulting respectable people and escaping punishment by grasping an effigy of the emperor. Thereby even ex-slaves and slaves had intimidated their patrons and masters with threatening words and gestures. The junior senator Gaius Cestius Gallus (I) raised the matter. Emperors were certainly godlike, he said, but even gods only listened to virtuous petitioners; the Capitol and other Roman temples were not sanctuaries to encourage crime; and it was the height of illegality when Annia Rufilla, convicted for fraud by his agency, should menace and abuse him in the Forum, actually outside the senate, while he could not risk legal proceedings because she clutched an image of the emperor. Similar stories, some more serious, came from all sides. Drusus was begged to inflict exemplary punishment; and summoning Annia, he had her convicted and gaoled in the State prison.

Next, two knights, Considius Aequus and Caelius Cursor, who had made fictitious accusations of treason against the praetor Magius Caecilianus, were punished at the emperor's instigation by a senatorial decree. Both decisions improved Drusus' reputation. Living sociably in Rome, he seemed a moderating influence on his father's solitary designs. Even his youthful extravagances were not unpopular. Better to spend the day enjoying shows and the night banqueting than to lead the emperor's isolated, joyless life of gloomy watchfulness and sinister machinations.

For Tiberius and the accusers were untiring. Ancharius Priscus had impeached the governor of Crete and Cyrene, Caesius Cordus, for extortion – to which was added a charge of treason, now the complement of every prosecution. Again, when a prominent man in Macedonia, Antistius Vetus, was acquitted of adultery, Tiberius rebuked the judges and haled the defendant back to be tried for treason as a seditious accomplice of the anti-Roman intentions of Rhescuporis, who had murdered his fellow-monarch Cotys IV. Antistius was outlawed, and banished to an island without access to Macedonia or Thrace.

Meanwhile Thrace, divided between Rhoemetalces II and the children of Cotys IV – with a Roman regent, Titus Trebellenus Rufus, during their minority – was in disorder. The country was unfamiliar with Roman rule; and Rhoemetalces was as forcibly criticized as the regent, for not avenging his people's wrong. Three strong tribes, the Coelaletae, Odrysae, and Dii, opened hostilities. But their leaders did not join forces, and were individually insignificant, so a coalition involving serious war was averted. One contingent plundered its own neighbourhood, another crossed the Balkan mountains to raise the outlying tribes, while the largest and best organized blockaded the king in Philippopolis, a city founded by King Philip II of Macedonia.

When the commander of the nearest Roman army, Publius Vellaeus, heard this news, he sent auxiliary cavalry and infantry against the marauding and recruiting forces, and himself took the main Roman infantry to raise the siege. Each operation was successful. The marauders were annihilated; quarrels broke out in the besieging force, and as the Roman brigade moved up Rhoemetalces made a timely sortie. What followed was not a battle or even a fight, but a massacre of half-armed stragglers, without Roman bloodshed.

In the same year heavy debts drove Gallic communities into rebellion. Its keenest instigators were Julius Florus among the Treviri and Julius Sacrovir among the Aedui – both noblemen, whose ancestors' services to Rome had earned them citizenship in days when this was scarce and conferred for merit. Secret conferences were attended by desperate characters and penniless, frightened men driven to crime by their evil records. It was agreed that Florus should raise the Belgae and Sacrovir the tribes farther south. There were treasonable gatherings and discussions about endless taxation, crushing rates of interest, and the brutality and arrogance of governors. 'Germanicus' death has demoralized the Roman army!' they cried. 'Besides, look at the contrast between your strength and Italy's weakness. Think of the unwarlike population of Rome. How the army needs us provincials! This is an ideal opportunity to regain independence.'

These seeds of rebellion were sown in almost every Gallic community. But the outbreak started among the Andecavi and Turoni. The imperial governor of Lugdunese Gaul, Acilius Aviola, suppressed both, the former with the city-police battalion which garrisoned Lugdunum, and the latter with regular troops sent by his colleague in Lower Germany, Gaius Visellius Varro. To hide their rebellious aims – for which the time was not yet ripe – certain Gallic chiefs supported the disciplinary measures. Sacrovir himself was to be seen encouraging the fighters – on the Roman side. He was bare-headed, ostensibly to attract attention to his valour; but prisoners said it was to show his identity and so avoid being aimed at. Tiberius received this information but disregarded it: his indecision did no good to the war.

Florus, pursuing his plans, tempted a cavalry regiment – raised among the Treviri but serving with us in Roman fashion – to begin hostilities by massacring our business-men. The majority remained loyal, but a few went over. A crowd of debtors and dependants also took up arms. Making for the Arduenna Forest, they were intercepted by brigades sent from opposite directions by the imperial governors of Lower and Upper Germany. The Romans sent ahead a man of rebel nationality, Julius Indus by name, whose loyalty was stimulated by hatred for Florus. This man dispersed the still undisciplined crowd. But Florus escaped in the rout, and his hiding-place proved untraceable. Finally, however, seeing soldiers blocking every exit, he killed himself. So the rebellion among the Treviri ended.

The revolt of the Aedui was more formidable; for they were a

richer nation, and less accessible to counter-measures. Sacrovir with
an armed force occupied the capital, Augustodunum, and seized the
youthful Gallic noblemen who were being educated there. Holding
them as pledges to win over their parents and relations, he distributed
among them secretly manufactured weapons. His army was forty
thousand strong; one-fifth were equipped like Roman soldiers, the
rest with hunters' spears, knives, and other such arms. There was also
a party of slaves training to be gladiators. Completely encased in iron
in the national fashion, these Crupellarii, as they were called, were too
clumsy for offensive purposes but impregnable in defence. Reinforcements came in. The neighbouring communities had not yet openly
joined, but supplied keen volunters. And the Roman generals were
quarrelling; both claimed to control operations. Finally the aged and
infirm governor of Lower Germany yielded to his Upper German
colleague of more active years, Gaius Silius (I).

At Rome it was said that not the Treviri and Aedui alone but all the
sixty-four peoples of Gaul had revolted, that the Germans had joined
them, and the Spanish provinces were wavering. As usual, rumour
magnified everything. Every respectable Roman citizen deplored his
country's difficulties. But many disliked the existing régime and hoped
for change so greatly that they even welcomed danger for themselves.
They criticized Tiberius for devoting attention to accusers' reports
during so dangerous a rebellion. 'Was Sacrovir too', they inquired,
'going to appear before the senate for treason? Here at last are men to
put a forcible stop to these bloodthirsty imperial letters – and even
war is a welcome change from the miseries of peace!' The emperor,
however, took all the more pains to appear unperturbed. Profoundly
secretive, he allowed neither gesture nor expression to show he was
concerned. Or perhaps he knew that the gravity of the trouble had
been exaggerated.

Silius sent auxiliaries ahead to ravage villages of the Sequani (a
frontier people who were allies and neighbours of the Aedui). Then
he himself, with two brigades, moved rapidly against Augustodunum.
There was much rivalry among Roman sergeant-majors to reach it
first. Indeed, even the ordinary soldiers protested against the usual
halts and rests at night. They felt that, once they and the enemy saw
each other face to face, victory was as good as won.

On the open ground twelve miles from the town Sacrovir and his forces came into sight. He had stationed his heavily armoured men in front, the fully armed battalions on the wings, and half-armed supporters in the rear. He himself, finely mounted and accompanied by his chiefs, rode round and addressed his men, recalling the ancient triumphs of the Gauls and their successes against the Romans, and contrasting the glorious independence that victory would bring with the even more oppressive servitude that would await defeat.

His words were gloomily received – and cut short. For the Roman army was advancing in line. The Gallic townsmen lacked discipline and battle experience; their eyes and ears were no use to them. The Romans' confidence made exhortations unnecessary. However, Silius spoke. It was an affront to the conquerors of Germany, he suggested, to have to march against Gauls – a single battalion had recently suppressed the rebel Turoni, a single cavalry regiment the Treviri, a few troops from this very army the Sequani. 'The wealthy, luxurious Aedui look unwarlike enough', he said. 'You prove that they are what they look! And then when they run, you can spare their lives.'

There was a mighty shout in reply. Our cavalry enveloped the enemy's flanks, while the infantry made a frontal attack. The Gallic flanks were driven in. The iron-clad contingent caused some delay as their casing resisted javelins and swords. However, the Romans used axes and mattocks, and struck at their plating and its wearers like men demolishing a wall. Others knocked down the immobile gladiators with poles or pitchforks, and, lacking the power to rise, they were left for dead. Sacrovir and his closest associates fled first to Augustodunum and then, fearing betrayal, to a house nearby. There he killed himself; and his companions killed each other. The house was set on fire, and the bodies burnt inside it.

At this late stage Tiberius wrote informing the senate simultaneously of the outbreak of the war and its termination. He neither exaggerated nor minimized the facts, commenting that victory was due to the loyal courage of his generals and to his own policy. To explain why he and Drusus had not gone to the war, he stressed the size of the empire and the inadvisability of a ruler leaving the centre of government merely because of disturbances in one community or another. Now however (he added) that the motive for his going could not be ascribed to anxiety, he would go – to study the situation, and deal with it.

The senate decreed vows and prayers for his return, and other honours. Only Publius Cornelius Dolabella (I), determined to outshine everybody in ridiculous flattery, proposed that Tiberius should enter the city from Campania with an official ovation. This elicited a letter from Tiberius suggesting that, after conquering the most formidable nations and receiving or declining so many Triumphs in his youth, the emperor was not undistinguished enough to hanker after the empty honour of a suburban parade in his old age.

A little later, Tiberius asked the senate to award a public funeral to Publius Sulpicius Quirinius. He came from Lanuvium, and had no connection with the ancient patrician Sulpician family. But he was a fine soldier, whose zealous services had earned him a consulship and honorary Triumph from the divine Augustus for capturing the fortresses of the Homonadenses on the Cilician borders. Later, appointed adviser to Gaius Caesar during the latter's Armenian commission, Quirinius had treated Tiberius, then living at Rhodes, with respect – as the emperor now told the senate; and he coupled this praise of Quirinius' attentiveness with an attack on Marcus Lollius (I), whom he blamed for Gaius Caesar's perverse quarrelsomeness on that occasion. But others had less agreeable memories of Quirinius, who was a mean, over-influential old man, and (as I have mentioned) had persecuted Aemilia Lepida (II).

At the end of the year an informer attacked the knight Clutorius Priscus, who had been subsidized by Tiberius for writing a well-known poem about Germanicus' death. Clutorius was now accused of composing another poem while Drusus was ill, for even more lucrative publication if the prince died. Clutorius had bragged of this in the house of Publius Petronius, before his host's mother-in-law Vitellia and many leading women. When the accuser came forward, the other women were intimidated into admitting this. Vitellia alone said she had heard nothing. However, the damning evidence was more widely believed, and the consul-elect Decimus Haterius Agrippa moved for the death penalty.

Marcus Aemilius Lepidus (IV) opposed this motion. 'If, senators,' he argued, 'we only consider the outrageous utterance with which Clutorius Priscus has degraded himself and his hearers, prison and the noose – or even the tortures reserved for slaves – are not enough for him. Yet, however deplorable and outrageous the offence, the emperor's moderation and your own ancient and modern precedents indicate the mitigation of penalties. Besides, folly is distinguished from crime – and words from deeds. For these reasons, it is legitimate to propose a punishment which will cause us to regret neither over-leniency nor harshness. I have often heard our emperor deploring suicides, since they prevent the exercise of his clemency. Clutorius is still alive. His survival will not endanger the State; and his death will convey no lesson. His compositions are senseless, but they are insignificant and ephemeral. A man who betrays his own outrages to impress not men but mere females is no very great danger. I propose, therefore, that we expel him from the city, outlaw him, and confiscate his property, as if he were guilty under the treason law.'

A single ex-consul, Gaius Rubellius Blandus, agreed. But the rest supported Haterius. So Clutorius Priscus was imprisoned and immediately executed.

This drew from Tiberius a characteristically cryptic reproof of the senate. While praising their loyalty in so vigorously avenging even minor offences against the emperor, he deprecated so hasty a punishment of a mere verbal lapse. He commended Lepidus – but refrained from criticizing Haterius. The result was a decision that no senatorial decree should be registered at the Treasury for nine days, executions to be delayed for that period. But the senate lacked the freedom to reconsider. And the intervals never softened Tiberius.

The consuls of the following year were Gaius Sulpicius Galba and Decimus Haterius Agrippa. The year was peaceful abroad. But the capital was nervous – for it anticipated stern measures against the current extravagance, which extended unrestrainedly to every sort of outlay. Most of this, however enormous, could be concealed by suppressing prices. But the sums spent on gluttonous eating were widely discussed; and the emperor's old-fashioned austerity inspired fears of rigorous action. On the initiative of Gaius Calpurnius Bibulus, the aediles had argued that the law restricting expenditure was being ignored, that prohibited food prices were increasing daily, and that ordinary measures were helpless against this situation. When the matter was raised in the senate, it was referred without discussion to the emperor. Tiberius often privately doubted whether restraint of these immoderate appetites would be either practicable or beneficial. He knew how undignified it would be to start something which he could not maintain, or could only maintain by humiliating and disgracing eminent men. Finally, he wrote the senate a letter to this effect:

'On all other public questions, senators, it may be desirable for me to be asked, and express, my opinions in your presence. But in regard to this matter, it is well that my eyes are elsewhere. Otherwise, if you indicated the apprehensive faces of men guilty of shameful extravagance, I too might see them, and so find them out. If our energetic aediles had consulted me earlier, I should perhaps have advised them not to tackle such deep-set, flagrant evils – so as not to publish our helplessness against them.

'Yet they have done what I expect from every official, their duty. For me, however, although silence is unfitting, speech is not easy. For I am neither aedile, nor praetor, nor consul. Some grander, more impressive utterance is expected from the emperor. People praise themselves for their good actions but all blame their failings on a single man. And where should I begin my prohibitions and attempted reversions to antique standards? With the vast mansions, or the cosmopolitan hordes of slaves? Or with the ponderous gold and silver plate, the wonderful pictures and bronze-work, the men's clothes indistinguishable from women's? Or the feminine speciality – the export of our currency to foreign or enemy countries for precious stones?

'I know that at social gatherings these practices are criticized, and their limitation is demanded. But if they were penalized by a law, their present critics themselves would cry that it was a national disaster, a death-blow to distinction, and the conversion of everyone into a potential criminal. Yet the human body, when it has a long and persistently worsening illness, needs a vigorous, radical treatment. And the mind's feverish ailments, too, can only be relieved by remedies as severe as the infection. All our laws – those of our ancestors which are forgotten, those of the divine Augustus which are neglected (and that is worse) – have merely conferred immunity on extravagance. For when you want something that is not prohibited, you fear prohibition. But once you safely ignore a prohibition, fear and shame vanish. Frugality used to prevail because people had self-control – and because we were citizens of one city. Even our domination of Italy did not bring the same temptations. But victories abroad taught us to spend other people's money. Then civil wars showed how to spend our own.

'Besides, the matter to which the aediles' warning relates is inessential – relatively insignificant. Italy's dependence on external resources, Rome's subsistence continually at the mercy of sea and storm – those are problems about which there are no speeches. Yet without provincial resources to support master and slave, and supplement our agriculture, our woods and country-houses could not feed us. That, senators, is the emperor's anxiety. Its neglect would mean national ruin. For other troubles, the remedy lies with the individual. If we are decent, we shall behave well – the rich when they are surfeited, the poor because they have to.

'Nevertheless, any officials who can offer enough severity and energy may, with my compliments, relieve me of part of my burdens. But if they want to denounce misbehaviour, take the credit for it, and then leave me the enmities they have created, I intimate to you, senators, that I also do not want to make enemies. When national necessity demands I will face hostility, formidable and often unjust though it may be. But when it is useless and unprofitable – to you as well as myself – I have good reason to decline.' When the emperor's letter had been read, the aediles were excused from the task.

Since then, however, extravagant eating, which reached fantastic heights during the century between Actium and the disturbances which brought Galba to the throne,[1] has gradually become unfashionable. The reasons for the change are worth examining. Old rich families, noble and illustrious, were often ruined by their sumptuous tastes. For, in those days, to court (and be courted by) the public in Rome and the provinces, and by foreign monarchs, was allowed. Fortunes, palaces, and their contents dictated the size of dependent hordes and of reputations. But the reign of terror, when distinction meant death, induced prudence in survivors. At the same time too, the numerous self-made men admitted into the senate from Italian towns (and even from the provinces) brought frugal domestic habits, and, though by good fortune or hard work many of them were rich in later life, they did not change their ideas. No one promoted simplicity more than Vespasian, with his own old-fashioned way of life. For deference to the emperor

1. Galba came to the throne in A.D. 68 from Spain.

and the wish to imitate him were more effective than legal penalties and threats.

Or perhaps not only the seasons but everything else, social history included, moves in cycles. Not, however, that earlier times were better than ours in every way – our own epoch too has produced moral and intellectual achievements for our descendants to copy. And such honourable rivalry with the past is a fine thing.

Tiberius utilized the credit his resistance to the tyranny of informers had gained him by writing to ask the senate to grant Drusus a tribune's authority.[1] This was a designation of supremacy invented by Augustus, who had wanted some title other than 'king' or 'dictator' which would place him above other officials. In due course Augustus had chosen associates in this power – Marcus Agrippa, and on his death Tiberius. That was how he designated his successor, calculating that this would damp misguided aspirations in others. He was confident of Tiberius' unpretentiousness, and his own pre-eminence.

While Germanicus lived Tiberius had not decided between him and Drusus. But now he brought Drusus to the top. His letter began with a prayer that heaven might prosper his plans for the national advantage. Then he wrote in moderate, unexaggerated terms about his son's character, pointing out that Drusus was a married man with three children and had reached the age at which he himself had been called to the same responsibilities by the divine Augustus. Drusus' promotion, he added, was not premature – after eight years' probation, including the repression of mutinies, completion of wars, a Triumph and two consulships, the prince knew the work he was to share.

The senators, who had foreseen this request, had their complimentary reaction planned. Yet they could think of nothing better than statues of the Caesars, altars to the gods, temples, arches, and other hackneyed gestures. Marcus Junius Silanus (I) was the only exception. For his proposal was that all monuments, public and private, should no longer be dated by names of consuls, but by those of holders of this tribune's authority – to honour the rulers, he degraded the consulship. Quintus Haterius moved that the day's decrees should be engraved in the senate-house in gold lettering. His disgusting

1. See Key to Technical Terms, TRIBUNE OF THE PEOPLE.

sycophancy caused laughter. And since he was so old, it would earn him nothing – except dishonour.

Quintus Junius Blaesus' governorship of Africa was now prolonged. Servius Cornelius Lentulus Maluginensis, the priest of Jupiter, requested the governorship of Asia. It was a common fallacy, he said, that holders of his priesthood could not leave Italy; their legal position was identical with that of the priests of Mars and Quirinus, who were allowed provinces: so why should the priests of Jupiter not have them too? 'There is no law against it,' he said, 'and nothing in the religious archives. Ordinary priests have often performed the worship of Jupiter when his own priest has been unavailable owing to illness or public business. Moreover, for seventy-five years – after the suicide of Lucius Cornelius Merula[1] – the priesthood was unoccupied. Yet the ceremonies continued without interruption. If the post could remain vacant for so long without detriment to the rites, surely it is easier still for me to be away for one year's governorship! The Chief Priests used to deny governorships to the priests of Jupiter because of personal rivalries. But today the gods have given us a Chief Priest who is also chief citizen, superior to jealousy, ill-will, or personal considerations.' Various objections, however, were raised by Cnaeus Cornelius Lentulus (II) – the augur – and others, and it was decided to await the view of the imperial Chief Priest. He, however, postponed his investigation of the matter.

Meanwhile he wrote to the senate modifying the compliments to Drusus in honour of his tribunician power. Tiberius specifically censured the preposterous, un-Roman suggestion of golden lettering. A letter from Drusus also was read. Despite calculated modesty it gave an arrogant impression. Things had come to a pretty pass when a mere youth, awarded so great a distinction, stayed away from Rome's gods and the senate, and did not assume his duties on his native soil. 'He must be fighting or visiting distant countries.' But he was only touring the Campanian lakes and coasts. So this was the first lesson he learnt from his father – a fine training for the ruler of the world! It was felt that whereas an elderly emperor might shrink from the public

1. He had killed himself on the return of Marius and Cinna in 87 B.C., and the priesthood of Jupiter remained vacant until filled by Augustus' nomination in 11 B.C. Augustus himself became Chief Priest in 12 B.C., after the death of the former Triumvir Marcus Aemilius Lepidus (III).

gaze, pleading weariness and past labours, Drusus' motive could only be conceit.

Tiberius, while he tightened his control by this conferment on Drusus, allowed the senate a shadow of its ancient power by inviting it to discuss provincial petitions. In Greek cities criminals were increasingly escaping punishment owing to over-lavish rights of sanctuary. Delinquent slaves filled temples. Asylum was granted indiscriminately – to debtors escaping their creditors, even to men suspected of capital offences. Protecting religious observance, these communities were protecting crime itself; and interventions provoked outbreaks which no authority could control. So the cities were requested to submit their charters and their representatives to investigation at Rome.

Some cities then voluntarily abandoned their unfounded claims. Many however persisted, on the strength of ancient religious myths or their services to Rome. It was a splendid sight, that day, to see the senate investigating privileges conferred by its ancestors, treaties with allies, edicts of kings who had reigned before Rome was a power, even divine cults; and it was free, as of old, to confirm or amend.

The Ephesians were the first to arrive. They asserted that Apollo and Diana were not, as commonly believed, born at Delos: at Ephesus there was a river Cenchrius, with an Ortygian grove – it was here that the pregnant Latona, leaning upon an olive-tree which was still standing, had given birth to the twin deities. The grove, they said, had been consecrated by divine order, and there Apollo himself, after killing the Cyclops, had taken refuge from Jupiter's anger. Later Bacchus, after defeating the Amazons, had pardoned those who begged for mercy at the altar, and the temple's sanctity had been further enhanced by permission of Hercules, during his conquest of Lydia. Its privileges had been respected by the Persian governors, Macedonians, and Romans, in turn.

Magnesia on the Maeander – the next delegation – based its claims on the pronouncements of Lucius Cornelius Scipio Asiaticus and Sulla.[1] After their victories over Antiochus III and Mithridates VI respectively, they had rewarded the Magnesians for their loyalty and bravery by granting inviolable right of asylum to the temple of Diana

1. Magnesia resisted Antiochus III – the Seleucid monarch – and Mithridates VI of Pontus in 190 and 88 B.C. respectively.

Leucophryene. Then Aphrodisias on behalf of its cult of Venus produced a decree of Julius Caesar, commending its long-standing loyalty to his cause. Stratonicea, too, in support of its shrine of Jupiter and Diana of the Crossroads, quoted a later ordinance of Augustus praising the unshakable devotion to Rome with which they had resisted the Parthian invasion.[1]

The representatives of Hierocaesarea had earlier stories of their Persian Diana and her shrine dedicated in the reign of Cyrus I.[2] They recalled that many Roman generals, including Marcus Perperna and Publius Servilius Vatia Isauricus,[3] had recognized the sanctity, not only of the temple, but of the land for two miles round. Then the people of Cyprus made claims for three shrines, the oldest built by Aerias to Venus of Paphos, the next by his son Amathus to Venus of Amathus, and the third by Teucer – fleeing from his father Telamon's anger[4] – to Jupiter of Salamis. Delegations from other cities also were heard.

However, the extensive material and local rivalries proved wearisome. So the senate requested the consuls to investigate the charters for flaws and then report back to itself. Their report approved the cases I have quoted, and added to them an authentic sanctuary of Aesculapius at Pergamum, but intimated that all other stories went back to a past too dim for consideration. Smyrna, for instance, attributed its temple of Venus Stratonicis to instructions from an oracle of Apollo, and Tenos cited another pronouncement from him ordering the dedication of a statue and shrine to Neptune. The deputation from Sardis, recalling more recent history, ascribed their privilege to the victorious Alexander, and Miletus with equal confidence cited King Darius I.[5] In these cases the cults were of Diana and Apollo respectively. The Cretans made similar claims for a statue of the divine Augustus.

Decrees were then passed in highly honorific terms, but imposing limits. Bronze tablets, too, were to be set up inside the temples as a solemn record – and a warning not to allow religion to become a cloak for inter-city rivalries.

1. In 40 B.C.   2. King of Persia 559–529 B.C.
3. Perperna crushed Aristonicus of Pergamum in 130 B.C., and Isauricus reduced pirates in Southern Anatolia in 78–5 B.C.
4. All mythical or legendary figures.   5. King of Persia 521–486 B.C.

At about this time the Augusta fell dangerously ill; and the emperor had to return urgently to Rome. Either mother and son were still good friends or, if they were not, they concealed it. Indeed shortly beforehand, when dedicating a statue, near the Theatre of Marcellus, to the divine Augustus, she had inscribed Tiberius' name after her own. This was believed to have given him grave, though unexpressed, offence as a slur on his imperial dignity. However, the senate now decreed national prayers and major Games, to be organized by the Pontifical Order, the augurs, and the Board of Fifteen for Religious Ceremonies, assisted by the Board of Seven for Sacrificial Banquets and the Brotherhood of Augustus. Lucius Apronius had proposed that the Fetials should also be among the organizers. But Tiberius opposed this, distinguishing between the functions of the various priesthoods and citing precedents. The Fetials, he said, had never enjoyed such dignity; the priests of Augustus had only been included because their Brotherhood was attached to the family for which the vows were being fulfilled.

The only proposals in the senate that I have seen fit to mention are particularly praiseworthy or particularly scandalous ones. It seems to me a historian's foremost duty to ensure that merit is recorded, and to confront evil deeds and words with the fear of posterity's denunciations. But this was a tainted, meanly obsequious age. The greatest figures had to protect their positions by subserviency; and, in addition to them, all ex-consuls, most ex-praetors, even many junior senators competed with each other's offensively sycophantic proposals. There is a tradition that whenever Tiberius left the senate-house he exclaimed in Greek, 'Men fit to be slaves!' Even he, freedom's enemy, became impatient of such abject servility.

Then, gradually, self-abasement turned into persecution. Gaius Junius Silanus, accused of extortion by the people of Asia of which he had been governor, was simultaneously assailed by the former consul Mamercus Aemilius Scaurus, the praetor Junius Otho, and the aedile Bruttedius Niger. They charged him with offences against the divinity of Augustus and the imperial majesty of Tiberius. Mamercus quoted as ancient precedents[1] charges made by Scipio Africanus (II), Cato the Censor, and Marcus Aemilius Scaurus against Lucius

1. The three precedents quoted by Mamercus Scaurus date from 132–29, 149, and 116 B.C. respectively.

Aurelius Cotta, Servius Sulpicius Galba (I), and Publius Rutilius Rufus respectively – as if there was any comparison with the crimes attacked by Scipio, Cato, or the famous Scaurus, whom this blot on his family, his great-grandson, was now dishonouring with his sordid activities! Junius Otho had formerly kept a school. Later, admitted to the senate by Sejanus' influence, he disgraced even those humble origins by his impudent audacity. Bruttedius Niger was a highly cultured man who, if he had gone straight, would have attained great eminence. But impatience spurred him to outstrip first his equals, then his superiors – and finally his own former ambitions. Impatience has ruined many excellent men who, rejecting the slow, sure way, court destruction by rising too quickly.

The accusers were joined by the two senior members of Silanus' staff in Asia, Gellius Publicola and Marcus Paconius. He was unquestionably guilty of brutality and extortion. But he was involved in circumstances which might have crushed even an innocent man. His enemies in the senate were formidable; and they were supported by the best speakers in the whole province of Asia, selected for this very purpose. Against them he stood alone, an inexperienced speaker, in mortal fear – which incapacitates even practised orators.

Tiberius' words and looks were unrelievedly menacing. So was the persistence of his interrogations, and the impossibility of negative answers or evasions – even confession was sometimes necessary, so that the emperor should not have asked in vain. Moreover, Silanus' slaves were sold to the Treasury Agent for examination under torture. And not one friend could help him in his peril; for supplementary charges of treason, which were preferred against him, reduced them to compulsory silence. So Silanus, after requesting a few days' adjournment, abandoned his defence. But he ventured to write Tiberius a letter of reproachful entreaty.

The emperor, feeling that a precedent would better justify his proposed action against Silanus, ordered the reading of Augustus' letter and the senate's decree about an earlier governor of the same province, Lucius Valerius Messalla Volesus. Then he asked Lucius Calpurnius Piso (I) for his opinion. Beginning with a prolonged eulogy of the emperor's mercifulness, Piso proposed that Silanus should be outlawed and banished to the island of Gyaros. There was general assent, except for one proposal by Cnaeus Cornelius Lentulus (II) – with which

Tiberius concurred – that the property inherited by Silanus from his mother, Atia by name,¹ should be treated separately and allowed to his son.

Publius Cornelius Dolabella (I), elaborately sycophantic, included in a denunciation of Silanus the proposal that no one of scandalous life and evil reputation should be eligible for a governorship – the emperor to be judge. For whereas (Dolabella observed) the law punishes offences, it would be much kinder, to offenders and provincials alike, to forestall them. Tiberius, however, disagreed. 'I am aware', he said, 'of the rumours about Silanus. But decisions should not be based on rumours. Many governors have belied people's hopes and fears: important positions stimulate some natures and blunt others. An emperor's knowledge cannot be all-embracing, and intrigues against rivals should not influence him. The law is concerned with what has been done. What *will* be done is unknown. That is why our ancestors ruled that punishment should follow crime. This was wise, and has always been accepted. Do not reverse it. Emperors have enough burdens – and enough power. Strengthen the executive, and you weaken the law. When one can act by law, the use of official authority is a mistake.'

These constitutional sentiments were welcome, the more so since they were not characteristic of Tiberius. And capable, as he was, of mercy (when not impelled by anger), he proposed that, since Gyaros was a grim, uninhabited island, Silanus – as a concession to his Junian family and former membership of the senate – should be allowed to retire to Cythnos instead. This had been requested, he added, by Silanus' sister Junia Torquata, a priestess of Vesta and a woman of old-fashioned saintliness. It was agreed without discussion.

The people of Cyrene were heard next, and Caesius Cordus, accused by Ancharius Priscus, was condemned for extortion. A knight called Lucius Ennius was charged with treason for melting down a silver statue of the emperor for use as plate. Tiberius forbade the prosecution. But Gaius Ateius Capito made a show of independence by openly objecting. He argued that the decision ought not to be taken away from the senate, that so grave a misdeed must not go unpunished, and that the emperor's generosity concerning his personal wrongs should not be extended to condoning offences against the State. But Tiberius

1. If the mother of Gaius Junius Silanus was an Atia (the text is somewhat uncertain), she was presumably related to Augustus' mother of the same name.

understood the sinister implications of this attitude and persisted in his veto. Capito's degradation was especially conspicuous: for he was a learned secular and religious lawyer whose words disgraced his personal talents as well as his official distinction.

A religious problem next arose. In what temple were the knights to lodge the gift vowed by them to Fortune-on-Horseback for the Augusta's recovery from illness? Rome had many temples of Fortune but none with this title. It was discovered, however, that a temple at Antium had the designation – and that all rites, temples, and statues of the gods in Italian towns were under Roman jurisdiction and control. So the gift was deposited at Antium.

Since religious matters were being discussed, Tiberius now produced his deferred answer to the application of Servius Cornelius Lentulus Maluginensis, priest of Jupiter, for the governorship of Asia. Tiberius read a priestly ordinance decreeing that whenever the priest of Jupiter was ill he might at the Chief Priest's discretion stay away for a period exceeding two nights, provided that it was not on days of public sacrifice or oftener than twice in one year. This ruling – formulated under Augustus – showed that priests of Jupiter were ineligible for provincial governorships, since these involved a year's absence: the precedent was the ban on the departure of Aulus Postumius[1] by the Chief Priest Lucius Caecilius Metellus. So Asia was allotted to the ex-consul next after Maluginensis.

At about this time Marcus Aemilius Lepidus (IV) asked the senate's leave to strengthen and beautify, at his own expense, the Hall that was the family monument of the Aemilii, built by Lucius Aemilius Paullus (II).[2] For public munificence was still fashionable. Augustus had allowed enemy spoils, or great resources, to be devoted by Titus Statilius Taurus (I), Lucius Marcius Philippus, and Lucius Cornelius Balbus (II) to the adornment of Rome for the applause of posterity.[3] Now Lepidus, though of moderate means, followed their example by repairing his family memorial. When, however, the Theatre of Pom-

1. Aulus Postumius had been forbidden to leave in 242 B.C. However, he was priest of Mars, not Jupiter.

2. Consul 50 B.C. and grandfather of Marcus Aemilius Lepidus (IV), he had reconstructed the Hall (Basilica) of the Aemilii.

3. Taurus and Balbus had constructed the first stone amphitheatre and a theatre respectively. Philippus restored the temple of Hercules of the Muses.

pey was accidentally burnt down, Tiberius undertook to rebuild it himself on the grounds that no Pompeius had the means to do so; but its name was to remain unchanged.

Tiberius commended Sejanus' energy and watchfulness in preventing the fire from spreading beyond Pompey's Theatre; and the senate voted that his statue be erected there. Again, shortly afterwards, when Tiberius awarded an honorary Triumph to Quintus Junius Blaesus, governor of Africa, the emperor indicated that this was a compliment to the latter's nephew Sejanus. Yet Blaesus' achievements had earned the distinction. For Tacfarinas, despite frequent defeats, had raised reinforcements in the interior and was insolent enough to send representatives to Tiberius demanding land for himself and his army. As the alternative, he offered endless war. No personal or national slur, it is said, ever provoked the emperor more than the sight of this deserter and brigand behaving like a hostile sovereign. Even Spartacus (reflected Tiberius), burning Italy unavenged – at a time when he had destroyed consuls' armies and the nation was convulsed by terrible wars overseas against Quintus Sertorius and Mithridates VI of Pontus – had not been allowed conditions for his surrender.[1] And now, with Roman power at its height, was this bandit Tacfarinas to be bought off by a treaty granting lands?

Tiberius entrusted the matter to the governor Quintus Junius Blaesus. By promising pardon he was to induce the rebels to lay down arms – except the leader, who was to be captured by any means possible. The amnesty brought many over. Moreover, Tacfarinas was now confronted by methods like his own. Since his army was inferior in fighting power but superior in raiding capacity, he operated with independent groups, avoiding engagements and setting traps. So the Romans, too, attacked with three separate formations. Each had a target of its own. One, under the divisional commander Publius Cornelius Lentulus Scipio (I), blocked the route by which the enemy had raided Lepcis, with the Garamantes to fall back upon. On the other flank, a detachment commanded by Blaesus' son protected the communities of Cirta against raids. In the centre was the governor and commander-in-chief himself with selected troops. By planting forts and defences at appropriate spots, he cramped and harassed the enemy.

1. Spartacus led the slave-revolt of 73–1 B.C., Quintus Sertorius a rebellion in Spain in 82–72 B.C.

In whatever direction they moved, they found part of the Roman army on front, flanks, and often rear. By these methods many rebels were killed and taken prisoner.

Then Blaesus split up his three formations into smaller bodies, each under a company-commander of distinguished record. It had been customary to withdraw the troops when summer was over, and quarter them in winter camps in Africa proper.[1] Blaesus abolished this custom. Instead he established a chain of forts – the usual procedure at the beginning, not the end, of a campaigning season. Then, employing mobile columns with desert training, he kept Tacfarinas in a continual state of movement.

Finally, Blaesus captured the rebel leader's brother. Then, however, he withdrew – too soon for the interests of the province, since enough of the enemy were left to revive hostilities. Nevertheless Tiberius treated the war as ended, and even allowed Blaesus the honour of being hailed victor by his army, a traditional distinction granted to successful generals by the spontaneous acclamation of their victorious troops. The distinction was not limited to one commander at a time, and did not confer precedence over others. It had been granted on certain occasions by Augustus. After this award by Tiberius to Blaesus it was never conferred again.

Two eminent men died this year. One was Asinius Saloninus,[2] noteworthy as grandson of Marcus Agrippa and Gaius Asinius Pollio (I), half-brother of Drusus, and intended husband of one of Tiberius' granddaughters. The other death that occurred was of Gaius Ateius Capito, whom I have mentioned already. By his distinction as a jurist he had achieved national eminence. Yet his grandfather had only been a company-commander of Sulla, and his father a praetor. Augustus had made him consul before age to give him precedence over another distinguished lawyer, Marcus Antistius Labeo.[3] For these two paragons of the arts of peace were the simultaneous products of a single generation. Labeo's incorruptible independence gave him the finer reputa-

---

1. The original province of Africa, annexed after the capture of Carthage in 146 B.C., roughly corresponded with Tunisia.

2. Saloninus was the son of Vipsania (previously married to Tiberius), and so was Drusus' half-brother; he was to have married a daughter of Germanicus.

3. Gaius Ateius Capito and Marcus Antistius Labeo founded two competing legal schools, the *Sabiniani* and *Proculiani*.

tion; Capito's obedience secured him the greater imperial favour. Labeo stopped short at the praetorship. This seemed unfair – and increased his popularity. Capito's consulship, on the other hand, earned him jealousy and dislike. Another death was that of Junia Tertulla, niece of Cato, wife of Gaius Cassius, sister of Brutus – a full sixty-three years after Philippi. Her will caused much discussion, because although she was very rich and included complimentary references to almost every leading Roman she omitted the emperor. However, he showed no autocratic resentment, and did not refuse her a ceremonial funeral, including a eulogy from the official dais. The effigies of twenty highly distinguished families, Manlii, Quinctii, and others equally aristocratic, headed the procession. But Cassius and Brutus were the most gloriously conspicuous – precisely because their statues were not to be seen.

CHAPTER 7

'Partner of My Labours'

*

IN the consulships of Gaius Asinius Pollio (II) and Gaius Antistius Vetus (I), Tiberius now began his ninth year of national stability and domestic prosperity (the latter, he felt, augmented by Germanicus' death). But then suddenly Fortune turned disruptive. The emperor himself became tyrannical – or gave tyrannical men power. The cause and beginning of the change lay with Lucius Aelius Sejanus, commander of the Guard. I have said something of his influence, and will now describe his origins and personality – and his criminal attempt on the throne.

Sejanus was born at Vulsinii. His father, Lucius Seius Strabo, was a Roman knight. After increasing his income – it was alleged – by a liaison with a rich debauchee named Marcus Gavius Apicius, the boy joined, while still young, the suite of Augustus' grandson Gaius Caesar. Next by various devices he obtained a complete ascendancy over Tiberius. To Sejanus alone the otherwise cryptic emperor spoke freely and unguardedly. This was hardly due to Sejanus' cunning; in that he was outclassed by Tiberius. The cause was rather heaven's anger against Rome – to which the triumph of Sejanus, and his downfall too, were catastrophic. Of audacious character and untiring physique, secretive about himself and ever ready to incriminate others, a blend of arrogance and servility, he concealed behind a carefully modest exterior an unbounded lust for power. Sometimes this impelled him to lavish excesses, but more often to incessant work. And that is as damaging as excess when the throne is its aim.

The command of the Guard had hitherto been of slight importance. Sejanus enhanced it by concentrating the Guard battalions, scattered about Rome, in one camp. Orders could reach them simultaneously, and their visible numbers and strength would increase their self-confidence and intimidate the population. His pretexts were, that scattered quarters caused unruliness; that united action would be needed in an emergency; and that a camp away from the temptations of the city would improve discipline. When the camp was ready, he gradually insinuated himself into the men's favour. He would talk with them addressing them by name. And he chose their company- and battalion-commanders himself. Senators' ambitions, too, he tempted with offices and governorships for his dependants.

Tiberius was readily amenable, praising him in conversation – and even in the senate and Assembly – as 'the partner of my labours', and allowing honours to his statues in theatres, public places, and brigade headquarters. Yet Sejanus' ambitions were impeded by the well-stocked imperial house, including a son and heir – in his prime – and grown-up grandchildren.[1] Subtlety required that the crimes should be spaced out: it would be unsafe to strike at all of them simultaneously. So subtle methods prevailed. Sejanus decided to begin with Drusus, against whom he had a recent grudge. For Drusus, violent-tempered and resentful of a rival, had raised his hand against him during a for-tuitous quarrel and, when Sejanus resisted, had struck him in the face.

After considering every possibility, Sejanus felt most inclined to rely on Drusus' wife Livilla, the sister of Germanicus. Unattractive in earlier years, she had become a great beauty. Sejanus professed devo-tion, and seduced her. Then, this first guilty move achieved – since a woman who has parted with her virtue will refuse nothing – he in-cited her to hope for marriage, partnership in the empire, and the death of her husband. So the grand-niece of Augustus, daughter-in-law of Tiberius, mother of Drusus' children, degraded herself and her ancestors and descendants with a small-town adulterer; she sacrificed her honourable, assured position for infamy and hazard. The plot was communicated to Eudemus, Livilla's friend and doctor, who had professional pretexts for frequent interviews. Sejanus encouraged his mistress by sending away his wife Apicata, the mother of his three children. Nevertheless the magnitude of the projected crime caused misgivings, delays, and (on occasion) conflicting plans.

Meanwhile, at the beginning of the year Drusus Caesar, one of Germanicus' children, assumed adult clothing, and the senate's decrees in honour of his brother Nero Caesar were repeated. Tiberius

1. Nero Caesar and Drusus Caesar, sons of his adoptive son Germanicus.

spoke as well, warmly praising his own son Drusus for his fatherly affection to the sons of his 'brother' Germanicus. For, though lofty positions are not easily compatible with friendliness, Drusus was believed to like the young men or at least not to dislike them.

Next there was a revival of the old idea of a tour in the provinces by Tiberius. The emperor justified his proposal (the object of frequent lip-service by him) on the grounds of the numerous soldiers due for release, and the need to fill their places by conscription. There were not enough volunteers, he said, and they lacked the old bravery and discipline, since voluntary enlistment mostly attracted penniless vagrants. Then he briefly enumerated the army formations and the provinces under their protection. I now propose to do the same – in order to give an idea of the Roman armed forces and dependent monarchs at that time, when the empire was so much smaller.

Italy was guarded by two fleets, one on each sea-board, at Misenum and Ravenna; and other warships – Augustus had captured them in his victorious battle of Actium and sent them, strongly manned, to Forum Julii – defended the near coast of Gaul. But our main strength lay on the Rhine: eight brigades, for protection against Germans or Gauls. Three more occupied the recently pacified Spanish provinces, two each Africa and Egypt (Mauretania had been presented by the Roman State to King Juba II). Then the huge stretch of territory between this end of Syria and the Euphrates was controlled by four brigades, while on the frontiers Roman might also maintained certain monarchies against foreign states, the Iberian and Albanian and others. Another four brigades were on the Danube, two in Pannonia and two in Moesia: Thrace belonged to Rhoemetalces II and the children of Cotys IV. There were two reserve brigades in Dalmatia which had easy access to Italy in an emergency. However, the capital had its own troops; three battalions of city police, and nine of the Guard, mostly recruited in Etruria, or Umbria, or the old territory of Latin rights and early Roman settlements. Then, at appropriate points outside Italy, the provincials contributed naval crews, and auxiliary cavalry and infantry. Altogether these were about as numerous as the regular army. But I cannot enumerate them since, as circumstances required, they changed stations, or their numbers rose or fell.

This, the year in which Tiberius' rule began to deteriorate, seems an appropriate moment to review the other branches of the government also, and the methods by which they had been administered since his accession. In the first place, public business – and the most important private business – was transacted in the senate. Among its chief men, there was freedom of discussion: their lapses into servility were arrested by the emperor himself. His conferments of office took into consideration birth, military distinction, and civilian eminence, and the choice manifestly fell on the worthiest men. The consuls and praetors maintained their prestige. The lesser offices, too, each exercised their proper authority. Moreover, the treason court excepted, the laws were duly enforced.

Levies of grain, indirect taxation, and the other revenues belonging to the State were managed by associations of Roman knights. But the imperial property was entrusted by the emperor to carefully selected agents – some known to him by reputation only. Once appointed, these were kept on indefinitely, often becoming old in the same jobs. The public suffered, it is true, from oppressive food prices. But that was not the emperor's fault. Indeed, he spared neither money nor labour in combating bad harvests and stormy seas. He ensured also that the provinces were not harassed by new impositions and that old impositions were not aggravated through official acquisitiveness or brutality; beatings and confiscations did not exist. His estates in Italy were few, his slaves unobtrusive, his household limited to a few ex-slaves. Any disputes that he had with private citizens were settled in the law courts.

Tiberius, in his ungracious fashion – grim and often terrifying as he was – maintained this policy until the death of Drusus reversed it. While Drusus lived, the same methods were employed, because Sejanus in the early stages of his power wanted to gain a reputation for enlightened policy. Moreover, there was an alarming potential avenger in Drusus, who openly showed his hatred and repeatedly complained that the emperor, though he had a son, went elsewhere for his collaborator. Soon, Drusus reflected, the collaborator would be called a colleague – the first steps of an ambitious career are difficult, but once they are achieved helpers and partisans emerge. 'Already Sejanus has secured this new camp – where the Guard are at the disposal of their commander. His statue is to be seen in Pompey's Theatre. The grandsons of us Drususes will be his grandsons too.[1] What can

1. Sejanus' daughter was intended to marry Claudius' son.

we do now except trust his moderation and pray he will be for-bearing?' Drusus often talked like this and many heard him. But even his confidences were betrayed by his wife – to her lover.

So Sejanus decided to act. He chose a poison with gradual effects resembling ordinary ill-health. It was administered to Drusus (as was learnt eight years later) by the eunuch Lygdus. All through his son's illness, Tiberius attended the senate. Either he was unalarmed or he wanted to display his will-power. Even when Drusus had died and his body was awaiting burial, Tiberius continued to attend. The consuls sat on ordinary benches as a sign of mourning. But he reminded them of their dignity and rank. The senators wept. But he silenced them with a consoling oration. 'I know', he said, 'that I may be criticized for appearing before the senate while my affliction is still fresh. Most mourners can hardly bear even their families' condolences – can hardly look upon the light of day. And that need not be cen-sured as weakness. I, however, have sought sterner solace. The arms in which I have taken refuge are those of the State.'

After referring sorrowfully to the Augusta's great age, his grandson's immaturity, and his own declining years, he said that the sons of Germanicus were his only consolation in his grief; and he requested that they should be brought in. The consuls went out, reassured the boys, and conducted them before Tiberius. He took them by the hand, and addressed the senate. 'When these boys lost their father', he said, 'I entrusted them to their uncle Drusus, begging him – though he had children of his own – to treat them as though they were his blood, and, for posterity's sake, to fashion them after himself. Now Drusus has gone. So my plea is addressed to you. The gods and our country are its witnesses.

'Senators: on my behalf as well as your own, adopt and guide these youths, whose birth is so glorious – these great-grandchildren of Augustus. Nero and Drusus Caesars: these senators will take the place of your parents. For, in the station to which you are born, the good and bad in you is of national concern.' This speech was greeted by loud weeping among the senators, followed by heartfelt prayers for the future. Indeed, if Tiberius had stopped there, he would have left his audience sorry for him and proud of their responsibility. But by reverting to empty discredited talk about restoring the Republic and handing the government to the consuls or others, he undermined belief even in what he had said sincerely and truthfully. However, Drusus was voted the same posthumous honours as Germanicus – with the additions expected of flattery's second attempt. The funeral was noteworthy for its long procession of ancestral effigies – Aeneas, originator of the Julian line; all the kings of Alba Longa; Romulus, founder of Rome; then the Sabine nobility with Attus Clausus;[1] finally the rest of the Claudian house.

In describing Drusus' death I have followed the most numerous and reputable authorities. But I should also record a contemporary rumour, strong enough to remain current today. According to this, Sejanus, after seducing Livilla into crime, similarly corrupted the eunuch Lygdus, whose youthful looks had endeared him to his master Drusus and raised him high in the latter's household. Next – the story continues – when the plotters had fixed the place and time for the poisoning, Sejanus had the audacity to change his plan and warn the emperor privately that when dining with his son Tiberius must refuse the first drink offered him, since Drusus intended to poison him. The old emperor, it is alleged, believed this fiction, and at the dinner-party passed the cup he had received to Drusus, who tossed it off as a young man would – in all innocence, but this dyed suspicion deeper since it seemed that Drusus, terrified and ashamed, was inflicting on himself the fate he had designed for his father.

This was widely rumoured. But it is not backed by any reliable authority – and it can be confidently refuted. For no one even of ordinary sense, much less Tiberius with his great experience, would kill his son unheard, by his own hand, leaving no opportunity for second thoughts. Surely Tiberius would rather have tortured the server of the poison and extracted the originator's name. Against his only son – never before convicted of wrong-doing – he would only have proceeded with the characteristic slowness and deliberation which he showed even to strangers. But Sejanus, too much loved by Tiberius and hated by everyone else, passed for the author of every crime; and rumours always proliferate around the downfalls of the great. For such reasons even the most monstrous myths found believers.

Besides, the real story of the murder was later divulged by Sejanus' wife Apicata, and corroborated under torture by Eudemus and Lygdus; and no historian, however unfriendly to Tiberius, however ten-

1. The legendary founder of the Claudian family.

dentious an investigator of his doings, has accused him of this crime. My own motive in mentioning and refuting the rumour has been to illustrate by one conspicuous instance the falsity of hearsay gossip, and to urge those who read this book not to prefer incredible tales – however widely current and readily accepted – to the truth unblemished by marvels.

When Tiberius pronounced his son's funeral eulogy from the platform, the attitudes and tones of mourning exhibited by the senate and public were insincere and unconvincing. Secretly they were glad that the house of Germanicus was reviving. However, this awakening popularity, and Agrippina's ill-concealed maternal ambitions, only hastened the family's ruin. For when Sejanus saw that Drusus' death brought no retribution upon the murderers and no national grief, his criminal audacity grew. The succession of the children of Germanicus was now certain. So he considered how they could be removed.

To poison all three was impracticable, since their attendants were loyal – and the virtue of their mother Agrippina unassailable. Her insubordination, however, gave Sejanus a handle against Agrippina. He played on the Augusta's longstanding animosity against her, and on Livilla's new complicity. These ladies were to notify Tiberius that Agrippina, proud of her large family and relying on her popularity, had designs on the throne. To this end Sejanus employed skilful slanderers. Notable among them was Julius Postumus, whose adulterous liaison with Mutilia Prisca made him a close friend of the Augusta and particularly apt for Sejanus' purposes; for Prisca had great influence over the old lady, whose jealousy she could use against Agrippina, her granddaughter not by blood like Livilla, but by marriage. Meanwhile Agrippina's closest friends were induced to accentuate her restlessness by malevolent talk.

Tiberius derived comfort from his work. He remained fully occupied with public business – legal cases concerning citizens, and petitions from the provinces. On his initiative, the senate decreed three years' remission of tribute to two cities ruined by earthquakes, Cibyra and Aegium. A governor of Farther Spain, Gaius Vibius Serenus (I), was convicted of violence and deported as a bad character to the island of Amorgos. Carsidius Sacerdos, accused of supplying grain to the enemy Tacfarinas, was acquitted. So was Gaius Sempronius Gracchus (II). He had been taken as a baby by his father to share his banishment on the isle of Cercina. There the son grew up among uneducated expatriates, and later made a living by small trading in Africa and Sicily. Even so, he did not escape the perils of high rank. Indeed, unless his innocence had been vouched for by two governors of Africa, Lucius Aelius Lamia and Lucius Apronius, he would have been destroyed by his famous, tragic name and his father's downfall.

Delegations came this year from two Greek communities, Samos and Cos. They requested the confirmation of sanctuary rights for their temples of Juno and Aesculapius respectively. The Samians relied on a decree of the Amphictyonic Council, the principal arbiter of all matters in the epoch when the Greeks had founded their settlements in Asia and ruled its coast. Cos put forward considerations of equal antiquity, together with a local point. For they had sheltered Roman citizens in the temple of Aesculapius at the time when, on the orders of king Mithridates VI of Pontus, these were being massacred in every island and city in Asia.

Next, after numerous and generally unsuccessful complaints by the praetors, Tiberius addressed the senate on the ill-behaviour of ballet-dancers and their offences against public order and private morality. The emperor commented that their frivolous popular entertainment, the old Oscan farce, had become so degraded and influential that the senate's authority was needed to repress it. The dancers were then ejected from Italy.

This year also brought the emperor further bereavement. For one of Drusus' twins died. So did a friend. This was Lucilius Longus, Tiberius' comrade in good and evil fortune, and the only senator who had shared his retirement to Rhodes. So, in spite of his humble origin, Lucilius received a state funeral, and a statue in the Forum of Augustus was allotted him at the national expense by the senate. The senate still handled all manner of business. Even the emperor's agent in Asia, Lucilius Capito, had to defend himself before it when the people of the province prosecuted him. Tiberius insisted that he had only given the agent power over his personal slaves and revenues, and if Capito had assumed the governor's authority and employed military force he was exceeding his instructions: the provincials must be heard. The case was tried, and Capito condemned.

For this act of justice, and the punishment of Gaius Junius Silanus in the previous year, the cities of Asia decreed a temple to Tiberius, his mother, and the senate. Permission was granted. Germanicus' son Nero Caesar expressed the thanks of the cities to the senate and his grandfather – a welcome experience to his listeners, whose still fresh memories of Germanicus created the illusion that it was he whom they were seeing and hearing. And the young man's princely looks and modest bearing were all the more attractive because Sejanus was known to hate him.

At about the same time Tiberius raised the question of replacing the lately deceased priest of Jupiter, Servius Cornelius Maluginensis, and of amending the law governing these appointments. This should be done, he said, either by senatorial decree or by legislation initiated by himself, just as Augustus had modernized other equally hoary usages. Tiberius recalled that the selection had to be made from three simultaneously nominated patricians, born from formal marriages 'by cake and spelt'. This was the tradition, he said, but there were no longer enough candidates since the old wedding ceremony was obsolete or very rare; and he suggested various explanations of this – notably the indifference of both sexes, and their deliberate avoidance of the complicated ritual. Besides, he added, parents objected that their authority no longer applied to holders of this priesthood, or to their wives (who were in such cases transferred to their husbands' control). Consequently, a remedy must be applied either by senatorial decree or by law, just as Augustus, too, had modernized certain heavy relics. After discussion of the religious considerations it was decided not to alter the constitution of the priesthood; but a law was carried providing that the priest's wife, though subject to her husband in regard to her sacred functions, should in other respects have the same legal rights as other women. And so the late priest's son was appointed in his father's place. To increase the dignity of priestly offices – and willingness to undertake their ritual – two million sesterces were allocated to the priestess of Vesta, Cornelia, appointed to succeed Scantia. It was also decided that the Augusta, whenever she visited the theatre, should sit in the seats reserved for the Vestal priestesses.

In the next year the consuls were Servius Cornelius Cethegus and Lucius Visellius Varro. Starting with the Pontifical Order, the priestly corporations included Nero Caesar and Drusus Caesar in their prayers for the safety of the emperor. Servility, rather than affection, was the cause. But in a degraded society exaggerated servility is as dangerous as none at all. Tiberius, never warm-hearted to the house of Germanicus, was now particularly irritated that these youths should be coupled with himself, at his advanced age. He sent for the priests and asked them whether they had been influenced by Agrippina's pleas – or threats. They took the blame themselves. However, since many of them were his own relations or distinguished figures, they were only mildly rebuked. But Tiberius warned the senate that in future the young men's susceptible characters should not be tempted to become conceited by premature distinctions. Actually his protest had been prompted by pressure from Sejanus, who declared that Rome was split asunder as though there was civil war: people were calling themselves 'Agrippina's party' – the deepening disunity could only be arrested if some of the ringleaders were removed.

With this motive Sejanus attacked Gaius Silius (I) and Titius Sabinus. They both owed their ruin to Germanicus' friendship. Silius had also been head of a great army for seven years, winner cf an honorary Triumph in Germany, conqueror of Sacrovir. So his downfall would be the more spectacular and alarming. Many thought that he had aggravated his offence by imprudence. For he had boasted excessively of his own army's unbroken loyalty when others had lapsed into mutiny. 'If the revolt had spread to my brigades,' he said, 'Tiberius could not have kept the throne.' The emperor felt that these assertions of an obligation beyond all recompense damaged his own position. For services are welcome as long as it seems possible to repay them, but when they greatly exceed that point they produce not gratitude but hatred.

The emperor also disliked Silius' wife Sosia Galla, because she was a friend of Agrippina. So Sejanus decided that this couple should be the victims. Titius Sabinus could wait a little. The consul Lucius Visellius Varro was set in motion, and with his father's feud against Silius as a pretext sacrificed his own honour to gratify Sejanus' enmity. When accused, Silius requested a brief adjournment until the accuser's consulship should end. But Tiberius opposed this, arguing that officials often proceeded against private citizens, and that there must be no limitation of the rights of the consuls, on whose watchfulness it depended 'that the State takes no harm'. It was typical of Tiberius to use antique terms to veil new sorts of villainy.

So, with many solemn phrases, the senate was summoned as though the charges against Silius had a legal foundation – as though Varro were a real consul, or Rome a Republic! At first, the defendant said nothing. Then, attempting some sort of a defence, he made it clear whose malevolence was ruining him. The prosecution developed its case – longstanding connivance with Sacrovir and cognizance of his rebellion; victory ruined by rapacity; failure to check his wife's criminal acts. In extortion they were undoubtedly both involved. But the case was conducted as a treason trial.

Silius anticipated imminent condemnation by suicide. But his property was dealt with unmercifully. It is true that the provincial tax-payers received nothing back (and none of them requested a refund). But gifts by Augustus were deducted, and the claims of the emperor's personal estate enforced item by item. Never before had Tiberius gone to such pains regarding other men's property. Gaius Asinius Gallus proposed Sosia's banishment, moving that half of her property should be confiscated and the other half left to her children. Marcus Aemilius Lepidus (IV), however, counter-proposed that a quarter should go to the accusers – as the law required – but that her children should have the rest.

I find that this Marcus Lepidus played a wise and noble part in events. He often palliated the brutalities caused by other people's sycophancy. And he had a sense of proportion – for he enjoyed unbroken influence and favour with Tiberius. This compels me to doubt whether, like other things, the friendships and enmities of rulers depend on destiny and the luck of a man's birth. Instead, may not our own decisions play some part, enabling us to steer a way, safe from intrigues and hazards, between perilous insubordination and degrading servility?

However, Lepidus was contradicted by Marcus Aurelius Cotta Maximus Messallinus, who was of equally noble birth but very different character. At his proposal the senate decreed that officials, however free of guilt or knowledge of guilt themselves, should be punished for their wives' wrongdoing in the provinces as though it were their own.

Then came the case of the aristocratic and independent-minded Lucius Calpurnius Piso (II). This was the man who (as I have mentioned) had insisted to the senate that he would leave the city because of the intrigues of prosecutors, and who, defying the Augusta's might, had dared to hale her friend Urgulania into court from the palace itself. Tiberius had taken this reasonably for the moment. However, though his original bursts of anger might die down, he would turn over resentments in his mind, and did not forget. Quintus Granius charged Piso with treasonable private conversation, adding that he had poison in his house and wore a sword entering the senate-house. The last charge was passed over as too dreadful to be true. But the others – and there was no lack of them – were made into a prosecution, which Piso only avoided by his timely death.

The senate next considered the case of the exiled Cassius Severus. A vicious man of humble origin but an effective speaker, he had earned from the senate, by his unrestrained aggressiveness, a sworn verdict of banishment to Crete. There, by continuing the same practices, he brought upon himself so many enmities, new on top of old, that he was deprived of his property, outlawed, and ended his days on the rock of Seriphos.

At about this time the praetor Plautius Silvanus, for some unknown reason, threw his wife Apronia out of a window. Haled before the emperor by his father-in-law Lucius Apronius, he answered confusedly that he had been asleep and knew nothing, and his wife must have killed herself. Tiberius instantly proceeded to the house and inspected the bedroom. There signs of violence and resistance were detectable. So Tiberius referred the case to the senate, and it was entered for trial. Then Silvanus was sent a dagger by his grandmother Urgulania. In view of her intimacy with the Augusta, this was regarded as a hint from the emperor. So the accused, after an unsuccessful attempt with the dagger, had his veins opened. Soon afterwards his first wife Numantina was acquitted of driving her husband insane by incantations and philtres.

This year at last freed Rome from the long war with the Numidian Tacfarinas. Previous generals, when they thought they had achieved enough to win honorary Triumphs (already there were three laurelled statues in the city), had let the enemy alone. Yet Tacfarinas continued to ravage Africa; and Mauretanian auxiliaries flocked to him. Their king Ptolemy,[1] the son of Juba II, was too young for responsibility, and they evaded the tyrannical rule of his household's ex-slaves by coming

1. The last dependent King of Mauretania (A.D. 23 to 40).

to fight. The king of the Garamantes acted as receiver of Tacfarinas' plunder and joined his raids, not to the extent of heading an army, but by sending light-armed troops – on their long journey, rumour exaggerated their numbers. Moreover, from the province of Africa itself, destitute and disreputable characters flocked to Tacfarinas. This was largely because, after the achievements of Quintus Junius Blaesus, Tiberius had removed one of the garrison's two brigades, the ninth, as though Africa were clear of enemies. The governor at the time, Publius Cornelius Dolabella (I), had not dared to detain it – fearing the emperor's orders more than the hazards of war.

So Tacfarinas spread rumours that other peoples, too, were dismembering the empire, and so Africa was being gradually evacuated. He declared that such garrison as remained could be cut off – if all who preferred freedom to slavery made a united exertion. His army strengthened, he established an encampment and blockaded the town of Thubuscum. Dolabella, collecting all available troops, managed to raise the siege at the first onset, owing to the terror inspired by Rome – and the Numidians' inability to face an infantry charge. The next stage was to fortify strong points, and execute rebelliously inclined Musulamian chiefs. Then, since several expeditions against Tacfarinas had proved that a single heavy-armed force could never catch so mobile an enemy, Dolabella mobilized Ptolemy and his compatriots as well. Four columns were organized, under Roman generals or colonels; and Mauretanian officers were selected to lead raiding parties. Dolabella himself attended and directed the different units in turn.

It was soon reported that the Numidians had stationed themselves by the half-ruined fort of Auzea (which they themselves had burnt earlier), and pitched their encampment there. This seemed a safe poisition, because of large woods all round. But Dolabella, without revealing a destination, dispatched quick-moving light infantry and cavalry against them. At dawn, with fierce shouts and trumpet-blasts, they fell on the sleepy Numidians, whose horses were still tied up or feeding at a distance. The Roman infantry was in close order, their cavalry troops duly spaced, everything ready for battle. The enemy were taken unawares. They had no weapons, order or plan and were dragged to death or captivity like sheep.

The Roman soldiers resented their hardships, and the enemy's repeated refusals to fight. So they all took their fill of bloody vengeance. The word went round to make for Tacfarinas, a familiar figure after all this warfare: only the leader's death could end the war. His bodyguard fell around him, his son was taken prisoner, and he himself, as the Romans hemmed him in, rushed on to their spearpoints and escaped capture by his death. It had cost the Romans dearly.

But Dolabella's request for an honorary Triumph was rejected by Tiberius out of consideration for Sejanus – to avoid diminishing the glory of the latter's uncle, the former governor Quintus Junius Blaesus. This did not help Blaesus' reputation; but the rebuff increased that of Dolabella, who (with a smaller army) had to his credit important prisoners, the enemy commander's death, and the termination of the war. Accompanying him was a delegation of the Garamantes – an unfamiliar spectacle. Disturbed by Tacfarinas' death but regarding themselves as innocent, the tribe had sent the mission to make amends to Rome. Then, in recognition of the loyal conduct of King Ptolemy of Mauretania during the hostilities, an ancient compliment was revived and a senator dispatched to award him an ivory sceptre and embroidered triumphal robe, and greet him as king, ally, and friend.

In the same summer an incipient slave-war in Italy was only averted by an accident. The instigator was Titus Curtisius, a former Guardsman. By secret meetings at Brundusium and neighbouring towns, followed by openly published declarations, he started inciting the ferocious backwoods slaves to break free. Providentially three patrol ships for the protection of traders in those waters put into harbour. Also in that area was a quaestor, Cutius Lupus, occupying the traditional control-post of the pasture-land.[1] Organizing the crews into a force, he suppressed the rising in its initial stages. A colonel of the Guard called Staius, hastily sent by Tiberius with a strong force, took the ringleader and his most formidable helpers to Rome. There alarm had developed – owing to its vastly increased slave population, in contrast to the continual diminution of free-born inhabitants.

This year also witnessed a terrible instance of tragic heartlessness. Before the senate appeared two men called Vibius Serenus – a son prosecuting his father. The father, dragged back from exile, dirty and shabby and now manacled, had to face the charges of his elegant, brisk

1. One of the ancient administrative 'provinces' of Italy (finally abolished by Claudius) comprised the pasture-land and cattle-tracks of the south.

young son. Informer and witness in one, he accused his father of plotting against the emperor. Subversive agents, he explained, had been sent to the Gallic rebellion from Spain; funds had been provided by an ex-praetor, Marcus Caecilius Cornutus. Cornutus, finding the anxiety unbearable and regarding prosecution as equivalent to ruin, speedily committed suicide. But the defendant, undaunted, shook his manacles in his son's face and called on the gods of vengeance. 'Give me back my exile,' he prayed them, 'where such fashions were far away! And one day punish my son!'

The elder Serenus insisted that Cornutus was innocent – his panic was caused by a lying charge – if that was not so, let them produce the names of other accomplices besides himself: for surely he had not planned the emperor's murder and revolution with only one associate! The prosecutor, however, then cited Cnaeus Cornelius Lentulus (II) and Lucius Seius Tubero. This greatly embarrassed the emperor, whose close friends – one extremely old and the other sick – were thus charged with rebellious disturbance of the peace. Both were immediately exonerated.

Subsequent examinations of the elder Serenus' slaves went against the prosecution. Thereupon the accuser, demented with guilt and terrified by clamorous threats of imprisonment, the Tarpeian rock and a parricide's death, fled from Rome. But he was fetched back from Ravenna and forced to continue the prosecution. For the emperor made no secret of his own longstanding malevolence against the exile. After the condemnation of Marcus Scribonius Libo Drusus, the elder Serenus had written to Tiberius protesting that his efforts alone had gone unrewarded, and adding comments too insolent for safe address to that haughty, easily offended ear. Now, eight years later, although the stubbornness of the slaves had made their torture disappointing, Tiberius revived the matter, finding additional complaints from the intervening years.

Senators proposed the ancient punishment[1] for the elder Serenus, but the emperor, to mollify ill-feeling, vetoed it. He also rejected Gaius Asinius Gallus' counter-proposal of confinement on Gyaros or Donusa, observing that both islands were waterless and if a man were granted his life he must be allowed the means to live. So Serenus was returned to Amorgos.

1. Execution preceded by flogging.

Cornutus having committed suicide, it was proposed that the accusers should forfeit their rewards whenever a man prosecuted for treason killed himself before the trial was finished. This proposal was practically carried when Tiberius, quite sharply and with unaccustomed frankness, backed the accusers, protesting that such a measure would invalidate the laws and endanger the nation. 'Better cancel the laws', he said, 'than remove their guardians!' So that breed created for the country's ruin and never sufficiently penalized, the informers, kept their incentives.

These tragedies were interrupted by a comparatively agreeable event. Gaius Cominius, a Roman knight convicted of a poem slandering the emperor, was spared by Tiberius as a concession to the pleas of Cominius' brother, a member of the senate. This made it all the more surprising that Tiberius, who was no stranger to better things and understood that mercy was popular, should generally prefer grimmer courses. And his failures were not because he was unobservant: it is not difficult, when emperors' doings are concerned, to tell whether applause is genuine or insincere. Moreover he himself, usually by no means a fluent speaker – his words seemed to struggle for delivery – spoke more readily and easily when he urged mercy.

However, when Publius Suillius Rufus, formerly assistant of Germanicus overseas, was convicted of judicial corruption and banned from Italy, Tiberius proposed his relegation to an island, feeling strongly enough to declare on oath that the national interest so required. This was badly received at the time. But later, when Suillius returned, it was favourably regarded. For the next generation was to know him as exceedingly powerful and corrupt, exploiting long and ably – but never beneficially – the friendship of Claudius. The same penalty was imposed on the junior senator Firmius Catus for falsely accusing his sister of treason. It was he, as I have recorded, who trapped Marcus Scribonius Libo Drusus and then produced evidence to destroy him. Recalling this service, but alleging other reasons, Tiberius excused Catus from banishment, not objecting, however, to his expulsion from the senate.

I am aware that much of what I have described, and shall describe, may seem unimportant and trivial. But my chronicle is quite a different matter from histories of early Rome. Their subjects were great wars, cities stormed, kings routed and captured. Or, if home affairs were their choice, they could turn freely to conflicts of consuls with tribunes, to land- and corn-laws, feuds of conservatives and commons. Mine, on the other hand, is a circumscribed, inglorious field. Peace was scarcely broken – if at all. Rome was plunged in gloom, the ruler uninterested in expanding the empire.

Yet even apparently insignificant events such as these are worth examination. For they often cause major historical developments. This is so whether a country (or city) is a democracy, an oligarchy, or an autocracy. For it is always one or the other – a mixture of the three is easier to applaud than to achieve, and besides, even when achieved, it cannot last long. When there was democracy, it was necessary to understand the character of the masses and how to control them. When the senate was in power, those who best knew its mind – the mind of the oligarchs – were considered the wisest experts on contemporary events. Similarly, now that Rome has virtually been transformed into an autocracy, the investigation and record of these details concerning the autocrat may prove useful. Indeed, it is from such studies – from the experience of others – that most men learn to distinguish right and wrong, advantage and disadvantage. Few can tell them apart instinctively.

So these accounts have their uses. But they are distasteful. What interests and stimulates readers is a geographical description, the changing fortune of a battle, the glorious death of a commander. My themes on the other hand concern cruel orders, unremitting accusations, treacherous friendships, innocent men ruined – a conspicuously monotonous glut of downfalls and their monotonous causes. Besides, whereas the ancient historian has few critics – nobody minds if he over-praises the Carthaginian (or Roman) army – the men punished or disgraced under Tiberius have numerous descendants living today. And even when the families are extinct, some will think, if their own habits are similar, that the mention of another's crimes is directed against them. Even glory and merit make enemies – by showing their opposites in too sharp and critical relief.

But I must return to my subject. In the following year the consuls were Cossus Cornelius Lentulus (I) and Marcus Asinius Agrippa. The year began with the prosecution of Aulus Cremutius Cordus on a new and previously unheard-of charge: praise of Brutus in his *History*, and the description of Cassius as 'the last of the Romans'. The prosecutors were Satrius Secundus and Pinarius Natta, dependants of Sejanus; that was fatal to the accused man. So was the grimness of Tiberius' face as he listened to the defence. This is how Cremutius, resigned to death, conducted it:

'Senators, my words are blamed. My actions are not blameworthy. Nor were these words of mine aimed against the emperor or his parent, whom the law of treason protects. I am charged with praising Brutus and Cassius. Yet many have written of their deeds – always with respect. Livy, outstanding for objectivity as well as eloquence, praised Pompey so warmly that Augustus called him "the Pompeian". But their friendship did not suffer. And Livy never called Quintus Caecilius Metellus Pius Scipio, Lucius Afranius,[1] and this same pair, bandits and parricides – their fashionable designations today. He described them in language appropriate to distinguished men.

'Gaius Asinius Pollio (I) gave a highly complimentary account of them. Marcus Valerius Messalla Corvinus (I)[2] called Cassius "my commander". Both lived out wealthy and honoured lives. When Cicero praised Cato to the skies, the dictator Julius Caesar reacted by writing a speech against him – as in a lawsuit. Antony's letters, Brutus' speeches, contain scathing slanders against Augustus. The poems of Marcus Furius Bibaculus and Catullus – still read – are crammed with insults against the Caesars. Yet the divine Julius, the divine Augustus endured them and let them be. This could well be interpreted as wise policy, and not merely forbearance. For things unnoticed are forgotten; resentment confers status upon them.

'I am not speaking of the Greeks. For they left licence unpunished as well as freedom – or, at most, words were countered by words. But among us, too, there has always been complete, uncensored liberty to speak about those whom death has placed beyond hatred or partiality. Cassius and Brutus are not in arms at Philippi now. I am not on the platform inciting the people to civil war. They died seventy years ago! They are known by their statues – even the conqueror did not remove them. And they have their place in the historian's pages. Posterity gives everyone his due honour. If I am condemned, people will remember me as well as Cassius and Brutus.'

1. Metellus Pius was Pompey's father-in-law, Lucius Afranius one of his leading generals.
2. The orator and patron of letters, who became a supporter of Augustus.

Cremutius walked out of the senate, and starved himself to death. The senate ordered his books to be burnt by the aediles. But they survived, first hidden and later republished. This makes one deride the stupidity of people who believe that today's authority can destroy tomorrow's memories. On the contrary, repressions of genius increase its prestige. All that tyrannical conquerors, and imitators of their brutalities, achieve is their own disrepute and their victims' renown.

So continuous was the succession of prosecutions this year that even at the Latin Festival Drusus, as he mounted the platform to be inducted as honorary mayor, was approached with a charge – Calpurnius Salvianus lodged an accusation against Sextus Marius. However, Calpurnius was publicly reprimanded by Tiberius and banished.

Next the community of Cyzicus was accused of neglecting the worship of the divine Augustus and of using violence against Roman citizens. It lost the freedom it had earned during the war against Mithridates VI of Pontus when its bravery (as much as the help of Lucius Licinius Lucullus) beat off the king's besieging force. However Gaius Fonteius Capito (I), former governor of Asia, was acquitted, charges laid by the younger Vibius Serenus being demonstrated as fictitious. But this did not hurt Serenus. Widespread detestation actually protected him. For the really aggressive prosecutors became almost impregnable – reprisals only fell upon the insignificant and unknown.

This was the time when Farther Spain sent a delegation to the senate, applying to follow Asia's example and build a shrine to Tiberius and his mother. Disdainful of compliment, Tiberius saw an opportunity to refute rumours of his increasing self-importance. 'I am aware, senators,' he said, 'that my present opposition has been widely regarded as inconsistent with my acquiescence in a similar proposal by the cities of Asia. So I will justify both my silence on that occasion and my intentions from now onwards.

'The divine Augustus did not refuse a temple at Pergamum to himself and the City of Rome. So I, who regard his every action and word as law, followed the precedent thus established – the more readily since the senate was to be worshipped together with myself. One such acceptance may be pardonable. But to have my statue worshipped among the gods in every province would be presumptuous and arrogant. Besides, the honour to Augustus will be meaningless if it is debased by indiscriminate flattery. As for myself, senators, I emphasize to you that I am human, performing human tasks, and content to occupy the first place among men.

'That is what I want later generations to remember. They will do more than justice to my memory if they judge me worthy of my ancestors, careful of your interests, steadfast in danger and fearless of animosities incurred in the public service. Those are my temples in your hearts, those my finest and most lasting images. Marble monuments, if the verdict of posterity is unfriendly, are mere neglected sepulchres. So my requests to provincials and Roman citizens, and heaven, are these. To heaven – grant me, until I die, a peaceful mind and an understanding of what is due to gods and men. To mortals – when I am dead, remember my actions and my name kindly and favourably.'

Later, too, even in private conversation, he persisted in rejecting such veneration. Some attributed this to modesty, but most people thought it was uneasiness. It was also ascribed to degeneracy, on the grounds that the best men aimed highest – that was how Romulus, like Hercules and Liber (Bacchus) among the Greeks, had been admitted to the gods. 'Augustus had done better than Tiberius', it was said, 'by hoping. Rulers receive instantly everything else they want. One thing only needs to be untiringly worked for – a fair name for the future. Contempt for fame means contempt for goodness.'

Sejanus' judgement now became affected by too great success; and feminine ambition hustled him, since Livilla was demanding her promised marriage. He wrote a memorandum to the emperor. (It was customary at that time to address him in writing even when he was at Rome.) This is what Sejanus said:

'The kindness of your father Augustus, and your own numerous marks of favour, have accustomed me to bringing my hopes and desires to the imperial ear as readily as to the gods. I have never asked for brilliant office. I would rather watch and work, like any soldier, for the emperor's safety. Yet I have gained the greatest privilege – to be thought worthy of a marriage-link with your house. That inspired me to hope: besides, I have heard that Augustus, when marrying his daughter, had not regarded even knights as beneath his consideration. So please bear in mind, if you should seek a husband for Livilla, your friend who would gain nothing but prestige from the relationship. For

I am content with the duties I have to perform; satisfied – for my children's sake – if my family is safeguarded against the unfounded malevolence of Agrippina. For myself, to live my appointed span under so great an emperor is all the life I desire.'

In reply Tiberius praised Sejanus' loyalty, touched lightly on his own favours to him, and asked for time, ostensibly for unbiased reflection. Finally, he answered. 'Other men's decisions', he wrote, 'may be based on their own interests, but rulers are situated differently, since in important matters they need to consider public opinion. So I do not resort to the easy answer, that Livilla can decide for herself whether she should fill Drusus' place by remarrying, or stay in the same home. Nor shall I reply that she has a mother and grandmother who are her more intimate advisers than myself. I shall be more frank. In the first place Agrippina's ill-feelings will be greatly intensified if Livilla marries: this would virtually split the imperial house in two. Even now, the women's rivalry is irrepressible, and my grandsons are torn between them. What if the proposed marriage accentuated the feud?

'You are mistaken, Sejanus, if you think that Livilla, once married to Gaius Caesar and then to Drusus, would be content to grow old as the wife of a knight – or that you could retain your present status. Even if I allowed it, do you think it would be tolerated by those who have seen her brother and father, and our ancestors, holding the great offices of state? You do not want to rise above your present rank. But the officials and distinguished men who force their way in upon you and consult you on all matters maintain openly that you have long ago eclipsed all other knights and risen above any friend of my father's. Moreover, envying you, they criticize me.

'Augustus, you say, considered marrying his daughter to a knight. But he foresaw that the man set apart by such an alliance would be enormously elevated; and is it surprising, therefore, that those he had in mind were men like Gaius Proculeius,[1] noted for their retiring abstention from public affairs? Besides, if we are noting Augustus' delay in making up his mind, the decisive consideration is that the sons-in-law whom he actually chose were Marcus Agrippa and then, in due course, myself. I have spoken openly, as your friend. However, what you and Livilla decide, I shall not oppose. Of certain

1. A knight who was a close friend of Augustus.

projects of my own, and additional ties by which I plan to link you with me, I shall not speak now. This only shall I say: for your merits and your devotion to me, no elevation would be too high. When the time comes to speak before the senate and public, I shall not be silent.'

Sejanus was alarmed, not just for his marriage but on graver grounds. He replied urging Tiberius to eschew suspicion and ignore rumour and malignant envy. Then, unwilling either to shut out his stream of visitors – which would mean loss of influence – or by receiving them to give his critics a handle, he turned his attention to persuading Tiberius to settle in some attractive place far from Rome. He foresaw many advantages in this. He himself would control access to the emperor – as well as most of his correspondence, since it would be transmitted by Guardsmen. Besides, the ageing monarch, slackening in retirement, would soon be readier to delegate governmental functions. Meanwhile Sejanus himself would become less unpopular when his large receptions ceased – by eliminating inessentials, he would strengthen his real power. So he increasingly denounced to Tiberius the drudgeries of Rome, its crowds and innumerable visitors, and spoke warmly of peace and solitude, far from vexation and friction: where first things could come first.

Tiberius wavered. At this moment, a trial happened to take place which made him anxious to avoid the senate's meetings. For the evidence included offensive (and often accurate) remarks about himself, repeated to his face. For while the able and well-known Votienus Montanus was being tried for abusing the emperor, a soldier called Aemilius who was one of the witnesses, eager to prove the case, perseveringly spared no detail. Despite loud protests, Tiberius had to hear the insults to which, in private, he was subject. Greatly upset, he cried that he must clear his reputation immediately, or at least before the case ended. He was only calmed with difficulty by his friends' entreaties and a chorus of flattery. Votienus paid the penalty of treason. Imputations of his excessive severity to defendants only made Tiberius severer still. He exiled a lady named Aquilia for adultery – though one of the consuls-designate, Cnaeus Cornelius Lentulus Gaetulicus, had only requested condemnation under the Julian law – and struck a senator called Apidius Merula off the roll for not swearing obedience to the acts of the divine Augustus.

Deputations from Sparta and Messene were now heard concerning the ownership of the temple of Diana Limnatis. The Spartan assertion, backed by historical records and poems, was that whereas their ancestors had consecrated it on their own territory, it had been forcibly taken from them by Philip II of Macedon during their war against him; and afterwards they had received it back by rulings of Julius Caesar and Antony. The Messenians, on the other hand, cited the ancient partition of the Peloponnese among the descendants of Hercules, by which the Denthaliate area – in which the shrine stands – had been allotted to their king. This, they added, was confirmed by ancient bronze and stone records; if appeal was to be made to poets and historians, the more numerous and reliable authorities were on their side; and Philip's judgement had not been arbitrary but objective – King Antigonus III Doson[1] and the Roman commander Lucius Mummius had decided similarly, and the same verdict had been reached by the city of Miletus, officially appointed as arbitrator, and again by Atidius Geminus governor of Achaia. The Messenians won their case.

Segesta appealed for the reconstruction of its temple of Venus on Mount Eryx. When the well-known story of this antique ruin was repeated, Tiberius was pleased and on grounds of kinship gladly undertook the task. Next, a petition from Massilia was considered. Volcacius Moschus, an exile at that city, had become naturalized and left his property to it as his own country. His bequest was confirmed in view of the precedent of an earlier exile, Publius Rutilius Rufus, who had become a citizen of Smyrna.

This year witnessed the deaths of two noblemen, Cnaeus Cornelius Lentulus (II) and Lucius Domitius Ahenobarbus (I). Lentulus, in addition to his consulship and honorary Triumph won against the Getae, was honoured for poverty patiently endured, followed by great wealth respectably acquired and modestly employed. Domitius derived prestige from his father's sea-power during the civil war: subsequently he had joined first Antony and then the future Augustus. His grandfather had fallen on the aristocratic side at Pharsalus.[2] He himself had been chosen as husband for Augustus' niece, Octavia's daughter, Antonia (I). Later he had won an honorary Triumph by conducting

1. King of Macedonia from 229 to 220 B.C.
2. In Thessaly; the scene of Pompey's decisive defeat by Caesar in 48 B.C.

an army across the Elbe and penetrating deeper into Germany than anyone before him.

Another death was that of Lucius Antonius, of famous but ill-starred family. Only a boy when his father Iullus Antonius was executed for adultery with Augustus' daughter Julia (III), that emperor (his great-uncle) had dismissed him to Massilia, where study could be a cloak for exile. However, he was given an honourable funeral, and by the senate's decree his remains were placed in the tomb of the Octavii.

In the same year a savage crime was committed in Nearer Spain. As Lucius Calpurnius Piso (III), imperial governor of the province, was travelling – unguarded, since conditions were peaceful – he was suddenly attacked by a peasant from Termes, and killed with one blow. His assailant escaped to wooded country on a swift horse, which he there turned loose, evading pursuit in steep pathless country. But not for long. The horse was found and taken round the neighbouring villages, until its master was identified. Arrested, and tortured to reveal his associates, he shouted in his native tongue that investigation was useless – his partners could safely stand by and watch; no amount of pain would make him confess. Next day while he was being dragged back for further torture, he tore himself away from his guards and dashed his head against a rock, dying immediately. Nevertheless, Piso's death is attributed to conspirators from Termes. For public funds had been stolen, and he was recovering them with a strictness which seemed intolerable to natives.

Next year the consuls were Cnaeus Cornelius Lentulus Gaetulicus and Gaius Calvisius Sabinus. The year began with the award of an honorary Triumph to Gaius Poppaeus Sabinus for suppressing Thracian mountain tribesmen. The causes of the rebellion were their uncivilized and intractable temperaments, and their refusal of the conscription system which drafted their best men into our forces. Their loyalty even to their own kings was capricious – such contingents as they sent the kings were under their own chieftains and only employed against neighbours. It was now rumoured that the tribes were to be broken up, mixed with other peoples, and transported to far countries.

However, before opening hostilities the Thracians sent envoys to stress their friendship and obedience, which would remain intact, they said, if no new burdens were imposed. But if, they added, they were enslaved like conquered men, they had the weapons, warriors, and determination to be free or to die. They pointed to their fortresses on hilltops, where their parents and wives were lodged; and they threatened a difficult, arduous, bloody war.

Sabinus gave conciliatory replies until his forces were collected. But when a brigade under Pomponius Labeo reached him from Moesia and King Rhoemetalces II added loyal native auxiliaries, he led them and his own troops against the enemy. These had collected in wooded ravines. A few ventured to show themselves on open hillsides, but Sabinus attacked and easily routed them – inflicting little loss, however, since cover was near. Next Sabinus made his headquarters into a fortified camp. Then, taking a considerable force, he seized a narrow mountain-ridge which stretched, even and unbroken, to the nearest enemy fortress. This was defended by numerous armed Thracians, including irregulars. Against the fiercest of them, as they capered and chanted in front of their lines according to national custom, he detached picked archers. At long range these archers scored many hits without loss. But at closer quarters an unexpected sortie routed them. They were rescued by a battalion of Sugambri stationed by Sabinus nearby owing to its effectiveness in emergencies; it was as savage as the enemy in its chanting and clashing of arms.

Then the camp was moved closer to the enemy. The Thracian auxiliaries who, as I mentioned, had joined our side were left in the previous camp, and allowed to ravage, burn, and loot, provided that their plundering was restricted to the daylight and that they spent the night safe and watchful in the camp. At first this proviso was observed. But later, loaded with booty, they became self-indulgent and abandoned sentry duty in favour of dissipation, or lay drunkenly sleeping. The enemy learnt of their slackness and organized two detachments, one to attack the Thracian plunderers while the other assaulted the Roman camp. They did not expect to capture it but hoped that amid the shouting and clash of weapons every soldier would be too intent on his own peril to hear the other battle. To intensify the alarm the attack was to be by night. However, the attempt on the Roman fortifications was easily driven off. But the Thracian auxiliaries, lying along the earthworks, or in most cases drifting about outside, were terrified by the sudden raid, and slaughtered – with particular savagery, since they were condemned as traitorous deserters fighting to enslave themselves and their country.

On the next day Sabinus paraded his force on the plain. He hoped that the natives might be tempted by the night's success to risk battle. But they would not leave the fortress and its surrounding hills. So he proceeded to hem them in by strong-points, which – conveniently enough – he had already begun to construct. Linking these by a ditch and breastwork four miles in circumference, he gradually narrowed and tightened the loop, to cut off the defenders' water and fodder. He also began work on a mound from which boulders, spears, and torches could reach the now adjacent enemy. But their worst hardship was thirst, since there was now only one spring for a great crowd of warriors and non-combatants. Meanwhile, their horses and cattle, shut in with them in accordance with native custom, were dying of starvation. Beside them lay corpses, victims of wounds and thirst. The whole place stank with putrefaction and infection.

The troubles of the Thracians were intensified by the supreme misfortune of dissension. One party favoured surrender, another death at each other's hands, while a further section, insisting that a price should be paid for their deaths, demanded a sortie. Opposing views were not limited to the ranks, but came from a chieftain the aged Dinis, whose long experience of Roman power and mercy led him to urge that the only solution to their plight was surrender. He took the initiative by giving himself up to the victors with his wife and children. The old and young and the women, and those who preferred life to glory, followed him.

The younger men, however, were split between Tarsa and Turesis. Both were determined to die rather than lose their freedom. Tarsa cried out for a quick end, an end of fears as well as hopes, and set the example by plunging his sword into his breast. Others followed his lead. But Turesis and his supporters waited for darkness. The Roman commander, aware of their plan, reinforced his outposts. Night fell stormily. On the enemy's side savage cries alternated with complete stillness. The besiegers were perplexed. But Sabinus went round warning them not to let mysterious noises or pretended inactivity make them vulnerable to surprise – every man must stand firmly at his post and not throw weapons at non-existent targets.

Then the Thracians, in groups, charged down the slope. Some hurled boulders, fire-hardened stakes, and boughs hacked from trees at the palisade. Another party filled the ditch with branches, hurdles, and corpses. A small detachment brought ready-made gangways and ladders up to the turrets, which they grasped and overturned in hand-to-hand fighting. The Romans pushed them back with spears and shields, and hurled siege-javelins and showers of stones. Our men felt confident that the battle was won – and knew the disgrace (more conspicuous on our side) that defeat would bring upon them. As for the enemy, this was their supreme crisis. Moreover, many of them were spurred on by the wailing of their mothers and wives nearby.

Night gave the Thracians fresh heart. But it terrified the Romans. Striking out aimlessly, struck unpredictably, they could not tell friend and enemy apart. Shouts echoing back from the mountain clefts seemed to come from the rear; and they abandoned some of their defences, believing them overrun. However, only very few Thracians broke through. The remainder, their best men dead or wounded, were pushed back at dawn to their hill-fortress. There they were finally forced to surrender. The surrounding population submitted voluntarily. The remaining rebels were saved from successful assault or blockade by the severe, untimely winter of the Balkan mountains.

In Rome, convulsions shook the imperial house. The chain of events leading to Agrippina's end was initiated by the trial of her second cousin Claudia Pulchra. The prosecutor was Cnaeus Domitius Afer – an undistinguished recent praetor, ready to commit any crime for advancement. The charges were immorality (adultery with Furnius), attempted poisoning of the emperor, and magic spells against him. Agrippina, always violent, was upset by her relative's predicament, and hastened to Tiberius. She found him sacrificing to his adoptive father, and used this as the text of her reproaches. 'The man who offers victims to the deified Augustus', she said, 'ought not to persecute his descendants. It is not in mute statues that Augustus' divine spirit has lodged – I, born of his sacred blood, am its incarnation! I see my danger; and I wear mourning. Claudia Pulchra is an idle pretext. Her downfall, poor fool, is because she chooses Agrippina as friend! She forgot Sosia Galla – who suffered for just that.'

These words goaded the secretive Tiberius to one of his infrequent pronouncements. Grasping her, he quoted a Greek line: it was not *an injury that she did not reign*. Pulchra and Furnius were condemned. Afer became a leading advocate. His talents had been seen; and Tiberius had commented that he was a born speaker. Subsequently, in prosecution and defence alike, Afer's speeches greatly deteriorated in old age. It lessened his powers, but not his inability to remain silent.

Agrippina, resentful as ever, became physically ill. When Tiberius visited her, at first she wept long and silently. Then she broke into embittered appeals. 'I am lonely', she said. 'Help me and give me a husband! I am still young enough,[1] and marriage is the only respectable consolation. Rome contains men who would welcome Germanicus' wife and children.' Tiberius recognized the political implications of this – but did not want to show either anger or fear. So her persistence remained unanswered. This incident, ignored by the historians, I found in the memoirs of Agrippina's daughter (mother of the emperor Nero), in which she recorded for posterity her life and her family's fortunes.

Distressed and impetuous, Agrippina was further upset by Sejanus. His agents now warned her – ostensibly as friends – against schemes to poison her: she must avoid dining with her father-in-law Tiberius. Agrippina was bad at pretending. Next to the emperor at table, she remained silent and expressionless, her food untouched, until he happened to notice (or perhaps he was told). When fruit was placed before him, the emperor – requiring a more conclusive test – praised it and himself offered it to her. This accentuated her suspicions and she passed it to her slaves uneaten. Tiberius said nothing publicly. But he turned to his mother and asked if it was surprising that he envisaged somewhat stern measures against a woman who alleged he was poisoning her. It was accordingly rumoured that the emperor planned Agrippina's death, but – not daring to murder her openly – was trying to find a secret method.

To distract gossip, Tiberius attended the senate regularly. He spent several days hearing deputations from Asia arguing about which community should erect his temple. Eleven cities, of varying importance, competed with uniform keenness for this privilege. Their pleas all dwelt on ancient origins and services to Rome in the wars against

1. Agrippina was probably about forty.

Perseus, Aristonicus[1] and other foreign princes. Four, Hypaepa, Tralles, Laodicea on the Lycus, and Magnesia on the Maeander, were passed over as too unimportant. Even Ilium, boasting Troy as Rome's mother-city, was insignificant apart from its glorious antiquity. The assertion of Halicarnassus that it had stood firm, undisturbed by earthquakes, for twelve hundred years, and that the foundations of its temple would rest on natural rock, attracted attention briefly. The delegates from Pergamum cited their temple of Augustus; but this was thought distinction enough. Ephesus and Miletus were adjudged fully occupied with their state-cults of Diana and Apollo respectively.

So the choice rested between Sardis and Smyrna. The Sardians claimed kinship with the Etruscans, quoting a decree of the latter. They explained that the original nation, owing to its size, had been divided between the sons of King Atys – Tyrrhenus, who had been dispatched to create new homes, and Lydus, who had stayed in his fatherland – the two countries, in Italy and Asia, taking the names of their rulers; while the Lydians had extended their power by planting settlements in that part of Greece later called the Peloponnese after Pelops. The Sardians went on to quote Roman commanders' letters and treaties made with Rome during the Macedonian war; and they stressed their rich rivers, temperate climate, and fertile surrounding territory.

The deputation from Smyrna traced back their origins – whether Jupiter's son Tantalus, or Theseus (also of divine birth), or an Amazon was their founder – and then passed to their most confident arguments: their services to Rome, including the dispatch of naval forces[2] for wars abroad and even in Italy; and their initiative in founding a Temple of Rome, in the consulship of Marcus Porcius Cato the Censor,[3] at a time when our power although already considerable had not reached its height, since Carthage still existed and Asia still had powerful kings. They also cited Sulla's acknowledgement that, when his army was suffering critically from inadequate clothing in a bitter winter, a public

1. The Romans defeated Perseus of Macedonia in 168 B.C., and Aristonicus in Asia in 130 B.C.

2. The forces to which the delegation from Smyrna referred must have been sent during the Marsian (Social) War (91–88 B.C.).

3. In 195 B.C.

announcement of this fact at Smyrna caused the whole audience to strip off its clothes and send them to our soldiers.[1]

The senate voted in favour of Smyrna. It was proposed by Gaius Vibius Marsus that the governor of Asia, Marcus Aemilius Lepidus (IV), should be allotted a supernumerary official in charge of the new temple. As the governor modestly declined to make the choice himself, lots were cast and a former praetor, Valerius Naso, was appointed.

Now, after long consideration and frequent postponements, Tiberius at last left for Campania. His ostensible purpose was the dedication of temples to Jupiter and Augustus at Capua and Nola respectively. But he had decided to live away from Rome. Like most historians, I attribute his withdrawal to Sejanus' intrigues. Yet, since he maintained this seclusion for six years after Sejanus' execution, I often wonder whether it was not really caused by a desire to hide the cruelty and immorality which his actions made all too conspicuous. It was also said that in old age he became sensitive about his appearance. Tall and abnormally thin, bent and bald, he had a face covered with sores and often plaster. His retirement at Rhodes had accustomed him to unsociability and secretive pleasures.

According to another theory he was driven away by his mother's bullying: to share control with her seemed intolerable, to dislodge her impracticable – since that control had been given him by her. For Augustus had considered awarding the empire to his universally loved grand-nephew Germanicus. But his wife had induced him to adopt Tiberius instead (though Tiberius was made to adopt Germanicus). The Augusta harped accusingly on this obligation – and exacted repayment.

Tiberius left with only a few companions: one senator and ex-consul, Marcus Cocceius Nerva the jurist, one distinguished knight, Curtius Atticus – and Sejanus. The rest were literary men, mostly Greeks whose conversation diverted him. The astrologers asserted that the conjunction of heavenly bodies under which he had left Rome precluded his return. This proved fatal to many who deduced, and proclaimed, that his end was near. For they did not foresee the unbelievable fact that his voluntary self-exile would last eleven years. Time was to show how narrow is the dividing-line between authentic prediction

1. Presumably in the first war against Mithridates VI of Pontus (87–5 B.C.), who had sacked the cities in 88 B.C.

and imposture: truth is surrounded by mystery. For the first assertion proved authentic – though he came to adjacent points of the country-side or coast, and often approached the city's very walls. But the prophets' foreknowledge was limited, for he lived to a great age.

A dangerous accident to Tiberius at this time stimulated idle gossip, and gave him reason for increased confidence in Sejanus' friendship and loyalty. While they were dining at a villa called The Cave, in a natural cavern between the sea at Amyclae and the hills of Fundi, there was a fall of rock at the cave-mouth. Several servants were crushed, and amid the general panic the diners fled. But Sejanus, braced on hands and knees, face to face, warded the falling boulders off Tiberius. That is how the soldiers who rescued them found him. The incident increased Sejanus' power. Tiberius believed him dis-interested and listened trustingly to his advice, however disastrous.

Towards Germanicus' family Sejanus adopted the role of judge. Agents suborned as accusers were to direct their main onslaught against Nero Caesar, heir to the throne, who though youthfully un-pretentious often forgot the care which the circumstances demanded. His ex-slaves and dependants, impatient for power, urged him to show vigour and confidence. Rome and the armies wanted it, they said, and no counter-stroke would be risked by Sejanus, whose targets were juvenile ineffectiveness and senile passivity.

Nero Caesar listened. His intentions were harmless. But he some-times made thoughtless, disrespectful remarks. Spies noted, reported, and exaggerated these, and he was given no opportunity to explain. People began to show disquiet in various ways. They avoided him, or turned away after greeting him, or, very often, broke off conversa-tions abruptly. Sejanus' partisans stood and watched, sneering. Tibe-rius treated Nero Caesar grimly, or smiled insincerely – the young man seemed equally guilty whether he spoke or remained silent. Even night-time was not safe. For whether he slept, or lay awake, or sighed, his wife Livia Julia told her mother Livilla, and she told Sejanus. Sejanus even made an accomplice of the young man's brother Drusus Caesar – tempting him with supreme power if only he could elimi-nate his already undermined elder brother. Drusus Caesar's degraded character was animated by power-lust, and the usual hatred between brothers – also jealousy, because his mother Agrippina preferred Nero Caesar. But Sejanus' cultivation of Drusus Caesar did not exclude plans to begin his destruction too, since the youth, as he knew, was hot-headed and could be trapped.

The end of the year witnessed the deaths of Marcus Asinius Agrippa, who had lived worthily of his distinguished (though not ancient) house, and Quintus Haterius, of senatorial family. His oratory impressed his contemporaries, though surviving examples are less esteemed today. Indeed, his success was due to vigour rather than pains. Other men's careful, laborious work attains posthumous repute. Conversely, Haterius' resonant fluency died with him.

In the following year the consuls were Marcus Licinius Crassus Frugi and Lucius Calpurnius Piso (IV). A sudden disaster which now occurred was as destructive as a major war. It began and ended in a moment. An ex-slave called Atilius started building an amphitheatre at Fidenae for a gladiatorial show. But he neither rested its foundations on solid ground nor fastened the wooden superstructure securely. He had undertaken the project not because of great wealth or municipal ambition but for sordid profits. Lovers of such displays, starved of amusements under Tiberius, flocked in – men and women of all ages. Their numbers, swollen by the town's proximity, intensified the tragedy. The packed structure collapsed, subsiding both inwards and outwards and precipitating or overwhelming a huge crowd of spectators and bystanders.

Those killed at the outset of the catastrophe at least escaped torture, as far as their violent deaths permitted. More pitiable were those, mangled but not yet dead, who knew their wives and children lay there too. In daytime they could see them, and at night they heard their screams and moans. The news attracted crowds, lamenting kinsmen, brothers, and fathers. Even those whose friends and relations had gone away on other business were alarmed, for while the casualties remained unidentified uncertainty gave free range for anxieties. When the ruins began to be cleared, people rushed to embrace and kiss the corpses – and even quarrelled over them, when features were unrecognizable but similarities of physique or age had caused wrong identifications.

Fifty thousand people were mutilated or crushed to death in the disaster. The senate decreed that in future no one with a capital of less than four hundred thousand sesterces should exhibit a gladiatorial show, and no amphitheatre should be constructed except on ground of proved solidity. Atilius was banished. Immediately after the catastrophe, leading Romans threw open their homes, providing medical attention and supplies all round. In those days Rome, for all its miseries, recalled the practice of our ancestors, who after great battles had lavished gifts and attentions on the wounded.

This calamity had not been forgotten when Rome suffered an exceptionally destructive fire, which gutted the Caelian Hill. This was a fatal year, people said. Fastening on a scapegoat for chance happenings (as the public does), they detected an evil omen in the emperor's decision to leave Rome. Tiberius disarmed criticism by distributing money in proportion to losses incurred. This earned him votes of thanks in the senate by eminent members, and, as the news got round, a feeling of gratitude among the general public, because the donations were made without respecting persons or favouring relatives' petitions: sometimes the beneficiaries were unknown victims applying in response to the emperor's invitation. It was proposed that the Caelian should in future be called the Augustan Hill, since while flames roared on all sides the one thing unharmed was a statue of Tiberius in the house of a senator named Junius. The same thing, it was remarked, had once happened to Claudia Quinta, whose image, twice spared by conflagrations, our ancestors had dedicated in the temple of the Mother of the Gods: the Claudian house was holy and honoured by heaven, and the place where the gods had so conspicuously favoured the emperor should be accorded increased veneration.

It may be appropriate to record here that the hill was originally called Oak Hill because of its dense growth of oak trees, and was later named 'Caelian' after Caeles Vibenna, an Etruscan chief who, for helping Rome, had been granted the hill as a residence by Tarquinius Priscus – or another king; here writers disagree. But there is no doubt about the extensive Etruscan settlement, which also comprised the flat ground near the Forum; it was after these immigrants that the Tuscan Street was given its name.

Accidents, then, were alleviated by leading men's public spirit and the emperor's generosity. But there was no alleviation of the accusers, who became more formidable and vicious every day. Quinctilius Varus, a wealthy relation of Tiberius, was accused by Cnaeus Domitius Afer who had secured his mother Claudia Pulchra's condemnation.

After long poverty Afer had made money and misused it, and it surprised no one that he now had further infamous designs. But it was remarkable that his partner in the prosecution was Publius Cornelius Dolabella (I), an aristocrat and Varus' relative – setting out to ruin his own class and blood. However, the senate sought their only temporary escape from tragedy by opposing action pending the emperor's return.

Tiberius was dedicating the temples in Campania. He issued an edict forbidding the disturbance of his privacy, and troops were posted in the towns to prevent crowds. He detested these towns, and indeed the whole mainland. So he took refuge on the island of Capreae, separated from the tip of the Surrentum promontory by three miles of sea. Presumably what attracted him was the isolation of Capreae. Harbourless, it has few roadsteads even for small vessels; sentries can control all landings. In winter the climate is mild, since hills on the mainland keep off gales. In summer the island is delightful, since it faces west and has open sea all round. The bay it overlooks was exceptionally lovely, until Vesuvius' eruption transformed the landscape. This was an area of Greek colonization, and tradition records that Capreae had been occupied by the Teleboi.[1]

On this island then, in twelve spacious, separately named villas, Tiberius took up residence. His former absorption in State affairs ended. Instead he spent the time in secret orgies, or idle malevolent thoughts. But his abnormally credulous suspicions were unabated. Sejanus, who had encouraged them even at Rome, whipped them up, and now openly disclosed his designs against Agrippina and Nero Caesar. Soldiers attached to them reported with a historian's precision their correspondence, visitors, and doings private and public. Agents incited them to flee to the German armies, or – in the Forum at its peak hour – to grasp the divine Augustus' statue, and appeal to senate and public. They dismissed such projects: but were accused of them.

The next year, in which the consuls were Gaius Appius Junius Silanus and Publius Silius Nerva, began deplorably. A distinguished knight called Titius Sabinus was dragged to gaol because he had been Germanicus' friend. Sabinus had maintained every attention to Germanicus' widow and children, visiting their home, escorting them in public – of their crowds of followers he was the only survivor. Decent

1. From a group of small islands off north-western Greece.

men respected this, but spiteful people hated him. His downfall was planned by four ex-praetors ambitious for the consulship, Lucanius Latiaris, Marcus Porcius Cato, Petilius Rufus and Marcus Opsius. For the only access to this lay through Sejanus; and only crimes secured Sejanus' goodwill.

The four arranged that, with the others present as witnesses, one of them, Lucanius Latiaris (who knew Sabinus slightly), should trap him with a view to prosecution. So Latiaris after some casual remarks complimented Sabinus on his unshaken adherence, in its misfortunes, to the family he had supported in its prosperity – and he commented respecfully about Germanicus, sympathetically about Agrippina. Sabinus burst into tearful complaints; for misery is demoralizing. Latiaris then openly attacked Sejanus as cruel, domineering, and ambitious – and did not even spare Tiberius. These exchanges of forbidden confidences seemed to cement a close friendship. So now Sabinus sought out Latiaris' company, frequenting his house and unburdening his sorrows to this outwardly reliable companion.

The four partners next considered how to make these conversations available to a larger audience. The meeting-place had to appear private. Even if they stood behind the doors, they risked being seen or heard or detected by some suspicious whim. So in between roof and ceiling they crammed three Roman senators. In this hiding-place – as undignified as the trick was despicable – they applied their ears to chinks and holes. Meanwhile Latiaris had found Sabinus out of doors and, pretending to have fresh news to report, escorted him home to Sabinus' bedroom. There Latiaris dwelt on the unfailing subject of past and present distresses, introducing some fresh terrors too. Sabinus embroidered at greater length on the same theme: once grievances find expression, there is no silencing them. Acting rapidly, the accusers wrote to Tiberius and disclosed the history of the trap and their own deplorable role. At Rome there was unprecedented agitation and terror. People behaved secretively even to their intimates, avoiding encounters and conversation, shunning the ears both of friends and strangers. Even voiceless, inanimate objects – ceilings and walls – were scanned suspiciously.

In a letter read in the senate on January 1st Tiberius, after the customary New Year formalities, rounded upon Sabinus, alleging that he had tampered with certain of the emperor's ex-slaves and plotted against his life. The letter unequivocally demanded retribution. This was hastily decreed. The condemned man was dragged away, crying (as loudly as the cloak muffling his mouth and the noose round his neck allowed) that this was a fine New Year ceremony – this year's sacrifice was to Sejanus! But wherever his eye rested or his words carried, there was a stampede: all roads and public places were evacuated and deserted. Some, however, reappeared and showed themselves again – alarmed because they had displayed alarm. For it seemed that no day would be free of convictions when, at a season in which custom forbade even an ominous word, sacrifices and prayers were attended by manacles and nooses. Tiberius had incurred this indignation deliberately, people said – it was a purposeful, premeditated action to show that the newly elected officials who opened the religious year could also open the death-cells.

The emperor wrote again, thanking the senate for punishing a public danger, and adding that he had grave anxieties and reasons to suspect disaffected persons of plotting. He mentioned no names. But Nero Caesar and Agrippina were undoubtedly meant. If I did not propose to record each event under its own year, I should have liked to anticipate and recount immediately the fates of the four criminal plotters against Sabinus – partly in the reign of Gaius, and partly also under Tiberius. For Tiberius, unwilling though he was for others to destroy his villainous agents, frequently wearied of them and, when new recruits became available, eliminated their distasteful predecessors. However, this punishment of guilty men, and other similar cases, I shall describe at the proper time.

Gaius Asinius Gallus, of whose children Agrippina was aunt,[1] now proposed that the emperor should indicate his fears to the senate, and permit their removal. Now of all his self-ascribed virtues Tiberius cherished none more dearly than dissimulation. So he greatly disliked disclosing what he had suppressed. However Sejanus calmed him, not from affection for Gallus, but to let the emperor's hesitations take their course. For, as Sejanus knew, Tiberius reached decisions slowly, but once the outburst occurred there was a rapid transition from grim words to terrible action.

This was about the time when Julia (IV) died. Convicted of adul-

1. Because the children's mother Vipsania was, like Agrippina, a daughter of Marcus Agrippa (the two women were half-sisters). See Table 3.

tery, she had been condemned by her grandfather Augustus to banishment on the island of Trimerum off the Apulian coast. There she had endured exile for twenty years. The Augusta had helped her: after secretly ruining her step-daughter's family when they prospered, she openly showed pity for them in their ruin.

In this year, across the Rhine, the Frisian tribe broke the peace. The cause was Roman rapacity rather than Frisian insubordination. Bearing their povety in mind, Nero Drusus had assessed their taxation leniently: ox-hides were requested, for military purposes. No one had stipulated their dimensions or quality until Olennius, a senior staff-officer who was in charge of them, interpreted the requirements as buffalo-hides. This demand, severe enough for any community, was particularly oppressive in Germany where, though the forests abound in huge beasts, domestic animals are small. So first the Frisians lost their cattle, next their lands, and finally their wives and children went into slavery. Distressful complaints produced no relief. So they resorted to war. Soldiers collecting the tax were gibbeted. Olennius anticipated the Frisians' angry intentions by taking refuge in a fort called Flevum, where a considerable concentration of Roman and auxiliary troops guarded the North Sea coast.

When Lucius Apronius, imperial governor of Lower Germany, heard the news, he summoned detachments from Roman brigades in Upper Germany, together with picked auxiliary horse and foot, and brought the combined force down the Rhine against the Frisians. Finding the siege of Flevum raised, and the rebels gone to defend their own property, he constructed causeways and bridges across the adjacent coastal marshes for the transportation of his heavy columns. A ford was discovered; and German cavalry belonging to the tribe of the Canninefates, together with such of their auxiliary infantry as was serving with us, were ordered to take the enemy in the rear. The Frisians however, in battle-formation, repulsed our cavalry – and also regular cavalry dispatched in support.[1] Then Apronius sent in three of the infantry battalions from Germany, followed by two more, and finally (after an interval) the main auxiliary cavalry. If they had

1. In addition to the provincial and foreign auxiliary cavalry, there was a regular cavalry force of four troops, each thirty strong, attached to every brigade (see Key to Technical Terms, DIVISION).

attacked simultaneously, this would have been sufficient strength. But, arriving piecemeal, they failed to rally the disorganized horsemen. Indeed, the reinforcements themselves became involved in the panic-stricken retreat.

Then Apronius put the remaining auxiliaries under Cethegus Labeo, commander of the fifth division. Labeo, seriously endangered by his men's plight, sent messengers urgently requesting extensive regular reinforcements. But his men rushed forward ahead of the rest, drove back the enemy after a vigorous fight, and rescued the wounded and exhausted cavalry and infantry. The Roman general did not attempt retaliation, or bury his dead, although many regular and auxiliary colonels and senior company-commanders were killed. Later deserters reported that nine hundred Romans who had prolonged the battle till next day had been slaughtered in the Baduhenna wood, while another body four hundred strong had occupied the villa of an ex-soldier of ours named Cruptorix, but fearing treachery had killed each other. Germany glorified the Frisians for these doings. However, rather than appoint a commander for the war, Tiberius suppressed the losses.

The senate, too, had more pressing concerns than a frontier setback. Metropolitan terrors were what preoccupied them. From these they sought relief in flattery. Though assembled to consider some unrelated business, they voted the erection of altars to Mercy and Friendship – the latter to be flanked by statues of Tiberius and Sejanus. The senate also repeatedly begged them to vouchsafe a view of themselves. But neither came into Rome, or near it. They thought it sufficient to leave their island and show themselves on the Campanian coast opposite. There flocked senators and knights and large crowds of ordinary people – anxiously regarding Sejanus.

Access to him was harder now. It was only procurable by intrigue and complicity. His arrogance obviously battened on the sight of this blatant subservience. At Rome people circulate, and the city's size conceals the purposes of their errands. But there in Campania, huddled indiscriminately on land and shore, men endured, day and night, the patronage and self-importance of his door-keepers. Finally they were denied even that, and returned to Rome. Anxiety gnawed those whom he had not deigned to address or see. Others were elated. But they were misguided, for their ill-omened friendship was soon to end disastrously.

Tiberius had personally entrusted his grandchild Agrippina (II), daughter of Germanicus, to Cnaeus Domitius Ahenobarbus. Now the emperor ordered the marriage to be celebrated in the capital. His choice, Domitius, was a man of ancient family and a blood-relation of the Caesars; for his grandmother was Octavia, and Augustus his great-uncle.

In the following year, when Gaius Fufius Geminus and Lucius Rubellius Geminus were consuls, the aged Augusta died. By her own Claudian family, and her adoption into the Livii and Julii, she was of the highest nobility. Her first husband, and the father of her children, had been Tiberius Claudius Nero, who, after emigrating in the Perusian war, returned to Rome when peace was concluded between Sextus Pompeius (I) and the Triumvirate.[1] The future Augustus, fascinated by her beauty, removed her from him – with or without her encouragement – and hastily conducted her to his own home even before the baby she was expecting (the future Nero Drusus) was born. That was her last child. But her connection with Augustus through the marriage of her grandson Germanicus to his granddaughter Agrippina gave them great-grandchildren in common. Her private life was of traditional strictness. But her graciousness exceeded old-fashioned standards. She was a compliant wife, but an overbearing mother. Neither her husband's diplomacy nor her son's insincerity could outmanoeuvre her.

The implementation of her will was long delayed. At her modest funeral, the obituary speech was pronounced by her great-grandson Gaius, soon to be emperor. Tiberius did not interrupt his own self-indulgences for his mother's last rites, but wrote excusing himself and pleading important business. Moreover, when the senate decreed extensive honours to her memory, he curtailed them in the name of moderation, conceding only a few. Tiberius added that she was not to be deified[2] – she herself had not wished it.

The same letter contained strictures on 'female friendships'. This was an implied criticism of the consul Gaius Fufius Geminus, whom

---

1. The Perusian War (41–40 B.C.) ended in the defeat of Antony's brother Lucius Antonius by Octavian. The Treaty of Misenum (39) was a temporary agreement between the Triumvirs and Sextus Pompeius.
2. The Augusta was officially 'deified' by Claudius in A.D. 42.

the Augusta's patronage had elevated. Fufius could attract women. Moreover, his sharp tongue had often ridiculed Tiberius with sarcastic jokes such as autocrats long remember.

Now began a time of sheer crushing tyranny. While the Augusta lived there was still a moderating influence, for Tiberius had retained a deep-rooted deference for his mother. Sejanus, too, had not ventured to outbid her parental authority. Now, however, the reins were thrown off, and they pressed ahead. A letter was sent to Rome denouncing Agrippina and Nero Caesar. It was read so soon after the Augusta's death that people believed it had arrived earlier and been suppressed by her.

Its wording was deliberately harsh. However, the youth was accused not of actual or intended rebellion but of homosexual indecency. Against his daughter-in-law Tiberius dared not invent similar charges, but attacked her insubordinate language and disobedient spirit. The senate listened in terrified silence. But opportunists can always turn national disasters to advantage, and finally a few men to whom integrity offered no incentives demanded that the question should be put. Marcus Aurelius Cotta Maximus Messallinus was ready enough with a savage proposal. Other leading men, especially officials, felt anxiety. For Tiberius, despite his savage strictures, left his intentions obscure.

One member of the senate, Junius Rusticus, had been chosen by Tiberius to keep its minutes[1] and was believed to understand his secret thoughts. Rusticus had never shown courage before. But fate now impelled him. Or perhaps, in his anxiety about future uncertainties, misplaced cunning blinded him to immediate peril. For Rusticus, joining the hesitant senators, advised the consuls not to put the question. Vital issues depend on a touch, he said – the aged emperor might one day regret the elimination of Germanicus' family. Meanwhile, crowds with statues of Agrippina and Nero Caesar pressed round the senate-house. Cheering Tiberius, they cried that the letter was a fabrication – the emperor could not favour plots to destroy his family!

So on that day there were no tragic developments. Forged attacks on Sejanus circulated, their alleged authors ex-consuls – anonymity lent impudence to many imaginations. This infuriated Sejanus and gave him fresh material for his charges. The senate, he said, had

---

1. The Roman senate's *Hansard* dated from Julius Caesar's first consulship (59 B.C.). Cf. the *acta diurna*, p. 120.

scorned the emperor's distress, and the populace had been disloyal. Rebellious speeches and senatorial decrees were being heard and read. Next they would be seizing arms and hailing as leaders and commanders those whose statues they had followed like standards.

Tiberius again denounced his grandson and daughter-in-law. Then he reprimanded the Roman populace by edict. To the senate he expressed regrets that a single member's duplicity should have resulted in a public affront to the imperial majesty. However, he reserved the entire matter for his own decision. Without further discussion the senate proceeded, not to death sentences (these had been forbidden them), but to protestations that only the emperor's command was restraining their eagerness for vengeance.

[*There is now a gap of two years in our manuscript of Tacitus. First Agrippina, Nero Caesar, and Drusus Caesar are exiled; and Nero Caesar dies. Then Tiberius, believing Sejanus himself (now consul) guilty of conspiracy, has him arrested in the senate and executed. Sejanus' divorced wife Apicata now reveals to Tiberius that his own son Drusus had been poisoned by Sejanus and Livilla; and Livilla too is killed or kills herself.*]

CHAPTER 8

The Reign of Terror

*

FORTY-FOUR speeches were delivered about the punishment of Livilla. A few were prompted by anxiety, most by routine servility. But a partisan of Sejanus defended himself. 'That Sejanus should be disgraced,' he said, 'and my friendship with him become shameful, did not cross my mind. Destinies are reversed! The man who called Sejanus his colleague and son-in-law[1] pardons himself. Everyone else proceeds from humiliating sycophancy to outrageous abuse. Which is the more lamentable, to accuse a friend or to be accused because of him? I do not know! I shall not test whether anybody is cruel or merciful. A free man, undisturbed in conscience, I shall forestall my destruction. Remember me, please, happily, not sorrowfully. Add my name to those who have honourably withdrawn themselves from the harrowing national scene.'

He spent part of the day with his friends. If they wished to stay and talk, he let them. When they left, he bade them farewell. Then, while many still remained, gazing on his unperturbed features and not knowing the end was near, he drew a sword concealed in his clothing and fell upon it. Tiberius did not assail the dead man with the slanders and insults with which he had so savagely attacked Sejanus' uncle, Quintus Junius Blaesus.[2]

Next came the cases of Publius Vitellius and Publius Pomponius Secundus. The former was charged with offering the keys of the Treasury (of which he was controller) and Military Treasury for seditious projects. Pomponius was accused by the former praetor Con-

1. Tiberius had apparently intended to make Sejanus his grandson-in-law (not son-in-law as stated here) by betrothing him to Drusus' daughter Livia Julia.

2. Blaesus had evidently been executed.

sidius of friendship with Aelius Gallus[1] who had sheltered in his garden, as the safest hiding-place, after Sejanus' execution. The only support of Vitellius and Pomponius in this predicament was the fearlessness of their brothers, who went bail for them. But after numerous adjournments Publius Vitellius found his hopes and fears unendurable. Requesting a pen-knife (he wanted to write, he said) he put an end to his distress by a slight incision of his veins. Pomponius, however – a distinguished, high-principled intellectual – patiently endured misfortune, and outlived Tiberius.

The general rage against Sejanus was now subsiding, appeased by the executions already carried out. Yet retribution was now decreed against his remaining children. They were taken to prison. The boy understood what lay ahead of him. But the girl uncomprehendingly repeated: 'What have I done? Where are you taking me? I will not do it again!' She could be punished with a beating, she said, like other children. Contemporary writers report that, because capital punishment of a virgin was unprecedented, she was violated by the executioner, with the noose beside her. Then both were strangled, and their young bodies thrown on to the Gemonian Steps.

At this juncture Asia and Achaia were alarmed by a short-lived but vigorous rumour that Drusus Caesar, Germanicus' son,[2] had been seen in the Cyclades archipelago, and then on the mainland. It was really a youth of similar age whom certain of the emperor's former slaves had seditiously pretended to recognize. Joining him, they collected an ignorant following, attracted by the great name and their Greek taste for novelties and marvels. The story was invented – and instantly believed – that he had escaped from prison and was making for his father's armies, to invade Egypt or Syria. Surrounded by young supporters and enthusiastic crowds, he was delighted with his progress and over-optimistic. The matter was now reported to Gaius Poppaeus Sabinus, imperial governor of Macedonia and also Achaia. Determined to nip the story in the bud – whether it was true or false – he moved rapidly. Hastening past the gulfs of Torone and Thermae, the island of Euboea in the Aegean, and Piraeus in Attica, then landing on the isthmus of Corinth and crossing it, he moved into the Ionian Sea, and proceeded to the Roman colony of Actium near Nicopolis. There

1. Evidently Sejanus' son.
2. He had been confined in the Palatine dungeons at Sejanus' prompting.

he learnt that skilful questioning about his identity had induced the impostor to describe himself as the son of Marcus Junius Silanus (I); and that after losing many of his adherents he had taken ship, ostensibly for Italy. Poppaeus reported this to Tiberius. But I have no further information about the incident, either in its early or its final phases.

At the end of the year, ill-feeling that had long been developing between the consuls found open expression. Lucius Fulcinius Trio, a quarrelsome lawyer, had implied criticism of Publius Memmius Regulus for slackness in suppressing Sejanus' partisans. Regulus, an unassuming man until provoked, not only refuted his colleague but proposed his investigation for complicity in the plot. Many senators begged them to drop this feud with its calamitous prospects. But they persisted in exchanging hostile threats until they went out of office.

When next year's consuls, Cnaeus Domitius Ahenobarbus and Lucius Arruntius Camillus Scribonianus, had assumed their functions, Tiberius crossed the channel between Capreae and Surrentum and coasted along Campania, undecided whether to enter Rome – or determined not to, and therefore pretending that he would. He made frequent landings near the city, and visited Caesar's Gardens on the Tiber. But then he regained his secluded sea-cliffs. For his criminal lusts shamed him. Their uncontrollable activity was worthy of an oriental tyrant. Free-born children were his victims. He was fascinated by beauty, youthful innocence, and aristocratic birth. New names for types of perversion were invented. Slaves were charged to locate and procure his requirements. They rewarded compliance, overbore reluctance with menaces, and – if resisted by parents or relations – kidnapped their victims, and violated them on their own account. It was like the sack of a captured city.

As the year began at Rome, one might have thought Livilla's long-punished crimes newly discovered, so savage were the measures against even her statues and her memory. Sejanus' property was to be withdrawn from the Treasury and transferred to the emperor's personal estate – not that it made any difference. These motions were being pressed in identical or similar language by men with the grand names of Scipio, Silanus, Cassius, when suddenly Togonius Gallus inserted his undistinguished person among them. He proposed that the emperor should be urged to nominate senators from whom twenty should be chosen by lot to protect his life, armed, whenever he entered the senate-house. His speech caused laughter. Evidently he had taken literally Tiberius' request for a consul as bodyguard when he travelled from Capreae to Rome.

Tiberius, who liked to blend seriousness and humour, thanked the senators for their kindness. 'But who among you', he asked, 'are to be included in my bodyguard, and who excluded? Are they always to be the same, or will there be rotation? Will they be junior or senior officials or private persons? And what a sight they will be, putting on their swords at the senate-house door! If my life needs arms to protect it, it does not seem to me worth having.' As regards Togonius the emperor's reply was lenient, no request being made other than the cancellation of the proposal.

Junius Gallio, on the other hand, who had moved that ex-Guardsmen should be entitled to sit in the fourteen rows at the theatre reserved for the knights,[1] was sternly reprimanded. What, wrote Tiberius – as if addressing him to his face – had Gallio to do with the soldiers? They were entitled to receive their orders and rewards from the emperor only. How clever of Gallio to discover something which the divine Augustus had neglected! Or was he an agent of Sejanus fomenting rebellion in simple hearts – seeming to offer privileges, his real aim the subversion of discipline? So the reward for Gallio's careful sycophancy was ejection from the senate immediately, from Italy later. He chose the famous and agreeable island of Lesbos for his exile. But it was protested that life would be too pleasant for him there. So he was dragged back to Rome and lodged in private custody by officials.

Tiberius' letter about Gallio also, to the senate's great satisfaction, assailed the former praetor Sextius Paconianus, an evil, violent rooter-out of secrets. The revelation that Sextius had been Sejanus' chosen participant in his plot against Gaius released pent-up hatreds, and he only escaped the death-sentence by turning informer. When he denounced Lucanius Latiaris, there was the agreeable spectacle of defendant as unpopular as his accuser. Latiaris, as I recorded, was chiefly responsible for the downfall of Titius Sabinus. He was also the first to pay for it.

1. The front fourteen rows in the theatre were reserved for knights by the Roscian law.

While this was under way, Decimus Haterius Agrippa attacked the consuls of the previous year. Why, he asked, after assailing each other with accusations, were they now quiet? Evidently, he observed, mutual fears and bad conscience bound them to silence – but the senate, after what it had heard, could not keep silence. Publius Memmius Regulus replied that he was biding his time for retaliation, and would pursue the matter before the emperor. Lucius Fulcinius Trio suggested that this friction between colleagues, and remarks provoked by their quarrel, had best be forgotten. When Haterius persisted, an ex-consul Quintus Sanquinius Maximus urged the senate not to multiply the emperor's worries by hunting up further troubles – when solutions were needed, the emperor was capable of providing them. This saved Regulus, and postponed Trio's fate. Haterius, a somnolent creature (and, when awake, depraved), was all the more loathsome because, as he over-ate and debauched – too inactive for any imperial atrocity to threaten himself – he plotted the downfall of his betters.

Next, at the first opportunity, Marcus Aurelius Cotta Maximus Messallinus was accused of uttering reflections on Gaius' manliness; of describing a priest's banquet, which he himself had attended on the Augusta's birthday, as a funeral feast; and, when complaining of the influence of Marcus Aemilius Lepidus (IV) and Lucius Arruntius, his opponents in a money-dispute, he was said to have added: 'The senate will back them. My sweet little Tiberius will back me!' The charges were brought home and pressed by outstanding figures; but Cotta appealed to the emperor. Soon afterwards Tiberius wrote to the senate. In self-defence he traced back to its beginning his friendship with Cotta, whose many services he recalled, urging that words maliciously distorted, or loosely uttered at table, should not be regarded as damning evidence.

The opening of Tiberius' letter attracted attention. 'If I know what to write to you at this time, senators,' he said, 'or how to write it, or what not to write, may heaven plunge me into a worse ruin than I feel overtaking me every day!' His crimes and wickedness had rebounded to torment himself. How truly the wisest of men used to assert that the souls of despots, if revealed, would show wounds and mutilations – weals left on the spirit, like lash-marks on a body, by cruelty, lust, and malevolence. Neither Tiberius' autocracy nor isolation could save him from confessing the internal torments which were his retribution.

The senate was then instructed to investigate one of its members, Gaius Caesilianus, who had provided the chief evidence against Cotta. He was condemned to the same penalty as Aruseius and Sangurius, who had accused Lucius Arruntius.[1] This was the climax of Cotta's honours. Beggared (though a nobleman) by extravagance, disgraced by evil-doing, he received the compliment of a vengeance which equated him with the immaculate Lucius Arruntius.

The next defendants were Quintus Servaeus, a former praetor who had been on Germanicus' staff, and a knight called Minucius Thermus. They attracted particular sympathy because both had been friends with Sejanus, and neither had abused the fact. But Tiberius denounced them as leading criminals. He then requested a senator, Gaius Cestius Gallus (I), who had written privately to the emperor, to communicate the contents of his letter to his colleagues. The senator duly prosecuted Servaeus and Thermus before them. It was, indeed, a horrible feature of the period that leading senators became informers even on trivial matters – some openly, many secretly. Friends and relatives were as suspect as strangers, old stories as damaging as new. In the Forum, at a dinner-party, a remark on any subject might mean prosecution. Everyone competed for priority in marking down the victim. Sometimes this was self-defence, but mostly it was a sort of contagion, like an epidemic. In this case the two condemned men turned informer, and two others, Julius Africanus of the Santones tribe in Gaul, and Seius Quadratus, were dragged into the net.

I realize that many writers omit numerous trials and condemnations, bored by repetition or afraid that catalogues they themselves have found over-long and dismal may equally depress their readers. But numerous unrecorded incidents, which have come to my attention, ought to be known. For instance at this juncture, when everyone else was untruthfully disclaiming friendship with Sejanus, a knight called Marcus Terentius bravely accepted the imputation. 'In my position', he observed to the senate, 'it might do me more good to deny the accusation than to admit it. And yet, whatever the results, I will confess that I was Sejanus' friend: I sought his friendship, and was glad to secure it. I had seen him as joint-commander of the Guard with his

1. The earlier reference to this case is missing.

father. Then I saw him conducting the civil as well as the military administration. His kinsmen, his relations by marriage, gained office. Sejanus' ill-will meant danger and pleas for mercy. I give no examples. At my own peril only, I speak for all who took no part in his final plans. For we honoured, not Sejanus of Vulsinii, but the member of the Claudian and Julian houses into which his marriage alliances had admitted him – your future son-in-law, Tiberius, your partner as consul, your representative in State affairs.

'It is not for us to comment on the man whom you elevate above others, and on your reasons. The gods have given you supreme control – to us is left the glory of obeying! Besides, we only see what is before our eyes: the man to whom you have given wealth, power, the greatest potentialities for good and evil – and nobody will deny that Sejanus had these. Research into the emperor's hidden thoughts and secret designs is forbidden, hazardous, and not necessarily informative. Think, senators, not of Sejanus' last day, but of the previous sixteen years. We revered even Satrius Secundus and Pomponius.[1] We thought it grand even if Sejanus' ex-slaves and door-keepers knew us. You will ask if this defence is to be valid for all, without discrimination. Certainly not. But draw a fair dividing-line! Punish plots against the State and the emperor's life. But, as regards friendship and its obligations, if we sever them at the same time as you do, Tiberius, that should excuse us as it excuses you.' This courageous utterance, publicly reflecting everyone's private thoughts, proved so effective that it earned Terentius' accusers, with their criminal records, banishment and execution.

Tiberius next wrote denouncing an intimate friend of his brother Nero Drusus – the former praetor Sextus Vistilius, whom he had transferred to his own entourage. Vistilius was charged, rightly or wrongly, with criticizing Gaius' morals. For this the emperor excluded him from his company. Vistilius made a senile attempt to cut his veins, then bound them up and wrote Tiberius an appeal. But the reply was unrelenting, and he opened them again.

Then five senators, including a father and son Gaius Annius Pollio and Lucius Annius Vinicianus, were bracketed in one comprehensive charge of treason. All were of leading families, some of the highest official rank. Other senators felt extremely nervous. For few of them

1. The earlier reference to these men is missing.

were unrelated by marriage or friendship to such distinguished men. However, two of them, Gaius Appius Junius Silanus and Gaius Calvisius Sabinus, were rescued by the evidence of a commander of a city police battalion, Julius Celsus, who was one of the informers. Tiberius adjourned the other three cases for investigation by himself in consultation with the senate. However, his letter contained ominous allusions to one of the defendants, Mamercus Aemilius Scaurus.

Even women were in danger. They could not be charged with aiming at supreme power. So they were accused of weeping: one old lady, Vitia, was executed for lamenting the death of her son, Gaius Fufius Geminus. The senate decided this case. The emperor, however, sentenced to death two of his oldest friends, Vescularius Flaccus and Julius Marinus, his inseparable companions at Rhodes and Capreae respectively. One had been the emperor's go-between in the plot against Marcus Scribonius Libo Drusus, the other Sejanus' associate in ruining Curtius Atticus. So there was particular satisfaction that their practices had recoiled on themselves.

At about this time, Lucius Calpurnius Piso (I), member of the Pontifical Order, died a natural death – a rare end for one so distinguished. He had never initiated any sycophantic proposal; and in face of irresistible pressure he had showed wise moderation. Son of a man whose censorship I have recorded,[1] he won an honorary Triumph in Thrace, and lived to eighty.

But his particular distinction was the outstanding discretion which he showed as City Prefect. This office was unpopular, and obedience to it grudging, since it had only recently become permanent. Long ago, when kings or later officials left Rome, continuity of government had been ensured by a temporary official to administer the law and meet emergencies. Thus Denter Romulius is said to have been appointed by Romulus, Numa Marcius by Tullus Hostilius, and Spurius Lucretius by Tarquinius Superbus. Subsequently consuls made similar appointments, and a relic still survives in the nomination of a man to act as consul during the Latin Festival. Then in the civil wars the future Augustus entrusted Rome and Italy to a knight, Gaius Maecenas, of the Cilnian family. Later, when Augustus became sole ruler, the size of the population and tardiness of legal remedies induced him to appoint a former consul to discipline the slaves and those other inhabitants who

1. The father-in-law of Julius Caesar. The earlier reference is missing.

need threats of force to keep them in order. The first to receive these powers was Marcus Valerius Messalla Corvinus (I); but he resigned them after a few days, alleging ignorance of their application. Then Titus Statilius Taurus (I), old though he was, had made an excellent Prefect. Finally Lucius Calpurnius Piso (I) occupied the post no less creditably for twenty years. The senate honoured him with a public funeral.

A tribune, Quinctilianus, now consulted the senate about a book of Sibylline oracles. Lucius Caninius Gallus, a member of the Board of Fifteen for Religious Ceremonies, desired the senate to vote its inclusion among the Sibyl's prophecies. The senate agreed without discussion. But Tiberius wrote mildly criticizing the tribune for juvenile ignorance of traditional custom, and reprimanding Caninius. For Caninius' familiarity with religious lore and ritual (the emperor said) should have warned him not to raise the matter in a poorly attended senate, and on unreliable authority; he had not awaited his Board's decision or the usual perusal and consideration by its executive committee. Tiberius also recalled that, because of the many forgeries circulating with the prestige of the Sibyl's name, Augustus had required their notification to the city praetor before a certain date, private retention becoming illegal. (A similar decision had been taken in an earlier generation – after the burning of the Capitol during the Social War[1] – when the poems of the Sibyl, or Sibyls, were collected from Samos, Ilium, Erythrae, and even Africa, Sicily, and Greek settlements in Italy, and the priests were charged to do everything humanly possible to identify authentic examples.) So the collection of oracles recommended by Caninius was duly referred to the Board of Fifteen.

In the same year the high price of corn nearly caused riots. In the theatre, for several days, sweeping demands were shouted with a presumption rarely displayed to emperors. Upset, Tiberius reproved the officials and senate for not using their authority to restrain popular demonstrations. He enumerated the provinces from which he was importing corn – more extensively than Augustus. So the senate passed a resolution of old-fashioned strictness censuring the public. The consuls too issued an equally severe edict. Tiberius was silent.

1. The Capitol was burnt down in 83 B.C., during the war between the Marians and Sulla.

However, this was taken not for modesty as he hoped, but for arrogance.

At the end of the year three knights, Geminius, Celsus and Pompeius, succumbed to charges of conspiracy. Geminius had gained Sejanus' friendship through his extravagance and effeminacy, but no serious offence was involved. Another defendant, the city police colonel Julius Celsus, loosened the chain with which he was bound and looping it round his own throat strained against it until he broke his neck. Rubrius Fabatus was arrested for attempting flight to the mercy of the Parthians – in despair of Rome. Intercepted at the Sicilian Strait and conducted back by a staff-officer, he could not plausibly explain his ambitious travelling plans. However, he was left alive, not pardoned but forgotten.

Tiberius had long been meditating the choice of husbands for his marriageable granddaughters, Julia Livilla and Drusilla. Next year, when the consuls were Servius Sulpicius Galba (II) and Marcus Vinicius, he selected Lucius Cassius Longinus and Marcus Vinicius. Vinicius came from the town of Cales. His father and grandfather had become consuls, the rest of the family were knights. He was mild in character, with an elaborate oratorical style. Cassius came of an ancient and respected, though plebeian, family. Although sternly brought up by his father, he was more conspicuous for pliancy than vigour. To these men, then, Tiberius gave Germanicus' daughters; and he wrote to the senate perfunctorily complimenting the bridegrooms.

Next, after vague excuses for his absence, he turned to graver matters. Emphasizing the enmities he had incurred in the national interest, he requested that whenever he entered the senate a small escort should attend him – including the Guard commander, Quintus Naevius Cordus Sutorius Macro, colonels, and staff-officers. The senate passed a comprehensive resolution without specifying the numbers or composition of this bodyguard. Even so, Tiberius never again entered Rome, much less an official meeting. He often circled round his city by devious routes – only to recoil.

Accusers were now intensely active. Their present targets were men who enriched themselves by usury, infringing the law by which the dictator Julius Caesar had controlled loans and land-ownership in Italy. Since patriotism comes second to private profits, this law had long been ignored. Money-lending is an ancient problem in Rome, and a frequent cause of disharmony and disorder. Even in an earlier, less corrupt society steps had been taken against it. At first, interest had been determined arbitrarily by the rich, but then the Twelve Tables had fixed the maximum at 10 per cent.[1] Next, a tribune's law had halved the rate. Finally loans on compound interest were forbidden completely. Fraudulence, attacked by repeated legislation, was ingeniously revived after each successive counter-measure.

Now, however, the praetor Sempronius Gracchus (II), responsible for the investigation, was compelled by the numbers of potential defendants to refer the matter to the senate. That body – being implicated to a man – nervously entreated the emperor's indulgence. It was granted. Eighteen months were allowed in which all private finances had to be brought into line with the law. The result was a shortage of money. For all debts were called in simultaneously; besides, the many convictions and sales of confiscated property had concentrated currency in the Treasury and its imperially controlled branches. To meet this situation the senate had instructed that creditors should invest two-thirds of their capital in Italy, and debtors immediately pay the same proportion of their debts.

However, creditors demanded payment in full, and debtors were morally bound to respond. The first results were importunate appeals to money-lenders. Next, the praetor's court resounded with activity. The decree requiring land purchases and sales, envisaged as relief, had the opposite effect since when the capitalists received payment they hoarded it, to buy land at their convenience. These extensive transactions reduced prices. But large-scale debtors found it difficult to sell; so many of them were ejected from their properties, and lost not only their estates but their rank and reputation.

Then Tiberius came to the rescue. He distributed a hundred million sesterces among specially established banks, for interest-free three-year state loans, against security of double the value in landed property. Credit was thus restored; and gradually private lenders, too, reappeared. However, land transactions failed to adhere to the provisions of the senatorial decree. As usual, the beginning was strict, the sequel slack.

1. The provision attributed to the Twelve Tables (451–450 B.C.) is elsewhere ascribed to 357 B.C., and the veto on interest to 342 B.C.

Earlier fears now revived. Considius Proculus was accused of treason. While unperturbedly celebrating his birthday, he was dragged to the senate-house, and instantly condemned and executed. His sister Sancia was outlawed. Her accuser was Quintus Pomponius, a neurotic who claimed that he undertook these and similar cases in order to gain the emperor's favour and rescue his brother Publius Pomponius Secundus from danger. Another woman, Pompeia Macrina, was exiled. Tiberius had already ruined her husband and father-in-law, Argolicus and Laco, leading Greeks. Now her father, a distinguished knight, and her brother a former praetor, saw condemnation ahead and killed themselves. Their offence was that the latter's Mytilenean great-grandfather Theophanes had been a close friend of Pompey and had been deified posthumously by sycophantic Greeks. Then Sextus Marius, the richest man in Spain, was thrown from the Tarpeian Rock. The charge was incest with his daughter. But the real cause of his ruin was his wealth. This became clear from Tiberius' personal appropriation of his gold- and copper-mines – though the State was ostensibly their confiscator.

Frenzied with bloodshed, the emperor now ordered the execution of all those arrested for complicity with Sejanus. It was a massacre. Without discrimination of sex or age, eminence or obscurity, there they lay, strewn about – or in heaps. Relatives and friends were forbidden to stand by or lament them, or even gaze for long. Guards surrounded them, spying on their sorrow, and escorted the rotting bodies until, dragged into the Tiber, they floated away or grounded – with none to cremate or touch them. Terror had paralysed human sympathy. The rising surge of brutality drove compassion away.

This was about the time when Gaius, who had accompanied his grandfather to Capreae, received in marriage Junia Claudilla, a daughter of Marcus Junius Silanus (I). A deceitful discretion concealed Gaius' horrible character. His mother's condemnation, his brother's destruction, elicited no word from him. He faithfully reflected Tiberius' daily moods – almost his words. This later prompted the famous epigram by Gaius Sallustius Passienus Crispus[1] that there had never been a better slave or a worse master.

Tiberius' prophecy about the consul Servius Sulpicius Galba (II) deserves mention. After sending for Galba and sounding him in

1. He later married Gaius' sister Agrippina (II) (before she married Claudius).

various fashions Tiberius said to him in Greek: 'You too, Galba, shall one day have a taste of empire.' This prophecy of Galba's late, brief principate was based on Tiberius' knowledge of Chaldaean astrology, taught him at Rhodes by Thrasyllus. He had tested Thrasyllus' knowledge in this way. When seeking occult guidance Tiberius would retire to the top of his house, with a single tough, illiterate former slave as confidant. Those astrologers whose skill Tiberius had decided to test were escorted to him by this man over pathless, precipitous ground; for the house overhung a cliff. Then, on their way down, if they were suspected of unreliability or fraudulence, the ex-slave hurled them into the sea below, so that no betrayer of the secret proceedings should survive.

Thrasyllus, after reaching Tiberius by this steep route, had impressed him, when interrogated, by his intelligent forecasts of future events – including Tiberius' accession. Tiberius then inquired if Thrasyllus had cast his own horoscope. How did it appear for the current year and day? Thrasyllus, after measuring the positions and distances of the stars, hesitated, then showed alarm. The more he looked, the greater became his astonishment and fright. Then he cried that a critical and perhaps fatal emergency was upon him. Tiberius clasped him, commending his divination of peril and promising he would escape it. Thrasyllus was admitted among his closest friends; his pronouncements were regarded as oracular.

When I hear this and similar stories I feel uncertain whether human affairs are directed by Fate's unalterable necessity – or by chance. On this question the wisest ancient thinkers and their disciples differ. Many insist that heaven is unconcerned with our births and deaths – is unconcerned, in fact, with human beings – so that the good often suffer, and the wicked prosper. Others disagree, maintaining that although things happen according to fate, this depends not on astral movements but on the principles and logic of natural causality.

This school leaves us free to choose our lives. But once the choice is made, they warn that the future sequence of events is immutable. Yet in regard to those events they claim that the popular ideas of good and evil are mistaken: many who seem afflicted are happy, if they endure their hardships courageously; others (however wealthy) are wretched, if they employ their prosperity unwisely. Most men, however, find it natural to believe that lives are predestined from birth, that the science of prophecy is verified by remarkable testimonials, ancient and modern; and that unfulfilled predictions are due merely to ignorant impostors who discredit it. Not here – for I must not extend this digression – but in its place I will record the forecast of Nero's reign made by Thrasyllus' son.

In the same year it became known that Gaius Asinius Gallus[1] was dead. He died of starvation – whether self-inflicted or forcible was undiscovered. Tiberius, asked if he would permit the burial of Asinius, unblushingly authorized it, adding his regrets at the circumstances which removed the defendant before investigation by himself. In three years, apparently, no time had been found to try this elderly ex-consul and father of consuls.

The next to perish was Drusus Caesar. For eight days he had staved off death on pitiable nourishment – by gnawing the stuffing of his mattress. It has been suggested that the emperor had ordered Macro, if Sejanus attempted rebellion, to free the youth from the Palatine – where he was incarcerated – and display him to the people as a leader. Later, however, because of rumours that Tiberius had relented towards Drusus Caesar and his mother Agrippina, the emperor's lenient second thoughts were again superseded by severity.

Even when Drusus Caesar was dead, Tiberius attacked him. The charges included immorality, plots to murder his relatives, designs against the government. He also ordered reports of the prince's daily doings and sayings to be posthumously recited. This seemed the supreme cruelty. That agents had stood by Drusus all these years noting every look and groan, even private mutterings; and that his grandfather could have heard, read, and published the whole story, was scarcely credible. Yet there were the reports of a staff-officer of the Guard and an ex-slave, named Attius and Didymus respectively, and in them the names of the slaves who had struck and intimidated Drusus Caesar whenever he tried to leave his room. The officer had even noted his own brutal language – as something creditable.

He also recorded the dying man's words. First, feigning madness, Drusus Caesar had screamed apparently delirious maledictions upon Tiberius. Then, despairing of his life, he had uttered an elaborate and

1. He had been condemned and imprisoned three years earlier.

formal curse: that for deluging his family in blood, for massacring his daughter-in-law, nephew, and grandchildren, Tiberius might pay the penalty due to his house – to his ancestors and descendants. The senators interrupted, as though horrified. What really horrified them – and amazed them – was that one formerly so astute, so secretive a concealer of his crimes as Tiberius should unflinchingly snatch away the prison walls and show his grandson battered by an officer, beaten by slaves, vainly begging the bare necessities of life.

This tragedy was still fresh when news came of Agrippina's end.[1] After Sejanus' death hope, I suppose, was what had kept her alive. But even then her cruel treatment was not mitigated. So she killed herself – unless food was denied so that her death should look like suicide. From Tiberius came an outburst of filthy slanders, accusing her of adultery with Gaius Asinius Gallus, and asserting that she had wearied of living when Asinius died. (Actually, Agrippina knew no feminine weaknesses. Intolerant of rivalry, thirsting for power, she had a man's preoccupations.) It should be recorded, Tiberius continued, that she died on the very day of Sejanus' execution two years earlier. He claimed credit for not having Agrippina strangled or hurled on to the Gemonian Steps. For this, he was voted thanks, and it was resolved that henceforward on every eighteenth of October, the day of both deaths, a sacrifice should be made to Jupiter.

Shortly afterwards Marcus Cocceius Nerva, the emperor's companion, an expert in secular and religious law, decided to die – his position unthreatened, his health sound. When Tiberius heard this he sat beside Nerva, inquired his reasons, and implored him to desist, declaring that his own feelings and reputation would suffer grievously if his most intimate friend chose to die without cause. Nerva declined to speak, and persisted in refusing nourishment. Those who knew his mind asserted that his close sight of Rome's calamities had impelled him, in indignation and terror, to seek an honourable death.

Curiously enough Agrippina's destruction brought down Plancina, widow of Cnaeus Calpurnius Piso. Openly delighting at Germanicus'

---

1. Agrippina (I) and Nero Caesar had been exiled in A.D. 29 to the islands of Pontia and Pandateria respectively. Nero Caesar had been starved to death like his brother.

death, she had been rescued, after Piso's downfall, by the Augusta's intercessions and Agrippina's hostility. Now that her patroness and her enemy were both gone, justice prevailed. Charged with her notorious offences, Plancina met by her own hand her well-deserved, overdue end.

As the country mourned its calamities, it was a contributory grievance that Livia Julia, daughter of Drusus and widow of Nero Caesar, married into the family of Gaius Rubellius Blandus, whose grandfather was widely remembered as a mere knight from Tibur. The last days of the year witnessed the death and state funeral of Lucius Aelius Lamia, who, finally released from his fictitious imperial governorship of Syria,[1] had become City Prefect. Nobly born, vigorous in old age, he had gained in prestige by not being allowed to take up his governorship. Then, on the death of Lucius Pomponius Flaccus who had succeeded Lamia in Syria, a letter was read from Tiberius complaining that every distinguished man capable of commanding an army declined the post, and that he was reduced to entreaties in order to persuade former consuls to accept a province. He forgot that Lucius Arruntius was, for the tenth successive year, being prevented from proceeding to his Spanish governorship.

The death of Marcus Aemilius Lepidus (IV) also occurred in this year. I have already commended on his good sense and wisdom – and his aristocratic origin needs little description. The Aemilii have always produced good Romans. Even the family's bad characters have shared its distinction.

Next year the consuls were Paullus Fabius Persicus and Lucius Vitellius (I). It was now, at the conclusion of an age-long cycle, that the phoenix appeared in Egypt, a remarkable event which occasioned much discussion by Egyptian and Greek authorities.[2] I will indicate the facts on which there is agreement, and certain others which are doubtful but not wholly fantastic. The phoenix is sacred to the sun. Those who have depicted it agree that its head and the markings of its plumage distinguish it from other birds. Regarding the length of its life accounts vary. The commonest view favours 500 years. But some estimate that it appears every 1461 years, and that the three last seen

---

1. Appointed imperial governor of Syria in A.D. 20, he had not been allowed to assume his duties.

2. Other writers place the visit of the phoenix two years earlier.

flew to Heliopolis in the reigns of Sesosis, Amasis, and Ptolemy III (of the Macedonian dynasty) respectively,[1] escorted by numerous ordinary birds astonished by its unfamiliar aspect. Its earliest appearances are unverifiable; but since between Ptolemy and Tiberius there were less than 250 years some have denied the authenticity of the Tiberian phoenix, which did not, they say, come from Arabia or perform the traditionally attested actions. For when its years are complete and death is close, it is said to make a nest in its own country and shed over it a procreative substance – from which rises a young phoenix. Its first function after growth is the burial of its father. This is habitually done as follows. After proving, by a long flight with a load of myrrh, that it is capable of the burden and the journey, it takes up its father's body, carries it to the Altar of the Sun, and burns it. The details are disputed and embellished by myths. But that the bird sometimes appears in Egypt is unquestioned.

At Rome the massacre was continuous. Pomponius Labeo, whose imperial governorship of Moesia I have mentioned, opened his veins and bled to death, followed by his wife Paxaea. Such deaths were readily resorted to. They were due to fears of execution, and because people sentenced to death forfeited their property and were forbidden burial, whereas suicides were rewarded for this acceleration by burial and recognition of their wills. Tiberius, however, wrote to the senate recalling that Romans of earlier days, when excluding someone from their friendship, had terminated relations by forbidding him their houses. That, he said, was what he had done in this case: but Labeo, charged with misgovernment of his province and other offences, had tried to conceal his crime by maliciously implying persecution and unnecessarily alarming his wife, who – though guilty – had been in no danger.

Next came the second indictment of Mamercus Aemilius Scaurus. This aristocratic and eloquent, but dissolute, personage was ruined not by Sejanus' friendship but by the no less lethal enmity of Macro. Stealthily imitating his predecessor, Macro had denounced the sub-ject-matter of a tragedy written by Scaurus, citing verses alleged to

1. These earlier epiphanies are dated to the thirty-third (though most tradi-tions about Sesosis-Sesostris are a millennium later), sixth, and third centuries B.C.

reflect on Tiberius. But the ostensible charges, brought by Servilius and Cornelius, were adultery with Livilla and magic. Scaurus, worthily of the Aemilii of old, anticipated his condemnation, encouraged and joined by Sextia his wife. And yet, when occasion arose, retribution overcame accusers too. The ill-famed destroyers of Scaurus were outlawed and banished to the islands for accepting bribes to drop a charge against Varius Ligur. Likewise an ex-aedile named Abudius Ruso was actually condemned and banned from Rome, while menacing Cnaeus Cornelius Lentulus Gaetulicus (under whom he had commanded a brigade) for having betrothed his own daughter to a son of Sejanus. At this time Gaetulicus commanded the army of Upper Germany. It loved him dearly for his generous kindness and leniency. He was also popular with the neighbouring army of Lucius Apronius, his father-in-law. It was persistently asserted that Gaetulicus had ventured to write to Tiberius. 'My connection with Sejanus,' he was believed to have said, 'was not my idea, but yours. I could be deceived as easily as you. The same mistake could not be considered harmless in some, a capital offence in others. My own loyalty is undiminished and permanent – unless I am plotted against. But I should regard my supersession as a death-warning. Let us strike a bargain – that you rule everywhere else, and I keep my province.'

The story is remarkable. Yet it is corroborated by Gaetulicus' retention – alone among Sejanus' connections – of life and favour. Tiberius knew that he himself, old and unpopular, reigned by prestige more than by actual power.

*

In the next year, when the consuls were Gaius Cestius Gallus (I) and Marcus Servilius Nonianus (II), certain Parthian noblemen visited Rome, unknown to their king Artabanus III. That monarch, while he had Germanicus to fear, had been faithful to Rome and just towards his own people. But then successful warfare against neighbouring nations encouraged him – and he despised Tiberius as old and unwarlike. So Artabanus became insolent to us, and brutal to his subjects. He wanted Armenia, and on the death of its monarch Artaxias III installed his eldest son Arsaces on its throne, sending delegates with an insulting demand for the treasure the exiled King Vonones I had left in Syria and

Cilicia.[1] Artabanus added menacing boasts about the old frontiers of the Persian and Macedonian empires, promising to seize the lands that Cyrus and Alexander had ruled.

The secret Parthian mission to Rome was chiefly inspired by the wealthy nobleman Sinnaces, supported by Abdus, a eunuch (for among orientals that condition, far from being despised, is actually a source of power). Other leading men, too, had been consulted. They could find no one of the Parthian royal house to elevate to the throne – Artabanus had killed many of them, and the rest were minors. So they requested Prince Phraates (son of Phraates IV, a former Parthian king) from Rome. All that was needed, they said, was a name and an authorization: the name of a Parthian royalty – to show himself on the Euphrates – and the authorization of Tiberius. This was what Tiberius wanted. True to his policy of manipulating foreign affairs by astute diplomacy without warfare, he subsidized and equipped Phraates.

Meanwhile Artabanus discovered the conspiracy. Panic and passion for revenge seized him in turn. Though natives regard hesitation as servile, and expect instant action from a king, Artabanus acted prudently. Abdus, invited with ostensible friendliness to dinner, was disabled by a slow poison. Disingenuous tactics, including presents, distracted Sinnaces; and he was kept busy. Then, in Syria, Phraates, abandoning the Roman way of life – to which he had been accustomed for many years – in favour of his Parthian countrymen's customs, could not tolerate these, fell ill, and died.

But Tiberius persevered. Another royal prince, Tiridates III, was selected to dispute Parthia with Artabanus. Simultaneously Mithridates, a brother of Pharasmanes the king of Iberia in the Caucasus, was reconciled with his brother and sent to recover Armenia from Artabanus' son Arsaces. The eastern situation as a whole was entrusted to Lucius Vitellius (I). Though his reputation at Rome was admittedly bad, and much scandalous behaviour was attributed to him, his provincial government showed old-fashioned integrity. But after his recall, fear of Gaius and friendship with Claudius were to make Vitellius so deplorably servile that, to subsequent generations, he is a byword for degraded sycophancy. His first doings are effaced by his last – his youthful distinction by his scandalous later years.

1. Probably an earlier mention of the treasure is missing.

The violent and treacherous princeling Mithridates took the initiative in persuading his brother Pharasmanes to help him recover the Armenian throne. Agents were found to induce the Armenians (at a heavy price) to murder Arsaces. Simultaneously a strong Iberian force broke into Armenia and seized the capital, Artaxata. Artabanus, learning the news, appointed another son Orodes to exact retribution, gave him Parthian troops, and sent representatives to hire auxiliaries.

Pharasmanes responded by enlisting the Albani and calling on the Sarmatians, whose chiefs, as is the national custom, accepted gifts from, and enlisted on, both sides. But the Iberians controlled the strong-points and speedily rushed their Sarmatians over the Caucasian pass into Armenia. They easily blocked those of the Sarmatians who had joined the other side. For the Iberians closed every pass except one, and that one – between the outermost Albanian mountains and the sea – is impassable in summer since the seaboard is flooded by Etesian gales: in winter south winds drive back the water, and the sea's recession drains the shallows.

Orodes, short of allies, was now challenged to fight by the heavily reinforced Pharasmanes. He refused. However, the enemy harassed Orodes, riding close to the camp, plundering his sources of forage, and often virtually blockading him with a ring of outposts. Orodes' Parthians, unaccustomed to such insolence, pressed round him and demanded battle. Their whole strength lay in their cavalry. But Pharasmanes had useful infantry as well as cavalry, since the highland life of the Iberians and Albanians has given them exceptional toughness and endurance. They claim Thessalian origin, dating from the time when Jason, after leaving with Medea and their children, returned to the empty palace of Aeetes and the kingless Colchians. They have many stories about him, and maintain an oracle of Phrixus; and as he is said to have been carried on a ram (whether it was the animal or a ship's figurehead), the sacrifice of rams is forbidden.

When both sides had drawn up their battle-line, Orodes addressed his men, glorifying the Parthian empire and its royal family's grandeur, in contrast with the humble Iberians and their mercenaries. Pharasmanes, however, reminded his troops that they had never submitted to Parthia – the loftier their aspirations, he said, the greater would be the honour of victory, and the disgrace and peril of defeat. Contrasting his own formidable warriors with the enemy in their gold-embroidered robes, he cried: 'Men on one side – on the other, loot!'

Nevertheless, among the Sarmatians, their Iberian commander's was not the only voice. This must not be a bowman's engagement, men shouted; better to rush matters by a charge, and then fight hand-to-hand! So the battle was confused. The Parthian cavalry, expert at withdrawals as well as pursuits, opened ranks to allow themselves room to shoot. But the Sarmatian horsemen on the other side, instead of shooting back – their bows being inferior in range – charged, with pikes and swords. At one moment it was like an orthodox cavalry battle, with successive advances and retreats. Next the riders, interlocked, shoved and hewed at one another. At this juncture, the Albanian and Iberian infantry struck. Gripping hold of the Parthian riders, they tried to unsaddle them. The Parthians were caught between two fires – infantry grappling with them at close quarters, and Sarmatian horsemen attacking them from higher ground.

Pharasmanes and Orodes were conspicuous, supporting the staunchest fighters and rescuing those in trouble. Then they recognized each other and charged. Pharasmanes' onslaught was the more violent, and he pierced the Parthian's helmet and wounded him. But he failed to deliver a second blow, since his horse carried him past; and the wounded man's bravest officers protected him. Still, false reports of Orodes' death were believed; the Parthians were panic-stricken, and conceded victory.

Artabanus then mobilized his kingdom's entire resources for retaliation. But the Iberians had the better of the fighting, since they knew the Armenian terrain. Nevertheless, the Parthians were only induced to retire because Lucius Vitellius concentrated his divisions in a feint against Mesopotamia. Artabanus could not face war against Rome, and he evacuated Armenia. Vitellius then secured his downfall by enticing his subjects to abandon him. For indeed Artabanus was as disastrously unsuccessful in war as he was savage in peace. So Sinnaces, already (as I have mentioned) the enemy of Artabanus, persuaded his own father Abdagaeses to revolt, together with other accomplices encouraged to rebel by continuous Parthian reverses. They were gradually joined by men who had supported Artabanus from fear rather than goodwill and plucked up courage now that leaders had appeared. Soon all that Artabanus had left were his foreign guards, expatriates unconcerned with right and wrong – paid instruments of crime. With these he hastily fled to the remote borders of Scythia, hoping to obtain help from marriage connections among the Hyrcanians and Carmanians of that region. Meanwhile the Parthians – always impatient of present rulers, fond of absent ones – might penitently change their minds.

However, Artabanus had fled, and his countrymen were now inclined for a new king. So Vitellius advised Tiridates III to seize his opportunity, and led the bulk of his regular and auxiliary troops to the Euphrates. There sacrifices were performed. Vitellius offered to Mars the Roman boar, ram, and bull;[1] Tiridates propitiated the river with a finely harnessed horse. Though no rain had fallen, the inhabitants reported a spontaneous and remarkable rise in its waters. Moreover, its white foam seemed to form circles, like diadems, which were said to prophesy a successful crossing. Others offered a shrewder interpretation – the enterprise would prosper at first, but briefly; omens of earth or sky were more reliable, but rivers being fluid no sooner displayed a portent than they obliterated it.

A bridge of boats was constructed, and the army crossed. The first to join them was Ornospades, with a large force of cavalry. Formerly an exile, he had seen distinguished service under Tiberius in the Dalmatian war[2] and received Roman citizenship, and later, restored to his king's friendship and high favour, had become governor of Mesopotamia, the plain enclosed by the famous Tigris and Euphrates. Soon afterwards Tiridates was joined by Sinnaces and Abdagaeses. The latter, the pillar of their cause, brought the court treasure and regalia. Vitellius concluded that his display of Roman might was sufficient. Exhorting Tiridates to remember all the great qualities of his royal grandfather Phraates IV and his imperial foster-father, he urged his supporters to remain loyal to their king, respectful to Rome, and true to their own honour and good faith. Then Vitellius marched his army back to Syria.

I have merged the events of two summers, to allow some respite from Roman miseries. Three years had passed since Sejanus' execution. But influences which soften other hearts – time, entreaties, satiety – did not dissuade Tiberius from punishing disputable, out-

1. This national Roman offering was called the *suovetaurilia*.
2. Tiberius had fought against the Illyrian and Pannonian rebels in A.D. 6–9.

dated offences as though they were fresh and terrible. Lucius Fulcinius Trio, alarmed, escaped imminent prosecution by killing himself. He left a will savagely criticizing Naevius Sutorius Macro and Tiberius' leading ex-slaves, and attacking the emperor himself as a dotard who, by reason of his long absence, was virtually an exile. Fulcinius' heirs wanted this suppressed. But Tiberius had it read to show his toleration of free speech – and indifference to his own reputation. Or perhaps, warned by his long unawareness of Sejanus' crimes, he now favoured publicity for every kind of assertion, so that abuse – failing other methods – should reveal the truth which servility hides.

Further senators now fell. One, Granius Marcianus, accused by Gaius Sempronius Gracchus (II) of treason, committed suicide. A former praetor called Tarius Gratianus was sentenced to death for the same offence. Two others, Titus Trebellenus Rufus and Sextius Paconianus, met similar ends, one killing himself, the other strangled in gaol for verses he had composed there criticizing the emperor. When Tiberius heard of these events he was not, as hitherto, across the sea, receiving messengers from afar, but near the city where he could answer the consuls' letters on the same day – or after a single night – and could almost gaze at the homes deluged in blood, and the executioners at work.

The last days of the year witnessed the death of Gaius Poppaeus Sabinus. Humbly born, he had owed his consulship and honorary Triumph to the friendship of emperors. He had been retained as imperial governor of important provinces for twenty-four years – not for any outstanding talent, but because he was competent and no more.

The following year the consuls were Quintus Plautius and Sextus Papinius Allenius. Tragedies had now become so frequent that the executions of Lucius Aruseius[1] and others caused little shock. Yet it was alarming when the knight Vibulenus Agrippa, after the completion of a hearing against him, drew poison from his clothing, swallowed it in the senate-house itself, collapsed, and was rapidly taken by attendants to prison. There the noose was tightened round his neck – though he was already dead. Not even ex-king Tigranes IV of Armenia was saved by his royal rank from prosecution and the fate common to Roman citizens. The former consul Gaius Sulpicius Galba

1. The name is uncertain. Part of this passage is lost.

and the two sons of Quintus Junius Blaesus[1] died by suicide. Galba had received an ominous letter from Tiberius excluding him from the ballot for governorships. As for the Blaesi, priesthoods destined for them while their family prospered, and deferred when the crash came, had now been treated by Tiberius as vacant and given to others. They saw that this meant death, and acted accordingly. Aemilia Lepida (III), whose marriage with Drusus Caesar I have recorded,[2] had showered slanders on her husband and lived, execrable but unpunished, while her father Marcus Aemilius Lepidus (IV) survived. Now accusers prosecuted her for adultery with a slave. Since her guilt was beyond question, she did not defend herself but committed suicide.

At this period the Cietae, a tribe subject to the Cappadocian prince Archelaus the younger, resisted compulsion to supply property-returns and taxes in Roman fashion by withdrawing to the heights of the Taurus mountains where, aided by the nature of the country, they held out against the prince's unwarlike troops. But the divisional commander Marcus Trebellius, sent by Lucius Vitellius (imperial governor of Syria) with 4,000 regulars and picked auxiliary forces, constructed earthworks round two hills held by the natives (the smaller called Cadra, the larger Davara). After killing some who attempted to break out, Trebellius forced the rest to surrender.

Meanwhile with Parthian approval Tiridates III occupied Mesopotamian towns, including Macedonian foundations (Nicephorium, Anthemusias, and others with Greek names) and some places of Parthian origin (Halus and Artemita). This caused satisfaction among those who loathed the cruelty of the Scythia-bred Artabanus III and hoped Tiridates had been civilized by Roman culture. The supreme sycophancy came from Seleucia on the Tigris, a powerful walled city which, remembering its founder Seleucus, had not decayed into barbarism. Its senate numbers three hundred men, selected for their wealth or intelligence. The public, too, have prerogatives of their own. When senate and public agree, Seleucia despises Parthia. When they disagree, each calls in help against the other, and one side's external helper overwhelms both sides alike. That had recently happened during the reign of Artabanus III. He had sacrificed the public to their

1. They were Sejanus' cousins.
2. The account of the marriage is lost.

leaders; this was in his interests, since democracy approximates to freedom, whereas arbitrary absolutism feels closer to oligarchy.

So the Seleucian people welcomed Tiridates with royal honours, ancient and modern. They abused Artabanus as low-born, being royal on his mother's side only. Tiridates established democratic government at Seleucia. Then however, as he was considering which day to select for his formal accession to the throne, he received letters from two of the most powerful governors, Phraates and Hiero, requesting a brief postponement. It was decided to move to the capital Ctesiphon and there to await these important personages. One deferment followed another, but finally the hereditary commander-in-chief (or Surenas) with traditional ritual, before a large and enthusiastic crowd, crowned Tiridates with the royal diadem.

If he had immediately proceeded to the other peoples in the interior, all waverers' doubts would have vanished and the Parthian empire would have been his. Instead he besieged the fortress in which Artabanus had lodged his treasury and harem. This allowed time for agreements to be broken; and Phraates and Hiero, with others who had not participated in the coronation, went over to Artabanus – some because they feared him, others through jealousy of Abdagaeses (now Court Minister) and Tiridates. Artabanus was discovered in Hyrcania, a grimy figure, eating what his bow procured him. At first, in alarm, he suspected a trap. Convinced, finally, that the aim of their visit was his restoration, he recovered confidence and inquired the cause of this sudden change. Hiero criticized Tiridates as a mere boy, and complained that the power was not in the hands of the royal family: Tiridates had the empty title, but foreign luxury had made him effeminate – and Abdagaeses' family was supreme.

Artabanus' experience of rulership told him that, however spurious their affection, their hatreds were genuine. Waiting only to collect Scythian allies, he took the field – too quickly to allow enemy intrigues, or second thoughts by friends. To enlist popular sympathy, he retained his filthy appearance. Using every means – appeals and menaces alike – to attract waverers and encourage supporters, he approached Seleucia with a large force.

Unnerved by news of his approach, and by his arrival very soon afterwards, Tiridates hesitated. Should he engage Artabanus, or aim at a war of attrition? Those favouring battle and a speedy decision argued that the enemy troops, dispersed and weary after their long march, were not even psychologically united in loyalty to Artabanus – they backed him now, but recently they had betrayed and opposed him. Abdagaeses, however, counselled retreat to Mesopotamia, where, protected by the Tigris, they could first raise the Armenians and other outlying peoples such as the Elymaei, and then, with allied and Roman support, put matters to the test. This advice prevailed. For Abdagaeses was all-powerful – and Tiridates had no taste for danger. But the retirement virtually became a flight. First the Arabians, then the rest, left for their homes – and for Artabanus' camp. Finally Tiridates relieved them from the dishonour of desertion by returning, with a few followers, to Syria.

In the same year there was a serious fire at Rome. The Aventine and adjacent parts of the Circus Maximus were devastated. Tiberius acquired prestige from the calamity by defraying the value of the houses and apartment-blocks destroyed. This generosity cost him one hundred million sesterces. It was all the more popular because his own building activities were slight. His only two public works were the Temple of Augustus and a new stage for Pompey's Theatre – and even these he was too contemptuous of his reputation to dedicate, or too old. To estimate individual losses in the fire, he appointed a commission comprising the husbands of his four granddaughters, Cnaeus Domitius Ahenobarbus, Lucius Cassius Longinus, Marcus Vinicius, and Gaius Rubellius Blandus, with one additional member, Publius Petronius, nominated by the consuls. The emperor was voted every compliment that senators' ingenuity could devise. But his reactions, favourable or negative, were never known. For his end was near.

Shortly afterwards, the last consuls of his reign, Cnaeus Acerronius Proculus and Gaius Petronius Pontius Nigrinus, entered office.

Macro had become excessively powerful. Never neglectful of Gaius' favour, now Macro cultivated him more strenuously every day. After the death of Junia Claudilla – whose wedding with Gaius I recorded elsewhere – Macro induced his own wife Ennia to pretend she loved the prince and entice him into a promise of marriage. Gaius had no objection if it helped him towards the throne. Temperamental though he was, intimacy with his grandfather had taught him dissimulation.

The emperor knew this – and hesitated about the succession. First, there were his grandsons. Drusus' son Tiberius Gemellus was nearer to him in blood, and dearer. But he was still a boy. Gaius was in the prime of early manhood. He was also popular, being Germanicus' son. So his grandfather hated him. Claudius too was considered. He was middle-aged and well-meaning, but his weakmindedness was an objection. Tiberius feared that to nominate a successor outside the imperial house might bring contempt and humiliation upon Augustus' memory and the name of the Caesars. He cared more for posthumous appreciation than for immediate popularity.

Soon, irresolute and physically exhausted, Tiberius left the decision to fate. It was beyond him. Yet, by certain comments, he showed understanding of the future. When he reproached Macro for abandoning the setting for the rising sun, his meaning was clear. And when Gaius, in casual discussion, slighted the memory of Sulla, Tiberius foretold that Gaius would have all Sulla's faults and none of his virtues. Then, weeping bitterly and clasping his grandson Tiberius Gemellus, he said to the frowning Gaius: 'You will kill him! And someone else will kill you!' However, despite failing health, Tiberius did not ration his sensualities. He was making a show of vigour to conceal his illness; and he kept up his habitual jokes against the medical profession, declaring that no man over thirty ought to need advice about what was good or bad for him.

At Rome, meanwhile, were sown the seeds of bloodshed in later reigns. Acutia, the former wife of Publius Vitellius, was charged with treason by Decimus Laelius Balbus. But after her conviction, the proposal to reward her accuser was vetoed by a tribune, Junius Otho – whose downfall the feud thus created ultimately brought about. Then Albucilla, earlier married to Satrius Secundus, who had divulged Sejanus' conspiracy,[1] was denounced for disloyalty to the emperor. She was notorious for her many lovers, and Cnaeus Domitius Ahenobarbus, Gaius Vibius Marsus, and Lucius Arruntius were cited for complicity and adultery with her. Of Ahenobarbus' lineage I have spoken. Marsus too could claim ancient family, as well as literary distinction. Memoranda submitted to the senate indicated that the interrogation of witnesses and torture of the slaves had been supervised

1. He had denounced Sejanus for planning to murder Tiberius and Gaius and seize the throne.

by Macro. But there was reason to suspect that Macro, known to hate Arruntius, had forged much of the evidence.

Perhaps the invalid emperor did not know this. For no instructions came from him. So Ahenobarbus and Marsus were able to stay alive – the former preparing his defence, the latter ostensibly starving himself to death. Arruntius' friends urged him, too, to procrastinate. But his answer was that different things suited different people. 'I have lived long enough', he said. 'My only regret is that insults and perils have made my old age unhappy. Sejanus long hated me; and Macro does now. There is always some powerful figure against me. It is not my fault; it is because I dislike criminality.

'Certainly I might survive the few days until Tiberius dies. But in that case, how can I avoid the young emperor ahead? If Tiberius, in spite of all his experience, has been transformed and deranged by absolute power, will Gaius do better? Almost a boy, wholly ignorant, with a criminal upbringing, guided by Macro – the man chosen to suppress Sejanus, though Macro is the worse man of the two and responsible for more terrible crimes and national suffering. I foresee even grimmer slavery ahead. So from evils past, and evils to come, I am escaping.'

With these prophetic words he opened his veins. What followed showed the wisdom of his death. Albucilla, after unsuccessfully wounding herself, was consigned to prison by the senate. One of her lovers, a former praetor named Carsidius Sacerdos, was deported to an island, another, Pontius Fregellanus, deprived of senatorial rank. But so was her prosecutor Decimus Laelius Balbus – to the general satisfaction, since he was noted for his malignant eloquence, readily utilized against innocent men.

At this time, too, Sextus Papinius – son of a man who had been consul – hurled himself headlong to a sudden and undignified death. The blame fell on his mother. Long divorced, she had indulged his extravagances to a point at which death was his only escape. Charged in the senate, she prostrated herself before the senators and made a long and piteous appeal, pleading especially the anguish which anybody, particularly a weak woman, must feel at a bereavement such as hers. However, she was banned from Rome for ten years, until her younger son had passed the dangerous years of youth.

Tiberius' health and strength were now failing. But his stern will and vigorous speech and expression remained. So did his powers of dissimulation. To conceal his obvious decline, he assumed an affable manner. After numerous moves he settled in a villa on Cape Misenum which had belonged to Lucius Licinius Lucullus. There his end was discovered to be approaching. For an eminent doctor called Charicles, though not employed to treat the emperor's illnesses, had made himself available for consultation. Ostensibly taking his leave to attend to private affairs, he grasped the emperor's hand – and under cover of this respectful gesture felt his pulse. Tiberius noticed, ordered the dinner to be prolonged, and stayed up later than usual. This was allegedly in honour of his departing friend. But he may well have been annoyed, and so taken special pains to conceal his annoyance.

However, Charicles assured Macro that Tiberius was sinking and would not last more than two days. There were conferences, and dispatches to imperial governors and generals, hurriedly making all arrangements. On March 16th the emperor ceased to breathe, and was believed to be dead. Gaius, surrounded by a congratulatory crowd, issued forth to begin his reign. But then it was suddenly reported that Tiberius had recovered his speech and sight, and was asking for food to strengthen him after his fainting-fit. There was a general panic-stricken dispersal. Every face was composed to show grief – or unawareness. Only Gaius stood in stupefied silence, his soaring hopes dashed, expecting the worst. Marco, unperturbed, ordered the old man to be smothered with a heap of bed-clothes and left alone.

So Tiberius died, in his seventy-eighth year. The son of Tiberius Claudius Nero, he was a Claudian on both sides (his mother was successively adopted into the Livian and the Julian families). From birth he experienced contrasts of fortune. After following his proscribed father into exile, he entered Augustus' family as his stepson – only to suffer from many competitors, while they lived: first Marcellus and Agrippa, then Gaius Caesar and Lucius Caesar. His own brother Nero Drusus was more of a popular favourite. But Tiberius' position became most delicate of all after his marriage to Augustus' daughter Julia (III). For he had to choose between enduring her unfaithfulness or escaping it. He went to Rhodes. When he returned, he was undisputed heir in the emperor's home for twelve years. Then he ruled the Roman world for nearly twenty-three.

His character, too, had its different stages. While he was a private citizen or holding commands under Augustus, his life was blameless; and so was his reputation. While Germanicus and Drusus still lived, he concealed his real self, cunningly affecting virtuous qualities. However, until his mother died there was good in Tiberius as well as evil. Again, as long as he favoured (or feared) Sejanus, the cruelty of Tiberius was detested, but his perversions unrevealed. Then fear vanished, and with it shame. Thereafter he expressed only his own personality—by unrestrained crime and infamy.

PART TWO

CLAUDIUS AND NERO

CHAPTER 9

The Fall of Messalina

★

[*The manuscript breaks off at the death of Tiberius, and Tacitus' description of the four years' reign of the unbalanced Gaius (Caligula) is lost. So is his account of the first six years of Gaius' successor and uncle Claudius. Claudius has married his own cousin Messalina (his third wife). Their children are Octavia and Britannicus, who are about six and five respectively when Tacitus' surviving narrative is resumed. Poppaea Sabina is a wealthy and fashionable beauty of whom Messalina is jealous.*]

MESSALINA believed that Decimus Valerius Asiaticus, twice consul, had been Poppaea Sabina's lover. Messalina also coveted the park which had been begun by Lucius Licinius Lucullus, and which Asiaticus was beautifying with exceptional lavishness. So she directed Publius Suillius Rufus to prosecute both of them. He was to be associated in this with Britannicus' tutor, Sosibius. The task of the ostensibly well-meaning tutor was to warn Claudius to beware of another's power – of resources too formidable for an emperor's comfort. 'Asiaticus', declared Sosibius, 'was the principal instigator of the murder of Gaius! At an Assembly meeting he fearlessly admitted the crime, and claimed glory for it. So he is famous at Rome. Moreover, rumours throughout the provinces tell of a projected visit to the armies of Germany. For his birth at Vienna in Gaul, and his powerful connections in that country, make it easy for him to rouse his own people's tribes.'[1]

Without further inquiry Claudius sent the commander of the Guard, Rufrius Crispinus, with enough troops to suppress a rebellion.

---

1. Asiaticus came from Vienne (S. France). There is no evidence that he participated in Gaius' murder; he said he wished he had. His Gardens of Lucullus were on the Pincian Hill.

Proceeding at full speed, Crispinus found Asiaticus at Baiae and took him to Rome in chains. Refused access to the senate, Asiaticus was examined in a bedroom, with Messalina present. Publius Suillius Rufus accused him of corrupting the army and using bribes and sexual entanglements to commit the soldiers to unbounded atrocities. Adultery with Poppaea Sabina was a supplementary charge. Another was effeminacy. At this accusation the prisoner found his voice. 'Ask your sons, Suillius,' he said. 'They will confirm my masculinity.'

Then Asiaticus began his defence. It greatly moved Claudius – and even extracted tears from Messalina. She left the room to dry them, warning Lucius Vitellius (I) not to let the defendant elude her. Then she rapidly organized Poppaea Sabina's destruction. Agents were suborned to threaten Poppaea with imprisonment, and thus terrorize her into suicide. Claudius knew nothing of this. When Poppaea's husband Publius Cornelius Lentulus Scipio (I) was dining with him a few days later, the emperor asked him why he had come without his wife. The answer was that she was dead.

Lucius Vitellius, asked by Claudius whether he thought Asiaticus should be acquitted, first tearfully recalled their long friendship and partnership in devotion to the emperor's mother, Antonia (II). Then, reviewing Asiaticus' public services – including recent military activity against the British – and every other mitigating consideration, Vitellius urged that he should be allowed to choose his own death. Claudius' decision was to the same merciful effect. Asiaticus' friends recommended to him the unforcible method of self-starvation, but he proposed to dispense with that favour. After gymnastic exercises as usual, he bathed and dined cheerfully. Then, remarking that it would have been more honourable to die by the wiles of Tiberius or the violence of Gaius than by a woman's intrigues and Vitellius' obscene tongue, he opened his veins. First, however, he inspected his pyre and ordered it to be moved so that the flames should not damage the foliage of the trees. For he remained calm to the end.

The senate was then summoned, and Publius Suillius Rufus proceeded to add to the list of accused personages two distinguished knights of the name of Petra. The real reason for their deaths was the supposition that they had lent their house as a meeting-place for the ballet-dancer Mnester (I)[1] and Poppaea Sabina. But the ostensible

1. A former slave in the imperial service.

charge against one of the two men was a dream in which he had seen Claudius wearing a wheaten wreath with inverted ears.[1] This Petra had interpreted as portending a corn shortage. The wreath was otherwise described as of whitening vine leaves, predicting the emperor's death in the autumn. In any case, it was certainly some dream which destroyed him and his brother.

One and a half million sesterces, and an honorary praetorship, were voted to Rufrius Crispinus. Lucius Vitellius proposed the award of a further million to Sosibius for helping Britannicus with his instruction and Claudius with his advice. Publius Cornelius Lentulus Scipio (I), asked for his opinion, answered: 'Since I share the general view about Poppaea Sabina's misdeeds, take it that I say what everyone says' – a graceful compromise between husbandly love and senatorial compulsion.

Now Suillius continued his prosecutions with unremitting ferocity. Moreover, his unscrupulousness had many imitators. For the emperor's absorption of all judicial and magisterial functions had opened up extensive opportunities for illicit gain. The most readily purchasable commodity on the market was an advocate's treachery. One distinguished knight named Samius fell on his sword at Suillius' house after paying him four hundred thousand sesterces and then finding Suillius was in collusion with the other side.

After this the senators, led by the consul-designate Gaius Silius (II) (whose power and downfall I shall describe in the appropriate place), rose and demanded enforcement of the ancient Cincian law[2] forbidding the acceptance of money or gifts for legal services. Those affected by the measure protested. Silius, however, violently assailed Suillius – whom he hated. Silius recalled the ancient orators who had wanted no rewards for their eloquence except present and future fame. 'What would otherwise be the first and finest of talents', he said, 'is defiled by mercenary hire – an eye on profits means double-dealing. If no one paid a fee for lawsuits, there would be less of them! As it is, feuds, charges, malevolence, and slander are encouraged. For just as physical illness brings revenue to doctors, so a diseased legal system enriches advocates. Remember that the great orators reached the top

1. Claudius' accession in A.D. 41 had been at a time of serious corn shortage, which he took vigorous steps to meet.
2. The law dated from 204 B.C. and had been revived by Augustus.

of their profession without degrading themselves or their eloquence.'
And he cited Gaius Asinius Pollio (I) and Marcus Valerius Messalla
Corvinus (I), and among later figures Lucius Arruntius and Marcus
Claudius Marcellus Aeserninus.

This speech by the consul-designate was applauded, and a motion
was prepared inculpating offenders under the extortion law. Suillius
and Cossutianus Capito, and others like them, saw that this meant not
just trial – they were obviously guilty – but punishment. So they
flocked round Claudius urging forgiveness of the past. Allowed to
plead their case, they argued that advocates, like anyone else, cannot
just hope for eternal fame: they have to work to meet people's practical
needs, and ensure that nobody succumbs to a powerful litigant through
lack of an advocate.

'But eloquence', they added, 'is not acquired for nothing. To attend
to other people's affairs means neglecting one's own. Other senators
often earn their living by military service, or agriculture. No calling
attracts candidates unless they can reckon its emoluments beforehand.
It was easy for men like Gaius Asinius Pollio (I) and Marcus Valerius
Messalla Corvinus (I), gorged with the spoils of Augustus' war with
Antony, or for men such as Marcus Claudius Marcellus Aeserninus
and Lucius Arruntius, the heirs of wealthy families, to appear high-
minded. Besides, one can equally point to former orators like Publius
Clodius and Gaius Scribonius Curio[1] who received huge fees for
speeches. We, however, are senators of moderate means who, in a
peaceful state, only seek peace-time incomes. Besides, think of the
humble people who win distinction by pleading. Remove a profession's
incentives, and the profession perishes.' Less idealistic though these
arguments were, Claudius saw some point in them. He decided to
establish a maximum fee of ten thousand sesterces: those who accepted
more were to be guilty of extortion.

At this period Mithridates, whose accession to the Armenian throne
and imprisonment by Gaius[2] I have mentioned, returned to his kingdom with Claudius' encouragement, backed by the resources of his

1. Notorious politicians of the last years of the Republic.
2. Gaius had evidently recalled Mithridates and allowed Roman suzerainty
over Armenia to lapse. The struggle between Vardanes and Gotarzes took place
during the early years of Claudius' reign.

brother Pharasmanes, king of Iberia. The latter had reported that, since Parthia was again plunged in civil war, all lesser matters there were neglected in the fight for supremacy. For the king of Parthia Gotarzes II, among many other atrocities, had had one of his own brothers, Artabanus by name, murdered, together with his wife and son. So the other Parthians, alarmed, called in a further brother, Vardanes. Vardanes, always ready for adventures, covered 350 miles in two days,[1] routed the unsuspecting and panic-stricken Gotarzes, and speedily occupied the adjacent provinces. Only Seleucia on the Tigris refused homage. Less for immediate advantage than from irritation (it had deserted his father Artabanus III too), Vardanes involved himself in a siege of this powerful and well-provisioned city, with its protections of river and walls. Meanwhile Gotarzes, mobilizing reinforcements among the Dahae and Hyrcanians, renewed the struggle. Vardanes was forced to raise the siege, and withdrew to Bactria.

This major disunion in the east, and its uncertain outcome, gave Mithridates his chance of seizing Armenia. While Roman troops actively reduced mountain fortresses, Iberian forces overran the plains. The Armenians unsuccessfully risked an engagement under Demonax, and then laid down arms. Some delay was caused by Cotys, the king of Lesser Armenia, to whom certain Armenian leaders had turned. However, a letter from Claudius restrained him, and Mithridates established himself. But his severity was inadvisable for a new monarch.

The rival Parthian leaders were preparing for battle when Gotarzes II discovered a conspiracy among their followers – and revealed it to Vardanes. Thereupon the two brothers abruptly concluded a truce. Their first meeting was hesitant. But then they clasped hands and swore, over the altars of the gods, to punish the treachery of their enemies and achieve a compromise with each other. Vardanes was thought the more suitable to be king. Gotarzes, to avoid rivalry, withdrew into remote Hyrcania. Vardanes returned to Seleucia, which surrendered. Its revolt had lasted seven years. This prolonged defiance by one city had humiliated the Parthians.

Vardanes then toured the principal provinces. He was also enthusiastic to visit Armenia, but was checked by a threat of war from the imperial governor of Syria, Gaius Vibius Marsus. Meanwhile

1. The speed of Vardanes' progress is hardly credible for a large cavalry force.

Gotarzes had regretted giving up the throne. Invited back by the nobles – who find subordination particularly intolerable in peace-time – he collected an army. Vardanes marched against him and won a hard-fought battle at a crossing of the river Barferush. Then, by a series of further successes, he reduced one tribe after another up to the river Tedzhen, the frontier between the Dahae and Arii.

Finally, however, his conquests ended because the Parthians, though victorious, disliked distant service. So, after erecting monuments glorifying his power and the subjection of peoples never before under Parthian monarchs, Vardanes returned home. But his triumphs had made him more overbearing and autocratic. So, while unsuspectingly out hunting, he was assassinated. He was still very young; yet in renown he would have had few equals, however long-lived, if only he had sought to inspire as much affection in his people as terror in his enemies.

The murder of Vardanes created anarchy among the Parthians, who were divided concerning his successor. Many wanted Gotarzes II, others a descendant of King Phraates IV called Meherdates who was in our hands as a hostage. Gotarzes prevailed, and occupied the palace. But his cruelty and dissipation impelled the Parthians to dispatch a secret appeal to the Roman emperor, urging that Meherdates should be released to assume the crown of his forefathers.

This year being the eight hundredth since Rome's foundation, Secular Games were celebrated, sixty-four years after those of Augustus. The calculations undertaken by the two emperors I omit, since they have been sufficiently described in my account of Domitian's reign.[1] For he too celebrated Secular Games, with which I was closely concerned as a member of the Board of Fifteen for Religious Cere-monies and praetor for the year. I mention this not from vanity but because these celebrations have since ancient times been administered by the Board, special responsibility for the ceremonies falling to those of its members who are officials.

The Games held by Claudius included performances in the Circus, where in the emperor's presence youthful horsemen of noble birth performed the Troy Pageant.[2] Among them were the emperor's son

1. Tacitus wrote about Domitian's reign in the lost books of his *Histories*.
2. The 'Troy Pageant' was a cavalry 'field day' for young noblemen, with ritual movements. This was one of the ancient institutions revived by Augustus.

Britannicus and Lucius Domitius Ahenobarbus, soon to be adopted heir to the throne with the name of Nero. The greater applause received by the latter was regarded as prophetic. A further story, that in his infancy serpents had watched over him, was a fable adapted from foreign miracle-tales. Nero himself – who was not over-modest – used to say that just one snake had been seen in his bedroom.

His popularity was an inheritance from Germanicus, of whom he was the only surviving male descendant. Moreover, pity was increasingly felt for his mother Agrippina (II), owing to her persecution by Messalina. The latter, always Agrippina's enemy and now particularly virulent, was only distracted from launching prosecutions and prosecutors by a new and almost maniacal love affair. She was infatuated with the best-looking young man in Rome, Gaius Silius (II). Forced by Messalina to divorce his aristocratic wife Junia Silana – so that her own adulterer should be disengaged – Silius realized the scandal and the peril. But refusal meant certain death. Besides, there was some hope of avoiding detection. And the affair was lucrative. So, banishing thoughts of the future, he took comfort and enjoyment from the present. Messalina, spurning secrecy, repeatedly visited his house with numerous attendants, clung to him when he went out, showered wealth and distinction upon him. Finally, as though the empire had changed hands, there were to be seen in her lover's home imperial slaves and ex-slaves and furniture.

Claudius, unaware of his matrimonial complications, was busy with the functions of censor. A former consul and playwright Publius Pomponius Secundus, and high-ranking ladies, had been insulted in the theatre: the emperor issued edicts sternly rebuking audiences for their unruliness. He also passed a law against harsh treatment of debtors, forbidding loans to minors for repayment after their fathers' deaths. Claudius next ordered the construction of an aqueduct to convey streams from the Simbruine hills into Rome. Then, influenced by the discovery that even the Greek alphabet was a gradual creation, he introduced and popularized new Latin characters.

The first people to represent thoughts graphically were the Egyptians with their animal-pictures. These earliest records of humanity are still to be seen, engraved on stone. They also claim to have discovered the alphabet and taught it to the Phoenicians, who, controlling the seas, introduced it to Greece and were credited with inventing what they had really borrowed. The story is that Cadmus, arriving with a Phoenician fleet, taught the still uncivilized Greeks how to write. According to other accounts, Cecrops of Athens, or Linus of Thebes, or Palamedes of Argos in the Trojan war, invented sixteen letters, the rest being introduced later, notably by Simonides.[1] In Italy, the Etruscans learnt writing from Demaratus the Corinthian,[2] the Aborigines from Evander the Arcadian.[3] The Latin characters resemble those of the earliest Greeks. Their letters, like ours, were originally few, and subsequently increased – thus affording Claudius a precedent. However, after employment in his reign the three letters that he invented became obsolete. But they can still be seen on bronze inscriptions in public squares and temples.

Claudius then proposed to the senate the establishment of a Board of Soothsayers. 'This oldest Italian art', he said, 'ought not to die out through neglect. The advice of soothsayers, consulted in time of disaster, has often caused the revival and more correct subsequent observance of religious ceremonies. Moreover leading Etruscans, on their own initiative – or the Roman senate's – have kept up the art and handed it down from father to son. Now, however, public indifference to praiseworthy accomplishments has caused its neglect; and the advance of foreign superstitions has contributed to this. At present all is well. But gratitude for divine favour must be shown by ensuring that rites observed in bad times are not forgotten in prosperity.' So the senate decreed that the priests should consider which institutions of the soothsayers required upkeep or support.

In the same year the tribe of the Cherusci asked Rome for a king. Civil wars having annihilated their nobility, the only surviving royal prince was Italicus, son of Flavus (Arminius' brother) and of a daughter of Actumerus, chief of the Chatti. Italicus was kept at Rome – a handsome man, trained to fight and ride in both German and Roman style. Claudius subsidized him, provided an escort, and encouraged him to enter upon his heritage, adding that Italicus was the first man

1. The lyric and elegiac poet of Ceos (c. 556–468 B.C.).
2. Livy represents Demaratus, 'tyrant' of Corinth, as the father of the Roman king Tarquinius Priscus (traditionally sixth century B.C.).
3. According to Virgil, Evander was king of the Palatine when Aeneas arrived in Rome.

born at Rome as a citizen – not a hostage – to proceed to a foreign throne.

At first the Germans welcomed him. Free of partisanships, he favoured all equally, and gained prestige and respect – sometimes by the generally popular qualities of affability and moderation, more often by the drunkenness and lustfulness which natives admire. His reputation reached neighbouring states, and beyond. But men who had found disunion profitable envied his power. 'Rome is encroaching,' they said to the adjacent communities which they sought out. 'Germany's ancient freedom is being destroyed. Is there really no home-born person eligible for the kingship? Do we have to give first place to the son of Flavus, a mere Roman military policeman? It is no good talking of Arminius. Even if his own son had returned to reign after growing up in enemy country, there would be reason to fear the contagion of foreign upbringing, slave-labour, dress, and everything else. Besides, if Italicus takes after his father, no one ever fought against his own country and its god more violently than Flavus did!'

Such arguments attracted numerous supporters. Italicus' following, however, was just as large. He reminded them that he had not intruded against their will, but had been invited because his birth made him pre-eminent. A test of his courage, he added, would find him worthy of his uncle and grandfather – and he was not ashamed of his father, who had steadfastly maintained obligations to Rome which he had entered with German approval: the word 'freedom' was hypocritically put foward by low characters whose politics were a menace and whose only hope was national disunion.

These assertions were enthusiastically applauded. There followed a battle – important by native standards – which Italicus won. But success made him arrogant, and he was ejected. Subsequently, with the backing of the Langobardi, he was restored. But in good and bad fortune alike he proved disastrous to the Cherusci.

At this period the Chauci, free from internal dissension, took advantage of the death of the imperial governor of Lower Germany, Quintus Sanquinius Maximus, to raid that province before his successor Cnaeus Domitius Corbulo (II) arrived. Their commander was Gannascus of the tribe of the Canninefates, an auxiliary deserter and now a pirate with small ships plundering, in particular, the Gallic coast, which he knew to be both wealthy and unwarlike. On arrival

in the province Corbulo's careful methods soon won him the fame
that dates from this campaign. Bringing up warships by the main
channel of the Rhine, and other craft (according to their build) by
creeks and canals, he sank the enemy's boats and ejected Gannascus.[1]

His Roman soldiers were enthusiastic looters but slack and reluctant workers. So, when the immediate situation was remedied,
Corbulo revived traditional standards of discipline. Falling out on the
march, and fighting without orders, were prohibited. Picket and sentry
duty – all tasks day and night – were performed under arms. One
soldier is said to have been executed for digging at the earthwork without side-arms, another for wearing his dagger only. These stories are
exaggerated, and perhaps invented. But Corbulo's strictness inspired
them; and a man credited with such severity over details must have
been vigilant and, for serious offences, inexorable.

The terror he caused had opposite effects on our men and the Germans. It made the Romans better soldiers, and weakened the morale
of the natives. The Frisians, hostile or disloyal since the revolt they
had launched by defeating Lucius Apronius, gave hostages and settled
on lands delimited by Corbulo. He also allocated to them a senate,
officials, and laws – and constructed a fort to ensure obedience.

Then Corbulo sent agents to induce the Greater Chauci (the eastern
branch) to surrender, and to trap and kill Gannascus. The trap was
successful. Being directed against a deserter who had broken faith, it
was not dishonourable. Yet it upset the Chauci, and provoked them
to rebellion. Some Romans welcomed this policy, others deplored it.
'Why provoke the enemy?' they said. 'If he fails, Rome will be the
loser. If he wins, such a distinguished soldier will offend the inactive
emperor – and so endanger peace.'

And indeed Claudius forbade further aggression against the Germans, and even ordered the withdrawal of our garrisons to the west
bank of the Rhine. These instructions took Corbulo by surprise. He
received them when he was already building a camp in enemy
country. Many consequences crowded into his mind – peril from the
emperor, scorn from the natives, ridicule from provincials. However,
his only comment was: 'Earlier Roman commanders were fortunate!'
Then he sounded the retreat. But to keep the troops occupied he made

1. The ships of Cnaeus Domitius Corbulo (II) belonged to the Rhine fleet
created by Nero Drusus.

them dig a twenty-three-mile Meuse–Rhine canal, to bypass the hazards of the North Sea.

Though he had forbidden the war, Claudius awarded Corbulo an honorary Triumph. Soon afterwards the same honour was awarded in Upper Germany to Curtius Rufus. He had sunk a mine in the territory of the Mattiaci to find silver. Its products were scanty and short-lived, though the troops suffered and toiled, digging channels and doing underground work which would have been laborious enough in the open. This forced labour covered several provinces. Worn out by it, the men secretly appealed to the emperor, in the name of all the armies, begging him to grant honorary Triumphs to commanders *before* giving them their armies.

Some said Curtius Rufus was a gladiator's son. I do not want to lie about his origin but would be embarrassed to tell the truth. When he grew up he had been employed by the assistant to the governor of Africa. At Hadrumetum, while he was strolling alone at midday in a deserted colonnade, a female figure of superhuman stature appeared to him and said: 'Rufus, you will come to this province as governor.' Encouraged by the omen he left for Rome, where his energetic personality, aided by subsidies from friends, won him the quaestorship. Then, defeating noble competitors, he became praetor. Tiberius backed him, palliating his inglorious birth with the remark 'Curtius Rufus' achievements are paternity enough.' Surly though cringing to his superiors, bullying to his inferiors, ill at ease with his equals, Curtius lived to an advanced age, gained the consulship, an honorary Triumph, and finally the governorship of Africa – where, his destiny fulfilled, he died.

Meanwhile at Rome a knight called Cnaeus Nonius was found wearing a sword at the emperor's morning reception. No motive became evident, then or later. Under torture, he did not deny his guilt. But he revealed no accomplices; whether he had any to hide is unknown.

In the same year Publius Cornelius Dolabella (II) proposed that an annual gladiatorial display should be defrayed by the quaestors. Offices had traditionally been the reward of merit, and every respectable citizen, however young, could stand for them. There had been no lower age-limit for consulships or dictatorships. The quaestorship had been founded in the regal period, as is shown by Lucius Junius Brutus'

restatement of the Assembly's original law.¹ Selection remained with
the consuls until this and other offices passed to popular vote. The first
quaestors to be appointed by the new method – sixty-three years after
the expulsion of the Tarquins – were Valerius Potitus and Aemilius
Mamercus (to supervise the war-chest). Then, as business increased,
two more quaestors were added for duties at Rome. Soon, with
taxes coming in from Italy and the provinces, the number was again
doubled. Next, twenty more were appointed by Sulla – to enlarge
the senate, which he had invested with criminal jurisdiction. Later
these judicial functions were recovered by the order of knights. Yet,
even after that, quaestorships still depended not on payment but on
merit and popularity. But Dolabella's proposal virtually put them up
for auction.

In the following year the consuls were Aulus Vitellius and Lucius
Vipstanus Poplicola. During debates that were now held about enlarging the senate, the chief men of 'long-haired' (northern and central)
Gaul² – belonging to tribes with long-standing treaties with Rome, of
which they themselves were citizens – claimed the right to hold office
in the capital. The question aroused much discussion, and the opposing
arguments were put to the emperor.

'Italy is not so decayed', said some, 'that she cannot provide her
own capital with a senate. In former times even peoples akin to us
were content with a Roman senate of native Romans only; and the
government of those days is a glorious memory. To this day, people
cite the ancient Roman character for their models of courage and
renown.

'Is it not enough that Venetian and Insubrian Gauls³ have forced
their way into the senate? Do we have to import foreigners in hordes,
like gangs of prisoners, and leave no careers for our own surviving

1. The Republic is described as having inherited from the kings, on their
expulsion (traditionally 510 B.C.), its legislation governing the offices of state.
The quaestorship (now believed to be of Republican origin) became elective in
447 B.C.
2. The tribes of northern and central Gaul (Gallia Comata – 'long-haired'
Gaul as opposed to the Romanized area of Narbonese Gaul in the south) possessed privileged ('federated') treaty relationship with Rome. Leading individual
Gauls were Roman citizens.
3. The Venetians and Insubrians represent the Gallic peoples of northernmost
Italy given Roman citizenship by Julius Caesar (49 B.C.).

ed together in formal marriage – 'for the purpose of rearing
dren'; that she should have listened to the diviners' words,
med the wedding-veil, sacrificed to the gods; that the pair
uld have taken their places at a banquet, embraced, and finally
nt the night as man and wife. But I am not inventing marvels.
hat I have told, and shall tell, is the truth. Older men heard and
corded it.

The imperial household shuddered – especially those in power, with
verything to fear from a new emperor. There were secret conferences. Then indignation was unconcealed. 'While a ballet-dancing
actor violated the emperor's bedroom', they said, 'it was humiliating
enough. Yet it did not threaten Claudius' life. Here, on the other
hand, is a young, handsome, intelligent nobleman, consul-to-be – but
with a loftier destiny in mind. For where such a marriage will lead is
clear enough.' When they thought of Claudius' sluggish uxoriousness, and the many assassinations ordered by Messalina, they were
terrified. Yet the emperor's very pliability gave them hope. If they
could convince him of the enormity of the outrage, Messalina might
be condemned and eliminated without trial. But everything, they felt,
turned on this – would Claudius give her a hearing? Could they
actually shut his ears against her confession?

Callistus, who has already been mentioned in connection with
Gaius' murder, Narcissus, who had contrived the death of Gaius
Appius Junius Silanus,[1] and Pallas, who was now basking in the
warmest favour, conferred together.[2] They discussed whether, pretending ignorance of everything else, they could secretly frighten
Messalina out of her affair with Silius. But this scheme was abandoned
by Pallas and Callistus as too dangerous for themselves. Pallas' motive
was cowardice. Callistus had learnt from his experience dating from
the previous reign that power was better safeguarded by diplomatic
than by vigorous methods. Narcissus, however, persevered in taking
action – with this new feature: she was to be denounced without

1. The assassination of Gaius (performed by Gaius Cassius Chaerea) and the
execution of Messalina's stepfather Gaius Appius Junius Silanus under Claudius
were described in the lost part of Tacitus' work.
2. The reign of Claudius witnessed an unprecedented increase in the power of
the great secretaries of state, ex-slaves such as Narcissus (Secretary-General),
Pallas (Financial Secretary), and Callistus (Petitions Secretary).

aristocracy, or for impoverished senators from Latium? Every post
will be absorbed by the rich men whose grandfathers and great-
grandfathers commanded hostile tribes, assailed our armies in battle,
besieged the divine Julius Caesar at Alesia.[1] Those are recent memories.
But are we to forget our men who, beside Rome's Capitoline citadel,
were killed by the ancestors of these very Gauls?[2] Let them, by all
means, have the title of Roman citizens. But the senate's insignia, the
glory of office, they must not cheapen.'

These and similar arguments did not impress Claudius. He contradicted them on the spot, and then summoned the senate and made this
speech:[3]

'The experience of my own ancestors, notably of my family's
Sabine founder Clausus who was simultaneously made a Roman citizen
and a patrician, encourage me to adopt the same national policy, by
bringing excellence to Rome from whatever source. For I do not
forget that the Julii came from Alba Longa, the Coruncanii from
Camerium, the Porcii from Tusculum; and, leaving antiquity aside,
that men from Etruria, Lucania, and all Italy have been admitted into
the senate; and that finally Italy herself has been extended to the Alps,
uniting not merely individuals but whole territories and peoples under
the name of Rome.

'Moreover, after the enfranchisement of Italy across the Po, our
next step was to make citizens of the finest provincials too: we added
them to our ex-soldiers in settlements throughout the world, and by
their means reinvigorated the exhausted empire. This helped to stabilize peace within the frontiers and successful relations with foreign
powers. Is it regretted that the Cornelii Balbi immigrated from Spain,
and other equally distinguished men from southern Gaul? Their
descendants are with us; and they love Rome as much as we do. What
proved fatal to Sparta and Athens, for all their military strength, was
their segregation of conquered subjects as aliens. Our founder Romulus, on the other hand, had the wisdom – more than once – to transform

1. The site of Julius Caesar's defeat of Vercingetorix in 52 B.C.
2. The traditional date of the destruction of Rome by the Senones was 390
B.C.
3. Claudius' speech has survived on a bronze tablet preserved at Lyon.
Tacitus does not reproduce it exactly or faithfully, but brings out the main
points.

whole enemy peoples into Roman citizens within the course of a single day. Even some of our kings were foreign. Similarly, the admission to former office of the sons of slaves is not the novelty it is alleged to be. In early times it happened frequently.

' "The Senonian Gauls fought against us," it is objected. But did not Italians, Vulsci and Aequi, as well? "The Gauls captured Rome" you say. But we also lost battles to our neighbours – we gave hostages to the Etruscans, we went beneath the Samnites' yoke.[1] Actually, a review of all these wars shows that the Gallic war took the shortest time of all – since then, peace and loyalty have reigned unbroken. Now that they have assimilated our customs and culture and married into our families, let them bring in their gold and wealth rather than keep it to themselves. Senators, however ancient any institution seems, once upon a time it was new! First, plebeians joined patricians in office. Next, the Latins were added. Then came men from other Italian peoples. The innovation now proposed will, in its turn, one day be old: what we seek to justify by precedents today will itself become a precedent.'

The senate approved the emperor's speech. The first Gauls who thereby obtained the right to become Roman senators were the Aedui. They owed this privilege to their ancient treaty with Rome and their position as the only Gallic community entitled 'Brothers of the Roman People'. At this period Claudius also elevated senators of particularly long standing and illustrious birth to patrician rank, which few surviving families possessed. They comprised what Romulus had called 'the Greater' and Lucius Junius Brutus 'the Lesser' Houses. Even the families which the dictator Caesar and Augustus promoted in their place, under the Cassian and Saenian laws respectively, had died out.[2] The action of Claudius was welcomed as beneficial, and the imperial censor enjoyed performing it.

But Claudius was worried about how to expel notorious bad characters from the senate. Rejecting old-fashioned severity in favour of a lenient modern method, he advised individuals concerned to consider their own cases and apply for permission to renounce senatorial

1. The Romans were defeated by the Samnites at Caudium in 321 B.C.

2. Other writers, while agreeing that Lucius Junius Brutus added 100 families to the patricians, ascribe the 100 Lesser Families to Tarquinius Priscus, traditionally the last but two of the Roman kings.

rank – which would readily be granted. He w
pulsions by the censors *and* resignations in a sin
humiliation of those expelled should be mitigated
those who had modestly volunteered to withdraw.
consuls, Lucius Vipstanus Poplicola, proposed tha
be called Father of the Senate – since others too wer
the Country, whereas new services to the country de
But the emperor vetoed the proposal as too flattering
cluded the ritual of the census, which showed a c
5,984,072 persons.[1]

And now ended Claudius' ignorance of his own dom
Now he had, ineluctably, to discover and punish his wi
(as a preliminary to coveting an incestuous substitute).
adultery was going so smoothly that she was drifting, thro
dom, into unfamiliar vices. But now fate seemed to have
Gaius Silius; or perhaps he felt that impending perils could
met by perilous action. He urged that concealment should be d
'We do not have to wait until the emperor dies of old age!'
her. 'Besides, only innocent people can afford long-term plans.
rant guilt requires audacity. And we have accomplices who shar
danger. I am without wife or child. I am ready to marry, and to a
Britannicus. Your power will remain undiminished. Peace of m
will only be yours if we can forestall Claudius. He is slow to disco
deception – but quick to anger.'

Messalina was unenthusiastic. It was not that she loved her husband
But she feared that Silius, once supreme, might despise his mistress,
and see the crime prompted by an emergency in its true colours. However, the idea of being called his wife appealed to her owing to its sheer outrageousness – a sensualist's ultimate satisfaction. So, waiting only until Claudius had left to sacrifice at Ostia, she celebrated a formal marriage with Silius.

It will seem fantastic, I know, that in a city where nothing escapes notice or comment, any human beings could have felt themselves so secure. Much more so that, on an appointed day and before invited signatories, a consul designate and the emperor's wife should have been

1. This total, like the figure of over four million given by Augustus, probably includes all citizens and their wives and children.

forewarning of charge or accuser. Narcissus watched for an opening. Then, as Claudius prolonged his stay at Ostia, he induced the emperor's two favourite mistresses to act as informers. They were persuaded by gifts, promises, and assurances of the increased influence that Messalina's downfall would bring them.

One of the women, Calpurnia (I), secured a private interview with Claudius. Throwing herself at his feet, she cried that Messalina had married Silius – in the same breath asking the other girl, Cleopatra (who was standing by ready), for corroboration: which she provided. Then Calpurnia urged that Narcissus should be summoned. 'I must excuse my earlier silences', said Narcissus, 'about Vettius Valens, Plautius Lateranus, and the like – and now, too, I do not propose to complain of her adulteries, much less impel you to demand back from Silius your mansion, slaves, and other imperial perquisites. *But are you aware you are divorced?* Nation, senate, and army have witnessed her wedding to Silius. Act promptly, or her new husband controls Rome!'

Claudius summoned his closest friends. First he interrogated Gaius Turranius, controller of the corn supply, then Lusius Geta, commander of the Guard. They confirmed the story. The rest of the emperor's entourage loudly insisted that he must visit the camp and secure the Guard – safety must come before vengeance. Claudius, it is said, was panic-stricken. 'Am I still emperor?' he kept on asking. 'Is Silius still a private citizen?'

Meanwhile, Messalina was indulging in unprecedented extravagances. It was full autumn; and she was performing in her grounds a mimic grape-harvest. Presses were working, vats overflowing, surrounded by women capering in skins like sacrificing or frenzied Maenads. She herself, hair streaming, brandished a Bacchic wand. Beside her stood Silius in ivy-wreath and buskins, rolling his head, while the disreputable chorus yelled round him. Vettius Valens, the story goes, gaily climbed a great tree. Asked what he saw, his answer was: 'A fearful storm over Ostia!' There may have been a storm. Or it could have been a casual phrase. But later it seemed prophetic.

Rumours and messengers now came pouring in. They revealed that Claudius knew all, and was on his way, determined for revenge. So the couple separated, Messalina to the Gardens of Lucullus, Silius – to disguise his alarm – to business in the Forum. The others too melted away in every direction. But they were pounced on and arrested separately by staff-officers of the Guard, in the streets or in hiding-places. Messalina was too shaken by the catastrophe to make any plans. But she instantly decided on the course that had often saved her – to meet her husband and let him see her.

She also sent word that Britannicus and Octavia should go and seek their father's embraces. She herself begged the senior priestess of Vesta, Vibidia, to obtain the ear of the emperor as Chief Priest and urge pardon. Meanwhile, with only three companions – so rapidly was she deserted – she walked from end to end of the city. Then she started along the Ostia road – in a cart used for removing garden refuse. People did not pity her, for they were horrified by her appalling crimes.

On Claudius' side there was just as much agitation. Lusius Geta, the Guard commander, followed his own caprices, regardless of right and wrong. No one trusted him. So Narcissus, supported by others as afraid as he was, asserted that there was only one hope of saving the emperor's life: the transference of the Guard, for that one day, to the command of a freed slave – himself; for he offered himself as commander. Then, afraid that Claudius, during the return journey to Rome, might have his mind changed by his companions Lucius Vitellius and Gaius Caecina Largus, Narcissus asked for a place in the same carriage, and sat with them.

Claudius, it was widely said afterwards, contradicted himself incessantly, veering from invective against Messalina's misconduct to reminiscences of their marriage and their children's infancy. Lucius Vitellius would only moan 'How wicked, how sinful!' When Narcissus pressed that he should reveal his mind honestly and unambiguously, Vitellius, undeterred, still responded with cryptic exclamations which could be taken in two ways. Caecina Largus did the same.

Now Messalina came into view. She cried and cried that Claudius must listen to the mother of Octavia and Britannicus. Narcissus shouted her down with the story of Silius and the wedding, simultaneously distracting the emperor's gaze with a document listing her immoralities. Soon afterwards, at a point near the city, the two children were brought forward. Narcissus ordered their removal. But he could not remove Vibidia, who demanded most indignantly that a wife should not be executed unheard. Narcissus replied that the emperor would hear Messalina – she would have a chance to clear herself – and that meanwhile Vibidia had better go and attend to her own religious duties.

Claudius remained strangely silent. Lucius Vitellius looked as if he did not know what was happening. The former slave, Narcissus, took charge. He ordered the adulterer's home to be opened and the emperor to be taken there. First, in the forecourt, Narcissus pointed out a statue of Silius' condemned father, placed there in defiance of senatorial decree. Then he pointed to the heirlooms of Neros and Drususes that had come to the house among the wages of sin. This angered the emperor; he became threatening. Narcissus conducted him to the camp and delivered a preliminary statement. Then Claudius addressed the assembled Guard – but only briefly, because, just though his indignation was, he could hardly express it for shame.

The Guardsmen shouted repeatedly for the offenders to be named and punished. Silius was brought on to the platform. Without attempting defence or postponement, he asked for a quick death. Certain distinguished knights showed equal courage. They too desired a speedy end. The execution of accomplices was ordered: Titius Proculus – appointed Messalina's 'guardian' by Silius – Vettius Valens, who confessed, and two further members of the order of knights, Pompeius Urbicus and Saufeius Trogus. The same penalty was visited on the commander of the watch, Decrius Calpurnianus, the superintendent of a gladiator's school, Sulpicius Rufus, and a junior senator, Juncus Vergilianus.

Only Mnester (I) caused hesitation. Tearing his clothes, he entreated Claudius to look at his whip-marks and remember the words with which the emperor had placed him under Messalina's orders. Others, he urged, had sinned for money or ambition, he from compulsion – and if Silius had become emperor he, Mnester, would have been the first to die. Claudius had an indulgent nature and this moved him. But the ex-slaves prevailed upon the emperor not, after executing so many distinguished men, to spare a ballet-dancer – when crimes were so grave it was irrelevant whether they were voluntary or enforced.

Rejection, too, awaited the defence of an unpretentious but good-looking young knight, Sextus Traulus Montanus, whom within a single night Messalina, as capricious in her dislikes as in her desires, had sent for and sent away. Plautius Lateranus escaped the death sentence owing to an uncle's distinguished record. So did Suillius Caesoninus, because of his own vices – at that repulsive gathering his had been merely a female part.

Meanwhile at the Gardens of Lucullus Messalina was fighting for her life. She composed an appeal. Its terms were hopeful and even at times indignant, so shameless was her insolence to the very end. Indeed, if Narcissus had not speedily caused her death, the fatal blow would have rebounded on her accuser. For Claudius, home again, soothed and a little fuddled after an early dinner, ordered 'the poor woman' (that is said to have been his phrase) to appear on the next day to defend herself. This was noted. His anger was clearly cooling, his love returning. Further delay risked that the approaching night would revive memories of conjugal pleasures.

So Narcissus hurried away. Ostensibly on the emperor's instructions, he ordered a Guard colonel, who was standing by, and some staff officers to kill Messalina. A former slave, name Euodus, was sent to prevent her escape and see that the order was carried out. Hastening to the Gardens ahead of the officers, he found her prostrate on the ground, with her mother Domitia Lepida sitting beside her. While her daughter was in power they had quarrelled. But in her extremity, Lepida was overcome by pity. She urged Messalina to await the executioner. 'Your life is finished,' she said. 'All that remains is to make a decent end.' But in that lust-ridden heart decency did not exist. Messalina was still uselessly weeping and moaning when the men violently broke down the door. The officer stood there, silently. The ex-slave, with a slave's foulness of tongue, insulted her. Then, for the first time, it dawned on Messalina what her position really was. Terrified, she took a dagger and put it to her throat and then her breast – but could not do it. And so the officer ran her through. The body was left with her mother. Claudius was still at table when news came that Messalina had died; whether by her own hand or another's was unspecified. Claudius did not inquire. He called for more wine, and went on with his party as usual.

On the days that followed, the emperor gave no sign of hatred, satisfaction, anger, distress, or any other human feeling – even when he saw the accusers exulting, and his children mourning. His forgetfulness was helped by the senate, which decreed that Messalina's name and statues should be removed from all public and private sites. It also aristocracy, or for impoverished senators from Latium? Every post will be absorbed by the rich men whose grandfathers and great-grandfathers commanded hostile tribes, assailed our armies in battle, besieged the divine Julius Caesar at Alesia.[1] Those are recent memories. But are we to forget our men who, beside Rome's Capitoline citadel, were killed by the ancestors of these very Gauls?[2] Let them, by all means, have the title of Roman citizens. But the senate's insignia, the glory of office, they must not cheapen.'

These and similar arguments did not impress Claudius. He contradicted them on the spot, and then summoned the senate and made this speech:[3]

'The experience of my own ancestors, notably of my family's Sabine founder Clausus who was simultaneously made a Roman citizen and a patrician, encourage me to adopt the same national policy, by bringing excellence to Rome from whatever source. For I do not forget that the Julii came from Alba Longa, the Coruncanii from Camerium, the Porcii from Tusculum; and, leaving antiquity aside, that men from Etruria, Lucania, and all Italy have been admitted into the senate; and that finally Italy herself has been extended to the Alps, uniting not merely individuals but whole territories and peoples under the name of Rome.

'Moreover, after the enfranchisement of Italy across the Po, our next step was to make citizens of the finest provincials too: we added them to our ex-soldiers in settlements throughout the world, and by their means reinvigorated the exhausted empire. This helped to stabilize peace within the frontiers and successful relations with foreign powers. Is it regretted that the Cornelii Balbi immigrated from Spain, and other equally distinguished men from southern Gaul? Their descendants are with us; and they love Rome as much as we do. What proved fatal to Sparta and Athens, for all their military strength, was their segregation of conquered subjects as aliens. Our founder Romulus, on the other hand, had the wisdom – more than once – to transform

1. The site of Julius Caesar's defeat of Vercingetorix in 52 B.C.
2. The traditional date of the destruction of Rome by the Senones was 390 B.C.
3. Claudius' speech has survived on a bronze tablet preserved at Lyon. Tacitus does not reproduce it exactly or faithfully, but brings out the main points.

whole enemy peoples into Roman citizens within the course of a single day. Even some of our kings were foreign. Similarly, the admission to former office of the sons of slaves is not the novelty it is alleged to be. In early times it happened frequently.

'"The Senonian Gauls fought against us," it is objected. But did not Italians, Vulsci and Aequi, as well? "The Gauls captured Rome" you say. But we also lost battles to our neighbours – we gave hostages to the Etruscans, we went beneath the Samnites' yoke.[1] Actually, a review of all these wars shows that the Gallic war took the shortest time of all – since then, peace and loyalty have reigned unbroken. Now that they have assimilated our customs and culture and married into our families, let them bring in their gold and wealth rather than keep it to themselves. Senators, however ancient any institution seems, once upon a time it was new! First, plebeians joined patricians in office. Next, the Latins were added. Then came men from other Italian peoples. The innovation now proposed will, in its turn, one day be old: what we seek to justify by precedents today will itself become a precedent.'

The senate approved the emperor's speech. The first Gauls who thereby obtained the right to become Roman senators were the Aedui. They owed this privilege to their ancient treaty with Rome and their position as the only Gallic community entitled 'Brothers of the Roman People'. At this period Claudius also elevated senators of particularly long standing and illustrious birth to patrician rank, which few surviving families possessed. They comprised what Romulus had called 'the Greater' and Lucius Junius Brutus 'the Lesser' Houses. Even the families which the dictator Caesar and Augustus promoted in their place, under the Cassian and Saenian laws respectively, had died out.[2] The action of Claudius was welcomed as beneficial, and the imperial censor enjoyed performing it.

But Claudius was worried about how to expel notorious bad characters from the senate. Rejecting old-fashioned severity in favour of a lenient modern method, he advised individuals concerned to consider their own cases and apply for permission to renounce senatorial

1. The Romans were defeated by the Samnites at Caudium in 321 B.C.
2. Other writers, while agreeing that Lucius Junius Brutus added 100 families to the patricians, ascribe the 100 Lesser Families to Tarquinius Priscus, traditionally the last but two of the Roman kings.

rank – which would readily be granted. He would then publish expulsions by the censors *and* resignations in a single list – so that the humiliation of those expelled should be mitigated by association with those who had modestly volunteered to withdraw. For this one of the consuls, Lucius Vipstanus Poplicola, proposed that Claudius should be called Father of the Senate – since others too were called Father of the Country, whereas new services to the country deserved new titles. But the emperor vetoed the proposal as too flattering. Then he concluded the ritual of the census, which showed a citizen body of 5,984,072 persons.[1]

And now ended Claudius' ignorance of his own domestic affairs. Now he had, ineluctably, to discover and punish his wife's excesses (as a preliminary to coveting an incestuous substitute). Messalina's adultery was going so smoothly that she was drifting, through boredom, into unfamiliar vices. But now fate seemed to have unhinged Gaius Silius; or perhaps he felt that impending perils could only be met by perilous action. He urged that concealment should be dropped. 'We do not have to wait until the emperor dies of old age!' he told her. 'Besides, only innocent people can afford long-term plans. Flagrant guilt requires audacity. And we have accomplices who share our danger. I am without wife or child. I am ready to marry, and to adopt Britannicus. Your power will remain undiminished. Peace of mind will only be yours if we can forestall Claudius. He is slow to discover deception – but quick to anger.'

Messalina was unenthusiastic. It was not that she loved her husband. But she feared that Silius, once supreme, might despise his mistress, and see the crime prompted by an emergency in its true colours. However, the idea of being called his wife appealed to her owing to its sheer outrageousness – a sensualist's ultimate satisfaction. So, waiting only until Claudius had left to sacrifice at Ostia, she celebrated a formal marriage with Silius.

It will seem fantastic, I know, that in a city where nothing escapes notice or comment, any human beings could have felt themselves so secure. Much more so that, on an appointed day and before invited signatories, a consul designate and the emperor's wife should have been

1. This total, like the figure of over four million given by Augustus, probably includes all citizens and their wives and children.

joined together in formal marriage – 'for the purpose of rearing children'; that she should have listened to the diviners' words, assumed the wedding-veil, sacrificed to the gods; that the pair should have taken their places at a banquet, embraced, and finally spent the night as man and wife. But I am not inventing marvels. What I have told, and shall tell, is the truth. Older men heard and recorded it.

The imperial household shuddered – especially those in power, with everything to fear from a new emperor. There were secret conferences. Then indignation was unconcealed. 'While a ballet-dancing actor violated the emperor's bedroom', they said, 'it was humiliating enough. Yet it did not threaten Claudius' life. Here, on the other hand, is a young, handsome, intelligent nobleman, consul-to-be – but with a loftier destiny in mind. For where such a marriage will lead is clear enough.' When they thought of Claudius' sluggish uxoriousness, and the many assassinations ordered by Messalina, they were terrified. Yet the emperor's very pliability gave them hope. If they could convince him of the enormity of the outrage, Messalina might be condemned and eliminated without trial. But everything, they felt, turned on this – would Claudius give her a hearing? Could they actually shut his ears against her confession?

Callistus, who has already been mentioned in connection with Gaius' murder, Narcissus, who had contrived the death of Gaius Appius Junius Silanus,[1] and Pallas, who was now basking in the warmest favour, conferred together.[2] They discussed whether, pretending ignorance of everything else, they could secretly frighten Messalina out of her affair with Silius. But this scheme was abandoned by Pallas and Callistus as too dangerous for themselves. Pallas' motive was cowardice. Callistus had learnt from his experience dating from the previous reign that power was better safeguarded by diplomatic than by vigorous methods. Narcissus, however, persevered in taking action – with this new feature: she was to be denounced without

1. The assassination of Gaius (performed by Gaius Cassius Chaerea) and the execution of Messalina's stepfather Gaius Appius Junius Silanus under Claudius were described in the lost part of Tacitus' work.

2. The reign of Claudius witnessed an unprecedented increase in the power of the great secretaries of state, ex-slaves such as Narcissus (Secretary-General), Pallas (Financial Secretary), and Callistus (Petitions Secretary).

forewarning of charge or accuser. Narcissus watched for an opening. Then, as Claudius prolonged his stay at Ostia, he induced the emperor's two favourite mistresses to act as informers. They were persuaded by gifts, promises, and assurances of the increased influence that Messalina's downfall would bring them. One of the women, Calpurnia (I), secured a private interview with Claudius. Throwing herself at his feet, she cried that Messalina had married Silius – in the same breath asking the other girl, Cleopatra (who was standing by ready), for corroboration: which she provided. Then Calpurnia urged that Narcissus should be summoned. 'I must excuse my earlier silences', said Narcissus, 'about Vettius Valens, Plautius Lateranus, and the like – and now, too, I do not propose to complain of her adulteries, much less impel you to demand back from Silius your mansion, slaves, and other imperial perquisites. *But are you aware you are divorced?* Nation, senate, and army have witnessed her wedding to Silius. Act promptly, or her new husband controls Rome!'

Claudius summoned his closest friends. First he interrogated Gaius Turranius, controller of the corn supply, then Lusius Geta, commander of the Guard. They confirmed the story. The rest of the emperor's entourage loudly insisted that he must visit the camp and secure the Guard – safety must come before vengeance. Claudius, it is said, was panic-stricken. 'Am I still emperor?' he kept on asking. 'Is Silius still a private citizen?'

Meanwhile, Messalina was indulging in unprecedented extravagances. It was full autumn; and she was performing in her grounds a mimic grape-harvest. Presses were working, vats overflowing, surrounded by women capering in skins like sacrificing or frenzied Maenads. She herself, hair streaming, brandished a Bacchic wand. Beside her stood Silius in ivy-wreath and buskins, rolling his head, while the disreputable chorus yelled round him. Vettius Valens, the story goes, gaily climbed a great tree. Asked what he saw, his answer was: 'A fearful storm over Ostia!' There may have been a storm. Or it could have been a casual phrase. But later it seemed prophetic.

Rumours and messengers now came pouring in. They revealed that Claudius knew all, and was on his way, determined for revenge. So the couple separated, Messalina to the Gardens of Lucullus, Silius – to disguise his alarm – to business in the Forum. The others too melted away in every direction. But they were pounced on and arrested separately by staff-officers of the Guard, in the streets or in hiding-places. Messalina was too shaken by the catastrophe to make any plans. But she instantly decided on the course that had often saved her – to meet her husband and let him see her.

She also sent word that Britannicus and Octavia should go and seek their father's embraces. She herself begged the senior priestess of Vesta, Vibidia, to obtain the ear of the emperor as Chief Priest and urge pardon. Meanwhile, with only three companions – so rapidly was she deserted – she walked from end to end of the city. Then she started along the Ostia road – in a cart used for removing garden refuse. People did not pity her, for they were horrified by her appalling crimes.

On Claudius' side there was just as much agitation. Lusius Geta, the Guard commander, followed his own caprices, regardless of right and wrong. No one trusted him. So Narcissus, supported by others as afraid as he was, asserted that there was only one hope of saving the emperor's life: the transference of the Guard, for that one day, to the command of a freed slave – himself; for he offered himself as commander. Then, afraid that Claudius, during the return journey to Rome, might have his mind changed by his companions Lucius Vitellius and Gaius Caecina Largus, Narcissus asked for a place in the same carriage, and sat with them.

Claudius, it was widely said afterwards, contradicted himself incessantly, veering from invective against Messalina's misconduct to reminiscences of their marriage and their children's infancy. Lucius Vitellius would only moan 'How wicked, how sinful!' When Narcissus pressed that he should reveal his mind honestly and unambiguously, Vitellius, undeterred, still responded with cryptic exclamations which could be taken in two ways. Caecina Largus did the same.

Now Messalina came into view. She cried and cried that Claudius must listen to the mother of Octavia and Britannicus. Narcissus shouted her down with the story of Silius and the wedding, simultaneously distracting the emperor's gaze with a document listing her immoralities. Soon afterwards, at a point near the city, the two children were brought forward. Narcissus ordered their removal. But he could not remove Vibidia, who demanded most indignantly that a wife should not be executed unheard. Narcissus replied that the emperor would hear Messalina – she would have a chance to clear herself – and that meanwhile Vibidia had better go and attend to her own religious duties.

Claudius remained strangely silent. Lucius Vitellius looked as if he did not know what was happening. The former slave, Narcissus, took charge. He ordered the adulterer's home to be opened and the emperor to be taken there. First, in the forecourt, Narcissus pointed out a statue of Silius' condemned father, placed there in defiance of senatorial decree. Then he pointed to the heirlooms of Neros and Drususes that had come to the house among the wages of sin. This angered the emperor; he became threatening. Narcissus conducted him to the camp and delivered a preliminary statement. Then Claudius addressed the assembled Guard – but only briefly, because, just though his indignation was, he could hardly express it for shame.

The Guardsmen shouted repeatedly for the offenders to be named and punished. Silius was brought on to the platform. Without attempting defence or postponement, he asked for a quick death. Certain distinguished knights showed equal courage. They too desired a speedy end. The execution of accomplices was ordered: Titius Proculus – appointed Messalina's 'guardian' by Silius – Vettius Valens, who confessed, and two further members of the order of knights, Pompeius Urbicus and Saufeius Trogus. The same penalty was visited on the commander of the watch, Decrius Calpurnianus, the superintendent of a gladiator's school, Sulpicius Rufus, and a junior senator, Juncus Vergilianus.

Only Mnester (I) caused hesitation. Tearing his clothes, he entreated Claudius to look at his whip-marks and remember the words with which the emperor had placed him under Messalina's orders. Others, he urged, had sinned for money or ambition, he from compulsion – and if Silius had become emperor he, Mnester, would have been the first to die. Claudius had an indulgent nature and this moved him. But the ex-slaves prevailed upon the emperor not, after executing so many distinguished men, to spare a ballet-dancer – when crimes were so grave it was irrelevant whether they were voluntary or enforced.

Rejection, too, awaited the defence of an unpretentious but good-looking young knight, Sextus Traulus Montanus, whom within a single night Messalina, as capricious in her dislikes as in her desires, had sent for and sent away. Plautius Lateranus escaped the death sentence owing to an uncle's distinguished record. So did Suillius Caesoninus, because of his own vices – at that repulsive gathering his had been merely a female part.

Meanwhile at the Gardens of Lucullus Messalina was fighting for her life. She composed an appeal. Its terms were hopeful and even at times indignant, so shameless was her insolence to the very end. Indeed, if Narcissus had not speedily caused her death, the fatal blow would have rebounded on her accuser. For Claudius, home again, soothed and a little fuddled after an early dinner, ordered 'the poor woman' (that is said to have been his phrase) to appear on the next day to defend herself. This was noted. His anger was clearly cooling, his love returning. Further delay risked that the approaching night would revive memories of conjugal pleasures.

So Narcissus hurried away. Ostensibly on the emperor's instructions, he ordered a Guard colonel, who was standing by, and some staff officers to kill Messalina. A former slave, name Euodus, was sent to prevent her escape and see that the order was carried out. Hastening to the Gardens ahead of the officers, he found her prostrate on the ground, with her mother Domitia Lepida sitting beside her. While her daughter was in power they had quarrelled. But in her extremity, Lepida was overcome by pity. She urged Messalina to await the executioner. 'Your life is finished,' she said. 'All that remains is to make a decent end.' But in that lust-ridden heart decency did not exist. Messalina was still uselessly weeping and moaning when the men violently broke down the door. The officer stood there, silently. The ex-slave, with a slave's foulness of tongue, insulted her. Then, for the first time, it dawned on Messalina what her position really was. Terrified, she took a dagger and put it to her throat and then her breast – but could not do it. And so the officer ran her through. The body was left with her mother. Claudius was still at table when news came that Messalina had died; whether by her own hand or another's was unspecified. Claudius did not inquire. He called for more wine, and went on with his party as usual.

On the days that followed, the emperor gave no sign of hatred, satisfaction, anger, distress, or any other human feeling – even when he saw the accusers exulting, and his children mourning. His forgetfulness was helped by the senate, which decreed that Messalina's name and statues should be removed from all public and private sites. It also awarded Narcissus an honorary quaestorship. But this was the least reason for conceit to a man who exceeded even Pallas or Callistus in power.

The vengeance on Messalina was just. But its consequences were grim.

CHAPTER 10

The Mother of Nero

*

MESSALINA's death convulsed the imperial household. Claudius was impatient of celibacy and easily controlled by his wives, and the ex-slaves quarrelled about who should choose his next one. Rivalry among the women was equally fierce. Each cited her own high birth, beauty, and wealth as qualifications for this exalted marriage. The chief competitors were Lollia Paulina,[1] daughter of the former consul Marcus Lollius (II), and Germanicus' daughter Agrippina (II). Their backers were Callistus and Pallas respectively. Narcissus supported Aelia Paetina,[2] who was of the family of the Aelii Tuberones. The emperor continually changed his mind according to whatever advice he had heard last.

Finally, he summoned the disputants to a meeting and requested them to give reasoned opinions. At the meeting, Narcissus reminded Claudius that he had been married to Aelia Paetina before; that the union had been productive (a daughter, Claudia Antonia, had been born to them); that remarriage would necessitate no domestic innovations; and that, far from entertaining a stepmother's dislike for Britannicus and Octavia, Paetina would cherish them next to her own children. Callistus objected that Claudius had divorced Paetina long ago and that this disqualified her – remarriage would make her arrogant, and Lollia was far more eligible since, being childless, she would be a mother to her stepchildren without jealousy. Pallas, proposing Agrippina, emphasized that the son whom she would bring with her was Germanicus' grandson,[3] eminently deserving of imperial rank; let the emperor ally himself with a noble race and unite two

1. At one time married to Gaius.
2. She had been Claudius's wife earlier.
3. The future emperor Nero.

branches of the Claudian house, rather than allow this lady of proved capacity for child-bearing, still young, to transfer the glorious name of the Caesars to another family.

These arguments prevailed. Agrippina's seductiveness was a help. Visiting her uncle frequently – ostensibly as a close relation – she tempted him into giving her the preference and into treating her, in anticipation, as his wife. Once sure of her marriage, she enlarged the scope of her plans and devoted herself to scheming for her son Lucius Domitius Ahenobarbus, whose father was Cnaeus Domitius Ahenobarbus. It was her ambition that this boy, the future Nero, should be wedded to the emperor's daughter Octavia. Here criminal methods were necessary, since Claudius had already betrothed Octavia to Lucius Junius Silanus Torquatus (I) – and had won popularity for his distinguished record by awarding him an honorary Triumph, and giving a lavish gladiatorial display in his name. But with an emperor whose likes and dislikes were all suggested and dictated to him, anything seemed possible.

Lucius Vitellius had an eye for future despots. Using his post as censor to cloak his servile fabrications, he sought Agrippina's favour by involving himself in her projects and prosecuting Lucius Junius Silanus Torquatus. Silanus' attractive but shameless sister, Junia Calvina, had until lately been married to Vitellius' son: using this as a handle, Vitellius put an unsavoury construction on the unguarded (but not incestuous) affection between Silanus and his sister. Claudius, particularly ready to suspect the future husband of the daughter he loved, gave attention to the charge. Silanus, unaware of the plot, happened to be praetor for the year. Suddenly, though the roll of senators and the ceremonies terminating the census were long complete, an edict of Vitellius struck him off the senate. Simultaneously, Claudius cancelled Octavia's engagement with Silanus, and he was forced to resign his office and was superseded for the one remaining day, in favour of Titus Clodius Eprius Marcellus.

Next year the consuls were Gaius Pompeius Longinus Gallus and Quintus Veranius (II). Rumour now strongly predicted Claudius' marriage to Agrippina; so did their illicit intercourse. But they did not yet dare to celebrate the wedding. For marriage with a niece was unprecedented – indeed it was incestuous, and disregard of this might, it was feared, cause national disaster. Hesitation was only overcome when Lucius Vitellius undertook to arrange matters by methods of his own. He asked Claudius if he would yield to a decree of the Assembly and the senate's recommendation. The emperor replied that he was a citizen himself and would bow to unanimity. Then Vitellius, requesting him to wait in the palace, entered the senate and stating that it was a matter of the highest national importance, asked permission to speak first.

'In his exceedingly arduous duties,' Vitellius said, 'which cover the whole world, the emperor needs support, to enable him to provide for the public good without domestic worries. Could there be a more respectable comfort to our Censor – a stranger to dissipation or self-indulgence, law-abiding since earliest youth – than a wife, a partner in good and bad fortune alike, to whom he can confide his inmost thoughts, and his little children?'

These winning preliminaries were warmly applauded by the senate. Then Vitellius proceeded. 'We agree unanimously, then, that the emperor should marry. The chosen lady must be aristocratic, capable of child-bearing, and virtuous. Agrippina's exceptionally illustrious birth is indisputable. She has demonstrated her fertility. Her morals are equally outstanding. For the emperor – who knows no man's wives but his own – her widowhood is welcome and providential. You have heard from your parents, indeed you have yourselves known, of the abduction of men's wives at an emperor's whim. The respectable arrangement which I propose is strikingly different. We can create a precedent: the nation presents the emperor with a wife! Marriage to a niece, it may be objected, is unfamiliar to us. Yet in other countries it is regular and lawful. Here also, unions between cousins, long unknown, have become frequent in course of time. Customs change as circumstances change – this innovation too will take root.'

At this, some senators ran out of the house enthusiastically clamouring that if Claudius hesitated they would use constraint. A throng of passers-by cried that the Roman public were similarly minded. Claudius delayed no longer. After receiving the crowd's congratulations in the Forum, he entered the senate to request a decree legalizing future marriages with a brother's daughter. However, only one other seeker after this sort of union is identifiable – a knight named Alledius Severus, whose motive was believed to be the hope of Agrippina's favour.

From this moment the country was transformed. Complete obedience was accorded to a woman – and not a woman like Messalina who toyed with national affairs to satisfy her appetites. This was a rigorous, almost masculine despotism. In public, Agrippina was austere and often arrogant. Her private life was chaste – unless power was to be gained. Her passion to acquire money was unbounded. She wanted it as a stepping-stone to supremacy.

On the wedding-day Lucius Junius Silanus Torquatus committed suicide. For that day finally terminated his hopes of life – or perhaps he chose it to increase ill-feeling. His sister Junia Calvina was banished from Italy. Claudius ordained ritual prescribed by King Tullus Hostilius, including expiatory ceremonies by priests at the Grove of Diana. The emperor's resuscitation, at this juncture, of punishments and expiations for Silanus' incest provoked universal ridicule. Agrippina, however, was anxious not to be credited with bad actions only. So she now secured the recall of Lucius Annaeus Seneca[1] from exile and his appointment to a praetorship. She judged that owing to his literary eminence this would be popular. She also had designs on him as a distinguished tutor for her young son Lucius Domitius Ahenobarbus (the future Nero). Seneca's advice could serve their plans for supremacy; and he was believed to be devoted to her – in gratitude for her favours – but hostile to Claudius whose unfairness he resented.

It was now decided to act without further delay. A consul-designate, Lucius Mammius Pollio, was induced by lavish promises to propose a petition to Claudius, begging him to betroth Octavia to Domitius – an arrangement compatible with their ages and likely to lead to higher things. The arguments used closely resembled those recently employed by Lucius Vitellius. The engagement took place. In addition to their previous relationship, Domitius was now Claudius' future son-in-law. By his mother's efforts – and the intrigues of Messalina's accusers, who feared vengeance from her son – he was becoming the rival of Britannicus.

I have mentioned that a Parthian delegation had been sent to Rome

1. Henceforward described as Seneca, i.e. the philosopher (son of Seneca I the rhetorician), exiled eight years earlier for adultery with Germanicus' daughter Julia Livilla.

to ask for Meherdates[1] – a hostage in our hands – as their king. It now
appeared before the senate. The delegates described their mission in
these terms:

'We know of the treaty between our two countries. Nor do we
come as rebels against the Parthian royal house. We are calling upon
the son of Vonones I, the grandson of Phraates IV, to destroy the
tyranny of Gotarzes II, which nobles and populace alike find unendurable. He has exterminated his brothers and other near relations –
not to speak of more distant kinsmen. Now he is turning even upon
pregnant women and small children. A slovenly administrator and
unsuccessful commander, he plunges into brutality to disguise his
inertia.

'You and we have an old, officially inaugurated friendship. We,
your allies, rival you in power but take second place out of respect.
Now we need your help. That is why Parthian kings' sons are given
you as hostages: so that, if our rulers at home become distasteful, we
can apply to emperor and senate and receive a monarch trained in
your culture.'

In response to these and similar assertions Claudius spoke about
Roman supremacy and Parthian homage. He compared himself to the
divine Augustus, recalling that Augustus too had been asked for a
Parthian king. (About Tiberius, who had likewise sent one, he said
nothing.) Meherdates was present: Claudius advised him to think of
himself not as an autocrat among slaves, but as a guide of free men,
and to be merciful and just – virtues all the more welcome to natives
because of their unfamiliarity. Then, turning to the deputation, he
commanded Rome's foster-son as having hitherto shown exemplary
character. But, he added, kings have to be endured however they are,
since continual changes are undesirable; and Rome, having taken her
fill of glory, wanted other countries also to be peaceful. He then instructed Gaius Cassius Longinus, imperial governor of Syria, to conduct the prince to the bank of the Euphrates.

At this period Cassius was pre-eminent as a jurist – military qualities
are unrecognized in peace-time, in which good and bad soldiers are
indistinguishable. Yet Cassius, as far as he could without a war,
revived ancient discipline, organized manoeuvres, and took as much
trouble and forethought as if an enemy were upon him. He felt he

1. Meherdates' father had been sent by Augustus to seize the Parthian throne.

owed this to his ancestors, the Cassian family, of which the fame extended to that area.[1] Summoning the men who had instigated the mission, Cassius encamped at Zeugma, the site of the most convenient river-crossing. The Parthian dignitaries joined him; so did Acbarus (Abgar V), the Arab king of Edessa.[2] Cassius warned Meherdates to press on, since delay cools oriental enthusiasm and produces treachery. But the advice was disregarded by the ingenuous young man, who thought kingship meant self-indulgence, and allowed himself to be detained for many days at Edessa by its deceitful ruler. Carenes, governor of Mesopotamia, invited him in, stressing that everything would be easy if he came quickly. Yet instead of taking the short route to Mesopotamia, Meherdates made a detour to Armenia, which in that season, at the outset of winter, is forbidding.

Finally, exhausted by snow-bound mountainous territory, he and his men joined up with Carenes' force near the plains. Crossing the Tigris, they went on through Adiabene; its king, Izates, had ostensibly allied himself with Meherdates but was privately a loyal supporter of Gotarzes. During the journey, Meherdates and Carenes captured the ancient Assyrian capital Ninos, and the famous fortress where the Persian Darius III had been finally defeated by Alexander.[3] Meanwhile Gotarzes offered vows to the mountain deities on Mount Sunbulah. The chief cult is that of Hercules. At regular intervals he warns his priests by dreams to prepare, beside his temple, horses equipped for hunting. With quivers full of arrows fastened on them, these are let loose in the forest and only return at night, panting violently, their quivers empty. In a second dream the god reveals the course he has followed in the woods; and all along it wild beasts are found struck down.

Since, however, Gotarzes' army was not yet strong enough, he took up a position protected by the river Adhaim (?), and, in spite of envoys taunting him to fight, contrived delays – moving from place to place, and sending agents to bribe the enemy forces to change sides. The monarchs of Adiabene and then Edessa deserted to him with their

---

1. Because, after the defeat and death of Marcus Licinius Crassus at Carrhae (53 B.C.), Gaius Cassius (the later murderer of Caesar) had successfully defended Syria.
2. Capital of Osroene (N. Iraq).
3. At Gaugamela, north-east of Nineveh (331 B.C.).

armies. Disloyalty was their national habit; besides, experience has shown that natives are readier to invite kings from Rome than to keep them.

Deprived of these powerful allies, and suspecting treason in his other associates too, Meherdates decided that his only hope was to stake everything on an engagement. Gotarzes felt confident after these defections, and accepted battle. The struggle was bloody, and long undecided. But finally Carenes, after routing his opponents, advanced too far; and fresh troops cut off his return. Meherdates, desperate, listened to the promises of a vassal of his father, Parraces, who then treacherously surrendered him in chains to the victorious Gotarzes. Gotarzes, sneering at Meherdates as no relative of his, no Parthian royalty but an alien Roman, allowed him to live – with his ears cut off. This was a demonstration of his clemency and our humiliation.

Gotarzes II soon fell ill and died. He was succeeded by the king of Media Atropatene, Vonones II, whose short and undistinguished reign contained no noteworthy victories or reverses. His successor was his son Vologeses I.

The king of the Crimean Bosphorus, Mithridates,[1] had been deposed and was homeless. He now learnt that most of the kingdom's Roman garrison under Aulus Didius Gallus had been withdrawn. Only a few battalions, under a Roman knight, Gaius Julius Aquila, were left with the exile's young and inexperienced brother, King Cotys I. Mithridates despised both. He raised the tribes, enticed deserters, and finally collected an army and seized control of the neighbouring tribe, the Dandaridae, expelling its king. At this news Cotys and Aquila feared invasion was imminent. But they were conscious of their weakness. Zorsines, chief of the Siraci, had resumed hostilities against them; and now they too sought outside assistance, sending envoys to Eunones, chief of the Aorsi. Cotys and Aquila could point to the power of Rome, ranged against the rebel Mithridates; and an alliance was easily negotiated.

It was arranged the Eunones should fight cavalry battles, while all sieges were undertaken by the Romans. The combined forces ad-

1. The ejection by the Romans of this Mithridates from the important corn-producing dependent kingdom of the Bosphorus (Crimea), which Claudius had given him, is not recorded in the surviving portions of Tacitus' narrative.

vanced, Eunones' tribesmen in the van and rear, auxiliary battalions and Bosphorans (armed in Roman fashion) forming the main body. They drove back the enemy and took Soza, a town of the Dandaridae which Mithridates had evacuated. Owing to the dubious loyalty of its inhabitants they decided to garrison it. Then they made for Zorsines' tribe, crossed the river Panda, and besieged Uspe. This hill-town possessed a wall and moat. But the wall, being made not of stone but of wickerwork hurdles with earth between, was poor protection against attack; and it suffered from our firebrands and spears launched from lofty siege-towers. Indeed, only the interruption of hostilities by night-fall prevented the conclusion of the battle within a single day.

Next day, the townsmen of Uspe sent envoys asking for the free population to be spared but offering to hand over ten thousand slaves.[1] The victorious Romans rejected this proposal on the grounds that it was barbarous to slaughter men who had surrendered, but hard to provide guards for such large numbers – better that they should be slain in normal warfare. So the soldiers, who had scaled the defences on ladders, were given orders to kill; and the inhabitants were exterminated.

This terrified the surrounding population. Armaments, fortifications, natural heights and obstacles, rivers, and cities had all failed to check invasion; nothing seemed safe. Zorsines long hesitated whether to support Mithridates in his extremity or save his own ancestral kingdom. Finally he put his own people's interests first, gave hostages, and prostrated himself before the emperor's statue. This was an important success for the Roman army. Unscathed and triumphant, it is reliably reported to have reached a point only three days from the river Don. But its return was less satisfactory. For on the voyage back, some ships went aground on the Crimean coast, where natives surrounded them and killed a battalion commander and numerous auxiliaries.

Resistance being hopeless, Mithridates considered to whose mercy he should appeal. He distrusted his brother Cotys I, who had betrayed him and then fought against him. And no Roman of sufficient importance for his promises to carry weight was available. So Mithridates turned to Eunones, who had no personal feud with him and had be-

1. These were probably native serfs working for their masters the Sarmatian Siraci.

come stronger since his alliance with Rome. Adapting his dress and appearance as best he could to his critical situation, Mithridates entered Eunones' palace and fell at his feet, crying: 'Mithridates, whom the Romans have sought on land and sea for many years, voluntarily presents himself! Treat as you will the descendant of mighty Achaemenes.[1] That descent is all my enemies have left me.'

Eunones was moved by his distinction, reversed fortunes, and dignified plea. Raising the suppliant, he congratulated Mithridates for trusting him and his tribe with such an appeal. Eunones then sent envoys to Claudius with a letter. 'Friendships between Roman emperors and the kings of great nations', he wrote, 'originate from their comparable grandeur. You and I are also partners in victory. The happiest ending of a war is a pardon; Zorsines, for example, though conquered, was not despoiled. Mithridates deserves harder treatment, and for him I ask no power or royal position. But spare him a triumphal procession or capital punishment.'

Claudius was generally conciliatory to foreign notables. But he could not decide whether to accept Mithridates as a prisoner, with the promise of his life, or to recapture him by force. Resentment of his aggression, and the desire for revenge, inclined the emperor to the latter course. But on the other side it was argued that the war involved would be in a land without roads or harbours, against savage chieftains of nomad tribes in barren country. Delays would be wearisome, haste perilous – victory inglorious, but defeat humiliating. Better, ran this argument, to seize the opportunity offered, and let Mithridates live, as a destitute exile to whom every further day of life would be an additional punishment.

Claudius was impressed by these points, and wrote informing the ex-king's captor that though Mithridates merited a death sentence, and the emperor had the means to enforce it, it was traditional Roman policy to show mercy to suppliants no less than resolution against enemies: 'it was against whole nations and kingdoms, not individuals, that Triumphs were earned'. Then Mithridates was handed over and conducted to Rome by the imperial finance agent in Pontus, Junio Chilo.

However, he is reported to have addressed the emperor with more

1. Achaemenes was the traditional ancestor of Cyrus and Darius and the other Achaemenid rulers of the Persian empire (*c.* 559–330 B.C.).

spirit than his situation warranted. One observation became publicly known: 'I have not been brought back to you; I have come back. If you disbelieve this, let me go – and then try to catch me!' When he was displayed to the public beside the platform in the Forum among his guards, his expression remained undaunted. The insignia of consul and praetor respectively were conferred upon Junius Chilo and Gaius Julius Aquila.

Agrippina hated Lollia Paulina as a rival for the emperor's hand; and Agrippina was a relentless enemy. In this same year she found an accuser to prosecute Lollia. The charges were association with Chaldaean astrologers and magicians, and the consultation of Apollo's statue at Clarus concerning Claudius' marriage. The emperor did not give the defendant a hearing. He himself spoke at length about her noble connections – omitting her marriage with Gaius, but pointing out that her mother was the sister of Lucius Volusius Saturninus (I), her great-uncle Marcus Aurelius Cotta Maximus Messallinus, and she herself the former wife of Publius Memmius Regulus. But he added that her projects were a national danger and that her potentialities for mischief must be eliminated. She must therefore, he said, have her property confiscated and leave Italy. She was left with five million sesterces out of her vast property. Another noblewoman, Calpurnia (II), was struck down because the emperor had praised her looks. Since, however, he had spoken casually and without designs on her, Agrippina's anger stopped short of extreme measures. In Lollia Paulina's case, however, a colonel of the Guard was sent to enforce her suicide.

Also condemned at this time was Gaius Cadius Rufus, a governor of Bithynia, who was charged by its people for extortion. Another province, Narbonese Gaul, received a privilege for its deferential attitude to the senate: senators originating from it were allowed to visit their homes without the emperor's permission, as was already permitted to members from Sicily. Ituraea and Judaea, on the deaths of their monarchs, Sohaemus and Agrippa (I)[1] respectively, were incorporated in the province of Syria.

It was decided to reintroduce and perpetuate the 'Augury for the Welfare of Rome', suspended for the last seventy-five years. Claudius

1. Agrippa (I), grandson of Herod the Great, had died in A.D. 44.

also extended the city boundary:[1] Here he followed an ancient custom whereby those who have expanded the empire are entitled to enlarge the city boundary also. Yet no Roman commander except Sulla and the divine Augustus had ever exercised this right, however great their conquests.

There are various traditions concerning the pretensions or renown of the kings in this respect. The original foundation, and Romulus' boundary, are noteworthy. The furrow indicating the city's limits started from the Cattle Market, because oxen are employed for ploughing (the bronze statue of a bull is displayed there), and ran outside the great altar of Hercules. Then there were stones at regular intervals marked along the base of the Palatine Hill to the altar of Consus, the old Council House, the shrine of the Lares, and the Forum. The Forum and Capitol are believed to have been included in the city not by Romulus but by Titus Tatius.[2] Subsequently the city boundaries grew as Roman territory expanded. The limits established by Claudius are easily traceable and are indicated in public records.

In the following year Gaius Antistius Vetus (II) and Marcus Suillius Nerullinus became consuls. The adoption of Lucius Domitius Ahenobarbus was now hurried forward. Pallas, pledged to Agrippina as organizer of her marriage and subsequently her lover, took the initiative. He pressed Claudius to consider the national interests and furnish the boy Britannicus with a protector: 'Just as the divine Augustus, though supported by grandsons, advanced his stepsons, and Tiberius, with children of his own, adopted Germanicus; so Claudius too ought to provide himself with a young future partner in his labours.' The emperor was convinced. Echoing the ex-slave's arguments in the senate, he promoted Lucius Domitius Ahenobarbus above his own son, who was three years younger.

Thanks were voted to the emperor. More remarkable was the compliment that the young man received: legal adoption into the Claudian family with the name of Nero. Authorities noted that this was the

1. The official, religious boundary of the city consisted of a strip of holy ground outside the wall.
2. The legendary Sabine opponent and then co-ruler of Romulus. Archaeology shows that the Forum served as a cemetery for the earliest hill-settlements and was not drained and incorporated into the city until later. The Capitol was believed to have been at first a home for political refugees.

first known adoption into the patrician branch of the Claudii,[1] which had come down without a break from Attus Clausus. And now Agrippina, too, was honoured with the title of Augusta. After these developments no one was hard-hearted enough not to feel distressed at Britannicus' fate. Gradually deprived even of his slaves' services, Britannicus saw through his stepmother's hypocrisy and treated her untimely attentions cynically. He is said to have been intelligent. This may be true. But it is a reputation which was never tested, and perhaps he only owes it to sympathy with his perils.

Agrippina now advertised her power to the provincials. She had a settlement of ex-soldiers established at the capital of the Ubii and named after her. This was her birthplace. Incidentally, it had been her grandfather Agrippa to whom the tribe had submitted after crossing the Rhine.

At this time, too, a marauding raid by the Chatti alarmed Upper Germany. The imperial governor Publius Pomponius Secundus sent German levies from the tribes of the Vangiones and Nemetes, and auxiliary cavalry, with orders to cut off the raiders or, if they dispersed, to surround them unawares. The troops carried out his orders keenly. They divided into two columns. The left-hand column surprised a newly returned enemy band, somnolent after an orgy over the spoils. Particularly satisfactory was the recovery, after forty years of enslavement, of a few survivors from the disaster of Publius Quinctilius Varus. The contingent which had taken the shorter, right-hand, route inflicted a worse defeat on the enemy, which had risked an open engagement. Laden with plunder after this achievement, the column returned to the Taunus mountains.

Pomponius was waiting there with his Roman brigades. He hoped that eagerness to retaliate might induce the Chatti to risk battle. But they were afraid of being trapped between the Romans and their perpetual enemies the Cherusci. So they sent a delegation to Rome with hostages. Pomponius was awarded an honorary Triumph – a small part of his reputation with posterity, which values his poetry more.

At the same period Vannius was ejected from the kingdom of the Suebi which Drusus had given him. In the early years of his reign his people had loved and honoured Vannius. Then continuous power had

1. The patrician Claudii were the Neros and Drususes, the non-patricians the Marcelli.

made him tyrannical; and internal disputes, combined with the enmity of his neighbours, brought him down. His downfall was due to Vibilius, king of the Hermunduri, and to his own sister's sons, Vangio and Sido. Claudius received repeated appeals from Vannius, but refused to intervene between the native combatants. However, he promised Vannius a safe refuge if he were ejected. The emperor also instructed the imperial governor of Pannonia, Sextus Palpellius Hister, to post a division with picked local auxiliaries on the Danube bank, in order to protect the losers – and intimidate the winners, in case success emboldened them to break the peace with Rome also.

For numberless hordes, Lugii and other tribes, were closing in, drawn by the reputation of the opulent kingdom which Vannius had enriched for thirty years by plunder and taxation. Since his own infantry and Sarmatian cavalry from the tribe of the Jazyges were no match for the enemy's numbers, he decided to gain time by conducting defensive warfare from his strongholds. His cavalry, however, had no patience for sieges, and wandered over the surrounding plains. There the hostile Lugii and Hermunduri converged on them, and a battle became unavoidable. Vannius came down from his fortresses, but was defeated – though applauded, in his misfortune, for fighting personally at close quarters and receiving frontal wounds.

Vannius took refuge with the Roman fleet waiting on the Danube. His dependants soon followed and were settled, with grants of land, in Pannonia. His nephews shared his kingdom. To us they were steadfastly loyal. With their subjects, they were popular while winning power, unpopular (more markedly) after they had won it. Their characters had changed – or absolutism was producing its results.

*

In Britain[1] the situation inherited by the imperial governor Publius Ostorius Scapula was chaotic. Convinced that a new commander, with an unfamiliar army and with winter begun, would not fight them, hostile tribes had broken violently into the Roman province. But Ostorius knew that initial results are what produce alarm or confidence. So he marched his light auxiliary battalions rapidly ahead, and stamped out resistance. The enemy were dispersed and hard

1. British affairs from A.D. 47 to 58 are described consecutively here.

pressed. To prevent a rally, or a bitter treacherous peace which would give neither general nor army any rest, Ostorius prepared to disarm all suspects and reduce the whole territory as far as the Trent[1] and Severn.

The first to revolt against this were the Iceni. We had not defeated this powerful tribe in battle, since they had voluntarily become our allies. Led by them, the neighbouring tribes now chose a battlefield at a place protected by a rustic earthwork, with an approach too narrow to give access to cavalry. The Roman commander, though his troops were auxiliaries without regular support, proposed to carry these defences. At the signal, Ostorius' infantry, placed at appropriate points and reinforced by dismounted cavalrymen, broke through the embankment. The enemy, imprisoned by their own barrier, were overwhelmed – though with rebellion on their consciences, and no way out, they performed prodigies of valour. During the battle the governor's son, Marcus Ostorius Scapula, won the Citizen's Oak-Wreath for the saving of a Roman's life.

This defeat of the Iceni quieted others who were wavering between war and peace. The Roman army then struck against the Decangi,[2] ravaging their territory and collecting extensive booty. The enemy did not venture upon an open engagement and, when they tried to ambush the column, suffered for their trickery. Ostorius had nearly reached the sea facing Ireland when a rising by the Brigantes recalled him. For, until his conquests were secured, he was determined to postpone further expansion. The Brigantes subsided; their few peace-breakers were killed, and the rest were pardoned.

But neither sternness nor leniency prevented the Silures from fighting. To suppress them, a brigade garrison had to be established.[3] In order to facilitate the displacement of troops westward to man it, a strong settlement of ex-soldiers was established on conquered land at Camulodunum. Its mission was to protect the country against revolt and familiarize the provincials with law-abiding government. Next Ostorius invaded Silurian territory.

1. The interpretation of Trisantona = Trent is based on a small emendation of an otherwise incomprehensible text.

2. Inscribed pieces of lead found in north-east Wales suggest that the tribe which Tacitus knows as the Decangi may have called themselves 'Degeangli'.

3. The site of the camp among the Silures (S.E. Wales or borders) is uncertain.

The natural ferocity of the inhabitants was intensified by their belief in the prowess of Caratacus,[1] whose many undefeated battles – and even many victories – had made him pre-eminent among British chieftains. His deficiency in strength was compensated by superior cunning and topographical knowledge. Transferring the war to the country of the Ordovices, he was joined by everyone who found the prospect of a Roman peace alarming. Then Caratacus staked his fate on a battle. He selected a site where numerous factors – notably approaches and escape-routes – helped him and impeded us. On one side there were steep hills. Wherever the gradient was gentler, stones were piled into a kind of rampart. And at his front there was a river without easy crossings. The defences were strongly manned.

The British chieftains went round their men, encouraging and heartening them to be unafraid and optimistic, and offering other stimulants to battle. Caratacus, as he hastened to one point and another, stressed that this was the day, this the battle, which would either win back their freedom or enslave them for ever. He invoked their ancestors, who by routing Julius Caesar had valorously preserved their present descendants from Roman officials and taxes – and their wives and children from defilement. These exhortations were applauded. Then every man swore by his tribal oath that no enemy weapons would make them yield – and no wounds either.

This eagerness dismayed the Roman commanders disconcerted as he already was by the river-barrier, the fortifications supplementing it, the overhanging cliffs, and the ferocious crowds of defenders at every point. But our soldiers shouted for battle, clamouring that courage could overcome everything; and their colonels spoke to the same effect, to encourage them further.

After a reconnaissance to detect vulnerable and invulnerable points, Ostorius led his enthusiastic soldiers forward. They crossed the river without difficulty, and reached the rampart. But then, in an exchange of missiles, they came off worse in wounds and casualties. However, under a roof of locked shields, the Romans demolished the crude and clumsy stone embankment, and in the subsequent fight at close quarters the natives were driven to the hill-tops. Our troops pursued them closely. While light-armed auxiliaries attacked with javelins, the heavy

1. Caratacus was the son of Cunobelinus. They are better known as Caractacus and Cymbeline.

regular infantry advanced in close formation. The British, unprotected by breastplates or helmets, were thrown into disorder. If they stood up to the auxiliaries they were cut down by the swords and spears of the regulars, and if they faced the latter they succumbed to the auxiliaries' broadswords and pikes. It was a great victory. Caratacus' wife and daughter were captured: his brother surrendered. He himself sought sanctuary with Cartimandua, queen of the Brigantes. But the defeated have no refuge. He was arrested, and handed over to the conquerors.

The war in Britain was in its ninth year. The reputation of Caratacus had spread beyond the islands and through the neighbouring provinces to Italy itself. These people were curious to see the man who had defied our power for so many years. Even at Rome his name meant something. Besides, the emperor's attempts to glorify himself conferred additional glory on Caratacus in defeat. For the people were summoned as though for a fine spectacle, while the Guard stood in arms on the parade ground before their camp. Then there was a march past, with Caratacus' petty vassals, and the decorations and neck-chains and spoils of his foreign wars. Next were displayed his brothers, wife, and daughter. Last came the king himself. The others, frightened, degraded themselves by entreaties. But there were no downcast looks or appeals for mercy from Caratacus. On reaching the dais he spoke in these terms.

'Had my lineage and rank been accompanied by only moderate success, I should have come to this city as friend rather than prisoner, and you would not have disdained to ally yourself peacefully with one so nobly born, the ruler of so many nations. As it is, humiliation is my lot, glory yours. I had horses, men, arms, wealth. Are you surprised I am sorry to lose them? If you want to rule the world, does it follow that everyone else welcomes enslavement? If I had surrendered without a blow before being brought before you, neither my downfall nor your triumph would have become famous. If you execute me, they will be forgotten. Spare me, and I shall be an everlasting token of your mercy!'

Claudius responded by pardoning him and his wife and brothers. Released from their chains, they offered to Agrippina, conspicuously seated on another dais nearby, the same homage and gratitude as they had given the emperor. That a woman should sit before Roman standards was an unprecedented novelty. She was asserting her partnership in the empire her ancestors had won.

Then the senate met. It devoted numerous complimentary speeches to the capture of Caratacus. This was hailed as equal in glory to any previous Roman general's exhibition of a captured king. They cited the display of Syphax by Publius Cornelius Scipio Africanus and of Perseus by Lucius Aemilius Paullus (I).[1] Ostorius received an honorary Triumph. But now his success, hitherto unblemished, began to waver. Possibly the elimination of Caratacus had caused a slackening of energy, in the belief that the war was over. Or perhaps the enemy's sympathy with their great king had whetted their appetite for revenge.

In Silurian country, Roman troops left to build forts under a divisional chief of staff were surrounded, and only saved from annihilation because neighbouring fortresses learnt of their siege and speedily sent help. As it was, casualties included the chief of staff, eight company-commanders, and the pick of the men. Shortly afterwards a Roman foraging party was put to flight. So were cavalry toops sent to its rescue. Ostorius threw in his light auxiliary battalions, but even so did not check the rout until the regular brigades joined in. Their strength made the struggle equal and eventually gave us the advantage. However, night was coming on, so the enemy escaped almost undamaged.

Battle followed battle. They were mostly guerrilla fights, in woods and bogs. Some were accidental – the results of chance encounters. Others were planned with calculated bravery. The motives were hatred or plunder. Sometimes these engagements were ordered by the generals; sometimes they knew nothing of them.

The Silures were exceptionally stubborn. They were enraged by a much-repeated saying of the Roman commander that they must be utterly exterminated, just as the Sugambri[2] had once been annihilated or transplanted to the Gallic provinces. Two auxiliary battalions, which their greedy commanders had taken plundering with insufficient precautions, fell into a trap laid by the Silures. Then they began,

1. Syphax of Numidia (N. Africa) was defeated in the Second Punic War (ended 201 B.C.), Perseus of Macedonia in 168 B.C.
2. Tiberius had transplanted the remnants of the Sugambri across the Rhine in 8 B.C.

by gifts of spoils and prisoners, to tempt other tribes to join their rebellion.

At this point, exhausted by his anxious responsibilities, Ostorius died. The enemy exulted that so considerable a general, if not defeated in battle, had at least been eliminated by warfare. On hearing of the governor's death the emperor, not wanting to leave the province masterless, appointed Aulus Didius Gallus to take over. Didius made for Britain rapidly. But he found a further deterioration. For in the interval a Roman brigade commanded by Manlius Valens had suffered a reverse. Reports were magnified – the enemy magnified them, to frighten the new general; and the new general magnified them to increase his glory if he won, and improve his excuse if resistance proved unbreakable. Again the damage was due to the Silures: until deterred by Didius' arrival, they plundered far and wide.

However, since Caratacus' capture the best strategist was Venutius who as I mentioned earlier, was a Brigantian.[1] While married to the tribal queen, Cartimandua, he had remained loyal and under Roman protection. But divorce had immediately been followed by hostilities against her and then against us. At first, the Brigantes had merely fought among themselves. Cartimandua had astutely trapped Venutius' brother and other relatives. But her enemies, infuriated and goaded by fears of humiliating feminine rule, invaded her kingdom with a powerful force of picked warriors. We had foreseen this, and sent auxiliary battalions to support her. The engagement that followed had no positive results at first but ended more favourably. A battle fought by a regular brigade under Caesius Nasica likewise had a satisfactory ending. Didius, of impressive seniority and incapacitated by age, was content to act through subordinates and on the defensive.

(These campaigns were conducted by two imperial governors over a period of years. But I have described them in one place since piecemeal description would cast a strain on the memory. Now I return to the chronological succession of events.)

Next came the year when Claudius held his fifth consulship (his colleague was Servius Cornelius Salvidienus Orfitus); Nero now prematurely assumed adult costume, to qualify himself for an official career. The emperor willingly yielded to the senate's sycophantic pro-

1. The earlier reference to Venutius has not survived.

posal that Nero should hold the consulship at nineteen and meanwhile, as consul-designate, already possess its status outside the city, and be styled Prince of Youth.[1] Furthermore gifts were made to the troops and public in Nero's name, and at Games held in the Circus he was allowed to attract popular attention by wearing triumphal robes, whereas Britannicus was dressed as a minor. So the crowd, seeing one in the trappings of command and the other in boy's clothes, could deduce their contrasted destinies.

Now, too, all colonels, staff-officers, and company-commanders of the Guard who showed sympathy with Britannicus' predicament were eliminated on various fictitious grounds; sometimes promotion was the pretext. Even former slaves loyal to him were removed. The excuse for this was a meeting between the two boys at which Nero had greeted Britannicus by that name, but Britannicus addressed him as 'Domitius'. Agrippina complained vigorously to her husband. This was a first sign of unfriendliness, she said, a contemptuous neglect of the adoption, a contradiction – in the emperor's own home – of a national measure, voted by the senate and enacted by the people. Disaster for Rome would ensue, she added, unless malevolent and corrupting teachers were removed. Disturbed by these implied accusations, the emperor banished or executed all Britannicus' best tutors and put him under the control of his stepmother's nominees.

Nevertheless, Agrippina did not yet venture to make her supreme attempt until she could remove the commanders of the Guard, Lusius Geta and Rufrius Crispinus, whom she regarded as loyal to the memory of Messalina and to the cause of Messalina's children. So Agrippina asserted to Claudius that the Guard was split by their rivalry and that unified control would mean stricter discipline. Thereupon the command was transferred to Sextus Afranius Burrus, who was a distinguished soldier but fully aware whose initiative was behind his appointment. Agrippina also enhanced her own status. She entered the Capitol in a ceremonial carriage.[2] This distinction, traditionally reserved for priests and sacred emblems, increased the reverence felt

1. The first 'princes of youth' had been Augustus' grandsons Gaius and Lucius Caesar.

2. The carriage (*carpentum*) had been allowed by the senate to Messalina and had appeared on a coin of Tiberius in honour of Livia.

for a woman who to this day remains unique as the daughter of a great commander and the sister, wife, and mother of emperors.

However, her chief supporter, Lucius Vitellius, greatly influential but extremely old, was now prosecuted by a junior senator, Junius Lupus – so precarious is a great man's position. The charges were treason and designs on the throne. The emperor would have listened but for the pleas, or rather menaces, of Agrippina, who instead induced him to outlaw the accuser. Vitellius had not asked for more than that.

This year witnessed many prodigies. Ill-omened birds settled on the Capitol. Houses were flattened by repeated earthquakes, and as terror spread the weak were trampled to death by the panic-stricken crowd. Further portents were seen in a shortage of corn, resulting in famine. The consequent alarm found open expression when Claudius, administering justice, was surrounded by a frenzied mob; driven to the far corner of the Forum, he was hard pressed until a detachment of troops forced a way for him through the hostile crowd. It was established that there was no more than fifteen days' supply of food in the city. Only heaven's special favour and a mild winter prevented catastrophe. And yet surely Italy once exported food for the army to distant provinces! The trouble, now, is not infertile soil. The fact is that we prefer to cultivate Africa and Egypt – thereby staking Rome's survival on the hazards of navigation.

In this year war broke out between the Armenians and Iberians, and seriously disturbed relations between Rome and Parthia. The king of Parthia was now Vologeses I, a Greek concubine's son, who had obtained the throne with the agreement of his brothers. Pharasmanes had long ruled over Iberia. His brother Mithridates held Armenia with our support. Pharasmanes had a son Radamistus, a tall handsome youth of great physical strength, skilled in his countrymen's accomplishments and well thought of among the adjacent peoples. Frequently and violently – too much so for his ambitions to remain a secret – he complained that his father's longevity kept him off the humble Iberian throne.

Pharasmanes, in his advancing years, felt nervous about his son's popularity and eagerness for power. So he diverted the young man's hopes to Armenia – recalling that he himself, after routing the Parthians, had put his brother Mithridates there. But force, he said, must wait – better set a trap and catch Mithridates unawares. So Radamistus counterfeited a breach with his father and, alleging that he could not face his stepmother's hostility, proceeded to his uncle Mithridates. There he was treated with great friendliness and honoured as a son – while he seduced the Armenian noblemen into rebellion against his unsuspecting host.

The next step was a pretended reconciliation with his father. Radamistus returned to Pharasmanes, reporting that all that plotting could do had been done, and force must do the rest. Pharasmanes invented a pretext for war. He alleged that, during hostilities against the neighbouring king of Albania, his brother Mithridates had opposed his appeal for Roman help, and must pay for this with his life. Then, at the head of a large force given him by his father, Radamistus suddenly burst into Armenia.

He drove the terrified Mithridates out of the open country into the fortress of Gorneae. Strongly situated and well garrisoned, it was under the Roman commander of an auxiliary battalion, Caelius Pollio, and a company-commander Casperius. Natives are totally ignorant of that branch of military art which we understand so thoroughly, siege-equipment and tactics, and Radamistus' attacks on the fortifications proved costly failures. So he began a blockade. But force created no impression, so he tried tempting Caelius Pollio's acquisitiveness. Casperius protested against this criminal bribery, aimed at the overthrow of an allied king and the Armenian realm given him by Rome. But his superior officer pleaded the enemy's strength; and Radamistus pleaded his father's orders. Casperius arranged a truce and left, intending to deter Pharasmanes from war, or, failing that, to report the Armenian situation to the imperial governor of Syria.

Relieved of supervision now that the company-commander had gone, Caelius Pollio urged Mithridates to make terms. He stressed the bonds of brotherhood, Pharasmanes' seniority, and their other family ties (Mithridates was married to a daughter of Pharasmanes, and Radamistus to a daughter of Mithridates), and argued that the Iberians, though at present in the ascendancy, were inclined for peace. 'You know Armenian treachery,' he said. 'Your only protection is an ill-provisioned fort. Do not attempt the hazards of warfare! Accept a bloodless agreement.' Mithridates hesitated, suspecting the intentions of Caelius, who had seduced one of his royal concubines and was considered purchasable for any outrage.

Meanwhile Casperius reached Pharasmanes, and demanded that the Iberians should raise the siege. Their king's public answers were ambiguous but on the whole acquiescent. Privately, however, Pharasmanes warned Radamistus by messenger to prosecute the siege with all urgency. The wage of treachery was therefore raised, and Pollio by secret bribery induced his men to demand peace and threaten to lay down arms. Mithridates was forced to agree to a day and place for a meeting; and he left the fort.

When they met, Radamistus threw himself into Mithridates' arms with pretended devotion, greeting him as father-in-law and parent, and swearing that neither by the sword nor by poison would he attack him. Then Radamistus conducted him into a wood nearby; everything was ready for a sacrifice there, he said, so that the gods might witness and ratify their agreement. By tradition, kings meeting to become allies join hands and have their thumbs tied and fastened tightly by a knot. The blood, flowing into the extremities, is released by a slight cut and licked by the two participants. The exchange of blood is held to confer a mystic sanction on the alliance. On this occasion, the man fastening the cords pretended to slip, and grasping Mithridates round the knees pulled him down. Then others ran up and shackled him. He was dragged away by his fetters – natives consider this particularly degrading – amid insults and blows from the populace who had suffered from his stern rule. Others, however, felt pity for this overwhelming change of fortune.

Mithridates' wife followed with their small children, filling the air with her cries. They, too, were imprisoned, in separate covered carriages, to await Pharasmanes' orders. In his criminal heart brotherly and fatherly feelings were outweighed by acquisitiveness. However, Pharasmanes spared himself the sight of the murders. Radamistus apparently remembered his oath. He employed neither sword nor poison against his sister and uncle. Instead, he heaped heavy clothing on their prostrate bodies and smothered them. Mithridates' sons too were killed, for weeping at their parents' deaths.

When Gaius Ummidius Durmius Quadratus, imperial governor of Syria, learnt that Mithridates had fallen by treachery and that his murderers held Armenia, he summoned his council. Reporting what had happened, he asked for advice whether punitive action should be taken. A few members were concerned for our national honour. Most, however, advocated prudence. Their argument was that foreigners' crimes were to be welcomed and that discord should actually be inculcated: indeed emperors had often made a gift of this same Armenia, ostensibly from generosity, really to unsettle the natives. Let Radamistus, they suggested, keep his ill-gotten gains, secured at the price of loathing and infamy – that was better for Rome than if he had won them gloriously. This view was accepted. However, for fear of seeming to condone the crime – or receiving contrary orders from Claudius – a delegation was sent to bid Pharasmanes evacuate Armenia and recall his son.

The governor of Cappadocia was a knight called Julius Paelignus. Though as contemptible for his stupidity as for his absurd appearance, he was extremely intimate with Claudius, who before his accession had amused his idle leisure with the company of such buffoons. Paelignus now collected local auxiliaries with a view to recovering Armenia. However, his ravages caused the provincials worse suffering than the enemy. Then his troops deserted him. Left defenceless against native attacks he fled to Radamistus – who gave him costly presents. Captivated, Paelignus urged Radamistus to assume the insignia of kingship; and the ceremony took place, with Paelignus standing by as authorizer and henchman.

When this disgraceful news became known, Quadratus felt it must be shown that all Romans were not like Paelignus; and he sent a division to handle the disturbed position as circumstances suggested. Crossing the Taurus mountains rapidly, its commander, Helvidius Priscus (I), dealt with the situation, more by diplomacy than by force. But then he was recalled to Syria, in case he provoked a Parthian war.

For Vologeses believed that he had an opportunity to invade Armenia – once ruled by his ancestors, now criminally seized by a foreigner. He collected an army and prepared to establish his brother Tiridates on the throne (this would mean that every branch of his family had its kingdom[1]). The Parthians crossed the frontier. The Iberians were driven back without a fight, and Artaxata and Tigranocerta submitted. Then, however, followed a terrible winter; and the inefficient supply system of the Parthians caused an epidemic. Vologeses was

1. Vologeses' other brother Pacorus was king of Media Atropatene.

compelled to evacuate the country and Armenia was once more without a government. In came Radamistus, more savage than ever – treating the people as traitors who would, in time, revolt again. However, though slavery was nothing new, the patience of the Armenians was not unlimited. They surrounded the palace in arms. Swift horses were all that saved Radamistus. They carried him and his wife away. But she was pregnant. At first she endured the journey as best she could, for terror of her enemies and love of her husband. But the continuous galloping soon shook and jarred her so terribly that she begged to be rescued from the humiliations of captivity by an honourable death. Radamistus admired her courage: sick with fear of leaving her to someone else, he embraced, comforted and encouraged her. But he was a man of violence; and finally, in the vehemence of his love, he drew his sabre, stabbed her, dragged her to the bank of the river Aras, and hurled her in – so that even her corpse should not be taken. Then he rode full speed to his own land of Iberia.

But Zenobia (that was his wife's name) was found by shepherds in a backwater. She lived; she was still breathing. Concluding from her noble appearance that she was someone distinguished, they bandaged her wound and applied rustic remedies. When they learnt her name and story they took her to the city of Artaxata. From there she was officially conducted to Tiridates, who received her kindly and gave her royal honours.

In the following year the consuls were Faustus Cornelius Sulla Felix and Lucius Salvius Otho Titianus. Lucius Arruntius Furius Scribonianus was now exiled for inquiring from astrologers about the emperor's death. The charge was also extended to his mother, Vibia, recalcitrant (it was alleged) against her earlier sentence of expulsion. The fact that Scribonianus' father, Lucius Arruntius Camillus Scribonianus, had rebelled in Dalmatia[1] was cited by the emperor to illustrate his mercy in again sparing this disaffected family. But the exile did not survive long. Did Scribonianus die naturally or by poison? People spread their own beliefs. The senate passed a severe, but futile, decree banning astrologers from Italy.

The emperor, in a speech, praised senators who voluntarily abandoned their rank through poverty. Those however who, by not

1. This revolt against Claudius in A.D. 42 had been crushed within a few days.

retiring, showed shamelessness as well as indigence were expelled. Next Claudius proposed to the senate that women marrying slaves should be penalized. It was decided that the penalty for such a lapse should be enslavement, if the man's master did not know, and the status of an ex-slave if he did. The emperor revealed that this proposal was due to Pallas; to whom accordingly rewards of an honorary praetorship and fifteen million sesterces were proposed by the consuldesignate Marcius Barea Soranus. Publius Cornelius Lentulus Scipio (II) added the suggestion that Pallas should be given the nation's thanks because, though descended from Arcadian kings, he preferred the national interests to his antique lineage, and let himself be regarded as one of the emperor's servants. Claudius reported that Pallas was content with that distinction only, and preferred not to exceed his former modest means. So the senate's decree was engraved in letters of bronze; it loaded praises for old-world frugality on a man who had once been a slave and was now worth three hundred million sesterces.

Pallas' brother, the knight Antonius Felix,[1] who was the governor of Judaea, showed less moderation. Backed by vast influence, he believed himself free to commit any crime. However, the Jews had shown unrest and had rioted when Gaius ordered the erection of his own statue in the Temple. Gaius died before the order had been carried out, but there remained fears that a later emperor would repeat it. Moreover, Felix stimulated outbreaks by injudicious disciplinary measures. His bad example was imitated by Ventidius Cumanus, who controlled part of the province. For Judaea was divided: the Samaritans came under Felix and the Galileans under Ventidius.

These tribes had a long-standing feud, which their contempt for their present rulers now allowed to rage unrestrained. They ravaged each other's territory with invading robber gangs, setting traps for one another and sometimes openly clashing, and then depositing their thefts and plunder with the Roman officials. At first the two men were pleased. Then, as the situation became graver, they intervened with troops – which suffered reverses. War would have flamed up throughout the province if the imperial governor of Syria had not intervened.

Jews who had ventured to kill Roman soldiers were executed without hesitation. The cases of Cumanus and Felix were more embarrassing. For Claudius, learning the causes of the revolt, had empowered

1. This is the Felix of the *Acts of the Apostles*, xxiv.

Quadratus to deal with these officials himself. He displayed Felix as one of the judges, his position on the bench being intended to silence his accusers. Cumanus was condemned for the irregularities of both. Then the Judaean province was peaceful again.

Shortly afterwards the wild Cilician tribes of the Cietae, which had often caused disturbances, fortified a mountainous position under their chief Troxoboris, and descended from it upon the cities and the coast. There they boldly attacked cultivators, townsmen, and often traders and ship-owners. They besieged Anemurium, and defeated a cavalry force under Curtius Severus sent to its relief from Syria; for the rough ground impeded cavalry operations and favoured the Cilicians who were on foot. Finally Antiochus Epiphanes IV of Commagene, the dependent monarch who controlled the coast, by offering inducements to the rank and file and tricking their leader, split the native forces, and after executing the chief and a few of his associates pardoned and pacified the rest.

A tunnel through the mountain between the Fucine Lake and the river Liris had now been completed. To enable a large crowd to see this impressive achievement a naval battle was staged on the lake itself, like the exhibition given by Augustus on his artificial lake adjoining the Tiber, though his ships and combatants had been fewer. Claudius equipped warships manned with nineteen thousand combatants, surrounding them with a circle of rafts to prevent their escape. Enough space in the middle, however, was left for energetic rowing, skilful steering, charging, and all the incidents of a sea-battle. On the rafts were stationed double companies of the Guard and other units, behind ramparts from which they could shoot catapults and stone-throwers. The rest of the lake was covered with the decked ships of the marines.

The coast, the slopes, and the hill-tops were thronged like a theatre by innumerable spectators, who had come from the neighbouring towns and even from Rome itself – to see the show or pay respects to the emperor. Claudius presided in a splendid military cloak, with Agrippina in a mantle of cloth of gold. Though the fighters were criminals they fought like brave men. After much blood-letting, they were spared extermination.

After the display, the waterway was opened. But careless construction became evident. The tunnel had not been sunk to the bottom of the lake or even halfway down. So time had to be allowed for the deepening of the channel. A second crowd was assembled, this time to witness an infantry battle fought by gladiators on pontoons. But, to the horror of banqueters near the lake's outlet, the force of the out-rushing water swept away everything in the vicinity – and the crash and roar caused shock and terror even farther afield. Agrippina took advantage of the emperor's alarm to accuse Narcissus, the controller of the project, of illicit profits. He retorted by assailing her dictatorial, feminine excess of ambition.

Next year, when the consuls were Decimus Junius Silanus Tor-quatus and Quintus Haterius Antoninus, Nero, aged sixteen, married the emperor's daughter Octavia. Eager to make a brilliant name as learned and eloquent, Nero successfully backed Ilium's application to be exempted from all public burdens, fluently recalling the descent of Rome from Troy and of the Julii from Aeneas, and other more or less mythical traditions. Nero's advocacy also secured for the settle-ment of Bononia, which had been burnt down, a grant of ten million sesterces. Next the Rhodians – continually liberated or subjected in accordance with their services in foreign wars, or lapses into disorder at home – recovered their freedom. And Phrygian Apamea, over-whelmed by an earthquake, was granted remission of taxes for five years.

But Agrippina's intrigues were still driving Claudius to the most brutal behaviour. Titus Statilius Taurus (II), famous for his wealth, had gardens which she coveted. So she broke him. The prosecutor she used as her instrument was Tarquitius Priscus. When Taurus was governor of Africa, Tarquitius had been his deputy; now that they were back he accused Taurus of a few acts of extortion but more especially of magic. Unable any longer to endure undeserved humilia-tion by a lying accuser, the defendant, without awaiting the senate's verdict, took his own life. The senate, however, so detested the informer that they expelled him – although Agrippina was his sup-porter.

On several occasions this year the emperor was heard saying that the decisions of knights who were his agents should be as valid as his own judgements. And in case these should be regarded as chance utterances, the senate decreed on the subject in more detailed and comprehensive terms than hitherto. The divine Augustus had conferred jurisdiction on those who governed Egypt, their judgements to rank with those of senatorial officials. Later, in other provinces and in Rome as well, knights were ceded many judicial cases hitherto heard by governors and praetors respectively. Now Claudius handed over to the knights all the powers which had so often caused rioting and fighting, as, for instance, when the laws of Gaius Sempronius Gracchus (I) gave them a monopoly of places on the Bench and the law of Quintus Servilius Caepio restored them to the senate.[1] This was the principal issue in the fighting between Marius and Sulla. In earlier days, however, the struggle had been between classes, and the results extorted applied to a whole class. Julius Caesar's protégés, Gaius Oppius and Lucius Cornelius Balbus (I), were the first individuals important enough to decide issues of peace and war. Later names of powerful members of the order, such as Gaius Matius and Publius Vedius Pollio, are not worth mentioning since Claudius now gave even ex-slaves, placed in control of his personal estates, equal authority with himself and the law.

Next he proposed to exempt Cos from taxation. In a lengthy discourse about its ancient history, he said that its first inhabitants had been Argives – or perhaps Coeus, the father of the goddess Latona; then Aesculapius had brought the art of healing, which had achieved remarkable distinction among his descendants. The emperor indicated their names and the periods at which each had lived. Then he added that a member of the same family was his own doctor, Gaius Stertinius Xenophon: in response to whose petition the people of Cos would in future be exempted from all taxation, holding their island as a sacred place, and serving the god alone. Claudius might, of course, have recalled their frequent assistance to Rome, and the victories they had shared with us. But he preferred not to disguise behind external arguments the favour which, with his usual indulgence, he had conceded to an individual.

The Byzantines, on the other hand, when their protests against oppressive burdens were given a hearing, reviewed all their services to Rome. Beginning with their treaty with Rome at the time of our war

---

1. This law of Gaius Sempronius Gracchus is one of the Sempronian laws of 122 B.C. The law of Quintus Servilius Caepio (106 B.C.) partially restored the law-courts to the senate.

against the king of Macedonia known, owing to his dubious origin, as pseudo-Philip,[1] they then recounted their services against Antiochus III, Perseus, and Aristonicus, their assistance to Marcus Antonius Creticus in the Pirate War, to Sulla, Lucius Licinius Lucullus, and Pompey, and finally, in more recent times, to the Caesars. The reason for these services had been their situation at a convenient crossing-point for generals and their armies and supplies. For the Greeks had founded Byzantium at the narrowest part of the strait between Europe and Asia. When they asked Pythian Apollo where to found a city, the oracle replied 'opposite the land of the blind'. This riddle referred to Chalcedon, whose inhabitants had arrived in the region earlier and had seen the superb site first but chosen an inferior one. Byzantium had originally been rich and prosperous. It has a fertile soil and a productive sea, since great numbers of fish, coming from the Black Sea and scared by shelving rocks under the surface on the winding Asiatic coast, swim away from it into the harbours on the European side. But subsequently financial burdens became oppressive; and now they begged for exemption or alleviation. The emperor supported them, arguing that their exhaustion from recent wars in Thrace[2] and the Crimean Bosphorus entitled them to relief. A remission of tribute was granted for five years.

In the following year the consuls were Marcus Asinius Marcellus and Manius Acilius Aviola. A series of prodigies indicated changes for the worse. Standards and soldiers' tents were set on fire from the sky. A swarm of bees settled on the pediment of the Capitoline temple. Half-bestial children were born, and a pig with a hawk's claws. A portent, too, was discerned in the losses suffered by every official post: a quaestor, aedile, tribune, praetor, and consul had all died within a few months. Agrippina was particularly frightened – because Claudius had remarked in his cups that it was his destiny first to endure his wives' misdeeds, and then to punish them. She decided to act quickly.

First, however, out of feminine jealousy, she destroyed Domitia

1. The 'pseudo-Philip' of Macedonia was Andriscus, defeated in 148 B.C. Creticus, father of the Triumvir Antony, had fought the pirates in 74–72 B.C. Lucullus had continued the war against Mithridates VI of Pontus from 73 to 66 B.C. (the Third Mithridatic War).

2. After recent hostilities Thrace had become a province (A.D. 46).

Lepida,[1] who regarded herself as Agrippina's equal in nobility – she was daughter of Antonia (I), and grand-niece of Augustus; cousin once removed of Agrippina; and sister of Agrippina's former husband Cnaeus Domitius Ahenobarbus. In beauty, age, and wealth there was little between the two women. Moreover both were immoral, disreputable, and violent, so they were as keen rivals in vicious habits as in the gifts bestowed on them by fortune. But their sharpest issue was whether aunt or mother should stand first with Nero. Lepida sought to seduce his youthful character by kind words and indulgence. Agrippina on the other hand, employed severity and menaces – she could give her son the empire, but not endure him as emperor.

However, the charge against Lepida was attempting the life of the empress by magic, and disturbing the peace of Italy by failing to keep her Calabrian slave-gangs in order. On these charges she was sentenced to death – in spite of vigorous opposition by Narcissus. His suspicions of Agrippina continually grew deeper. 'Whether Britannicus or Nero comes to the throne', he was said to have told his friends, 'my destruction is inevitable. But Claudius has been so good to me that I would give my life to help him. The criminal intentions for which Messalina was condemned with Gaius Silius have re-emerged in Agrippina. With Britannicus as his successor the emperor has nothing to fear. But the intrigues of his stepmother in Nero's interests are fatal to the imperial house – more ruinous than if I had said nothing about her predecessor's unfaithfulness. And once more there is unfaithfulness. Agrippina's lover is Pallas. That is the final proof that there is nothing she will not sacrifice to imperial ambition – neither decency, nor honour, nor chastity.'

Talking like this, Narcissus would embrace Britannicus and pray he would soon be a man. With hands outstretched – now to the boy, now to heaven – he besought that Britannicus might grow up and cast out his father's enemies, and even avenge his mother's murderers. Then Narcissus' anxieties caused his health to fail. He retired to Sinuessa, to recover his strength in its mild climate and health-giving waters.

Agrippina had long decided on murder. Now she saw her opportunity. Her agents were ready. But she needed advice about poisons. A sudden, drastic effect would give her away. A gradual, wasting

1. Domitia Lepida was Messalina's mother (Table 3).

recipe might make Claudius, confronted with death, love his son again. What was needed was something subtle that would upset the emperor's faculties but produce a deferred fatal effect. An expert in such matters was selected – a woman called Locusta, recently sentenced for poisoning but with a long career of imperial service ahead of her. By her talents, a preparation was supplied. It was administered by the eunuch Halotus who habitually served the emperor and tasted his food.

Later, the whole story became known. Contemporary writers stated that the poison was sprinkled on a particularly succulent mushroom. But because Claudius was torpid – or drunk – its effect was not at first apparent; and an evacuation of his bowels seemed to have saved him. Agrippina was horrified. But when the ultimate stakes are so alarmingly large, immediate disrepute is brushed aside. She had already secured the complicity of the emperor's doctor Xenophon; and now she called him in. The story is that, while pretending to help Claudius to vomit, he put a feather dipped in a quick poison down his throat. Xenophon knew that major crimes, though hazardous to undertake, are profitable to achieve.

The senate was summoned. Consuls and priests offered prayers for the emperor's safety. But meanwhile his already lifeless body was being wrapped in blankets and poultices. Moreover, the appropriate steps were being taken to secure Nero's accession. First Agrippina, with heart-broken demeanour, held Britannicus to her as though to draw comfort from him. He was the very image of his father, she declared. By various devices she prevented him from leaving his room and likewise detained his sisters, Claudia Antonia and Octavia. Blocking every approach with troops, Agrippina issued frequent encouraging announcements about the emperor's health, to maintain the Guard's morale and await the propitious moment forecast by the astrologers.

At last, at midday on October the thirteenth, the palace gates were suddenly thrown open. Attended by Sextus Afranius Burrus, commander of the Guard, out came Nero to the battalion which, in accordance with regulations, was on duty. At a word from its commander, he was cheered and put in a litter. Some of the men are said to have looked round hesitantly and asked where Britannicus was. However, as no counter-suggestion was made, they accepted the choice offered them. Nero was then conducted into the Guards' camp. There, after saying a few words appropriate to the occasion – and promising gifts on the generous standard set by his father – he was hailed as emperor.[1] The army's decision was followed by senatorial decrees. The provinces, too, showed no hesitation.

Claudius was voted divine honours, and his funeral was modelled on that of the divine Augustus – Agrippina imitating the grandeur of her great-grandmother Livia, the first Augusta. But Claudius' will was not read, in case his preference of stepson to son should create a public impression of unfairness and injustice.

1. New emperors, like successful generals, were hailed as 'Imperator'.

CHAPTER II

The Fall of Agrippina

*

THE first casualty of the new reign was the governor of Asia, Marcus Junius Silanus (II). His death was treacherously contrived by Agrippina, without Nero's knowledge. It was not provoked by any ferocity of temper. Silanus was lazy, and previous rulers had despised him – Gaius used to call him 'the Golden Sheep'.[1] But Agrippina was afraid he would avenge her murder of his brother, Lucius Junius Silanus Torquatus (I). Popular gossip, too, widely suggested that Nero, still almost a boy and emperor only by a crime, was less eligible for the throne than a mature, blameless aristocrat who was, like himself, descended from the Caesars. For Silanus was a great-great-grandson of the divine Augustus – and this still counted. So he was murdered. The act was done by a knight, Publius Celer, and a former slave, Helius, the emperor's agents in Asia. Without the precautions necessary to maintain secrecy, they administered poison to the governor at dinner.

Equally hurried was the death of Claudius' ex-slave Narcissus. I have described his feud with Agrippina. Imprisoned and harshly treated, the threat of imminent execution drove him to suicide. The emperor, however, was sorry: Narcissus' greed and extravagance harmonized admirably with his own still latent vices.

Other murders were meant to follow. But the emperor's tutors, Sextus Afranius Burrus and Lucius Annaeus Seneca, prevented them. These two men, with a unanimity rare among partners in power, were, by different methods, equally influential. Burrus' strength lay in soldierly efficiency and seriousness of character, Seneca's in amiable high principles and his tuition of Nero in public speaking. They collaborated in controlling the emperor's perilous adolescence; their

1. Diogenes the Cynic (*c.* 400–325 B.C.) was said to have called rich fools 'golden sheep'.

policy was to direct his deviations from virtue into licensed channels of indulgence. Agrippina's violence, inflamed by all the passions of ill-gotten tyranny, encountered their united opposition.

She, however, was supported by Pallas, who had ruined Claudius by instigating his incestuous marriage and disastrous adoption. But Nero was not disposed to obey slaves. Pallas' surly arrogance, anomalous in a man of servile origin, disgusted him. Nevertheless, publicly, Agrippina received honour after honour. When the escort-commander made the customary request for a password, Nero gave: 'The best of mothers.' The senate voted her two official attendants and the Priesthood of Claudius.

For Claudius was declared a god. A public funeral was to come first. On the day of the funeral the emperor pronounced his predecessor's praises. While he recounted the consulships and Triumphs of the dead man's ancestors, he and his audience were serious. References to Claudius' literary accomplishments too, and to the absence of disasters in the field during his reign, were favourably received. But when Nero began to talk of his stepfather's foresight and wisdom, nobody could help laughing.

Yet the speech, composed by Seneca, was highly polished – a good example of his pleasant talent, which admirably suited contemporary taste. Older men, who spent their leisure in making comparisons with the past, noted that Nero was the first ruler to need borrowed eloquence. The dictator Julius Caesar had rivalled the greatest orators. Augustus spoke with imperial fluency and spontaneity. Tiberius was a master at weighing out his words – he could express his thoughts forcibly, or he could be deliberately obscure. Even Gaius' mental disorders had not weakened his vigorous speech; Claudius' oratory, too, was graceful enough, provided it was prepared. But from early boyhood Nero's mind, though lively, directed itself to other things – carving, painting, singing, and riding. Sometimes, too, he wrote verses, and thereby showed he possessed the rudiments of culture.

Sorrow duly counterfeited, Nero attended the senate and acknowledged its support and the army's backing. Then he spoke of his advisers, and of the examples of good rulers before his eyes. 'Besides, I bring with me no feud, no resentment or vindictiveness,' he asserted. 'No civil war, no family quarrels, clouded my early years.' Then, outlining his future policy, he renounced everything that had occasioned

recent unpopularity. 'I will not judge every kind of case myself', he
said, 'and give too free rein to the influence of a few individuals by
hearing prosecutors and defendants behind my closed doors. From
my house, bribery and favouritism will be excluded. I will keep personal and State affairs separate. The senate is to preserve its ancient
functions. By applying to the consuls, people from Italy and the senatorial provinces may have access to its tribunals. I myself will look after
the armies under my control.'

Moreover, these promises were implemented. The senate decided
many matters. They forbade advocates to receive fees or gifts. They
excused quaestors-designate from the obligation to hold gladiatorial
displays. Agrippina objected to this as a reversal of Claudius' legislation. Yet it was carried – although the meeting was convened in the
Palatine, and a door built at the back so that she could stand behind a
curtain unseen, and listen. Again, when an Armenian delegation was
pleading before Nero, she was just going to mount the emperor's
dais and sit beside him. Everyone was stupefied. But Seneca instructed
Nero to advance and meet his mother. This show of filial dutifulness
averted the scandal.

At the end of the year there were disturbing rumours that the Parthians had broken out and were plundering Armenia – Radamistus,
who had so often seized control of that country and been ejected, had
again given up the struggle. So in Rome, where gossip thrives, people
asked how an emperor who was only just seventeen could endure or
repel the shock. A youth under feminine control was not reassuring.
Wars, with their battles and sieges, could not be managed by tutors.

However, there was also a contrary view, which regarded it as
better than if the responsibilities of command had fallen to the lazy
old Claudius, who would have been ordered about by his slaves.
Burrus and Seneca, it was recalled, were known to be highly experienced men, and Nero was nearly grown up; Pompey had conducted
a civil war at seventeen, and the future Augustus at nineteen. 'At the
top', said supporters of this opinion, 'command and planning count
more than weapon-wielding and physique. We shall see whether his
advisers are good or bad if he appoints the best man as commander,
ignoring that man's jealous critics and pressure, from wealthy or
influential rivals.'

While this was the talk, Nero commanded the eastern divisions to be raised to full strength by drafts from the adjacent provinces, and to proceed towards Armenia. Two dependent kings, namely Agrippa II and Antiochus Epiphanes IV (of Commagene), were instructed to prepare an army to invade Parthia, and orders were given that the Euphrates should be bridged. Lesser Armenia and Sophene were given to Aristobulus and Sohaemus, with royal status. Opportunely, there was a revolt against Vologeses led by a son of Vardanes I; and the Parthians evacuated Armenia. Their intention was to fight later. But the senators performed exaggerated celebrations, proposing days of thanksgiving on which the emperor should wear the triumphal robe, enter the city in ovation, and have his statue in the temple of Mars the Avenger – of the same size as the god's. Besides habitual sycophancy there was satisfaction because the man appointed to secure Armenia was Cnaeus Domitius Corbulo (II) – a sign that promotions were to be by merit.

The disposition of the eastern armies was as follows. Two brigades[1] with part of the auxiliaries were to remain in the province of Syria under its imperial governor, Gaius Ummidius Durmius Quadratus. Corbulo was to have a combined regular and auxiliary force of the same size, with the addition of the auxiliary infantry and cavalry wintering in Cappadocia. The allied kings were instructed to serve wherever hostilities required; their inclination was to follow Corbulo. He, to follow up his prestige – a vital matter in new undertakings – rapidly proceeded to Cilicia. Quadratus came there to meet him at Aegeae, so that Corbulo should not enter Syria to take over his army, thus becoming the focus of attention. Corbulo's appearance was impressive, and so was his oratory – superficial advantages matching his experience and ability.

Both commanders sent messengers advising Vologeses to choose peace not war, and to demonstrate, by giving hostages, the respect his predecessors had been accustomed to show for Rome. Vologeses duly handed over leading Parthian royalties. He wanted to select his own time for hostilities. Perhaps, too, he wanted, under the guise of hostages, to eliminate suspected rivals. The hostages were received by Insteius Capito, a junior Roman staff officer, who chanced to have been sent by Quadratus to see Vologeses concerning some previous

1. Four brigades (plus auxiliaries) were the normal garrison of Syria.

matter. Corbulo, hearing this, ordered a battalion commander, Arrius Varus, to go and take over the hostages. This caused an altercation between the two envoys.

To cut short this exhibition before foreigners, the officers left the decision to the hostages themselves and their escorts. They chose Corbulo on account of his freshly won reputation (indeed, he was popular even among enemies). So the two generals quarrelled. Quadratus declared himself robbed of the fruits of his own negotiations. Corbulo asserted that the Parthian decision to give hostages had been subsequent to his own appointment to conduct the war – which had converted the king's optimism into alarm. To terminate the dispute Nero had it announced that the imperial fasces should be wreathed with laurel 'owing to the successes of Quadratus and Corbulo'. (I have here described events extending into the next year.)

In the same year the emperor requested the senate to authorize statues of his late father Cnaeus Domitius Ahenobarbus and his guardian Asconius Labeo. He declined an offer to erect statues of himself in solid gold or silver. The senate had decreed that future years should begin in December, the month of his birth. But he retained the old religious custom of starting the year on January 1st. He refused to allow the prosecution of a Roman knight, Julius Densus, for favouring Britannicus – or of a junior senator, Carrinas Celer, who was accused by a slave. Consul in the next year, Nero exempted his colleague Lucius Antistius Vetus from swearing allegiance, like the other officials, to the emperor's acts. The senate praised this vigorously; they hoped that if his youthful heart were elated by popularity for minor good deeds he might turn to greater ones. Then he showed leniency by readmitting to the senate Plautius Lateranus, who had been expelled for adultery with Messalina. Nero pledged himself to clemency in numerous speeches; Seneca put them into his mouth, to display his own talent or demonstrate his high-minded guidance.

Agrippina was gradually losing control over Nero. He fell in love with a former slave Acte. His confidants were two fashionable young men, Marcus Salvius Otho,[1] whose father had been consul, and Claudius Senecio, son of a former imperial slave. Nero's secret, surreptitious, sensual meetings with Acte established her ascendancy. When

1. This is the Otho who was to become emperor for a few months in A.D. 69.

Nero's mother finally discovered, her opposition was fruitless. Even his older friends were not displeased to see his appetites satisfied by a common girl with no grudges. Destiny, or the greater attraction of forbidden pleasures, had alienated him from his aristocratic and virtuous wife Octavia, and it was feared that prohibition of his affair with Acte might result in seductions of noblewomen instead.

Agrippina, however, displayed feminine rage at having an ex-slave as her rival and a servant girl as her daughter-in-law, and so on. She refused to wait until her son regretted the association, or tired of it. But her violent scoldings only intensified his affection for Acte. In the end, deeply in love, he became openly disobedient to his mother and turned to Seneca – one of whose intimates, Annaeus Serenus, had screened the first stages of the liaison by lending his own name as the ostensible donor of the presents which Nero secretly gave Acte. Agrippina now changed her tactics, and indulgently offered the privacy of her own bedroom for the relaxations natural to Nero's age and position. She admitted that her strictness had been untimely, and placed her resources – which were not much smaller than his own – at his disposal. This change from excessive severity to extravagant complaisance did not deceive Nero – and it alarmed his friends, who urged him to beware of the tricks of this always terrible and now insincere woman.

One day Nero was looking at the robes worn by the resplendent wives and mothers of former emperors. Picking out a jewelled garment, he sent it as a present to his mother – a generous, spontaneous gift of a greatly coveted object. But Agrippina, instead of regarding this as an addition to her wardrobe, declared that her son was doling out to her a mere fraction of what he owed her – all else but this one thing was kept from her. Some put a sinister construction on her words.

Nero, exasperated with the partisans of this female conceit, deposed Pallas from the position from which, since his appointment by Claudius, he had virtually controlled the empire. As the ex-slave left the palace with a great crowd of followers, the emperor penetratingly commented 'Pallas is going to swear himself out of his state functions'.[1]

1. On retirement high senatorial officials (not ex-slaves such as Pallas) had to swear, before a concourse of friends, that they had done nothing illegal.

In fact, Pallas had substituted for that customary oath of high officials
a stipulation that there should be no investigations of his past conduct,
and that his account with the State should be regarded as balanced.

Agrippina was alarmed; her talk became angry and menacing. She
let the emperor hear her say that Britannicus was grown up and was
the true and worthy heir of his father's supreme position – now held,
she added, by an adopted intruder, who used it to maltreat his mother.
Unshrinkingly she disclosed every blot on that ill-fated family, without sparing her own marriage and her poisoning of her husband. 'But
heaven and myself are to be thanked', she added, 'that my stepson is
alive! I will take him to the Guards' camp. Let them listen to Germanicus' daughter pitted against the men who claim to rule the whole
human race – the cripple Burrus with his maimed hand, and Seneca,
that deportee with the professorial voice!' Gesticulating, shouting
abuse, she invoked the deified Claudius, the spirits of the Silani below
– and all her own unavailing crimes.

This worried Nero. As the day of Britannicus' fourteenth birthday[1]
approached, he pondered on his mother's violent behaviour – also on
Britannicus' character, lately revealed by a small indication which had
gained him wide popularity. During the amusements of the Satur-
nalia the young men had thrown dice for who should be king, and
Nero had won. To the others he gave various orders causing no embarrassment. But he commanded Britannicus to get up and come into
the middle and sing a song. Nero hoped for laughter at the boy's
expense, since Britannicus was not accustomed even to sober parties,
much less to drunken ones. But Britannicus composedly sang a poem
implying his displacement from his father's home and throne. This
aroused sympathy – and in the frank atmosphere of a nocturnal party,
it was unconcealed. Nero noticed the feeling against himself, and
hated Britannicus all the more.

Though upset by Agrippina's threats, he could not find a charge
against his stepbrother or order his execution openly. Instead, he
decided to act secretly – and ordered poison to be prepared. Arrangements were entrusted to a colonel of the Guard, Julius Pollio, who was
in charge of the notorious convicted poisoner Locusta. It had earlier
been ensured that Britannicus' attendants should be unscrupulous and

1. He would officially assume manhood on this occasion.

disloyal. His tutors first administered the poison. But it was evacuated, being either too weak or too diluted for prompt effectiveness. Impatient at the slowness of the murder, Nero browbeat the colonel and ordered Locusta to be tortured. They thought of nothing but public opinion, he complained; they safeguarded themselves and regarded his security as a secondary consideration. Then they swore that they would produce effects as rapid as any sword-stroke; and in a room adjoining Nero's bedroom, from well-tried poisons, they concocted a mixture.

It was the custom for young imperial princes to eat with other noblemen's children of the same age at a special, less luxurious table, before the eyes of their relations: that is where Britannicus dined. A selected servant habitually tasted his food and drink. But the murderers thought of a way of leaving this custom intact without giving themselves away by a double death. Britannicus was handed a harmless drink. The taster had tasted it; but Britannicus found it too hot, and refused it. Then cold water containing the poison was added. Speechless, his whole body convulsed, he instantly ceased to breathe.

His companions were horrified. Some, uncomprehending, fled. Others, understanding better, remained rooted in their places, staring at Nero. He still lay back unconcernedly – and he remarked that this often happened to epileptics; that Britannicus had been one since infancy; soon his sight and consciousness would return. Agrippina tried to control her features. But their evident consternation and terror showed that, like Britannicus' sister Octavia, she knew nothing. Agrippina realized that her last support was gone. And here was Nero murdering a relation. But Octavia, young though she was, had learnt to hide sorrow, affection, every feeling. After a short silence the banquet continued.

Britannicus was cremated the night he died. Indeed, preparations for his inexpensive funeral had already been made. As his remains were placed in the Field of Mars,[1] there erupted a violent storm. It was widely believed that the gods were showing their fury at the boy's murder – though even his fellow-men generally condoned it, arguing that brothers were traditional enemies and that the empire was indivisible. A number of contemporary writers assert that for a consider-

1. He was buried in the Mausoleum of Augustus.

able time previously Nero had corrupted his victim. If so, his death might have seemed to come none too soon, and be the lesser outrage of the two.

Such was this hurried murder of the last of the Claudians, physically defiled, then poisoned right among the religious emblems on the table, before his enemy's eyes – without time even to give his sister a farewell kiss. Nero justified the hasty funeral by an edict recalling the traditional custom of withdrawing untimely deaths from the public gaze and not dwelling on them with eulogies and processions. Now that he had lost his brother's help, he added, all his hopes were centred on his country; senate and people must give all the greater support to their emperor, the only remaining member of his family, exalted by destiny. Then he distributed lavish gifts to his closest friends. Some were shocked when, at such a juncture, men of ethical pretensions accepted his distribution of town and country mansions like loot. Others thought they had no choice since the emperor, with his guilty conscience, hoped for impunity if he could bind everyone of importance to himself by generous presents.

However, no generosity could mollify his mother. She became Octavia's supporter. Constantly meeting her own friends in secret, Agrippina outdid even her natural greed in grasping funds from all quarters to back her designs. She was gracious to officers, and attentive to such able and high-ranking noblemen as survived. She seemed to be looking round for a Party, and a leader for it. Learning this, Nero withdrew the military bodyguard which she had been given as empress and retained as the emperor's mother, and also the German guardsmen by which, as an additional compliment, it had recently been strengthened. Furthermore, he terminated her great receptions, by giving her a separate residence in the mansion formely occupied by Antonia (II). When he visited her there, he would bring an escort of staff-officers, hurriedly embrace her, and leave.

Veneration of another person's power, if it is ill-supported, is the most precarious and transient thing in the world. Agrippina's house was immediately deserted. Her only visitors and comforters were a few women, there because they loved her – or hated her. One of them was Junia Silana, whose separation from her husband Gaius Silius (II) by Messalina I have described. Noble, beautiful, and immoral, she had long been an intimate friend of Agrippina. Recently, however, an unspoken enmity had arisen between them, because Agrippina had deterred a young nobleman, Titus Sextius Africanus, from marrying Silana by describing her as immoral and past her prime. Agrippina did not want him for herself, but wanted to keep him from obtaining the childless Silana's wealth.

Silana now saw her chance of revenge. She put up two of her dependants, Iturius and Calvisius, to prosecute Agrippina. They avoided the old, frequently heard charges of her mourning Britannicus' death or proclaiming Octavia's wrongs. Instead they accused her of inciting Rubellius Plautus to revolution. This man, through his mother, possessed the same relationship to the divine Augustus as Nero did. Agrippina, the allegation was, proposed to marry Plautus and control the empire again. Nero's aunt Domitia – who was Agrippina's deadly rival – had a freed slave Atimetus who heard this story from the two prosecutors and urged the ballet-dancer Paris (another of Domitia's former slaves) to go speedily and divulge the plot to the emperor, in sensational terms.

It was late at night when Paris entered. Nero had long been drinking. This was the time Paris usually came, to enliven the emperor's dissipations. Tonight, however, Paris wore a gloomy expression; and he told his story in detail. The emperor, listening in terror, resolved to kill his mother, to kill Plautus, and also to depose Burrus from the command of the Guard, as being a supporter and nominee of Agrippina. One historian, Fabius Rusticus, claims that Nero had actually written a letter of appointment to a proposed successor of Burrus, Gaius Caecina Tuscus, and that it was only through Seneca's influence that Burrus retained his post. But this authority favours Seneca, whose friendship had made his career; and two others writers, Pliny the Elder and Cluvius Rufus, report no doubts of Burrus' loyalty. (My plan is to indicate such individual sources only when they differ. When they are unanimous, I shall follow them without citation.)[1]

Nero was so alarmed and eager to murder his mother that he only agreed to be patient when Burrus promised that, if she was found guilty, she should die. But Burrus pointed out that everyone must be given an opportunity for defence – especially a parent; and that at present there were no prosecutors but only the report of one man,

1. The extent of Tacitus' dependence on the lost histories of Fabius Rusticus, Marcus Cluvius Rufus, and Pliny the elder has long been disputed.

from a household unfriendly to her. Nero should reflect, he added, that it was late and they had spent a convivial night, and that the whole story had an air of recklessness and ignorance.

This calmed the emperor's fears. Next morning, Burrus visited Agrippina to acquaint her with the accusation and tell her she must refute it or pay the penalty. Burrus did this in Seneca's presence; certain ex-slaves were also there as witnesses. Burrus named the charges and the accusers, and adopted a menacing air. But Agrippina displayed her old spirit. 'Junia Silana has never had a child', she said, 'so I am not surprised she does not understand a mother's feelings! For mothers change their sons less easily than loose women change their lovers. If Silana's dependants Iturius and Calvisius, after exhausting their means, can only repay the hag's favours by becoming accusers, is that a reason for darkening my name with my son's murder, or loading the emperor's conscience with mine?

'As for Domitia, I should welcome her hostility if she were competing with me in kindness to my Nero – instead of concocting melodramas with her lover Atimetus and the dancer Paris. While I was planning Nero's adoption and promotion to consular status and designation to the consulship, and all the other preparations for his accession, she was beautifying her fish-ponds at her beloved Baiae.

'I defy anyone to convict me of tampering with city police or provincial loyalty, or of inciting slaves and ex-slaves to crimes. If Britannicus had become emperor could I ever have survived? If Rubellius Plautus or another gained the throne and became my judge, there would be no lack of accusers! For then I should be charged, not with occasional indiscretions – outbursts of uncontrollable love – but with crimes which no one can pardon except a son!'

Agrippina's listeners were touched, and tried to calm her excitement. But she demanded to see her son. To him, she offered no defence, no reminder of her services. For the former might have implied misgivings, the latter reproach. Instead she secured rewards for her supporters – and revenge on her accusers. Junia Silana, on the other hand, was exiled, her dependants Iturius and Calvisius expelled, Atimetus executed. Paris played too important a part in the emperor's debaucheries to be punished. Rubellius Plautus was left unnoticed – for the present. Publius Anteius, appointed imperial governor of Syria, was put off by various devices and finally kept in Rome. Faenius Rufus was given control of the food supply, Arruntius Stella given the Games projected by the emperor, and Tiberius Claudius Balbillus made imperial governor of Egypt.

Pallas and Burrus were charged with conspiring to give the empire to Faustus Cornelius Sulla Felix, because of his great name and marriage link with Claudius, whose daughter Claudia Antonia was his wife. The accusation originated with a certain Paetus, notorious for acquiring confiscated properties from the Treasury. His story was clearly untrue. But Pallas's innocence did not cause much satisfaction because of the disgust provoked by his arrogance. For when certain ex-slaves in his household were denounced as his accomplices, Pallas replied that all orders in his home were given by nods or waves of the hand – when more detailed instructions were required he wrote them, to avoid personal contact. Burrus, though himself among the accused, was one of the judges, and pronounced acquittal. The informer was banished, and his records unearthing forgotten debts to the Treasury were burnt.

At the end of the year the battalion of the Guard customarily present at the Games was withdrawn. The intention was to give a greater impression of freedom, to improve discipline by removing the Guardsmen from the temptations of public displays, and to test whether the public would behave respectably without their restraint.

The temples of Jupiter and Minerva were struck by lightning. The emperor consulted diviners and on their recommendation conducted a purification of the city.

The consuls for the following year were Quintus Volusius Saturnius and Publius Cornelius Lentulus Scipio (II). The year was a time of peace abroad, but disgusting excesses by Nero in Rome. Disguised as a slave, he ranged the streets, brothels, and taverns with his friends, who pilfered goods from shops and assaulted wayfarers. Their identity was unsuspected: indeed, as marks on his face testified, Nero himself was struck. When it became known that the waylayer was the emperor, attacks on distinguished men and women multiplied. For, since disorderliness was tolerated, pseudo-Neros mobilized gangs and behaved similarly, with impunity. Rome by night came to resemble a conquered city.

A senator called Julius Montanus, who had not yet held office, assaulted by the emperor in the dark, hit back vigorously. But then

Montanus recognized his assailant and apologized. However his apology was interpreted as a slur, and he was forced to commit suicide. Yet the incident diminished Nero's boldness. In future he surrounded himself with soldiers and masses of gladiators, and these, while holding aloof from minor semi-private brawls, intervened forcibly whenever the victims showed vigorous resistance.

In the theatre, there were brawls between gangs favouring rival ballet-dancers. Nero converted these disorders into serious warfare. For he waived penalties and offered prizes – watching in person, secretly and on many occasions even openly. Finally, however, public animosities and fears of worse disturbances left no alternative but to expel these dancers from Italy and station troops in the theatre again.

About this time the senate discussed the offences of former slaves. It was demanded that patrons should be empowered to re-enslave undeserving ex-slaves. The proposal had widespread support. But the consuls did not dare to put the motion without consulting the emperor, to whom they wrote stating the senate's view. Since his advisers, though few, were divided, Nero hesitated to give a ruling. One side denounced the disrespectfulness of liberated slaves. 'It goes to such lengths', they said, 'that former slaves confront their patron with the choice of yielding them their rights by legal argument, as equals, or by force. Freed slaves even lift their hands to strike their former master – and sarcastically urge their own punishment. For all that an injured patron may do is to send his freed slave away beyond the hundredth milestone – to the Campanian beaches! In all other respects the two men are legally equal and identical. Patrons ought to be given a weapon which cannot be disregarded. It would be no hardship for the liberated to have to keep their freedom by the same respectful behaviour which won it for them. Indeed, blatant offenders ought to be enslaved again, so as to frighten the ungrateful into obedience.'

The opposite argument went thus: 'The guilty few ought to suffer, but not to the detriment of freed slaves' rights in general. For ex-slaves are everywhere. They provide the majority of the voters, public servants, attendants of officials and priests, watchmen, firemen. Most knights, many senators, are descended from former slaves. Segregate the freed – and you will only show how few free-born there are! When our ancestors fixed degrees of rank, they were right to make everyone free. Besides, two sorts of liberation were instituted to leave room for second thoughts or favour. Some were liberated "by the wand", those who were not remained half-slaves. Slave-owners ought to consider individual merits, but be slow to grant what is irrevocable.'

This opinion prevailed. Nero wrote asking the senate to give separate consideration to every charge by a patron, but not to diminish the rights of ex-slaves in general. Soon afterwards his aunt Domitia was deprived of the patronage of her former slave Paris, ostensibly on legal grounds. He was pronounced free-born, on the orders of the emperor -- whose reputation suffered thereby.

Nevertheless there were still signs of a free country. A dispute arose between a praetor, Vibullius, and a tribune, Antistius Sosianus, because the latter had ordered the release of some of the disorderly followers of ballet-dancers. The praetor had imprisoned these hangers-on, and the senate backed him, censuring the tribune for irregularity. They also forbade tribunes to encroach on the authority of praetors and consuls, or to summon Italian litigants to Rome in cases where local settlement was practicable. The consul-designate Lucius Calpurnius Piso (V) added proposals that tribunes should not exercise their powers in their own homes, and that fines imposed by them should not be entered in the Treasury records for four months, during which time objections could be lodged for adjudication by the consuls. The powers of aediles, too, were curtailed, limits being fixed to the sums which 'curule' aediles and aediles of the people could distrain or fine. Moreover a quaestor in charge of the Treasury, Helvidius Priscus (II), was quarrelling with a tribune, Obultronius Sabinus, who charged him with over-rigorous compulsory sales of poor men's property. Thereupon the emperor transferred the Treasury and public accounts from quaestors to commissioners who were experienced former praetors. The control of the Treasury has undergone numerous changes. Augustus entrusted it to commissioners selected by the senate. Later, when improper canvassing was suspected, they were chosen by lot from the praetors. But the lot could fall on incompetent men, so this arrangement too was short-lived. Claudius returned the post to quaestors. However, thinking they might prove inactive through fear of giving offence, he promised them exceptional promotion. But the young men lacked the maturity for so important a first post.

A governor of Sardinia, Vipsanius Laenas, was found guilty of

fraudulence (also in this year). However, a governor of Achaia, Cestius Proculus, charged by the Cretans with extortion, was exonerated. The fleet-commander at Ravenna, Publius Palpellius Clodius
Quirinalis, who had inflicted his savagery and debauchery on Italy as
if it were the humblest of subject territories, poisoned himself to
forestall condemnation. Caninius Rebilus, outstanding in legal learning
and wealth, escaped the miseries of invalid old age by opening his
veins. No one had thought he had the courage for this, because of his
notorious effeminacy. Lucius Volusius Saturninus (II) also died, leaving a distinguished reputation and a great fortune, honestly won. He
had lived to ninety-three and avoided the malevolence of every
emperor.

Next year, when the consuls were Nero (for the second time) and
Lucius Calpurnius Piso (V), little worth recording occurred, except
in the eyes of historians who like filling their pages with praise of the
foundations and beams of Nero's huge amphitheatre in the Field of
Mars.[1] But that is material for official gazettes, whereas it has traditionally been judged fitting to Rome's grandeur that its histories should
contain only important events. Drafts of ex-soldiers were sent to two
Italian settlements, Capua and Nuceria. The city population were
given a bonus of four hundred sesterces a head. Forty million sesterces
were paid into the Treasury to maintain public credit. The 4 per cent
tax on the purchase of slaves was waived (though its removal was a
fiction, since the tax was only shifted to the dealers, who increased
their prices accordingly).

The emperor also published instructions that no provincial official,
in his province, should give shows of gladiators or wild beasts, or any
other display. For hitherto this ostensible generosity had been as
oppressive to provincials as extortion, the governors' intention being
to win partisans to screen their irregularities. The senate also passed a
punitive and precautionary measure. If a man was murdered by his
slaves, those liberated by his will – if they were in the house – were to
be executed with the rest.

At this time a former consul Lurius Varus, formerly convicted of
extortion, was restored to his rank. The distinguished lady Pomponia
Graecina, wife of Aulus Plautius – whose official ovation for British

1. This reference to the structure of Nero's amphitheatre seems to recall, not
very amiably, its description by Pliny the elder in his *Natural History*.

victories I have mentioned[1] – was charged with foreign superstition and referred to her husband for trial. Following ancient tradition he decided her fate and reputation before her kinsmen, and acquitted her. But her long life was continuously unhappy. For after the murder, by Messalina's intrigues, of her relative Livia Julia – daughter of Drusus – she wore mourning and grieved unceasingly for forty years. This escaped punishment under Claudius, and thereafter gave her prestige.

The same year witnessed several prosecutions. Publius Celer was accused by the province of Asia. He, as I have mentioned, had been the murderer of his governor Marcus Junius Silanus (II) – a great enough crime to overshadow his other misdeeds. Nero could not acquit him. Instead he protracted the case until Celer died of old age. Cossutianus Capito was indicted by the Cilicians. This vicious and disreputable individual believed he could behave as outrageously in his province as in Rome. Defeated, however, by determined prosecutors, he abandoned his defence and was condemned under the extortion law. The Lycians claimed damages from Titus Clodius Eprius Marcellus.[2] But his intrigues were so effective that some of his accusers were exiled for endangering an innocent man.

Nero's colleague in his third consulship was Marcus Valerius Messalla Corvinus (II), whose great-grandfather, the orator of the same name, a few old men remembered as consular colleague of Nero's great-great-grandfather the divine Augustus. The reputation of Messalla's distinguished family was now buttressed by an annual grant of half a million sesterces to enable him to support his poverty honestly. The emperor also conferred annuities on two other senators, Aurelius Cotta and Quintus Haterius Antoninus, though both had squandered their inherited fortunes by extravagance.

At the beginning of the year the war between Rome and Parthia for the possession of Armenia,[3] in abeyance after a half-hearted start, was energetically resumed. For Vologeses I of Parthia would allow

1. The ovation of Aulus Plautius must have been mentioned in the lost part of the book. His wife Pomponia Graecina may have been a Christian. Her link with Livia Julia may have been due to the marriage of the latter's great-grandfather Marcus Agrippa to the daughter of Titus Pomponius Atticus.

2. Eprius Marcellus was one of the most formidable speakers of his age.

3. In handling these provincial and foreign affairs Tacitus abandons the strict division between years.

his brother Tiridates neither to lose the Armenian throne, which he had given him, nor to hold it as the gift of a foreign power; whereas Cnaeus Domitius Corbulo (II) felt that the grandeur of Rome required the recovery of the territories once conquered by Lucius Licinius Lucullus and Pompey. Furthermore, the Armenians were divided in allegiance and asked both sides in. But their geographical position and way of life inclined them to the Parthians; and with Parthians they had intermarried. So those were the masters they preferred. Of freedom they knew nothing.

Corbulo found his own men's slackness a worse trouble than enemy treachery. His troops had come from Syria. Demoralized by years of peace, they took badly to service conditions. The army actually contained old soldiers who had never been on guard or watch, who found ramparts and ditches strange novelties, and who owned neither helmet nor breastplate – flashy money-makers who had soldiered in towns. Corbulo discharged men who were too old or too weak, and filled their places with Galatian and Cappadocian recruits, augmented by a brigade from Germany with auxiliary infantry and cavalry. The whole army was kept under canvas through a winter so severe that ice had to be removed and the ground excavated before tents could be pitched. Frostbite caused many losses of limbs. Sentries were frozen to death. A soldier was seen carrying a bundle of firewood with hands so frozen that they fell off, fastened to their load.

Corbulo himself, thinly dressed and bare-headed, moved among his men at work and on the march, encouraging the sick and praising efficiency – an example to all. But the harsh climate and service produced many shirkers and deserters. Corbulo's remedy was severity. In other armies, first and second offences were excused: Corbulo executed deserters immediately. Results showed that this was salutary and preferable to indulgence. For he had fewer deserters than lenient commanders.

Corbulo kept his troops in camp until spring was under way. Auxiliary infantry were suitably distributed, with orders not to provoke battle. These outposts were put under a senior staff-officer, Paccius Orfitus. He reported that the natives were unguarded and conditions were suitable for an engagement; but he was instructed to stay behind his defences and await reinforcements. When, however, a few small units reached him from neighbouring forts and ignorantly clamoured to fight, Paccius flouted his orders and attacked. He was routed. The troops who should have supported him took fright at his defeat and withdrew headlong to their respective entrenchments. Corbulo was angry. Reprimanding Paccius, he ordered him and his staff and men to encamp outside the fortifications, and in that degrading position they were kept until a unanimous petition secured their release.

Tiridates, now supported by his brother Vologeses' forces as well as his own dependants, dropped concealment and openly ravaged Armenia. As he moved rapidly, plundering communities he believed to be pro-Roman and evading detachments sent against him, his reputation (rather than any warlike feats) terrorized the country. Corbulo tried persistently to force an engagement, but failed. Instead he was forced to imitate the enemy and enlarge the theatre of war, dispersing his formations so that their commanders could deliver co-ordinated attacks at different points. So the king of Commagene, Antiochus Epiphanes IV, was ordered to invade the regions nearest his border. Pharasmanes, king of Iberia, also demonstrated his friendship to us by reviving his longstanding feud with the Armenians; he had executed his son Radamistus as a traitor. The tribe of the Heniochi, too, inaugurated their record of keen loyalty to Rome by overrunning certain remote areas.

Tiridates' plans were upset. Envoys from him demanded, in his and Parthia's name, why after he had recently given hostages and reaffirmed friendship he was being expelled from his longstanding occupancy of Armenia. Vologeses, they added, had not acted yet because they preferred to rely on their rights rather than force; but if the Romans persisted in fighting, then the Parthian royal house would again be as valorous and successful as numerous Roman disasters had proved it. But Corbulo knew that Vologeses was occupied with a rebellion in Hyrcania. So he urged Tiridates to petition the emperor. 'You might win a secure throne bloodlessly', he suggested, 'if you abandon distant far-off ambitions and take the better chance that is now offered you.'

These exchanges, however, did not bring peace any nearer. So it was decided to fix the place and time for a meeting. Tiridates said he would bring a thousand cavalry as escort – Corbulo could bring as many men as he liked, of whatever kind, provided that they came peaceably, without breastplates or helmets. Anyone, and best of all a wary veteran commander, could see a cunning native trick in the proposal to restrict his own numbers but allow Corbulo more. For any number of unarmed men, exposed to trained bowmen on horseback, would be useless. Pretending not to understand, Corbulo replied that these national issues were best discussed in front of their whole armies. The site he chose was between gently sloping hills suitable for infantry movements and level ground on which cavalry could deploy.

On the appointed day Corbulo arrived first. On his flanks were auxiliaries from the provinces and dependent kingdoms, in the centre the sixth brigade strengthened by an admixture of three thousand men from the third – these summoned from another camp by night but put under the same Eagle to look like a single brigade. It was evening when Tiridates appeared; but he stayed in the distance – visible yet not audible. So there was no meeting. Corbulo ordered his men to return to their respective camps. Tiridates moved away hastily. Either the dispersal of the Roman army made him suspect treachery, or he wanted to intercept provisions reaching us by the Black Sea by way of Trapezus. In this, however, he failed since the supply-line across the mountains was in Roman hands.

To avoid a long unprofitable campaign and put the Armenians on the defensive, Corbulo prepared to destroy their forts. Leaving smaller ones to two subordinates, the divisional commander Cornelius Flaccus and Insteius Capito, now chief-of-staff, he himself tackled the strongest in the region, Volandum by name. After reconnoitring its fortifications he planned the assault. He urged his men to strike for glory and also for plunder, and expel this shifty enemy who wanted neither war nor peace but admitted their treachery and cowardice by fleeing. Corbulo divided his force into four detachments. One he massed in tortoise-formation and set to destroying the rampart. Another had orders to move ladders to the walls. A further large party was to shoot torches and javelins from engines. Finally, two kinds of slingers were allotted positions to discharge lead bullets at long range.

The intention was to press the enemy at every point so that no unit in difficulties could be relieved from elsewhere. The attack was so energetic that, before the day was one-third gone, the Armenian defenders were swept from the walls, their barricades at the gates flattened, fortifications scaled and taken, every adult male killed – without the loss of one Roman soldier, and with very few wounded.

The non-combatant population were sold as slaves. Everything else went as spoils to the victors. The other two commanders were equally successful. The storming of three forts in one day caused the remaining garrisons to surrender in panic – or in some cases willingly.

This encouraged Corbulo to attack the Armenian capital Artaxata. But the direct route would have involved crossing the river Aras by a bridge right under the city walls and exposed to missiles. So his force instead crossed by a wider ford some way off. Tiridates was torn between pride and fright. Acquiescence in a siege would make him look helpless. But intervention would mean entangling himself and his cavalry on difficult ground. Finally he decided to display battle order and, as opportunity offered, to fight or lure the enemy into an ambush, by pretending to retreat. By the latter means he suddenly enveloped the Roman army.

But Corbulo was not taken by surprise. His forces were as ready for fighting as for marching; on the right flank stood the third brigade, on the left the sixth, with picked troops of the tenth in the centre. The baggage was brought within the lines. A thousand cavalry protected the rear, with orders to resist hand-to-hand attack but not to follow if the enemy withdrew. On the wings were the remaining cavalry and foot-archers. The left wing was extended along the foot of the hills so that enemy penetration could be outflanked as well as met frontally. Tiridates approached the Roman front line. He kept out of range, but by alternately threatening attack and simulating alarm tried to detach our formations so that he could fall on them separately. However, the Roman ranks remained cautiously closed. Only the commander of a cavalry section advanced too impetuously; he fell transfixed. But this example merely strengthened the general obedience. As darkness approached, Tiridates withdrew.

Corbulo pitched camp where he was. Supposing Tiridates to have retired to Artaxata, he thought of marching his forces there by night without heavy baggage and investing the town. But intelligence reports indicated that the king was on a long journey, either to Media Atropatene or to Albania. So Corbulo awaited daytime. Meanwhile he sent light-armed auxiliaries ahead to surround the walls and begin the siege from a distance. But the inhabitants of Artaxata voluntarily opened the gates and surrendered themselves and their property to the Romans, thus saving their lives.

The city was set on fire and razed to the ground. Its extensive walls could only have been held by a considerable garrison, and the Roman army was not numerous enough to provide garrisons as well as fighting. If, however, the town had been left unscathed and unguarded, its capture would have brought neither glory nor benefit. Besides, a divine portent seemed to occur. While the sun shone brightly all round the walls, the area of the city itself was suddenly enveloped in a dark cloud with unearthly lightning-flashes. It was believed that the angry gods were consigning Artaxata to destruction.

*

For these achievements Nero was officially hailed as victor. The senate decreed thanksgivings. They voted the emperor statues, arches, and a succession of consulships. The days of the victory and its announcement were to rank as festivals. Following further extravagant decrees of the same sort, Gaius Cassius Longinus – who had supported the other honours – observed that if the gods were to be thanked worthily for their favours the whole year was too short for their thanksgivings: so a distinction should be made between religious festivals and working days on which people might perform religious duties without neglecting mundane ones.

Now came the condemnation of Publius Suillius Rufus. He had earned much hatred in his stormy career. Nevertheless his fall brought discredit upon Seneca. Under Claudius the venal Suillius had been formidable. Changed times had not brought him as low as his enemies wished. Indeed, he envisaged himself as aggressor rather than suppliant. It was to suppress him – so it was said – that the senate had revived an old decree under the Cincian law, penalizing advocates who accepted fees. Suillius protested abusively, reviling Seneca with characteristic ferocity and senile outspokenness.

'Seneca hates Claudius' friends,' said Suillius. 'For under Claudius he was most deservedly exiled! He only understands academic activities and immature youths. So he envies men who speak out vigorously and unaffectedly for their fellow-citizens. I was on Germanicus' staff – while Seneca was committing adultery in his house! Is the acceptance of rewards a dependant offers voluntarily, for an honourable job, a worse offence than seducing imperial princesses? What branch of learning, what philosophical school, won Seneca three hundred million sesterces during four years of imperial friendship? In Rome, he entices into his snares the childless and their legacies. His huge rates of interest suck Italy and the provinces dry. I, on the other hand, have worked for my humble means. I will endure prosecution, trial, and everything else rather than have my lifelong efforts wiped out by this successful upstart!'

There were people to tell Seneca of these words, or exaggerated versions of them. Accusers were found. They charged Suillius with fleecing the provincials as governor of Asia, and embezzling public funds. The prosecution was granted a year for investigation. Meanwhile it was thought quicker to begin with charges relating to Rome – for which witnesses were available. They accused Suillius of forcing a former consul, Quintus Pomponius Secundus, into civil war by his savage indictments, driving Livia Julia, daughter of Drusus, and Poppaea Sabina to their deaths, striking down Decimus Valerius Asiaticus and two other ex-consuls, Quintus Lutetius Lusius Saturninus and Cornelius Lupus, and convicting masses of knights – in a word, all the brutalities of Claudius.

Suillius' defence was that he had invariably acted not on his own initiative but on the emperor's orders. But Nero cut him short, declaring that his father Claudius had never insisted on any prosecutions – his papers proved it. Suillius then alleged instructions from Messalina. But this defence too broke down. For why (it was asked) had just Suillius, and no one else, been selected to speak for that barbarous harlot? – the instrument of atrocities, the man who was paid for crimes and then blamed them on others, must be punished.

Half his estate was confiscated. His son, Marcus Suillius Nerullinus, and granddaughter were allowed the other half, as well as what they had inherited from their mother and grandmother. Suillius himself was exiled to the Balearic islands. Neither ordeal nor aftermath broke his spirit. His retirement was known to be sustained by comfortable self-indulgence. When accusers, relying on Suillius' unpopularity, prosecuted his son for extortion, the emperor felt vengeance was satisfied and vetoed the proceedings.

At about this time the tribune Octavius Sagitta, madly in love with a married woman called Pontia, paid her vast sums to become his mistress and then to leave her husband. He promised to marry her, and secured a similar promise from her. But once she was free she procrastinated, pleading her father's opposition and evading her promise – a richer husband now being in prospect. Octavius remonstrated, threatened, and appealed – his reputation and money were both gone (he said), and his life, all that he had left, he put in her hands. But she remained unmoved.

He pleaded for one night – as a consolation and to help him control himself in future. The night was fixed. Pontia had a maid in attendance who knew of the affair. Octavius arrived with a former slave. Under his clothes was a dagger. Love and anger took their course. They quarrelled, pleaded, insulted each other, made it up. For part of the night they made love. Then, ostensibly carried away by passion, he stabbed the unsuspecting woman with his dagger. A maid ran in and fell wounded by him. Then he fled.

When day came the murder was discovered. They were proved to have been together; the murderer was unmistakable. The ex-slave, however, claimed that the action was his, undertaken to avenge his patron's wrongs. Many were convinced by his devotion. But the maid recovered from her wound and revealed the truth. Octavius was charged before the consuls by his victim's father. He ceased to be tribune and was condemned by senatorial decree and under the law of murder.

An equally conspicuous case of immorality in the same year brought grave national disaster. There was at Rome a woman called Poppaea. Friendship with Sejanus had ruined her father, Titus Ollius, before he held office, and she had assumed the name of her brilliant maternal grandfather, Gaius Poppaeus Sabinus, of illustrious memory for his consulship and honorary Triumph. Poppaea had every asset except goodness. From her mother, the loveliest woman of her day, she inherited distinction and beauty. Her wealth, too, was equal to her birth. She was clever and pleasant to talk to. She seemed respectable. But her life was depraved. Her public appearances were few; she would half-veil her face at them, to stimulate curiosity (or because it suited her). To her, married or bachelor bedfellows were alike. She was indifferent to her reputation – yet insensible to men's love, and herself unloving. Advantage dictated the bestowal of her favours.

While married to a knight called Rufrius Crispinus – to whom she had borne a son – she was seduced by Marcus Salvius Otho, an extravagant youth who was regarded as peculiarly close to Nero. Their liaison was quickly converted into marriage. Otho praised her charms and graces to the emperor. This was either a lover's indiscretion or a deliberate stimulus prompted by the idea that joint possession of Poppaea would be a bond reinforcing Otho's own power. As he left the emperor's table he was often heard saying he was going to his wife, who had brought him what all men want and only the fortunate enjoy – nobility and beauty.

Under such provocations, delay was brief. Poppaea obtained access to Nero, and established her ascendancy. First she used flirtatious wiles, pretending to be unable to resist her passion for Nero's looks. Then, as the emperor fell in love with her, she became haughty, and if he kept her for more than two nights she insisted that she was married and could not give up her marriage. 'I am devoted to Otho. My relations with him are unique. His character and way of living are both fine. *There* is a man for whom nothing is too good. Whereas you, Nero, are kept down because the mistress you live with is a servant, Acte. What a sordid, dreary, menial association!'

Otho lost his intimacy with the emperor. Soon he was excluded from Nero's receptions and company. Finally, to eliminate his rivalry from the Roman scene, he was made governor of Lusitania. There, until the civil war, he lived moderately and respectably – enjoying himself in his spare time, officially blameless.

At this juncture Nero stopped trying to justify his criminal misdeeds. He particularly distrusted Faustus Cornelius Sulla Felix, whose stupidity he wrongly interpreted as well-concealed cunning. This suspicion was intensified by the fabrication of an old former imperial slave Graptus, familiar with the palace since Tiberius' reign. At this time the Milvian Bridge was notorious for its night resorts. Nero used to go there; he could enjoy himself more riotously outside the city. On his way home by the Flaminian road one night, a few young revellers, typical of the times, caused groundless alarm among his attendants. 'There had been a plot to attack Nero!' lied Graptus. 'Only a providential detour to the Gardens of Sallust had saved him – and the plotter was Sulla!' No slave or dependant of Sulla was identified, and his wholly timid and despicable character was incapable of such an attempt. However, he was treated as if proved guilty, exiled, and confined to Massilia.

This year Puteoli sent two opposing delegations to the senate, one from the town council and one from the other citizens. The council complained of public disorderliness, and the populace of embezzlement by officials and leading men. There had been riots, with stone-throwing and threatened arson. Gaius Cassius Longinus was appointed to prevent armed warfare and find a solution. But the town could not stand his severity, and at his own request the task was transferred to two brothers, Publius Sulpicius Scribonius Proculus and Sulpicius Scribonius Rufus. They were allocated a battalion of the Guard, fear of which – supplemented by a few executions – restored harmony.

The senate also passed a decree authorizing the city of Syracuse to exceed the numbers allowed at gladiatorial displays. This would be too insignificant to mention had not the opposition of Publius Clodius Thrasea Paetus[1] given his critics a chance to attack his attitude. 'If', they said, 'Thrasea believes Rome needs a free senate, why does he pursue such trivial matters? Why does he not argue one way or the other about questions of war and peace, taxation, legislation, and other matters of national importance? When a senator is called upon to speak, he may speak about anything and demand a motion about it. Is the prevention of extravagance at Syracusan shows the only reform we need? Is everything else in the empire as good as if Thrasea and not Nero were its ruler? If significant matters are passed over and ignored, surely trivialities ought to be left alone.' Thrasea, asked by his friends to justify himself, replied that it was not through ignorance of the general situation that he offered criticism on such a subject, but because he respectfully credited the senate with understanding that men who attended to these details would not fail to show attention to important matters also.

In this year there were persistent public complaints against the companies farming indirect taxes[2] from the government. Nero contemplated a noble gift to the human race: he would abolish every indirect tax. But the senators whom he consulted, after loudly praising his noble generosity, restrained his impulse. They indicated that the empire could not survive without its revenues, and that abolition of

1. This introduces the principal member of the Republican-Stoic 'opposition' to Nero.
2. Indirect taxes in certain provinces were still 'farmed' by associations of Roman knights.

the indirect customs dues would be followed by demands to abolish direct taxation also. Many companies for collecting indirect taxes, they recalled, had been established by consuls and tribunes in the freest times of the Republic; since then such taxation had formed part of the efforts to balance income and expenditure. But Nero's advisers agreed that tax-collectors' acquisitiveness must be restrained, to prevent novel grievances from discrediting taxes long endured uncomplainingly.

So the emperor's orders were these. Regulations governing each tax, hitherto confidential, were to be published. Claims for arrears were to lapse after one year. Praetors at Rome, governors in the provinces, must give special priority to cases against tax-collectors. Soldiers were to remain tax-free except on what they sold. There were other excellent provisions too. But they were soon evaded – though the abolition of certain illegal exactions invented by tax-collectors, such as the two and a half per cent and two per cent duties,[1] is still valid. Overseas transportation of grain was facilitated, and it was decided to exempt merchant ships from assessment and property-tax.

At this juncture two ex-governors of Africa, Quintus Sulpicius Camerinus and Marcus Pompeius Silvanus, were tried by the emperor and acquitted. Camerinus was charged not with embezzlement but with brutal acts towards a few individuals; Silvanus was beset by a crowd of accusers who requested time to collect witnesses. But he insisted on an immediate hearing, and being rich, old, and childless, was successful. Moreover, he outlived the legacy-hunters whose scheming had secured his acquittal!

Up to now, Germany had been peaceful because, prodigal awards having cheapened the honorary Triumph, our generals looked for greater glory from maintaining peace. To keep the troops busy, the imperial governor of Lower Germany, Pompeius Paulinus, finished the dam for controlling the Rhine, begun sixty-three years previously by Nero Drusus. His colleague in Upper Germany, Lucius Antistius Vetus, planned to build a Saône-Moselle canal. Goods arriving from the Mediterranean up the Rhône and Saône would thus pass via the Moselle into the Rhine, and so to the North Sea. Such a waterway, joining the western Mediterranean to the northern seaboard, would

1. The character of these taxes is not known.

eliminate the difficulties of land transport. But the imperial governor of Gallia Belgica, Aelius Gracilis, jealously prevented his neighbour in Lower Germany from bringing his army into the province he governed. 'This would be currying favour in Gaul, and would worry the emperor,' he objected – using an argument which often blocks good projects.

The prolonged inaction of the Roman armies led to a rumour that their commanders had been forbidden to open hostilities. So the Frisians, led by Verritus and Malorix – their kings (in so far as Germans have any) – advanced to the Rhine bank. Moving their fighting men over swamps and woods, and shipping the young and old across the lakes, they settled in lands reserved for Roman troops. There they erected houses, sowed fields, and tilled the land as if they had inherited it. However, a new imperial governor of Lower Germany, Lucius Duvius Avitus, threatened them with the power of Rome unless they returned to their old lands or had new ones granted by the emperor.

Verritus and Malorix decided to appeal. They went to Rome. While waiting for Nero, who was engaged, they visited Pompey's Theatre – one of the sights usually shown barbarians – to see the huge crowd. There, to pass the time (for they had not the education to enjoy the show), they inquired about the seating arrangements and distinctions between orders – where senators had their places and where knights sat. They saw, seated among the senators, men in foreign clothes. On inquiry they learnt that these were delegates who received this compliment because their nations were conspicuous for courage, and friendship for Rome. Crying that no race on earth was braver and more loyal than the Germans, they moved down and sat among the senators. The spectators liked this fine, impulsive, old-fashioned pride of race; and Nero made them both Roman citizens. All the same, he ordered the Frisians to evacuate the land. And when they ignored this instruction, auxiliary cavalry arrived unexpectedly and enforced his commands, capturing or killing obstinate resisters.

Then the Ampsivarii occupied the territory. They were a larger tribe, and inspired sympathy in neighbouring peoples since they had been expelled from their lands by the Chauci, and were homeless petitioners for a safe place of exile. Their spokesman was the pro-Roman Boiocalus, a well-known figure among these tribes. 'When the Cherusci rebelled', he reminded us, 'Arminius imprisoned me. I served under Tiberius and Germanicus. Now, as the climax to fifty years of loyalty, I am bringing my people into your empire. How little of this land would ever be used for the eventual grazing of Roman soldiers' flocks and herds! Reserve pasturage for cattle – if you must – though men are starving: but not, surely, to the extent of thinking desert wastes more useful to you than friendly nations! This used to be the territory of the Chamavi tribe, and then the Tubantes, and then the Usipi. Just as heaven belongs to the gods, the earth belongs to man: and tenantless land can be occupied.' He raised his eyes to the sun; he invoked all the heavenly bodies. 'Do you like looking at empty land?' he pretended to ask them. 'Then flood it – rather than expel us! And drown those who take other men's soil!'

Lucius Duvius Avitus was impressed. But he replied that men must obey their betters, that the gods they invoked had empowered the Romans to decide what to give and take away and to tolerate no judges but themselves. That was his official answer to the Ampsivarii. To Boiocalus himself, however, he promised land on the strength of his loyal record. The German rejected this as the wage of treachery. 'We may have nowhere to live', he commented, 'but we can find somewhere to die!' And they parted on bad terms.

The Ampsivarii urged the Bructeri, the Tencteri, and even more distant tribes, to fight at their side. Avitus wrote requesting the imperial governor of Upper Germany, Titus Curtilius Mancia, to cross the Rhine and menace their rear. Then Avitus invaded their potential allies the Tencteri, successfully threatening annihilation if they joined in. The Bructeri were likewise intimidated, and the other tribes proved equally unwilling to involve themselves in other people's dangers. The Ampsivarii fell back on the Usipi and Tubantes, who compelled them, however, to move on to the Chatti and then to the Cherusci. In their protracted wanderings, the exiles were treated as guests, then as beggars, then as enemies. Finally, their fighting men were exterminated, their young and old distributed as booty.

The same summer, the Hermunduri and Chatti fought a great battle. Each wanted to seize the rich salt-producing river which flowed between them. Besides their passion for settling everything by force, they held a religious conviction that this region was close to heaven so that men's prayers received ready access. And by divine favour, they believed, salt in this river and these woods was produced, not as in other countries by the evaporation of water left by the sea, but by pouring it on heaps of burning wood and thus uniting the two opposed elements, fire and water. In the battle, the Chatti were defeated – with catastrophic effects. For both sides, in the event of victory, had vowed their enemies to Mars and Mercury.[1] This vow implied the sacrifice of the entire beaten side with their horses and all their possessions. So the threats of this anti-Roman people recoiled on themselves.

But a friendly tribe also, the Ubii, were overwhelmed by a sudden disaster. Flames bursting out of the ground devoured farmhouses, crops, and villages far and wide, right up to the walls of the recently founded settlement named after Agrippina. Neither rain nor river nor any other water could quench the fire. Finally a few desperate and distraught peasants hurled rocks into the flames, and, as they subsided, advanced and fought them with clubs and other implements, as one would fight wild animals. Finally, they tore off their clothes and heaped them on. The oldest and dirtiest garments were most effective as extinguishers.

The fig-tree called 'Ruminalis', in the Place of Assembly, which 830 years earlier had sheltered the babies Romulus and Remus, suffered in this year. Its shoots died and its trunk withered. This was regarded as a portent. However, it revived, with fresh shoots.

When the new year came, and Gaius Vipstanus Apronianus and Gaius Fonteius Capito (II) became consuls, Nero ceased delaying his long-meditated crime. The longer his reign lasted, the bolder he became. Besides, he loved Poppaea more every day. While Agrippina lived, Poppaea saw no hope of his divorcing Octavia and marrying her. So she nagged and mocked him incessantly. He was under his guardian's thumb, she said – master neither of the empire nor of himself. 'Otherwise', she said, 'why these postponements of our marriage? I suppose my looks and victorious ancestors are not good enough. Or do you distrust my capacity to bear children? Or the sincerity of my love?

'No! I think you are afraid that, if we were married, I might tell you frankly how the senate is downtrodden and the public enraged by your mother's arrogance and greed. If Agrippina can only tolerate daughters-in-law who hate her son, let me be Otho's wife again! I

---

1. The German Tiu and Wotan.

will go anywhere in the world where I only need hear of the emperor's humiliations rather than see them – and see you in danger, like myself!' This appeal was reinforced by tears and all a lover's tricks. Nero was won. Nor was there any opposition. Everyone longed for the mother's domination to end. But no one believed that her son's hatred would go as far as murder.

According to one author, Cluvius Rufus, Agrippina's passion to retain power carried her so far that at midday, the time when food and drink were beginning to raise Nero's temperature, she several times appeared before her inebriated son all decked out and ready for incest. Their companions observed sensual kisses and evilly suggestive caresses. Seneca, supposing that the answer to a woman's enticements was a woman, called in the ex-slave Acte. She feared for Nero's reputation – and for her own safety. Now she was instructed to warn Nero that Agrippina was boasting of her intimacy with her son, that her boasts had received wide publicity, and that the army would never tolerate a sacrilegious emperor.

Another writer, Fabius Rusticus, agrees in attributing successful intervention to Acte's wiles, but states that the desires were not Agrippina's but Nero's. But the other authorities support the contrary version. So does the tradition. That may be because Agrippina really did intend this monstrosity. Or perhaps it is because no sexual novelty seemed incredible in such a woman. In her earliest years she had employed an illicit relationship with Marcus Aemilius Lepidus (V) as a means to power. Through the same ambition she had sunk to be Pallas' mistress. Then, married to her uncle, her training in abomination was complete. So Nero avoided being alone with her. When she left for her gardens or country mansions at Tusculum and Antium, he praised her intention of taking a holiday.

Finally, however, he concluded that wherever Agrippina was she was intolerable. He decided to kill her. His only doubt was whether to employ poison, or the dagger, or violence of some other kind. Poison was the first choice. But a death at the emperor's table would not look fortuitous after Britannicus had died there. Yet her criminal conscience kept her so alert for plots that it seemed impracticable to corrupt her household. Moreover, she had strengthened her physical resistance by a preventive course of antidotes. No one could think of a way of stabbing her without detection. And there was another danger:

that the selected assassin might shrink from carrying out his dreadful orders.

However, a scheme was put forward by Anicetus, an ex-slave who commanded the fleet at Misenum. In Nero's boyhood Anicetus had been his tutor; he and Agrippina hated each other. A ship could be made, he now said, with a section which would come loose at sea and hurl Agrippina into the water without warning. Nothing is so productive of surprises as the sea, remarked Anicetus; if a shipwreck did away with her, who could be so unreasonable as to blame a human agency instead of wind and water? Besides, when she was dead the emperor could allot her a temple and altars and the other public tokens of filial duty.

This ingenious plan found favour. The time of year, too, was suitable, since Nero habitually attended the festival of Minerva at Baiae.[1] Now he enticed his mother there. 'Parents' tempers must be borne!' he kept announcing. 'One must humour their feelings.' This was to create the general impression that they were friends again, and to produce the same effect on Agrippina. For women are naturally inclined to believe welcome news.

As she arrived from Antium, Nero met her at the shore. After welcoming her with outstretched hands and embraces, he conducted her to Bauli, a mansion on the bay between Cape Misenum and the waters of Baiae. Some ships were standing there. One, more sumptuous than the rest, was evidently another compliment to his mother, who had formerly been accustomed to travel in warships manned by the imperial navy. Then she was invited out to dinner. The crime was to take place on the ship under cover of darkness. But an informer, it was said, gave the plot away; Agrippina could not decide whether to believe the story, and preferred a sedan-chair as her conveyance to Baiae.

There her alarm was relieved by Nero's attentions. He received her kindly, and gave her the place of honour next himself. The party went on for a long time. They talked about various things; Nero was boyish and intimate – or confidentially serious. When she left, he saw her off, gazing into her eyes and clinging to her. This may have been a final piece of shamming – or perhaps even Nero's brutal heart was affected by his last sight of his mother, going to her death.

1. On 19–23 March.

But heaven seemed determined to reveal the crime. For it was a quiet, star-lit night and the sea was calm. The ship began to go on its way. Agrippina was attended by two of her friends. One of them, Crepereius Gallus, stood near the tiller. The other, Acerronia, leant over the feet of her resting mistress, happily talking about Nero's remorseful behaviour and his mother's re-established influence. Then came the signal. Under the pressure of heavy lead weights, the roof fell in. Crepereius was crushed, and died instantly. Agrippina and Acerronia were saved by the raised sides of their couch, which happened to be strong enough to resist the pressure. Moreover, the ship held together.

In the general confusion, those in the conspiracy were hampered by the many who were not. But then some of the oarsmen had the idea of throwing their weight on one side, to capsize the ship. However, they took too long to concert this improvised plan, and meanwhile others brought weight to bear in the opposite direction. This provided the opportunity to make a gentler descent into the water. Acerronia ill-advisedly started crying out, 'I am Agrippina! Help, help the emperor's mother!' She was struck dead by blows from poles and oars and whatever ship's gear happened to be available. Agrippina herself kept quiet and avoided recognition. Though she was hurt – she had a wound in the shoulder – she swam until she came to some sailing-boats. They brought her to the Lucrine lake, from which she was taken home.

There she realized that the invitation and special compliment had been treacherous, and the collapse of her ship planned. The collapse had started at the top, like a stage-contrivance. The shore was close by, there had been no wind, no rock to collide with. Acerronia's death and her own wound also invited reflection. Agrippina decided that the only escape from the plot was to profess ignorance of it. She sent an ex-slave Agerinus to tell her son that by divine mercy and his lucky star she had survived a serious accident. The messenger was to add, however, that despite anxiety about his mother's dangerous experience Nero must not yet trouble to visit her – at present rest was what she needed. Meanwhile, pretending unconcern, she cared for her wound and physical condition generally. She also ordered Acerronia's will to be found and her property sealed. Here alone no pretence was needed.

To Nero, awaiting news that the crime was done, came word that she had escaped with a slight wound – after hazards which left no doubt of their instigator's identity. Half-dead with fear, he insisted she might arrive at any moment. 'She may arm her slaves! She may whip up the army, or gain access to the senate or Assembly, and incriminate me for wrecking and wounding her and killing her friends! What can I do to save myself?' Could Burrus and Seneca help? Whether they were in the plot is uncertain. But they were immediately awakened and summoned.

For a long time neither spoke. They did not want to dissuade and be rejected. They may have felt matters had gone so far that Nero had to strike before Agrippina, or die. Finally Seneca ventured so far as to turn to Burrus and ask if the troops should be ordered to kill her. He replied that the Guard were devoted to the whole imperial house and to Germanicus' memory; they would commit no violence against his offspring. Anicetus, he said, must make good his promise. Anicetus unhesitatingly claimed the direction of the crime. Hearing him, Nero cried that this was the first day of his reign – and the magnificent gift came from a former slave! 'Go quickly!' he said. 'And take men who obey orders scrupulously!'

Agrippina's messenger arrived. When Nero was told, he took the initiative, and staged a fictitious incrimination. While Agerinus delivered his message, Nero dropped a sword at the man's feet and had him arrested as if caught red-handed. Then he could pretend that his mother had plotted against the emperor's life, been detected, and – in shame – committed suicide.

Meanwhile Agrippina's perilous adventure had become known. It was believed to be accidental. As soon as people heard of it they ran to the beach, and climbed on to the embankment, or fishing-boats nearby. Others waded out as far as they could, or waved their arms. The whole shore echoed with wails and prayers and the din of all manner of inquiries and ignorant answers. Huge crowds gathered with lights. When she was known to be safe, they prepared to make a show of rejoicing.

But a menacing armed column arrived and dispersed them. Anicetus surrounded her house and broke in. Arresting every slave in his path, he came to her bedroom door. Here stood a few servants – the rest had been frightened away by the invasion. In her dimly lit room a single maid waited with her. Agrippina's alarm had increased as nobody, not even Agerinus, came from her son. If things had been well there would not be this terribly ominous isolation, then this sudden uproar. Her maid vanished. 'Are you leaving me, too?' called Agrippina. Then she saw Anicetus. Behind him were a naval captain and lieutenant named Herculeius and Obaritus respectively. 'If you have come to visit me', she said, 'you can report that I am better. But if you are assassins, I know my son is not responsible. He did not order his mother's death.' The murderers closed round her bed. First the captain hit her on the head with a truncheon. Then as the lieutenant was drawing his sword to finish her off, she cried out: 'Strike here!' – pointing to her womb. Blow after blow fell, and she died.

So far accounts agree. Some add that Nero inspected his mother's corpse and praised her figure; but that is contested. She was cremated that night, on a dining couch, with meagre ceremony. While Nero reigned, her grave was not covered with earth or enclosed, though later her household gave her a modest tomb beside the road to Misenum, on the heights where Julius Caesar's mansion overlooks the bay beneath. During the cremation one of her former slaves, Mnester (II), stabbed himself to death. Either he loved his patroness, or he feared assassination.

This was the end which Agrippina had anticipated for years. The prospect had not daunted her. When she asked astrologers about Nero, they had answered that he would become emperor but kill his mother. Her reply was, 'Let him kill me – provided he becomes emperor!' But Nero only understood the horror of his crime when it was done. For the rest of the night, witless and speechless, he alternately lay paralysed and leapt to his feet in terror – waiting for the dawn which he thought would be his last. Hope began to return to him when at Burrus' suggestion the colonels and captains of the Guard came and cringed to him, with congratulatory handclasps for his escape from the unexpected menace of his mother's evil activities. Nero's friends crowded to the temples. Campanian towns nearby followed their lead and displayed joy by sacrifices and deputations.

Nero's insincerity took a different form. He adopted a gloomy demeanour, as though sorry to be safe and mourning for his parent's death. But the features of the countryside are less adaptable than those of men; and Nero's gaze could not escape the dreadful view of that sea and shore. Besides, the coast echoed (it was said) with trumpet blasts from the neighbouring hills – and wails from his mother's grave. So Nero departed to Neapolis.

He wrote the senate a letter. Its gist was that Agerinus, a confidential ex-slave of Agrippina, had been caught with a sword, about to murder him, and that she, conscious of her guilt as instigator of the crime, had paid the penalty. He added older charges. 'She had wanted to be co-ruler – to receive oaths of allegiance from the Guard, and to subject senate and public to the same humiliation. Disappointed of this, she had hated all of them – army, senate and people. She had opposed gratuities to soldiers and civilians alike. She had contrived the deaths of distinguished men.' Only with the utmost difficulty, added Nero, had he prevented her from breaking into the senate-house and delivering verdicts to foreign envoys. He also indirectly attacked Claudius' régime, blaming his mother for all its scandals. Her death, he said, was providential. And he even called the shipwreck a happy accident. For even the greatest fool could not believe it accidental – or imagine that one shipwrecked woman had sent a single armed man to break through the imperial guards and fleets. Here condemnation fell not on Nero, whose monstrous conduct beggared criticism, but on Seneca who had composed his self-incriminating speech.

Nevertheless leading citizens competed with complimentary proposals – thanksgivings at every shrine; annual games at Minerva's Festival (during which the discovery of the plot had been staged); the erection in the senate-house of gold statues of Minerva and (beside her) the emperor; the inclusion of Agrippina's birthday among ill-omened dates. It had been the custom of Publius Clodius Thrasea Paetus to pass over flatteries in silence or with curt agreement. But this time he walked out of the senate – thereby endangering himself without bringing general freedom any nearer.

Many prodigies occurred. A woman gave birth to a snake. Another woman was killed in her husband's arms by a thunderbolt. The sun suddenly went dark. All fourteen city-districts were struck by lightning. But these portents meant nothing. So little were they due to the gods that Nero continued his reign and his crimes for years to come.

However, to intensify his mother's unpopularity and indicate his increased leniency now she had gone, he brought back two eminent women, Junia Calvina and Calpurnia (II), and two former praetors,

Valerius Capito and Licinius Gabolus, whom she had exiled. He even permitted Lollia Paulina's ashes to be brought home, and a tomb erected. He also allowed back Junia Silana's two dependants, Iturius and Calvisius, whom he had recently banished. Silana herself had died at Tarentum, having returned from her distant exile when Agrippina, whose malevolence had struck her down, became less vindictive – or less powerful.

Nero lingered in the cities of Campania. His return to Rome was a worrying problem. Would the senate be obedient? Would the public cheer him? Every bad character (and no court had ever had so many) reassured him that Agrippina was detested, and that her death had increased his popularity. They urged him to enter boldly and see for himself how he was revered. Preceding him – as they had asked to – they found even greater enthusiasm than they had promised. The people marshalled in their tribes were out to meet him, the senators were in their gala clothes, wives and children drawn up in lines by sex and age. Along his route there were tiers of seats as though for a Triumph. Proud conqueror of a servile nation, Nero proceeded to the Capitol and paid his vows.

Then he plunged into the wildest improprieties, which vestiges of respect for his mother had hitherto not indeed repressed, but at least impeded.

CHAPTER 12

Nero and his Helpers

*

NERO had long desired to drive in four-horse chariot races. Another equally deplorable ambition was to sing to the lyre, like a professional. 'Chariot-racing', he said, 'was an accomplishment of ancient kings and leaders – honoured by poets, associated with divine worship. Singing, too, is sacred to Apollo: that glorious and provident god is represented in a musician's dress in Greek cities, and also in Roman temples.'

There was no stopping him. But Seneca and Burrus tried to prevent him from gaining both his wishes by conceding one of them. In the Vatican valley, therefore, an enclosure was constructed, where he could drive his horses, remote from the public eye. But soon the public were admitted – and even invited; and they approved vociferously. For such is a crowd: avid for entertainment, and delighted if the emperor shares their tastes. However, this scandalous publicity did not satiate Nero, as his advisers had expected. Indeed, it led him on. But if he shared his degradation, he thought it would be less; so he brought on to the stage members of the ancient nobility whose poverty made them corruptible. They are dead, and I feel I owe it to their ancestors not to name them. For though they behaved dishonourably, so did the man who paid them to offend (instead of not to do so). Well-known knights, too, he induced by huge presents to offer their services in the arena. But gifts from the man who can command carry with them an obligation.

However, Nero was not yet ready to disgrace himself on a public stage. Instead he instituted 'Youth Games'.[1] There were many volunteers. Birth, age, official career did not prevent people from acting – in Greek or Latin style – or from accompanying their performances

1. Instituted by Nero to celebrate the first shaving of his beard.

with effeminate gestures and songs. Eminent women, too, rehearsed indecent parts. In the wood which Augustus had planted round his Naval Lake, places of assignation and taverns were built, and every stimulus to vice was displayed for sale. Moreover, there were distributions of money. Respectable people were compelled to spend it; disreputable people did so gladly. Promiscuity and degradation throve. Roman morals had long become impure, but never was there so favourable an environment for debauchery as among this filthy crowd. Even in good surroundings people find it hard to behave well. Here every form of immorality competed for attention, and no chastity, modesty, or vestige of decency could survive.

The climax was the emperor's stage debut. Meticulously tuning his lyre, he struck practice notes to the trainers beside him. A battalion attended with its officers. So did Burrus, grieving – but applauding. Now, too, was formed the corps of Roman knights known as the Augustiani. These powerful young men, impudent by nature or ambition, maintained a din of applause day and night, showering divine epithets on Nero's beauty and voice. They were grand and respected as if they had done great things.

But the emperor did not obtain publicity by his theatrical talents only. He also aspired to poetic taste. He gathered round himself at dinner men who possessed some versifying ability but were not yet known. As they sat on, they strung together verses they had brought with them, or extemporized – and filled out Nero's own suggestions, such as they were. This method is apparent from Nero's poems themselves, which lack vigour, inspiration, and homogeneity. To philosophers, too, he devoted some of his time after dinner, enjoying their quarrelsome assertions of contradictory views. There were enough of such people willing to display their glum features and expressions for the amusement of the court.

At about this time there was a serious fight between the inhabitants of two Roman settlements, Nuceria and Pompeii. It arose out of a trifling incident at a gladiatorial show given by Livineius Regulus (II), whose expulsion from the senate I have mentioned elsewhere.[1] During an exchange of taunts – characteristic of these disorderly country towns – abuse led to stone-throwing, and then swords were drawn. The people of Pompeii, where the show was held, came off

1. The account of his expulsion from the senate has not survived.

best. Many wounded and mutilated Nucerians were taken to the capital. Many bereavements, too, were suffered by parents and children. The emperor instructed the senate to investigate the affair. The senate passed it to the consuls. When they reported back, the senate debarred Pompeii from holding any similar gathering for ten years. Illegal associations in the town were dissolved; and the sponsor of the show and his fellow-instigators of the disorders were exiled.

Cyrene secured the expulsion of a governor, Pedius Blaesus, from the senate for violating their treasury of Aesculapius and accepting bribes and solicitations to falsify the recruiting rolls. Cyrene also prosecuted another ex-praetor, Acilius Strabo, who had been sent by Claudius to adjudicate on the ancestral royal estates which had been left, with the whole kingdom, to Rome by King Ptolemy Apion.[1] Neighbouring landowners who had occupied these estates cited their longstanding usurpation as fair title. The adjudicator decided against them. So they reviled him. The senate answered that it did not know Claudius' instructions – reference must be made to the emperor. Nero upheld the adjudicator, but wrote that nevertheless he would help the provincial landowners by legalizing their occupation.

The deaths now occurred of two famous men, Cnaeus Domitius Afer and Marcus Servilius Nonianus (II). Both were great orators with distinguished records, Domitius as advocate, Servilius – after a long legal career – as Roman historian; also as man of taste, wherein he displayed a marked contrast with his otherwise equally brilliant rival.

In the following year, when Nero (for the fourth time) and Cossus Cornelius Lentulus (II) were consuls, a five-yearly stage-competition was founded at Rome on the Greek model. Like most innovations, its reception was mixed. Some recalled with approval the criticism of Pompey, among his elders, for constructing a permanent theatre, whereas previously performances had been held with improvised stage and auditorium, or (to go back to the remoter past) spectators had stood – since seats, it was feared, would keep them idle for days on end. 'As for the shows,' said objectors, 'let them continue in the old Roman way, whenever it falls to the praetors to celebrate them, and provided no citizen is obliged to compete. Traditional morals, already gradually deteriorating, have been utterly ruined by this imported

1. Ptolemy Apion, the last king of Cyrenaica, left it to Rome (as his father had planned) in 96 B.C.

laxity! It makes everything potentially corrupting and corruptible
flow into the capital – foreign influences demoralize our young men
into shirkers, gymnasts, and perverts.

'Responsibility rests with emperor and senate. They have given immorality a free hand. Now they are compelling the Roman upper class
to degrade themselves as orators or singers on the stage. It only remains to strip and fight in boxing-gloves instead of joining the army.
Does expert attention to effeminate music and songs contribute to
justice, or does it make the knights who serve as judges give better
verdicts? And this vileness continues even at night! Good behaviour
has no time left for it. In these promiscuous crowds, debauchees are
emboldened to practise by night the lusts they have imagined by
day.'

This licence was just what most people approved – though they put
it more respectably. 'But our ancestors, too,' they suggested, 'did not
shrink from such public entertainment as contemporary resources permitted. Ballet-dancers were imported from Etruria, horse-racing from
Thurii. Ever since the annexation of Greece and Asia,[1] performances
have become more ambitious. Two hundred years have passed since
the Triumph of Lucius Mummius – who first gave that sort of show
here – and during that time no upper-class Roman has ever demeaned
himself by *professional* acting. As for a permanent theatre, it was more
economical than the construction and demolition of a new one every
year, at vast expense.

'If – as now suggested – the State pays for shows, it will save the
purses of officials and give the public less opportunity to ask them for
Greek contests. Prizes for oratory and poetry will encourage talent.
And why should it be degrading even for a judge to listen with legitimate enjoyment to fine words? These nights – not many, out of a
period of five years – are for gaiety, not immorality. Besides, in such
a blaze of lights, surreptitious immorality is impossible.'

Certainly, the display took place without any open scandal. Nor
was there any partisan rioting, since the ballet-dancers, though allowed
back on the stage, were banned from these sacred contests. The first
prize for oratory was not awarded, but the emperor was declared

1. Achaia (Greece) and Asia (W. Anatolia) were annexed in 146 (Lucius
Mummius celebrated his Triumph in the following year) and 133 B.C. respectively.

winner. Greek clothes, which had been greatly worn during the competition, subsequently went out of fashion.

A brilliant comet now appeared. The general belief is that a comet means a change of emperor. So people speculated on Nero's successor as though Nero were already dethroned. Everybody talked of Rubellius Plautus, a Julian on his mother's side. His personal tastes were old-fashioned, his bearing austere, and his life respectable and secluded. Retirement, due to fear, had enhanced his reputation. The talk about the comet was intensified by equally superstitious reactions to a flash of lightning, which struck and broke the table at which Nero was dining in his mansion at Sublaqueum near the Simbruine Lakes. Since this was near Tibur, the birthplace of Plautus' father, the belief arose that the Divine Will had marked Plautus out. He was frequently courted by those whose devouring and often misguided ambitions attach them prematurely to new and hazardous causes. Nero was worried. He wrote asking Plautus, in the interests of the city's peace, to withdraw from malevolent gossip to enjoy his youthful years in the safety and calm of his family estates in Asia. So there Plautus went, with his wife, Antistia Pollitta, and his closest friends.

Nero, in these days, endangered and discredited himself by an extravagent eccentricity: he bathed in the source of the Marcian Aqueduct.[1] His immersion therein was held to have polluted the sanctity of its holy waters. The divine anger was apparent when he became seriously ill.

When Cnaeus Domitius Corbulo (II) had demolished Artaxata, he decided to utilize the panic thus created in order to capture Tigranocerta. For if he destroyed it, he would increase the enemy's terror; if he spared it, he would be praised as merciful. So he started out. Without relaxing precautions, he avoided hostilities so that the Armenians might hope to be pardoned. He knew they were unstable – slow to face danger, but quick to change sides when opportunity offered. The natives, according to their dispositions, offered submission, or evacuated their villages and withdrew into the wilds. Some hid themselves and their families in caves.

Corbulo varied his treatment. To suppliants he was lenient; fugitives he chased. Those in hiding he ruthlessly burnt out after stuffing

1. The aqueduct, still used, is now the Acqua Pia.

the mouths and exits of their caves with bushes and faggots. The Mardi, experienced brigands, harassed him as he skirted their borders. Mountains protect their country from attack, but Corbulo launched the Iberians to devastate it, and thus punished the tribe's rash hostility without sacrificing Roman lives. Nevertheless, though he and his army suffered no losses in battle, over-exertion was wearing them out – also inadequate rations, for meat was all that kept them alive. Moreover, water was short, it was a blazing summer, and marches were long. The only compensation was the endurance of the general, who bore as much as the rank and file, and more.

Finally, however, they reached cultivated territory, where they harvested the crops. Here the Armenians had taken refuge in two forts. One was successfully assaulted, the other taken by siege. When they passed on to the district of Tauraunitis, Corbulo escaped from an unexpected threat to his life. A native of some importance was discovered near his tent with a weapon. Under torture he disclosed a conspiracy to murder Corbulo, incriminating others as well as himself. These plotters of treachery behind friendly appearances were tried and executed.

Soon afterwards a deputation from Tigranocerta announced that its gates were open and its population awaited Corbulo's orders. They gave him a golden crown as a sign of welcome. He accepted it politely and spared the citizens' property, hoping thereby to win their loyalty. However, another fortress, Legerda, manned by a formidable garrison, was not overcome without a fight. The defenders even risked battle in the open. Then, driven inside their walls, they only capitulated when the Romans erected a siege-mound and forced an entrance.

These victories came the more easily because Parthia was engaged in a war with the Hyrcanians. These sent a mission to the emperor requesting an alliance and citing as a pledge of friendship their diversion of Vologeses. On their return journey Corbulo feared the Hyrcanian delegates would be intercepted by enemy forces if they crossed the Euphrates. So he gave them an escort to the Caspian sea, across which they returned home without entering Parthian territory.

However, Tiridates now entered Armenia on the far side, from Media Atropatene. But Corbulo, sending auxiliaries ahead under Lucius Verulanus Severus and himself following rapidly with Roman troops, forced him to withdraw and abandon all hope of fighting.

Burning and ravaging districts known to be unfriendly, Corbulo was occupying Armenia when Tigranes V – Nero's nominee for its throne – made his appearance. Through a member of the Cappadocian royal family (he was the great-grandson of Archelaus), Tigranes' long residence at Rome as a hostage had made him as docile as a slave. In any case, the Parthian royal house still had its supporters. So his welcome was not unanimous. However, the majority loathed Parthian arrogance and preferred a king appointed by Rome.

Tigranes was given a guard of a thousand Roman regulars, three auxiliary battalions of infantry, and two cavalry regiments. The new ruler was further protected by the allocation of Armenia's frontier zones to the adjoining kings, Pharasmanes of Iberia, Polemo II of Pontus, Aristobulus of Lesser Armenia, and Antiochus IV Epiphanes of Commagene. Corbulo retired to Syria, the imperial governorship of which was open to him, its incumbent, Gaius Ummidius Durmius Quadratus having died.

In the Asian province one of its famous cities, Laodicea, was destroyed by an earthquake in this year, and rebuilt from its own resources without any subvention from Rome.

In the same year, in Italy, the ancient town of Puteoli was given the status of a Roman settlement and named after Nero.[1] The settlements at Tarentum and Antium, too, were augmented by ex-soldiers. But this did not arrest their depopulation. For most of the settlers emigrated to the provinces in which they had served – leaving no children, since they were unaccustomed to marrying and bringing up families. Once these settlements had consisted of whole brigades of soldiers drawn up in their ranks behind their officers – a new community based on consent and comradeship. But now colonists came from various units and were unknown to each other. Without leaders, without loyalty, they were a mere concentration of aliens rather than a Roman settlement.

At this year's election of praetors at Rome there were three more candidates than posts,[2] and feelings were accordingly violent. Praetors were normally elected by the senate. Now, however, the emperor restored harmony by appointing the three supernumeraries to brigade

1. But the place had been a Roman settlement since 194 B.C.
2. i.e., there were fifteen candidates for twelve praetorships.

commands. He increased the senate's prerogatives by ordering that its appellants from civil courts must deposit the same sum as those appealing to himself (previously appeals to the senate had been unrestricted and subject to no sanction). At the end of the year a knight called Vibius Secundus was convicted for extortion on a charge brought by the Mauretanians, and expelled from Italy. The influence of his brother Quintus Vibius Crispus saved him from a worse sentence.

★

The following year, when the consuls were Lucius Caesennius Paetus and Publius Petronius Turpilianus, witnessed a serious disaster in Britain. The imperial governor Aulus Didius Gallus had, as I have said, merely held his own. His successor Quintus Veranius (II) had only conducted minor raids against the Silures when death terminated his operations. His life had been famous for its austerity. But his testamentary last words were glaringly self-seeking, for they grossly flattered Nero and added that Veranius, if he had lived two years longer, would have presented him with the whole province.

The new imperial governor of Britain was Gaius Suetonius Paulinus. Corbulo's rival in military science, as in popular talk – which makes everybody compete – he was ambitious to achieve victories as glorious as the reconquest of Armenia. So Suetonius planned to attack the island of Mona, which although thickly populated had also given sanctuary to many refugees.

Flat-bottomed boats were built to contend with the shifting shallows, and these took the infantry across. Then came the cavalry; some utilized fords, but in deeper water the men swam beside their horses. The enemy lined the shore in a dense armed mass. Among them were black-robed women with dishevelled hair like Furies, brandishing torches. Close by stood Druids, raising their hands to heaven and screaming dreadful curses.

This weird spectacle awed the Roman soldiers into a sort of paralysis. They stood still – and presented themselves as a target. But then they urged each other (and were urged by the general) not to fear a horde of fanatical women. Onward pressed their standards and they bore down their opponents, enveloping them in the flames of their own torches. Suetonius garrisoned the conquered island. The groves devoted to Mona's barbarous superstitions he demolished. For it was their religion to drench their altars in the blood of prisoners and consult their gods by means of human entrails.

While Suetonius was thus occupied, he learnt of a sudden rebellion in the province. Prasutagus, king of the Iceni, after a life of long and renowned prosperity, had made the emperor co-heir with his own two daughters. Prasutagus hoped by this submissiveness to preserve his kingdom and household from attack. But it turned out otherwise. Kingdom and household alike were plundered like prizes of war, the one by Roman officers, the other by Roman slaves. As a beginning, his widow Boudicca[1] was flogged and their daughters raped. The Icenian chiefs were deprived of their hereditary estates as if the Romans had been given the whole country. The king's own relatives were treated like slaves.

And the humiliated Iceni feared still worse, now that they had been reduced to provincial status. So they rebelled. With them rose the Trinobantes and others. Servitude had not broken them, and they had secretly plotted together to become free again. They particularly hated the Roman ex-soldiers who had recently established a settlement at Camulodunum. The settlers drove the Trinobantes from their homes and land, and called them prisoners and slaves. The troops encouraged the settlers' outrages, since their own way of behaving was the same – and they looked forward to similar licence for themselves. Moreover, the temple erected to the divine Claudius was a blatant stronghold of alien rule, and its observances were a pretext to make the natives appointed as its priests drain the whole country dry.

It seemed easy to destroy the settlement; for it had no walls. That was a matter which Roman commanders, thinking of amenities rather than needs, had neglected. At this juncture, for no visible reason, the statue of Victory at Camulodunum fell down – with its back turned as though it were fleeing the enemy. Delirious women chanted of destruction at hand. They cried that in the local senate-house outlandish yells had been heard; the theatre had echoed with shrieks; at the mouth of the Thames a phantom settlement had been seen in ruins. A blood-red colour in the sea, too, and shapes like human corpses left by the ebb tide, were interpreted hopefully by the Britons – and with terror by the settlers.

Suetonius, however, was far away. So they appealed for help to the

1. The spelling 'Boadicea' is unauthenticated.

imperial agent Catus Decianus. He sent them barely two hundred men, incompletely armed. There was also a small garrison on the spot. Reliance was placed on the temple's protection. Misled by secret pro-rebels, who hampered their plans, they dispensed with rampart or trench. They omitted also to evacuate old people and women and thus leave only fighting men behind. Their precautions were appropriate to a time of unbroken peace.

Then a native horde surrounded them. When all else had been ravaged or burnt, the garrison concentrated itself in the temple. After two days' siege, it fell by storm. The ninth Roman division, commanded by Quintus Petilius Cerialis Caesius Rufus, attempted to relieve the town, but was stopped by the victorious Britons and routed. Its entire infantry force was massacred, while the commander escaped to his camp with his cavalry and sheltered behind its defences. The imperial agent Catus Decianus, horrified by the catastrophe and by his unpopularity, withdrew to Gaul. It was his rapacity which had driven the province to war.

But Suetonius, undismayed, marched through disaffected territory to Londinium. This town did not rank as a Roman settlement, but was an important centre for business-men and merchandise. At first, he hesitated whether to stand and fight there. Eventually, his numerical inferiority – and the price only too clearly paid by the divisional commander's rashness – decided him to sacrifice the single city of Londinium to save the province as a whole. Unmoved by lamentations and appeals, Suetonius gave the signal for departure. The inhabitants were allowed to accompany him. But those who stayed because they were women, or old, or attached to the place, were slaughtered by the enemy. Verulamium suffered the same fate.

The natives enjoyed plundering and thought of nothing else. Bypassing forts and garrisons, they made for where loot was richest and protection weakest. Roman and provincial deaths at the places mentioned are estimated at seventy thousand. For the British did not take or sell prisoners, or practise other war-time exchanges. They could not wait to cut throats, hang, burn, and crucify – as though avenging, in advance, the retribution that was on its way.

Suetonius collected the fourteenth brigade and detachments of the twentieth, together with the nearest available auxiliaries – amounting to nearly ten thousand armed men – and decided to attack without further delay. He chose a position in a defile with a wood behind him. There could be no enemy, he knew, except at his front, where there was open country without cover for ambushes. Suetonius drew up his regular troops in close order, with the light-armed auxiliaries at their flanks, and the cavalry massed on the wings. On the British side, cavalry and infantry bands seethed over a wide area in unprecedented numbers. Their confidence was such that they brought their wives with them to see the victory, installing them in carts stationed at the edge of the battlefield.

Boudicca drove round all the tribes in a chariot with her daughters in front of her. 'We British are used to woman commanders in war,' she cried. 'I am descended from mighty men! But now I am not fighting for my kingdom and wealth. I am fighting as an ordinary person for my lost freedom, my bruised body, and my outraged daughters. Nowadays Roman rapicity does not even spare our bodies. Old people are killed, virgins raped. But the gods will grant us the vengeance we deserve! The Roman division which dared to fight is annihilated. The others cower in their camps, or watch for a chance to escape. They will never face even the din and roar of all our thousands, much less the shock of our onslaught. Consider how many of you are fighting – and why. Then you will win this battle, or perish. That is what I, a woman, plan to do! – let the men live in slavery if they will.'

Suetonius trusted his men's bravery. Yet he too, at this critical moment, offered encouragements and appeals. 'Disregard the clamours and empty threats of the natives!' he said. 'In their ranks, there are more women than fighting men. Unwarlike, unarmed, when they see the arms and courage of the conquerors who have routed them so often, they will break immediately. Even when a force contains many divisions, few among them win the battles – what special glory for your small numbers to win the renown of a whole army! Just keep in close order. Throw your javelins, and then carry on: use shield-bosses to fell them, swords to kill them. Do not think of plunder. When you have won, you will have everything.'

The general's words were enthusiastically received: the old battle-experienced soldiers longed to hurl their javelins. So Suetonius confidently gave the signal for battle. At first the regular troops stood their ground. Keeping to the defile as a natural defence, they launched their javelins accurately at the approaching enemy. Then, in wedge formation, they burst forward. So did the auxiliary infantry. The cavalry, too, with lances extended, demolished all serious resistance. The remaining Britons fled with difficulty since their ring of wagons blocked the outlets. The Romans did not spare even the women. Baggage animals too, transfixed with weapons, added to the heaps of dead.

It was a glorious victory, comparable with bygone triumphs. According to one report almost eighty thousand Britons fell. Our own casualties were about four hundred dead and a slightly larger number of wounded. Boudicca poisoned herself. Poenius Postumus, chief-of-staff of the second division which had not joined Suetonius, learning of the success of the other two formations, stabbed himself to death because he had cheated his formation of its share in the victory and broken regulations by disobeying his commander's orders.

The whole army was now united. Suetonius kept it under canvas to finish the war. The emperor raised its numbers by transferring from Germany two thousand regular troops, which brought the ninth division to full strength, also eight auxiliary infantry battalions and a thousand cavalry. These were stationed together in new winter quarters, and hostile or wavering tribes were ravaged with fire and sword. But the enemy's worst affliction was famine. For they had neglected to sow their fields and brought everyone available into the army, intending to seize our supplies. Still, the savage British tribesmen were disinclined for peace, especially as the newly arrived imperial agent Gaius Julius Alpinus Classicianus, successor to Catus Decianus, was on bad terms with Suetonius, and allowed his personal animosities to damage the national interests. For he passed round advice to wait for a new governor who would be kind to those who surrendered, without an enemy's bitterness or a conqueror's arrogance. Classicianus also reported to Rome that there was no prospect of ending the war unless a successor was appointed to Suetonius, whose failures he attributed to perversity – and his successes to luck.

So a former imperial slave, Polyclitus, was sent to investigate the British situation. Nero was very hopeful that Polyclitus' influence would both reconcile the governor and agent and pacify native rebelliousness. With his enormous escort, Polyclitus was a trial to Italy and Gaul. Then he crossed the Channel and succeeded in intimidating even the Roman army. But the enemy laughed at him. For them, freedom still lived, and the power of ex-slaves was still unfamiliar. The British marvelled that a general and an army who had completed such a mighty war should obey a slave.

But all this was toned down in Polyclitus' reports to the emperor. Retained as governor, Suetonius lost a few ships and their crews on the shore, and was then superseded for not terminating the war. His successor, the recent consul Publius Petronius Turpilianus, neither provoking the enemy nor provoked, called this ignoble inactivity peace with honour.

The same year witnessed two noteworthy crimes at Rome. One of the audacious perpetrators was a senator, the other a slave. Domitius Balbus was a former praetor whose age, wealth, and childlessness exposed him to fraudulence. His relative Valerius Fabianus (a man destined for an official career) forged Domitius' will. Two knights, Vinicius Rufinus and Terentius Lentinus, who were Valerius' accomplices, brought in Marcus Antonius Primus, a man ready for anything, and Marcus Asinius Marcellus, who had the distinction of being the great-grandson of Gaius Asinius Pollio (I) and was respected – apart from his belief that poverty was the supreme misfortune. So with these associates, and others of less account, Valerius sealed the document. When this was proved in the senate, the forgers were all convicted under the Cornelian law[1] against falsification, except Marcellus, who escaped punishment owing to the emperor's intervention in memory of his ancestors. Disgrace he did not escape.

On the same day a young ex-quaestor, Pompeius Aelianus, was condemned for complicity in the same crime and banned from Italy and his home country, Spain. Valerius Ponticus was excluded from Italy for conducting prosecutions before the praetor to avoid trial by the City Prefect – a procedure which, while preserving legality for the time being, aimed at ultimate acquittal by collusion. A clause was added to the relevant senatorial decree making anyone who bought or sold such connivance liable to the same penalty as if convicted by false accusation in a criminal case.

Soon afterwards the City Prefect, Lucius Pedanius Secundus, was murdered by one of his slaves. Either Pedanius had refused to free the murderer after agreeing to a price, or the slave, infatuated with some

1. Sulla's Cornelian law of 81 B.C. penalized fraud in regard to wills.

man or other, found competition from his master intolerable. After
the murder, ancient custom required that every slave residing under
the same roof must be executed. But a crowd gathered, eager to save
so many innocent lives; and rioting began. The senate-house was
besieged. Inside, there was feeling against excessive severity, but the
majority opposed any change. Among the latter was Gaius Cassius
Longinus, who when his turn came spoke as follows:

'I have often been here, senators, when decrees deviating from our
ancestral laws and customs were mooted. I have not opposed them.
Not that I had any doubts about the superiority – in every matter
whatsoever – of ancient arrangements, and the undesirability of every
change. But I did not wish, by exaggerated regard for antique usage,
to show too high an opinion of my own profession, the law. Nor did
I want, by continual opposition, to weaken any influence I may
possess. I wanted to keep it intact in case the country needed my
advice.

'It needs it today! A man who has held the consulship has been
deliberately murdered by a slave in his own home. None of his fellow-
slaves prevented or betrayed the murderer, though the senatorial
decree threatening the whole household with execution still stands.
Exempt them from the penalty if you like. But then, if the City Prefect
was not important enough to be immune, who will be? Who will
have enough slaves to protect him if Pedanius' four hundred were too
few? Who can rely on his household's help if even fear for their own
lives does not make them shield us?

'Or was the assassin avenging a wrong? For that is one shameless
fabrication. Tell us next that the slave had been negotiating about his
patrimony, or he had lost some ancestral property! We had better call
it justifiable homicide straightaway.

'When wiser men have in past times considered and settled the
whole matter, will you dare to refute them? Pretend, if you like,
that we are deciding a policy for the first time. Do you believe that a
slave can have planned to kill his master without letting fall a single
rash or menacing word? Or even if we assume he kept his secret – and
obtained a weapon unnoticed – could he have passed the watch,
opened the bedroom door, carried in a light, and committed the
murder, without anyone knowing? There are many advance notifica-
tions of crimes. If slaves give them away, we can live securely, though

one among many, because of their insecurity; or, if we must die, we can at least be sure the guilty will be punished.

'Our ancestors distrusted their slaves. Yet slaves were then born on the same estates, in the same homes, as their masters, who had treated them kindly from birth. But nowadays our huge households are international. They include every alien religion – or none at all. The only way to keep down this scum is by intimidation. Innocent people will die, you say. Yes, and when in a defeated army every tenth man is flogged to death, the brave have to draw lots with the others. Exemplary punishment always contains an element of injustice. But individual wrongs are outweighed by the advantage of the community.'

No one dared speak up against Cassius. But there were protesting cries of pity for the numbers affected, and the women, and the young, and the undoubted innocence of the majority. Yet those favouring execution prevailed. However, great crowds ready with stones and torches prevented the order from being carried out. Nero rebuked the population by edict, and lined with troops the whole route along which those condemned were taken for execution. Then it was proposed by Cingonius Varro that the ex-slaves, too, who had been under the same roof should be deported from Italy. But the emperor vetoed this – the ancient custom had not been tempered by mercy, but should not be aggravated by brutality.

Bithynia, this year, secured the condemnation of its governor, Tarquitius Priscus, for extortion. The senate, remembering that he had once accused his own governor, Titus Statilius Taurus (II), was delighted. In Gaul, a census was carried out by Quintus Volusius Saturninus, Titus Sextius Africanus, and Lucius Trebellius Maximus. The aristocratic Volusius and Sextius were rivals, and both despised Trebellius, who took advantage of their bickering to get the better of them.

Publius Memmius Regulus now died. His influence, dignity and good name had attained the greatest glory which the all-overshadowing imperial grandeur permits. Indeed, when Nero was ill, and sycophantic courtiers declared that his death would mean the end of the empire, the emperor answered that the State had a support; and when they asked what he meant, he replied: 'Memmius Regulus.' Yet Regulus survived unharmed. For he was inactive, his family was only

recently ennobled, and his resources were too insignificant to attract
envy.

Another event of this year was the dedication of a gymnasium by
Nero. Oil was distributed to senators and knights on a truly Greek
scale of extravagance. In the following year, when the consuls were
Publius Marius Celsus and Lucius Afinius Gallus, the praetor Antistius
Sosianus, whose disorderly behaviour as tribune I have mentioned,
wrote verses satirizing the emperor, and read them aloud at a large
dinner-party given by Marcus Ostorius Scapula. Antistius was
charged with treason by Cossutianus Capito, who on the entreaty of
his father-in-law Gaius Ofonius Tigellinus[1] had recently been made a
senator. This was the first revival of the treason law. The intention –
people believed – was not so much to ruin Antistius as to enable the
emperor to gain credit by using his tribune's authority to veto the
senate's adverse verdict.

The host testified that he had heard nothing. Yet contrary witnesses were believed, and one of the consuls-designate, Quintus Junius
Marullus, moved Antistius' deposition from the praetorship, to be
followed by execution in the ancient manner. There was general
agreement. But Thrasea, after highly complimenting Nero and
vigorously blaming Antistius, argued that under so excellent an
emperor the senate was liable to no compulsion, and need not inflict
the maximum punishment deserved. The executioner and the noose
were obsolete, said Thrasea; the laws had established penalties which
exempted judges from brutality and avoided undesirable anachro-
nisms; so let Antistius have his property confiscated and be sent to an
island, where every prolongation of his guilty life would intensify his
personal misery but splendidly illustrate official mercy.

Thrasea's independence made others less servile. So his proposal,
when the consul put the vote, was carried. Among the few dissen-
tients the worst sycophant was Aulus Vitellius.[2] Like other cowards he
insulted anyone decent, but kept quiet when answered back. However, the consuls did not venture to confirm the senate's decree, but
wrote informing Nero of the general view. Anger and discretion
fought within him. Finally he sent the following reply: 'Antistius,

1. This is the first mention of the joint commander of the Guard, Tigellinus,
who gained great influence over Nero.
2. This is the future emperor Vitellius (A.D. 69).

unprovoked, has grossly abused the emperor. The senate was asked to punish him. It ought to have fixed a punishment fitting the enormity of the crime. But I will not amend your leniency. Indeed, I should not have allowed anything else. Decide as you please. You could have acquitted him if you wished.'

These and similar comments were read out. Nero was clearly offended. Yet the consuls did not change the motion. Thrasea did not alter his proposal, and the others, too, adhered to their decision. Some wanted to avoid showing the emperor in an unfavourable light. The majority saw safety in numbers. Thrasea was showing his usual resolution – and conformity with his reputation.

Aulus Didius Gallus Fabricius Veiento fell to a similar charge, namely the inclusion in a so-called will of numerous insults against senators and priests. His accuser, Gaius Terentius Tullius Geminus, added that Veiento had accepted bribery, in return for his influence with the emperor regarding official promotions. This led Nero to deal with the case himself. He found Veiento guilty, expelled him from Italy, and ordered his writings to be burnt. These were eagerly sought for and read – while it was dangerous to have them. When, later, the ban became obsolete, they were forgotten.

The situation of the country was deteriorating every day; and a counteracting influence now vanished, with the death of Burrus. Whether natural causes or poison killed him is uncertain. The gradually increasing tumour in his throat, which blocked the passage and stopped his breathing, suggested natural causes. But the general view was that Nero, ostensibly proposing a medical treatment, had instructed that Burrus' throat should be painted with a poisonous drug. The patient, it was said, had detected the crime, and when the emperor visited him had turned his face away and only answered Nero's inquiries with the words: '*I* am doing all right.'

The death of Burrus caused great public distress. His merits were dwelt on – also the inferiority of his successors, one harmless but ineffective and the other a notorious criminal. For the emperor now appointed two commanders of the Guard – Faenius Rufus because he was popular (having managed the corn supply without personal profit), and Gaius Ofonius Tigellinus because Nero found his unending immoralities and evil reputation fascinating. Each commander behaved as expected. Tigellinus was the more influential with the emperor, in whose private debaucheries he participated. Rufus was liked by Guardsmen and civilians: which went against him with Nero. Burrus' death undermined the influence of Seneca. Decent standards carried less weight when one of their two advocates was gone. Now Nero listened to more disreputable advisers. These attacked Seneca, first for his wealth, which was enormous and excessive for any subject, they said, and was still increasing; secondly, for the grandeur of his mansions and beauty of his gardens, which outdid even the emperor's; and thirdly, for his alleged bids for popularity. They also charged Seneca with allowing no one to be called eloquent but himself. 'He is always writing poetry,' they suggested, 'now that Nero has become fond of it. He openly disparages the emperor's amusements, underestimates him as a charioteer, and makes fun of his singing. How long must merit at Rome be conferred by Seneca's certificate alone? Surely Nero is a boy no longer! He is a grown man and ought to discharge his tutor. His ancestors will teach him all he needs.' Seneca knew of these attacks. People who still had some decency told him of them. Nero increasingly avoided his company.

Seneca, however, requested an audience, and when it was granted, this is what he said. 'It is nearly fourteen years, Caesar, since I became associated with your rising fortunes, eight since you became emperor. During that time you have showered on me such distinctions and riches that, if only I could retire to enjoy them unpretentiously, my prosperity would be complete.

'May I quote illustrious precedents drawn from your rank, not mine? Your great-great-grandfather Augustus allowed Marcus Agrippa to withdraw to Mytilene, and allowed Gaius Maecenas the equivalent of retirement at Rome itself.[1] The one his partner in wars, the other the bearer of many anxious burdens at Rome, they were greatly rewarded, for great services. I have had no claim on your generosity, except my learning. Though acquired outside the glare of public life, it has brought me the wonderful recompense and distinction of having assisted in your early education.

'But you have also bestowed on me measureless favours, and boundless wealth. Accordingly, I often ask myself: "Is it I, son of a

1. Marcus Agrippa had retired temporarily to Mytilene in 23 B.C., and in the same year Maecenas partially lost Augustus' confidence owing to an indiscretion.

provincial knight[1], who am accounted a national leader? Is mine the unknown name which has come to glitter among ancient and glorious pedigrees? Where is my old self, that was content with so little? Laying out these fine gardens? Grandly inspecting these estates? Wallowing in my vast revenues?" I can only find one excuse. It was not for me to obstruct your munificence.

'But we have both filled the measure – you, of what an emperor can give his friend, and I, of what a friend may receive from his emperor. Anything more will breed envy. Your greatness is far above all such mortal things. But I am not; so I crave your help. If, in the field or on a journey, I were tired, I should want a stick. In life's journey, I need just such a support.

'For I am old and cannot do the lightest work. I am no longer equal to the burden of my wealth. Order your agents to take over my property and incorporate it in yours. I do not suggest plunging myself into poverty, but giving up the things that are too brilliant and dazzle me. The time now spent on gardens and mansions shall be devoted to the mind. You have abundant strength. For years the supreme power has been familiar to you. We older friends may ask for our rest. This, too, will add to your glory – that you have raised to the heights men content with lower positions.'

The substance of Nero's reply was this. 'My first debt to you is that I can reply impromptu to your premeditated speech. For you taught me to improvise as well as to make prepared orations. True, my great-great-grandfather Augustus permitted Agrippa and Maecenas to rest after their labours. But he did so when he was old enough to assure them, by his prestige, of everything – of whatever kind – that he had given them. Besides, he certainly deprived neither of the rewards which they had earned from him in the wars and crises of Augustus' youthful years. If my life had been warlike, you too would have fought for me. But you gave what our situation demanded: wisdom, advice, philosophy, to support me as boy and youth. Your gifts to me will endure as long as life itself! My gifts to you, gardens and mansions and revenues, are liable to circumstances.

'They may seem extensive. But many people far less deserving than you have had more. I omit, from shame, to mention ex-slaves who flaunt greater wealth. I am even ashamed that you, my dearest friend,

1. Seneca's family came from Corduba in Spain.

are not the richest of all men. You are still vigorous and fit for State
affairs and their rewards. My reign is only beginning. Or do you think
you have reached your limit? If so you must rank yourself below
Lucius Vitellius, thrice consul, and my generosity below that of
Claudius, and my gifts as inferior to the lifelong savings of Lucius
Volusius Saturninus (II).

'If youth's slippery paths lead me astray, be at hand to call me
back! You equipped my manhood; devote even greater care to guid-
ing it! If you return my gifts and desert your emperor, it is not your
unpretentiousness, your retirement, that will be on everyone's lips,
but *my* meanness, your dread of *my* brutality. However much your
self-denial were praised, no philosopher could becomingly gain credit
from an action damaging to his friend's reputation.'

Then he clasped and kissed Seneca. Nature and experience had
fitted Nero to conceal hatred behind treacherous embraces. Seneca
expressed his gratitude (all conversations with autocrats end like that).
But he abandoned the customs of his former ascendancy. Terminating
his large receptions, he dismissed his entourage, and rarely visited
Rome. Ill-health or philosophical studies kept him at home, he said.

After Seneca's elimination it was easy to bring down the commander of the Guard Faenius Rufus, who was accused of friendship
with Agrippina. Faenius' colleague Tigellinus became more powerful
every day. But he felt that his criminal aptitudes – the only qualities
he possessed – would influence the emperor more if he could make
them partners in crime. Studying Nero's fears, Tigellinus found he
chiefly dreaded Rubellius Plautus and Faustus Cornelius Sulla Felix.
One had been recently removed to Asia, the other to southern Gaul.
Tigellinus enlarged on their aristocratic origins, and their present
proximity to the armies of the east and of Germany respectively.

'I have no divided allegiance like Burrus,' he said. 'My only thought
is your safety! At Rome this may in some degree be ensured by vigilance on the spot. But how can one suppress sedition far away? The
dictator Sulla's name has excited the Gauls. For the peoples of Asia
Drusus' grandson is just as unsettling. Sulla's poverty increases his
daring. He pretends to be lazy – yet he is only biding his time for a
coup. Plautus is rich, and does not pretend to like retirement. He
parades an admiration of the ancient Romans, but he has the arrogance
of the Stoics, who breed sedition and intrigue.'

Action was not long delayed. Five days later, Sulla was murdered at dinner. Assassins had reached Massilia before the alarm. His head was transported to Nero, who joked that it was disfigured by premature greyness.

The plans for Plautus' death were less secret. More people were interested in his safety. Besides, the length and duration of the land and sea journeys encouraged rumours. The story was invented that Plautus had escaped to Corbulo who, having mighty armies behind him, would be in the gravest peril if there was to be a massacre of blameless notables. Asia, it was said, had risen in Plautus' support; the few, unenthusiastic, soldiers sent to murder him had failed to carry out their orders and had joined the rebellion. Idle credulity, as usual, amplified these fictitious rumours.

Meanwhile an ex-slave of Plautus, helped by favourable winds, outstripped the staff-officer of the Guard who had been sent against him, and brought a message from Plautus' father-in-law Lucius Antistius Vetus. 'Escape a passive end while there is a way out!' advised Antistius. 'Sympathy for your great name will make decent men back you and brave men help you. Meantime, disdain no possible support. Sixty soldiers have been sent. If you can repulse them, much can happen – even a war can develop – before Nero receives the news and sends another force. In short, either you save yourself by this action, or at least a bold end is as good as a timid one.'

But Plautus remained unimpressed. Either he felt helpless – an unarmed exile – or the suspense wearied him. Or perhaps he believed that his wife and children, whom he loved, would be more leniently treated if the emperor were not upset by an alarm. One account states that his father-in-law sent further messages saying that Plautus was in no danger. Or his philosophical friends, the Greek Coeranus and the Etruscan Gaius Musonius Rufus, may have recommended an imperturbable expectation of death rather than a hazardous anxious life.

The killers found him at midday, stripped for exercise. Supervised by the eunuch Pelago whom Nero had put in charge of the gang – like a slave set over a monarch's underlings – the officer slew him as he was. The victim's head was brought to Nero. I will quote the actual words he uttered when he saw it. 'Nero,' he said, 'how could such a long-nosed man have frightened you?'[1]

1. These words, missing in the text, are supplied from Dio.

Indeed, the fears which had caused the emperor to postpone his wedding with Poppaea were now dispelled. He planned to marry her quickly, after eliminating Octavia his wife. Octavia's conduct was unassuming; but he hated her, because she was popular and an emperor's daughter. First Nero wrote to the senate emphasizing his perpetual solicitude for the national interests, and – without admitting their murder – denouncing Sulla and Plautus as agitators. On these grounds the senate voted a thanksgiving, and the two men's expulsion from the senate. This was a mockery which caused greater disgust even than the crimes. Hearing of their decree, Nero concluded that all his misdeeds were accounted meritorious. So he divorced Octavia for barrenness, and married Poppaea.

Dominating Nero as his wife, as she had long dominated him as his mistress, Poppaea incited one of Octavia's household to accuse Octavia of adultery with a slave – an Alexandrian flute-player called Eucaerus was designated for the role. Octavia's maids were tortured, and though some were induced by the pain to make false confessions, the majority unflinchingly maintained her innocence. One retorted that the mouth of Tigellinus, who was bullying her, was less clean than any part of Octavia. Nevertheless, she was put away. First, there was an ordinary divorce: she received the ominous gifts of Burrus' house and Rubellius Plautus' estates. Soon, however, she was banished to Campania, under military surveillance.

Now indiscretion is safer for the Roman public than for their superiors, since they are insignificant; and they protested openly and loudly. This seemed to recall Nero to decency, and he proposed to make Octavia his wife again. Happy crowds climbed the Capitol, thankful to heaven at last. They overturned Poppaea's statues and carried Octavia's on their shoulders, showering flowers on them and setting them in the Forum and temples.

Even the emperor was acclaimed and worshipped again. Indeed a noisy crowd invaded the palace. But detachments of troops clubbed them and forced them back at the point of the sword. Then the changes the rioters had inspired were reversed, and Poppaea reinstated. Always a savage hater, she was now mad with fear of mass violence and Nero's capitulation to it. She fell at his feet crying: 'Now that things have reached this pass, it is not marriage I am fighting for, but what, to me, means less than my marriage – my life. It is in danger from Octavia's dependants and slaves! They pretend to be the people of Rome! They commit, in peace-time, outrages that could hardly happen even in war! The emperor is their target – they only lack a leader. And once disorders begin one will easily be found, when she leaves Campania and proceeds to the capital! Even her distant nod causes riots.

'What have *I* done wrong? Whom have I injured? Or is all this because I am going to give an authentic heir to the house of the Caesars? Would Rome prefer an Egyptian flute-player's child to be introduced into the palace? If you think it best, take back your directress voluntarily – do not be coerced into doing so. Or else, safeguard yourself! Punish suitably. No severity was needed to end the first troubles. But now, once they lose hope of Nero keeping Octavia, they will find her another husband.'

Poppaea's arguments, playing on Nero's alarm and anger in turn, duly terrified and infuriated him. But the suspicions concerning Octavia's slave came to nothing; the examination of her servants proved fruitless. So it was decided to extract a confession of adultery from someone against whom a charge of revolution could also be concocted. A suitable person seemed to be the aforementioned Anicetus, fleet-commander at Misenum and instrument of Nero's matricide. After the crime he had been fairly well regarded. Later, however, he was in serious disfavour; for the sight of a former accomplice in terrible crimes is a reproach.

Nero summoned him, and reminded him of his previous job – Anicetus alone had protected his emperor against his mother's plotting. Now, said Nero, he could earn equal gratitude by eliminating a detested wife. No violence or weapons were needed. Anicetus only had to confess adultery with Octavia. Great rewards were promised – though at present they were unspecified – and an agreed place of retirement. Refusal would mean death. Anicetus' warped character found no difficulty in a further crime. Indeed, the confession which he made to Nero's friends, assembled as a council of state, even exceeded his instructions. Then he was removed to comfortable exile in Sardinia, where he died a natural death.

Nero reported in an edict that Octavia had tried to win over the fleet by seducing its commander, and then, nervous about her unfaithfulness, had procured an abortion (the emperor forgot his recent charge of sterility). She was then confined on the island of Pandateria. No exiled woman ever earned greater sympathy from those who saw her. Some still remembered the banishment of the elder Agrippina by Tiberius and, more recently, of Julia Livilla by Claudius.[1] Yet they had been mature women with happy memories which could alleviate their present sufferings. But Octavia had virtually died on her wedding day. Her new home had brought her nothing but misery. Poison had removed her father, and very soon her brother. Maid had been preferred to mistress. Then she, Nero's wife, had been ruined by her successor. Last came the bitterest of all fates, this accusation.

So this girl, in her twentieth year, was picketed by company-commanders of the Guard and their men. She was hardly a living person any more – so certain was she of imminent destruction. Yet still she lacked the peace of death. The order to die arrived a few days later. She protested that she was a wife no longer – Nero's sister only. She invoked the Germanici, the relations she shared with Nero. Finally she even invoked Agrippina, in whose days her marriage had been unhappy, certainly, but at least not fatal. But Octavia was bound, and all her veins were opened. However, her terror retarded the flow of blood. So she was put into an exceedingly hot vapour-bath and suffocated. An even crueller atrocity followed. Her head was cut off and taken to Rome for Poppaea to see.

How long must I go on recording the thank-offerings in temples on such occasions? Every reader about that epoch, in my own work or others, can assume that the gods were thanked every time the emperor ordered a banishment or murder; and, conversely, that happenings once regarded joyfully were now treated as national disasters. Nevertheless, when any senatorial decree reaches new depths of sycophancy or abasement, I will not leave it unrecorded.

In the same year Nero was believed to have poisoned two of his most prominent ex-slaves – Doryphorus for opposing the emperor's marriage with Poppaea, and Pallas for reserving his own immense riches for himself by living so long.

Seneca was secretly denounced by Romanus as an associate of Gaius

1. The banishments of Julia Livilla in A.D. 37 and 41 (as of Agrippina in 29) were described in the lost parts of the work.

Calpurnius Piso. But Seneca more effectively turned the same charge against his accuser. However, the incident alarmed Piso – and by so doing initiated a far-reaching, disastrous conspiracy against Nero.

CHAPTER 13

Eastern Settlement

★

T H E Parthian king Vologeses I had now heard of Corbulo's activities and Rome's award of the Armenian throne to the foreigner Tigranes V. Vologeses wanted to avenge the slur cast on the Parthian royal house by the expulsion of his brother Tiridates from Armenia. Yet Roman power, and his respect for the longstanding treaty[1] with us, put him in two minds. Hesitant by nature, Vologeses was also embarrassed by the rebellion of the formidable Hyrcanian people and the numerous resultant campaigns. As he wavered, however, news of a further humiliation provoked him to action. Tigranes had left Armenia and subjected its neighbour Adiabene to devastation too protracted and comprehensive to be regarded as a mere raid.

This was too much for the Parthian grandees. 'Are we so utterly despised', they said, 'that we are invaded not even by a Roman commander but by an impudent hostage who has long been considered a slave?' The king of Adiabene, Monobazus, further inflamed their resentment. 'Where,' he asked, 'from what quarter, can I find protection? Armenia is gone! The borderlands are following! If Parthia will not help, we must give in to Rome, and make the best of it – avoid conquest by surrendering.' The silence, and restrained reproaches, of the dethroned exile Tiridates were even more effective. 'Passivity does not preserve great empires', he said. 'That needs fighting, with warriors and weapons. When stakes are highest, might is right. A private individual can satisfy his prestige by holding his own – but a monarch can only do it by claiming other people's property.'

Vologeses was moved by these pleas. Calling a council, he placed

1. The eastern events of about three years are here described together. The treaty which Vologeses I has in mind was the Romano–Parthian agreement of 20 B.C.

Tiridates next to himself. 'When this man,' said Vologeses, 'whose father was mine too, renounced the supreme position to me as the elder, I awarded him the third-ranking kingdom, Armenia; for Pacorus had already been given Media Atropatene. By abandoning the tradition of brotherly feuds and family strife, I thought I had settled the affairs of our family satisfactorily. But the Romans, though they have never broken the peace to their advantage, are breaking it once again. It will mean their destruction!

'I admit I should have preferred to rely on right and inheritance, not on sanguinary warfare, to keep what my ancestors won. But if I have delayed mistakenly, my prowess henceforward will make amends. Your might and renown, gentlemen, are undiminished. You have gained a name, also, for moderation. No man is exalted enough to scorn moderation; and the gods too honour it.' So saying, he placed the diadem on Tiridates' head. Then, entrusting his royal cavalry escort or auxiliaries from Adiabene to a nobleman called Monaeses, Vologeses ordered Tiridates to expel Tigranes from Armenia. Vologeses himself, waiving his dispute with the Hyrcanians, mobilized his home forces for major operations against the Roman provinces.

When Corbulo received reliable information of these measures, he sent two divisions to support Tigranes. But Corbulo secretly instructed their commanders, Lucius Verulanus Severus and Marcus Vettius Bolanus, to act warily and not to hustle. For he wanted to have a war on hand rather than to fight one. Moreover, since Syria would be the chief sufferer from invasion by Vologeses, he had written recommending Nero to appoint a separate commander to defend Armenia. Meanwhile Corbulo posted his remaining divisions on the Euphrates, improvised an armed force of provincials, and blocked every possible entrance-point with troops. Water being so scarce in the area, he built forts to protect certain springs, and destroyed others by filling them with sand.

During these preparations for the defence of Syria, Monaeses advanced rapidly, hoping to reach Tigranes before his approach was announced; but he did not catch Corbulo unawares or unprepared. Tigranes had occupied Tigranocerta. This city was powerfully garrisoned and fortified. Parts of its walls were protected by a considerable river, the Nicephorius, while a large fosse surrounded the remaining circumference. Inside were Roman troops, and stores already collected.

A few of their collectors, advancing rashly, had been surprised and
out off by the enemy. However, this irritated rather than intimidated
their fellow-soldiers.

The Parthians lacked the hand-to-hand courage to prosecute a
siege. Their sporadic discharge of arrows deluded no one but themselves; it did not frighten the Roman garrison. And when the Adia-
benians brought up ladders and siege-engines they were easily thrown
back, and then roughly handled by a sortie. But Corbulo decided to
take no great advantage of the successes. Instead he wrote to Vologeses protesting against his invasion of the province and blockade of
an allied, friendly king and Roman troops. Either Vologeses must
raise the siege, said Corbulo, or he himself would likewise occupy
enemy territory. The staff-officer Casperius who took the letter
found the Parthian king at Nisibis, thirty-seven miles from Tigranocerta, and spiritedly delivered his message in person.

It was Vologeses' longstanding and firm policy to avoid war with
Rome. Besides, his affairs were not going well. The siege had failed.
Tigranes was well-garrisoned and supplied. The assaulting party had
been routed. Moreover, Roman divisions had been dispatched to
Armenia, while others were on the Syrian frontier ready for an offensive. His own cavalry, however, was suffering from lack of fodder,
since an invasion of locusts had destroyed all leafage and grass. Afraid
– but hiding it – Vologeses gave a conciliatory reply: he would send
envoys to the Roman emperor, to discuss the Parthian claim to
Armenia and the conclusion of a stable peace. Then the king ordered
Monaeses to abandon the attempt on Tigranocerta, and also withdrew
himself.

This was generally regarded as a triumph, achieved by Corbulo's
threats and Vologeses' fears. Some, however, alleged a secret agreement whereby each side should suspend hostilities and both Vologeses
and Tigranes should leave Armenia. 'Otherwise', they argued, 'why
had the Roman army evacuated Tigranocerta? Was it better to have
wintered on the Cappadocian frontier, in hastily erected huts, rather
than in the capital of the kingdom they had just saved? No, surely the
war was postponed so that Vologeses should encounter a different
opponent. Corbulo clearly had no intention of hazarding any more
the honours that his long service had won him.'

For Corbulo, as already stated, had requested a separate appointment for the defence of Armenia. Lucius Caesennius Paetus was reported to be on his way. When he arrived, the forces were divided. Paetus received the first brigade which had recently been summoned from Moesia, and the fourth and twelfth, and all the auxiliaries from Pontus, Galatia, and Cappadocia. Corbulo retained the third, sixth and tenth brigades, and the original Syrian army. The remaining troops were to be shared or allotted as circumstances required. However, Corbulo was impatient of rivals. Paetus, for his part, might well in other circumstances have been satisfied to take second place – but he had formed a low estimate of what his colleague had achieved. There had been no killing or plundering, said Paetus – the storming of cities had been purely nominal: *he* intended to impose, not merely a phantom king, but the tribute and law and government of Rome.

At this juncture Vologeses' envoys, whose mission to the emperor I mentioned, returned unsuccessful. So Parthia started undisguised warfare. Paetus was willing, and entered Armenia with two divisions, the fourth under Lucius Funisulanus Vettonianus, and the twelfth under Calavius Sabinus. But the omens were sinister. For while crossing the Euphrates bridge the horse carrying the consular insignia took fright for no apparent reason, and bolted to the rear. Then a victim due for sacrifice (when the construction of the winter camp was complete) escaped outside the rampart before the work was done. Moreover, some soldiers' javelins caught fire – a particularly significant portent since the Parthian enemy fights with missiles.

But Paetus disregarded the omens. Without adequately fortifying his winter camp or arranging to store corn, he hurried his army across the Taurus range, proposing to recover Tigranocerta and devastate the areas which Corbulo had left unravaged. A few forts were captured and some credit gained, also loot; though Paetus claimed immoderate credit, and wasted the loot. But during his long marches over territory he could not hold, the corn he had seized became spoilt. Winter was approaching. So Paetus withdrew his army and composed a dispatch to Nero. It was grandly phrased – as if the war was over – but empty of substance.

Corbulo had guarded the Euphrates bank vigilantly. Now he reinforced its protection. A bridge was also constructed. To prevent interference by the enemy cavalry – already manoeuvring impressively nearby – he moved across the river large ships joined by poles and fortified with turrets. On these were stationed engines and catapults which repulsed the Parthians: their discharge of stones and spears outranged the enemy's arrows. The bridge was then completed, and the hills opposite occupied, first by auxiliaries and then by a brigade camp. The speed and power displayed were so imposing that the Parthians abandoned their preparations for invading Syria and concentrated all their hopes on Armenia.

Paetus was unaware of the threat. The fifth brigade was in distant Pontus. The others were weakened by excessive grants of leave. Then came news that Vologeses was approaching with a large and formidable force. Paetus summoned up the twelfth brigade. But this action, designed to give an impression of strength, only revealed his weakness. Yet with such a force, if only he had followed a consistent policy – his own or that of his advisers – he could have held the camp, or frustrated the Parthians by delaying action. As it was, emboldened to face the emergency by his staff, he adopted a different, inferior plan – to show his independent judgement. Asserting that the means given him to resist the enemy were not ditches and ramparts but men and weapons, he abandoned the winter camp and led out his army as though for a battle.

After losing a small reconnaissance detachment under a company-commander, he returned in alarm. But Vologeses' omission to press the pursuit restored his baseless confidence. So Paetus posted three thousand picked infantry on the nearest spur of the Taurus to bar Vologeses' approach, stationed the best of his cavalry from Pannonia on the neighbouring plain, and shut his wife and son into the fort of Arsamosata, which was garrisoned by one battalion. If concentrated, Paetus' troops might well have held the enemy's sporadic attacks; but he scattered them.

Only very reluctantly, it is said, did he agree to admit his danger to Corbulo. But Corbulo did not hurry. The graver the peril, he felt, the more glorious the rescue. Nevertheless, he told a thousand regular troops from each of his three brigades, eight hundred cavalry, and eight hundred auxiliary infantry, to stand by for marching orders.

Vologeses knew that Paetus had blocked his route with infantry on one flank and cavalry on the other. But the Parthian adhered to his plan. Frightening off the cavalry by a threat of force, he overwhelmed the Roman infantry. Only one company-commander, Tarquitius

Crescens, put up a fight for the tower he was defending. After numerous sorties, and the destruction of every oriental who approached, he fell beneath showers of firebrands. Surviving infantrymen fled far into the wilderness. The wounded regained the camp with terrified, exaggerated stories of the king's prowess and the ferocity of his numerous peoples. These tales were readily believed by listeners who felt the same terrors. The general himself collapsed under his difficulties. Paetus neglected every military duty, but wrote again to Corbulo, urging speed to save the Eagles, standards, and remaining prestige of his unhappy army – which would hold out loyally, he said, until it perished.

Corbulo was not alarmed. Leaving part of his army in Syria to hold the Euphrates defences, he proceeded to Armenia by the shortest provisioned route, by way of Commagene and Cappadocia. His usual military equipment was supplemented by numerous camels carrying corn; for measures to resist famine, as well as the enemy, were necessary. The first of the defeated force whom he encountered was a senior company-commander Paccius Orfitus, then numerous soldiers. They offered various excuses for their flight. But Corbulo ordered them to return to their units and see if Paetus would forgive them. Personally, he added, he was unindulgent, except to battle-winners.

Addressing his own troops, he encouraged them with reminders of past glories, and hopes of more. 'Our worthwhile objectives', he said, 'are not Armenian towns and villages but a Roman camp containing two Roman brigades. Any of you private soldiers can win from the emperor's own hand the glorious wreath for saving a citizen's life. But how infinitely honourable if this army could win it corporatively for saving a force as large as itself!' His address inspired unanimous enthusiasm. Besides, some soldiers had personal incentives – brothers and other relatives in danger. They marched at top speed, night and day.

Vologeses intensified the siege, bringing pressure alternately on the camp defences and the fort containing the non-combatants. He approached closer than Parthians usually do, hoping by this boldness to lure the enemy into an engagement. But the Romans could hardly be enticed out of their tents, other than to man the defences. In some cases the motive was obedience to their general. Others were cowards. They claimed to be waiting for Corbulo. But the prospect of an enemy onslaught made them think of past catastrophes like the Caudine Forks or Numantia[1] – 'and there the conquerors had been the Samnites, one Italian tribe, whereas the Parthians are a power rivalling imperial Rome itself. Even the brave, admired ancient Romans had taken thought for their lives when fortune deserted them.'

Paetus succumbed to the general hopelessness, and wrote to Vologeses. But his first letter was less a petition than a protest against this forcible support of Armenia, which, he claimed, had always been subject to Rome or to a king chosen by the emperor. Peace, he urged, was mutually beneficial. The king must look beyond the immediate circumstances. He had brought the whole strength of his kingdom against two brigades, but Rome had the rest of the world to support her warfare.

Vologeses replied evasively that he must await his brothers Pacorus and Tiridates, that this was the time and place fixed for deciding Armenia's future, and that heaven had added the task – befitting his house – of deciding the fate of the Roman army. Paetus then sent messengers requesting an interview with the king. Instead, Vologeses sent his cavalry-commander Vasaces. To him, Paetus emphasized the history of Rome's occupations and disposals of Armenia by Lucius Licinius Lucullus, Pompey, and the emperors. The Parthian objected that these had been purely nominal; the real power had belonged to his compatriots. After long discussion, Monobazus, the king of Adiabene, was brought in next day to witness an agreement. The siege was to be raised, all Roman troops evacuated from Armenia, forts and provisions ceded to the Parthians; after all of which, Vologeses was to be authorized to send envoys to Nero.

Paetus next bridged the river Arsania alongside the camp. Ostensibly this was for his own retreat, though in reality the Parthians had ordered its construction to commemorate their victory. For it was they who utilized it. Our army took a different route. Rumour added that the Roman troops suffered indignities befitting their humiliation, including the yoke. The behaviour of the Armenians was in keeping with such reports. They entered the defences before the Roman column left, and lined the roads, identifying and intercepting slaves and cattle our men had earlier plundered. Even clothing was torn off,

---

1. The defeats at the Caudine Forks by the Samnites and at Numantia in Spain by the Celtiberians were in 321 and 137 B.C. respectively.

and weapons seized from the terrified soldiers. To avoid any pretext for a battle, the Romans acquiesced.

To commemorate our defeat, Vologeses piled up the arms and corpses of the fallen. But he refrained from viewing the Roman army's withdrawal. His pride satisfied, he desired a name for moderation. He forded the river on an elephant, while horses swam across with his staff. For the rumour had spread that the bridge had been treacherously built to collapse beneath a weight. But those who ventured on it found it solid and reliable.

The besieged, it became known, had been so well provided with corn that they burned their granaries. The Parthians, however – according to Corbulo – were about to raise the siege owing to the exhaustion of their supplies and forage: and he was only three days' march away. He added that Paetus swore, before the standards (and witnesses sent by the kings), that no Roman should enter Armenia until Nero had written back saying whether he accepted the peace. Even assuming that these stories were invented to heighten Paetus' disgrace, the other reports are certainly true; in one day Paetus marched forty miles, abandoning his wounded as he went – a panic-striken flight as disgraceful as running away in battle.[1]

Corbulo and his troops met them at the Euphrates. There was no display of decorations or arms to point a censorious contrast. Corbulo's men, in sad sympathy for their fellow soldiers, wept so bitterly that they could hardly manage to utter a greeting. The incentives produced by success – rivalry in valour and ambition for glory – just were not there. Instead, in the lower ranks especially, the prevailing emotion was pity.

The generals had a brief conversation. 'My work is wasted!' said Corbulo. 'The war could have been ended, and the Parthians routed.' 'Nothing is lost for either of us,' replied Paetus. 'Let us turn our Eagles round and jointly invade Armenia, which is powerless now Vologeses has gone.' But Corbulo answered that the emperor had given him no such orders. 'I only left my province through anxiety for your army. Parthian plans are unpredictable! I must return to Syria. Even as it is, my infantry is exhausted by protracted marching – and we shall need luck to intercept their powerful cavalry, which moves so much faster on the level ground.'

1. Paetus' march was at twice, or nearly twice, the normal speed.

Paetus wintered in Cappadocia. Vologeses sent envoys to Corbulo requesting the suppression of his forts across the Euphrates and its re-establishment as the frontier. Corbulo then insisted that all Parthian garrisons should evacuate Armenia; and finally the king gave way. Corbulo's fortifications across the Euphrates were then demolished, and the Armenians were left without interference.

At Rome, however, trophies and arches for victory over Parthia were erected in the centre of the Capitoline hill. Voted by the senate while the war was still undecided, they were not abandoned now. Unmistakable facts were ignored in favour of appearances.

As a further distraction from the grave foreign situation, certain corn that had been intended for the inhabitants of Rome but had deteriorated in storage was dumped by Nero in the Tiber. This was to inspire confidence that supplies were abundant. However, nearly two hundred corn ships – actually in harbour – had been destroyed by a violent storm, and a hundred more were accidentally burnt when already up the Tiber. Yet the emperor did not increase the price. But he proceeded to appoint three ex-consuls, Lucius Calpurnius Piso (V), Aulus Ducenius Geminus, and Pompeius Paulinus, to control the national revenues. Nero utilized this occasion to criticize previous emperors for their ruinous expenditure in advance of income, and to emphasize his own annual gifts of sixty million sesterces to the nation.

At this period there was a widespread harmful practice whereby, when an election or ballot for governorships was impending, child-less persons fictitiously adopted sons,[1] and then, when they had won praetorships or provinces as fathers of families, immediately emanci-pated the adopted persons. The senate received angry appeals from real parents. These contrasted the unnatural, fraudulent brevity of these adoptions with the natural claims of themselves, who had suf-fered the anxieties of bringing up children. The childless were amply consoled, they argued, by the ready ease with which, carefree and un-burdened, they acquired influence and office; whereas their own legal privileges, after protracted waiting, became a farce when some irres-ponsible so-called father – whose lack of children did not come from bereavement – effortlessly achieved the longstanding ambitions of

1. The Lex Papia Poppaea of A.D. 9 gave preference to fathers of families in regard to promotion and inheritance.

authentic parents. So the senate decreed that, when offices or even inheritances were at stake, fictitious adoptions should carry no weight.

Next came the trial of a Cretan, Claudius Timarchus. Most of the charges against him were those habitually brought against mighty provincials whose enormous wealth inflates them into oppressors. But he had also made a remark (more than once) which constituted an insult to the senate: 'Whether a governor of Crete receives the thanks of our Provincial Assembly depends on me!' Thrasea utilized the occasion to the national advantage. Proposing the defendant's banishment from Crete, he reminded the senate how experience showed that, among right-thinking men, good laws and beneficial precedents are prompted by other men's misdeeds. Punishments, he pointed out, come after crimes, and rectifications after abuses. He quoted the Cincian bill originating from the excesses of advocates, the Julian laws from corruption among candidates, and the Calpurnian enactments from the rapacity of officials.[1]

'So let us face this unprecedented provincial arrogance', he urged, 'with a measure befitting Roman honour and dignity. Without diminishing our protection of provincials, we must recover the conviction that a Roman's reputation depends on Romans only. Once we used to send praetors and consuls, and even private citizens, to inspect provinces and report on everyone's loyalty. Then nations trembled for the verdict of one man! But now we court and flatter foreigners. Some individual makes a sign, and they thank our governor – or, more likely, prosecute him!

'But even granting that we must continue to let provincials display their power in this way, we should nevertheless frown on governors winning empty eulogies, extracted by entreaties. We should judge this as severely as ill-intentioned or brutal government. To oblige is often as harmful as to offend. Indeed, some virtues provoke hatred. Unbending strictness and incorruptibility do. That is why our officials usually start well and end badly; like election candidates, they begin looking round for support. Stop this, and provincial administration will be fairer and steadier. Prohibit votes of thanks, and popularity-

1. A Julian law of Augustus (18 B.C.) penalized bribery in elections. A Calpurnian law (149 B.C.) had established a permanent court to try cases of corruption.

hunting will collapse – just as acquisitiveness is repressed by fear of the extortion laws.'

These opinions received warm approval. But no senatorial decree could be carried, since the consuls ruled that no question on the subject was before the House. Later, however, on the emperor's initiative, a decree was passed forbidding votes of thanks to governors at Provincial Assemblies, or the participation by provincials in missions conveying such votes.

This, too, was the year in which the Gymnasium was struck by lightning and burnt down. A statue of Nero inside was melted into a shapeless bronze mass. An earthquake also largely demolished the populous Campanian town of Pompeii. Laelia, priestess of Vesta, died, and her place was taken by Cornelia, of the family of the Cossi.

Next year the consuls were Gaius Memmius Regulus and Lucius Verginius Rufus. Poppaea now bore Nero a daughter. His joy exceeded human measure, and mother and child were both named Augusta. The infant was born at Nero's own birthplace, the Roman settlement of Antium. The senate had already asked heaven's blessing on Poppaea's pregnancy and made official vows. Now these vows were discharged, with additions including a thanksgiving. A temple of Fertility was decreed, and a competition modelled on the Actian Victory Festival.[1] Golden statues of the Two Fortunes of Antium were to be placed on the throne of Capitoline Jupiter, and Antium was to have Circus Games in honour of the Claudian and Domitian houses, like the Games in honour of the Julian house at Bovillae.

But it was all ephemeral; for within less than four months the baby was dead. Then followed new forms of sycophancy. She was declared a goddess and voted a place on the gods' ceremonial couch, together with a shrine and a priest. The emperor's delight had been immoderate; so was his mourning.

Shortly after the birth, the whole senate had flocked out to Antium. But Thrasea had been forbidden to attend. It was noticed how calmly he received this affront – though it foreshadowed his own impending death. Nero, it is said, subsequently boasted to Seneca that he was reconciled with Thrasea; and Seneca congratulated Nero. The incident increased both these eminent men's prestige, but also their peril.

1. To celebrate his victory at Actium (N.W. Greece) Augustus had established five-yearly games at Nicopolis nearby.

At this time, the beginning of spring, there arrived the Parthian delegation bringing Vologeses' message and a letter confirming it. 'I say nothing now about my frequently repeated claim to Armenia,' ran the communication, 'since the gods, who direct the fates even of the greatest nations, have handed the country to the Parthians, not without Roman ignominy. When, recently, I besieged Tigranes, I could have destroyed Lucius Caesennius Paetus and his army. But I let them go free. I have sufficiently demonstrated my power; and I have also given proof of my clemency. Tiridates, too, would not decline to come to Rome and receive his diadem, if this were not prevented by taboos connected with his priesthood. He would attend the emperor's standards and statues, and inaugurate his reign before the Roman army.'

It was hard to reconcile this message with Paetus' report that the position was inconclusive. A Roman staff-officer escorting the delegates was interrogated concerning the situation. He replied that all Romans had left Armenia. The ironical character of the orientals' request for what they had already seized was clear. Nero consulted his council: was it to be a hazardous war, or a humiliating peace? The unhesitating decision was war. To prevent a further disaster from the incompetence of some new general – for they were disgusted with Paetus – the sole command was given to Corbulo, with his long experience of active service.

So the delegates were dismissed, their purpose unaccomplished. But they were given presents to encourage the hope that, if Tiridates made the same appeal in person, it would be favourably received. Corbulo's army was reinforced by a brigade from Pannonia under the command of Marius Celsus. Gaius Cestius Gallus (II) was made imperial governor of Syria. Instructions were sent to vassal kings and princes, and neighbouring governors of all ranks, to obey Corbulo's orders. His powers were virtually increased to those the state had granted to Pompey for the Pirate War.[1] Paetus, back in Rome, expected the worst. But Nero contented himself with a sarcastic rebuke. He was pardoning the general immediately, he intimated, because prolonged suspense would damage so timid a person's health.

Corbulo sent Paetus' fourth and twelfth brigades to Syria, considering that the loss of their best men and demoralization of the

1. In 67 B.C.

remainder had made them unfit to fight. His invasion force for Armenia included his own two fresh brigades, the sixth and third, toughened by long and successful service. To these Corbulo added the recently arrived fifteenth brigade from Pannonia, and the fifth which had been stationed in Pontus and so had escaped the disaster, picked detachments from Illyricum and Egypt, and auxiliary infantry and cavalry, including contingents from the dependent kings. These forces were concentrated in Melitene at the point where he planned to cross the Euphrates. Then – after the customary purification ritual – Corbulo addressed the army. His own achievements under the emperor's auspices received grandiloquent allusions. Reverses he blamed on Pactus' inexperience. His words had that authoritative ring which, in a military man, takes the place of eloquence.

Soon his advance began along the road originally opened up by Lucius Licinius Lucullus.[1] Obstructions formed in the course of time had to be cleared. When envoys arrived from Tiridates and Vologese to discuss peace, he did not rebuff them but sent them back with Roman staff-officers bearing conciliatory messages. 'Matters have not reached the point', he said, 'when war to the finish is unavoidable. Rome's many successes, Parthia's successes, too, are warnings against arrogance. To accept his kingdom as a gift, undevastated, is to Tiridates' advantage. Vologeses, too, will serve Parthian interests better by alliance with Rome than by a policy of mutual injury. I know the internal dissensions of your kingdom, with its formidable, lawless nations – a contrast to my emperor, whose territories are uniformly peaceful. This is his only war.'

Advice was reinforced by intimidation. The Armenian chiefs who had first revolted against Rome were driven from their homes, and their fortresses demolished. In highlands and lowlands, among strong and weak, there was panic. But the enemy felt no bitterness or hostility towards Corbulo. They trusted his advice. So Vologeses avoided showing intransigence on the main issue, and requested a truce in certain provinces; while Tiridates requested that a day and place should be fixed for a conference. An early date was arranged. As the place, the orientals selected the scene of Paetus' recent blockade with his army; this was to commemorate their victory. Corbulo did not object. Their contrasted fortunes seemed to accentuate his own glory.

1. He had marched along the same road to Tigranocerta in 69 B.C.

How little Paetus' discredit distressed him, he clearly showed by ordering the latter's son, a colonel, to take a detachment and bury the remains of the disastrous battle.

On the appointed day a distinguished knight, Tiberius Julius Alexander, who was attached to the campaign in an advisory capacity, and Corbulo's son-in-law, Annius Vinicianus, who, though below senatorial age, was acting as commander of the fifth brigade, entered Tiridates' camp. Their visit was both a compliment and a pledge against treachery. Then Tiridates and Corbulo, each with an escort of twenty cavalry, went to meet each other. When he saw the Roman, Tiridates was the first to dismount. Corbulo quickly did the same. On foot, they clasped hands. Corbulo began by complimenting the young ruler on his rejection of adventure and adoption of a safe, beneficial policy. The king, after long preliminaries concerning the nobility of his family, spoke in moderate terms. He would go to Rome, he said, and bring the emperor an unfamiliar distinction – the homage, following no Parthian reverse, of a Parthian royal prince. It was then arranged that Tiridates should lay the royal diadem before the emperor's statue, to resume it only from Nero's hand. The interview ended with an embrace.

A few days later both armies paraded in splendid array. On the Parthian side was troop after troop of cavalry, with their national ensigns. On the other side stood our brigades, with their glittering Eagles and standards; and all the images of gods made one think of a temple. On the dais in the middle was a Roman official chair, bearing Nero's effigy. To this Tiridates advanced. When the customary sacrifices had been made, he took the diadem from his head and laid it at the feet of the statue. This caused a profound and universal impression, the more so since the picture of Roman armies slaughtered and besieged had not faded from people's eyes. Now, it seemed, the situation was reversed. Tiridates was going to make a world-wide exhibition of himself; he was little short of a prisoner.

Corbulo improved his already glorious reputation by courtesy and entertainment. For every novelty he saw, the king requested explanations – for instance a company-commander announcing the new watch; the bugle-note terminating the banquet; the torch which lit the altar before the commander-in-chief's tent. Corbulo's grandiose replies fired Tiridates with admiration for ancient Roman customs.

Next day, however, he requested time to visit his brothers and mother before the long journey. Meanwhile, he gave his daughter as a hostage, and presented his petition for Nero.

Tiridates then went to find Vologeses and his other brother Pacorus, who were at Ecbatana and in Media Atropatene respectively. Concerned for Tiridates' interests, the Parthian king had sent envoys to Corbulo asking that his brother should not be exposed to any external signs of subjection – that he should keep his sword, be entitled to embrace governors, not be kept waiting at their doors, and at Rome receive a consul's honours. Vologeses was accustomed to foreign ostentatiousness. Clearly he did not understand how we Romans value real power but disdain its vanities.

Other events of this year were the award of Latin rights to the tribes of the Maritime Alps, and the allocation to Roman knights of places in the circus in front of the ordinary people's seats. Hitherto the order of knights had possessed no separate seats in the circus because the Roscian law allotting them 'the first fourteen rows' applied only to the theatre.

CHAPTER 14

The Burning of Rome

*

THE same year witnessed gladiatorial displays on a no less magnificent scale than before, but exceeding all precedent in the number of distinguished women and senators disgracing themselves in the arena. When the new year began, with Gaius Laecanius Bassus and Marcus Licinius Crassus Frugi (II) as consuls, Nero showed daily-increasing impatience to appear regularly on the public stage. Hitherto, he had sung at home, or at the Youth Games held in his Gardens. But he began to disdain such occasions as insufficiently attended and too restricted for a voice like his. Not venturing, however, to make his début at Rome, he selected Neapolis, as being a Greek city. Starting there, he planned to cross to Greece, win the glorious and long-revered wreaths of its Games, and thus increase his fame and popularity at home.

The Neapolitan theatre was filled. Besides the local population, it contained visitors from all around attracted by the notable occasion. Present, too, were those who attend the emperor out of respect or to perform various services – and even units of troops. The theatre now provided what seemed to most people an evil omen, but to Nero a sign of divine providence and favour. For when it was empty (the crowd having left), it collapsed. But there were no casualties; and Nero composed a poem thanking the gods for the happy outcome of the incident.

Then, on his way to cross the Adriatic, he stopped for a while at Beneventum. There large crowds were attending a gladiatorial display given by a certain Vatinius. This outstanding monstrosity of the court had originated from a shoe shop. Deformed in body and scurrilous in wit, he had first been taken up as a butt for abuse. But then he gained power enough to eclipse any scoundrel in influence, wealth, and capacity for damage. He rose by attacking decent people.

But even at his pleasures, attending this man's show, Nero took no vacation from crime. For enforced death now came to Decimus Junius Silanus Torquatus. This was because, in addition to the nobility of his Junian house, he could claim the divine Augustus as a great-great-grandfather. The accusers were instructed to charge Torquatus with generosity so extravagant that revolution had become his only hope. Censure was also to be directed against the titles which he gave some of his former slaves – Secretary-General, Petitions Secretary, and Financial Secretary. These, it was alleged, were titles of an imperial household: Torquatus must be preparing for one. His confidential ex-slaves were arrested and removed. Seeing conviction ahead, he opened his veins. Nero made the usual pronouncement indicating that, however guilty and rightly distrustful of his defence Torquatus had been, he would nevertheless – if he had awaited his judge's mercy – have lived.

Before long Nero, for some reason unknown, postponed his visit to Greece, and returned to Rome. But he still planned to visit the eastern provinces, particularly Egypt; and his secret thoughts dwelt on them. After announcing by edict that his absence would be brief and all branches of government would carry on with undiminished efficiency, he proceeded to the Capitol for consultation about his journey. After worshipping the Capitoline gods, he entered the shrine of Vesta. But there all his limbs suddenly began to tremble. The goddess frightened him. Or perhaps he was always frightened, remembering his crimes. At all events, he abandoned this journey too.

His patriotism came before everything, Nero asserted; he had seen the people's sad faces and heard their private lamentations about the extensive travels he planned – even his brief absences they found unendurable, being accustomed (he added) to derive comfort in life's misfortunes from the sight of their emperor. Just as in private relationships nearest are dearest, he said, so to him the inhabitants of Rome came first: he must obey their appeal to stay! The people liked such protestations. They loved their amusements. But their principal interest was the corn supply: and they feared it would run short if Nero went away. Senators and leading men were uncertain whether he was more abominable present or absent. Subsequently, as happens when men undergo terrifying experiences, the alternative that had befallen them seemed the graver.

Nero himself now tried to make it appear that Rome was his favourite abode. He gave feasts in public places as if the whole city were his own home. But the most prodigal and notorious banquet was given by Tigellinus. To avoid repetitious accounts of extravagance, I shall describe it, as a model of its kind. The entertainment took place on a raft constructed on Marcus Agrippa's lake. It was towed about by other vessels, with gold and ivory fittings. Their rowers were degenerates, assorted according to age and vice. Tigellinus had also collected birds and animals from remote countries, and even the products of the ocean. On the quays were brothels stocked with high-ranking ladies. Opposite them could be seen naked prostitutes, indecently posturing and gesturing.

At nightfall the woods and houses nearby echoed with singing and blazed with lights. Nero was already corrupted by every lust, natural and unnatural. But he now refuted any surmises that no further degradation was possible for him. For a few days later he went through a formal wedding ceremony with one of the perverted gang called Pythagoras. The emperor, in the presence of witnesses, put on the bridal veil. Dowry, marriage bed, wedding torches, all were there. Indeed everything was public which even in a natural union is veiled by night.

Disaster followed. Whether it was accidental or caused by a criminal act on the part of the emperor is uncertain – both versions have supporters. Now started the most terrible and destructive fire which Rome had ever experienced. It began in the Circus, where it adjoins the Palatine and Caelian hills. Breaking out in shops selling inflammable goods, and fanned by the wind, the conflagration instantly grew and swept the whole length of the Circus. There were no walled mansions or temples, or any other obstructions, which could arrest it. First, the fire swept violently over the level spaces. Then it climbed the hills – but returned to ravage the lower ground again. It outstripped every counter-measure. The ancient city's narrow winding streets and irregular blocks encouraged its progress.

Terrified, shrieking women, helpless old and young, people intent on their own safety, people unselfishly supporting invalids or waiting for them, fugitives and lingerers alike – all heightened the confusion. When people looked back, menacing flames sprang up before them or outflanked them. When they escaped to a neighbouring quarter, the fire followed – even districts believed remote proved to be involved. Finally, with no idea where or what to flee, they crowded on to the country roads, or lay in the fields. Some who had lost everything – even their food for the day – could have escaped, but preferred to die. So did others, who had failed to rescue their loved ones. Nobody dared fight the flames. Attempts to do so were prevented by menacing gangs. Torches, too, were openly thrown in, by men crying that they acted under orders. Perhaps they had received orders. Or they may just have wanted to plunder unhampered.

Nero was at Antium. He only returned to the city when the fire was approaching the mansion he had built to link the Gardens of Maecenas to the Palatine. The flames could not be prevented from overwhelming the whole of the Palatine, including his palace. Nevertheless, for the relief of the homeless, fugitive masses he threw open the Field of Mars, including Agrippa's public buildings, and even his own Gardens. Nero also constructed emergency accommodation for the destitute multitude. Food was brought from Ostia and neighbouring towns, and the price of corn was cut to less than $\frac{1}{4}$ sesterce a pound. Yet these measures, for all their popular character, earned no gratitude. For a rumour had spread that, while the city was burning, Nero had gone on his private stage and, comparing modern calamities with ancient, had sung of the destruction of Troy.

By the sixth day enormous demolitions had confronted the raging flames with bare ground and open sky, and the fire was finally stamped out at the foot of the Esquiline Hill. But before panic had subsided, or hope revived, flames broke out again in the more open regions of the city. Here there were fewer casualties; but the destruction of temples and pleasure arcades was even worse. This new conflagration caused additional ill-feeling because it started on Tigellinus' estate[1] in the Aemilian district. For people believed that Nero was ambitious to found a new city to be called after himself.

Of Rome's fourteen districts only four remained intact. Three were levelled to the ground. The other seven were reduced to a few scorched and mangled ruins. To count the mansions, blocks, and temples destroyed would be difficult. They included shrines of remote antiquity, such as Servius Tullius' temple of the Moon, the Great

1. Its site is uncertain.

Altar and holy place dedicated by Evander to Hercules, the temple vowed by Romulus to Jupiter the Stayer, Numa's sacred residence, and Vesta's shrine containing Rome's household gods. Among the losses, too, were the precious spoils of countless victories, Greek artistic masterpieces, and authentic records of old Roman genius. All the splendour of the rebuilt city did not prevent the older generation from remembering these irreplaceable objects. It was noted that the fire had started on July 19th, the day on which the Senonian Gauls had captured and burnt the city. Others elaborately calculated that the two fires were separated by the same number of years, months, and days.[1]

But Nero profited by his country's ruin to build a new palace. Its wonders were not so much customary and commonplace luxuries like gold and jewels, but lawns and lakes and faked rusticity – woods here, open spaces and views there. With their cunning, impudent artificialities, Nero's architects and engineers, Severus and Celer, did not balk at effects which Nature herself had ruled out as impossible.

They also fooled away an emperor's riches. For they promised to dig a navigable canal from Lake Avernus to the Tiber estuary, over the stony shore and mountain barriers.[2] The only water to feed the canal was in the Pontine marshes. Elsewhere, all was precipitous or waterless. Moreover, even if a passage could have been forced, the labour would have been unendurable and unjustified. But Nero was eager to perform the incredible; so he attempted to excavate the hills adjoining Lake Avernus. Traces of his frustrated hopes are visible today.

In parts of Rome unfilled by Nero's palace, construction was not – as after the burning by the Gauls – without plan or demarcation. Street-fronts were of regulated alignment, streets were broad, and houses built round courtyards. Their height was restricted, and their frontages protected by colonnades. Nero undertook to erect these at his own expense, and also to clear debris from building-sites before transferring them to their owners. He announced bonuses, in proportion to rank and resources, for the completion of houses and blocks before a given date. Rubbish was to be dumped in the Ostian marshes by corn-ships returning down the Tiber.

1. 418 years, 418 months, and 418 days had passed since the traditional date of the burning of Rome by the Gauls (390 B.C.).
2. Suetonius estimates the total length of the canal at about 172 miles.

A fixed proportion of every building had to be massive, untimbered stone from Gabii or Alba (these stones being fireproof). Furthermore, guards were to ensure a more abundant and extensive public water-supply, hitherto diminished by irregular private enterprise. House-holders were obliged to keep fire-fighting apparatus in an accessible place; and semi-detached houses were forbidden – they must have their own walls. These measures were welcomed for their practicality, and they beautified the new city. Some, however, believed that the old town's configuration had been healthier, since its narrow streets and high houses had provided protection against the burning sun, whereas now the shadowless open spaces radiated a fiercer heat.

So much for human precautions. Next came attempts to appease heaven. After consultation of the Sibylline books, prayers were addressed to Vulcan, Ceres, and Proserpina. Juno, too, was propitiated. Women who had been married were responsible for the rites – first on the Capitol, then at the nearest sea-board, where water was taken to sprinkle her temple and statue. Women with husbands living also celebrated ritual banquets and vigils.

But neither human resources, nor imperial munificence, nor appeasement of the gods, eliminated sinister suspicions that the fire had been instigated. To suppress this rumour, Nero fabricated scapegoats – and punished with every refinement the notoriously depraved Christians (as they were popularly called). Their originator, Christ, had been executed in Tiberius' reign by the governor of Judaea, Pontius Pilatus.[1] But in spite of this temporary setback the deadly superstition had broken out afresh, not only in Judaea (where the mischief had started) but even in Rome. All degraded and shameful practices collect and flourish in the capital.

First, Nero had self-acknowledged Christians arrested. Then, on their information, large numbers of others were condemned – not so much for incendiarism as for their anti-social tendencies.[2] Their deaths were made farcical. Dressed in wild animals' skins, they were torn to pieces by dogs, or crucified, or made into torches to be ignited after dark as substitutes for daylight. Nero provided his Gardens for the spectacle, and exhibited displays in the Circus, at which he mingled

1. This is the only mention in pagan Latin of Pontius Pilate's action.
2. But this phrase (*odio humani generis*) may instead mean 'because the human race detested them'.

with the crowd – or stood in a chariot, dressed as a charioteer. Despite their guilt as Christians, and the ruthless punishment it deserved, the victims were pitied. For it was felt that they were being sacrificed to one man's brutality rather than to the national interest.[1]

Meanwhile Italy was ransacked for funds, and the provinces were ruined – unprivileged and privileged communities alike. Even the gods were included in the looting. Temples at Rome were robbed, and emptied of the gold dedicated for the triumphs and vows, the ambitions and fears, of generations of Romans. Plunder from Asia and Greece included not only offerings but actual statues of the gods. Two agents were sent to these provinces. One, Acratus, was an ex-slave, capable of any depravity. The other, Secundus Carrinas, professed Greek culture, but no virtue from it percolated to his heart.

Seneca, rumour went, sought to avoid the odium of this sacrilege by asking leave to retire to a distant country retreat, and then – permission being refused – feigning a muscular complaint and keeping to his bedroom. According to some accounts one of his former slaves, Cleonicus by name, acting on Nero's orders intended to poison Seneca but he escaped – either because the man confessed or because Seneca's own fears caused him to live very simply on plain fruit, quenching his thirst with running water.

At this juncture there was an attempted break-out by gladiators at Praeneste. Their army guards overpowered them. But the Roman public, as always terrified (or fascinated) by revolution, were already talking of ancient calamities such as the rising of Spartacus. Soon afterwards a naval disaster occurred. This was not on active service; never had there been such profound peace. But Nero had ordered the

---

1. Tacitus seems to hesitate (as often) between two versions. Were the Christians persecuted as incendiaries or as Christians? Our other sources know nothing of the former charge. Probably they were persecuted as an illegal association potentially guilty of violence or subversiveness (i.e. treason), but although the attack created a sinister precedent its main purpose at the time was merely to distract attention from rumours against Nero by finding a suitable scapegoat. Christian beliefs are unlikely to have been attacked as such. It has often been disputed whether Nero's government regarded the Christians as a sect of the Jews (whose Roman community had been penalized by Tiberius and Claudius, but may now have obtained protection through the influence of Poppaea). The martyrdoms of St Peter and St Paul are attributed to this or later persecutions of Nero. In the later Roman empire the Christian writer Tertullian attacked Tacitus for this passage (and for his slanders on the Jews in the *Histories*).

fleet to return to Campania by a fixed date regardless of weather. So, despite heavy seas the steersmen started from Formiae. But when they tried to round Cape Misenum a south-westerly gale drove them ashore near Cumae and destroyed numerous warships and smaller craft.

As the year ended omens of impending misfortune were widely rumoured – unprecedentedly frequent lightning; a comet (atoned for by Nero, as usual, by aristocratic blood); two-headed offspring of men and beasts, thrown into the streets or discovered among the offerings to those deities to whom pregnant victims are sacrificed. Near Placentia a calf was born beside the road with its head fastened to one of its legs. Soothsayers deduced that a new head was being prepared for the world – but that it would be neither powerful nor secret since it had been deformed in the womb and given birth by the roadside.

CHAPTER 15

The Plot

*

THE consuls for the following year were Aulus Licinius Nerva
Silanus Firmus Pasidienus and Marcus Julius Vestinus Atticus. As
soon as they had assumed office, a conspiracy was hatched and instantly gained strength. Senators and knights, officers, even women,
competed to join. They hated Nero; and they liked Gaius Calpurnius
Piso. His membership of the aristocratic Calpurnian house linked him,
on his father's side, with many illustrious families. Among the masses,
too, he enjoyed a great reputation for his good qualities, real or
apparent. For he employed his eloquence to defend his fellow-citizens
in court; he was a generous friend – and gracious and affable even to
strangers; and he also possessed the accidental advantages of impressive
stature and a handsome face. But his character lacked seriousness or
self-control. He was superficial, ostentatious, and sometimes dissolute.
But many people are fascinated by depravity and disinclined for
austere morals on the throne. Such men found Piso's qualities attractive.

However, his ambitions were not what originated the conspiracy.
Who did, who initiated this enterprise which so many joined, I could
not easily say. Subrius Flavus, a colonel of the Guard, and Sulpicius
Asper, company-commander, were in the forefront – as their courageous deaths showed. Violent hatred was what brought in Lucan and
Plautius Lateranus.[1] Lucan's animosity was personal. For Nero had the
impudence to compete with Lucan as a poet, and had impeded his
reputation by vetoing his publicity. Lateranus joined from no personal
grievance; his motive was patriotism. Two other senators, Flavius
Scaevinus and Afranius Quintianus, belied their reputations by becoming leaders in so important a project. For Scaevinus' brain was

1. The Basilica of St John Lateran is named after the mansion of the Plautii
Laterani.

ruined by dissipation, and he led a languid sleepy life. Quintianus was a notorious degenerate who had been insulted by Nero in an offensive poem, and desired revenge. These men talked to each other, and to their friends, about the emperor's crimes and his reign's imminent close. They were joined by seven Roman knights: Claudius Senecio, Cervarius Proculus, Volcacius Araricus, Julius Augurinus, Munatius Gratus, Antonius Natalis and Marcius Festus. Senecio was Nero's close associate, and so his position was especially perilous since they were still ostensibly friends. Natalis shared all Piso's secrets. The rest looked to revolution for personal advancement. Nor were Flavus and Asper the only officers involved. Other accomplices were the Guard colonels Gaius Gavius Silvanus and Statius Proxpmus, and company-commanders, Maximus Scaurus and Venetus Paulus, were also in the plot. But the mainstay was felt to be Faenius Rufus, commander of the Guard. His respectability and good reputation had made less impression on Nero than the cruelty and depravity of his colleague Tigellinus – who persecuted Faenius with slanders, reiterating the alarming allegation that he had been Agrippina's lover and was intent on avenging her.

So when the conspirators were satisfied by Faenius' own repeated assurances that he was with them, serious discussion began about the date and place of Nero's murder. Subrius Flavus, it was said, had felt tempted to attack Nero when the emperor was singing on the stage or rushing from place to place during the night, unguarded, while his palace burned. Flavus had been attracted in the latter instance by Nero's opportune solitude, and in the former, conversely, by the large crowds which would witness the noble deed. But what held him back was that hindrance to all mighty enterprises, the desire for survival.

The plotters hesitated, still hoping and fearing. A woman called Epicharis, who had extracted their secret – it is not known how, for she had never before interested herself in anything good – kept urging them on and assailing them. Finally, happening to be in Campania and becoming impatient with the slowness of the conspirators, she attempted to unsettle and implicate the naval officers at Misenum. She began with a rear-admiral named Volusius Proculus, who had helped Nero with his mother's murder and felt his promotion had fallen short of so tremendous a crime. Whether their friendship was longstanding or recent is unknown. At all events Proculus told the woman of his services to Nero and their inadequate reward, and expressed not only discontent but the determination to have his own back if the chance occurred. This raised hopes that Proculus might be induced to act, and bring others in. The fleet could be extremely useful and provide valuable opportunities, since Nero enjoyed going to sea off Puteoli and Misenum.

So Epicharis went further. Enlarging on the emperor's abolition of the senate's rights and whole criminal record, she revealed the plan to avenge Rome's destruction at Nero's hands – only let Proculus make ready to do his part by winning over the best men, and he should be worthily rewarded. But she did not disclose the names of the conspirators. So, when Proculus proceeded – as he did – to report what he had heard to Nero, his information was useless. Epicharis was summoned and confronted with Proculus, but in the absence of witnesses easily refuted him. However, she herself was kept in custody. For Nero suspected that the story, though unproven, might not be untrue.

The conspirators were now tormented by fears of betrayal. They wanted to perform the assassination quickly – at Piso's villa at Baiae. For Nero appreciated its charms and often came for a bathe or banquet, without guards or imperial pomp. But Piso refused, arguing that to stain the sanctity of hospitality with the blood of an emperor, however evil, would cause a bad impression. The city would be a better place, he said – that detested palace Nero had plundered his people to build; or, since their deed would be in the public interest, a public centre.

That was what Piso said aloud. But secretly he was afraid of a rival claimant to the throne – Lucius Junius Silanus Torquatus (II). The illustrious birth of Torquatus, and his upbringing by Gaius Cassius Longinus, fitted him for the highest destiny. Moreover non-conspirators, who might pity Nero as the victim of a crime, would back Torquatus readily. Some thought that Piso had also wished to prevent the lively consul, Marcus Julius Vestinus Atticus, from leading a Republican movement or insisting that the next emperor should be chosen by himself. For Vestinus was not one of the conspirators – though Nero used the charge to gratify his longstanding hatred of an innocent man.

They finally decided to execute their design at the Circus Games, on the day dedicated to Ceres. For though Nero rarely left the seclusion of his palace and gardens, he often attended Circus performances, and was more accessible in their festive atmosphere. The attack was planned as follows. Plautius Lateranus, ostensibly petitioning for financial assistance, was to prostrate himself before the unsuspecting emperor and then – being both resolute and muscular – bring him down and hold him. As Nero lay pinned down, the military men among the plotters, and any others sufficiently daring, would rush up and kill him. The leading role was claimed by Flavius Scaevinus, who had taken a dagger from a temple of Safety or (according to other reports) from the Shrine of Fortune at Ferentum, and wore it as the dedicated instrument of a great enterprise.

Meanwhile Piso was to wait at the temple of Ceres, from which Faenius Rufus and the rest were to fetch him to the Guards' camp. The elder Pliny adds that, to win popular favour for Piso, Claudius' daughter Claudia Antonia was to accompany him. True or false, I have felt that this statement ought at least to be recorded. Yet it seems absurd either that Claudia Antonia should have staked her name and life on so hopeless a project, or that Piso, famous for his devotion to his wife, could have pledged himself to another marriage – unless indeed the lust for power outblazes all other feelings combined.

The secret was astonishingly well kept, considering the differences of the conspirators in social and financial position, rank, age, and sex. But betrayal came in the end – from the house of Flavius Scaevinus. The day before the attempt, he had a long conversation with Antonius Natalis. Then Scaevinus returned home and signed his will. Taking the aforesaid dagger from its sheath, and complaining that it was blunt with age, he gave it to his freed slave Milichus to be sharpened and polished on a stone. Then came a dinner-party, more luxurious than usual, at which Scaevinus freed his favourite slaves and gave others presents of money. He maintained a desultory conversation with superficial gaiety. But he was evidently anxious and seriously preoccupied. Finally, he instructed the same Milichus to prepare bandages and styptics for wounds.

Perhaps Milichus was in the secret, and had hitherto proved trustworthy. Alternatively (and this is the usual version) he knew nothing, but his suspicions were now aroused. At all events his slave's brain considered the rewards of treachery and conceived ideas of vast wealth and power. Then morality, his patron's life, gratitude for his freedom, counted for nothing. His wife's womanly, sordid advice implanted a further motive, fear. Many slaves and former slaves, she recalled, had been there and seen the same happenings – one man's silence would be useless, and the rewards would go to the informer who spoke first.

So at daybreak Milichus left for the Servilian Gardens. At first he was kept out. Finally, however, after insisting on the dreadful gravity of his news, he was taken by the doorkeepers to Nero's freed slave Epaphroditus – who conducted him to Nero. Milichus then revealed the resolute determination of the senators, the danger to Nero's life, and everything else he had heard or guessed. Exhibiting the dagger destined for Nero's murder, Milichus urged that the accused man be fetched. Scaevinus was arrested by soldiers. But he denied his guilt.

'The weapon concerned in the charge', he said, 'is a venerated heirloom kept in my bedroom. This ex-slave Milichus has stolen it. As to my will, I have often signed new clauses without particularly noting the date. I have given slaves their freedom and money-gifts before. This time the scale was larger because, with reduced means and pressing creditors, I feared my will would be rejected. My table has always been generous, my life comfortable – too comfortable for austere critics. Bandages for wounds I did not order. But the man's allegations of patent untruths are so unconvincing that he has added this charge merely because it rests wholly on his own evidence.'

Scaevinus spiritedly reinforced this defence by assailing the exslave as an infamous rascal. His self-possessed tones and features would have annihilated the accusation if Milichus' wife had not reminded her husband that Scaevinus had spoken privately and at length with Antonius Natalis, and that both of them were associates of Gaius Calpurnius Piso. So Natalis was summoned, and he and Scaevinus were interrogated separately about their conversation and its subject. The discrepancy between their replies aroused suspicion, and they were put in chains.

At the threat and sight of torture they broke down – Natalis first. With his more intimate knowledge of the whole conspiracy (and greater cunning as an accuser), he began by denouncing Piso – then Seneca. Either Natalis had really acted as intermediary between Seneca and Piso or he hoped to conciliate Nero, who loathed Seneca and sought every means to destroy him. Scaevinus was equally unheroic – or he may have thought that since all was known silence held no advantages. At all events, when told of Natalis' confession, he named the remaining conspirators. Of these, Lucan, Afranius Quintianus, and Claudius Senecio long refused to incriminate themselves. But finally, tempted by a bribe of impunity, they confessed. What they said explained their hesitation, for Lucan denounced his own mother Acilia, and his two partners implicated their closest friends, Glitius Gallus and Annius Pollio.

Nero now remembered the information of Volusius Proculus and consequent arrest of Epicharis. Thinking no female body could stand the pain, he ordered her to be tortured. But lashes did not weaken her denials, nor did branding – nor the fury of the torturers at being defied by a woman. So the first day's examination was frustrated. Next day her racked limbs could not support her, so she was taken for further torments in a chair. But on the way she tore off her breast-band, fastened it in a noose to the chair's canopy, and placed her neck inside it. Then, straining with all her weight, she throttled the little life that was still in her. So, shielding in direst agony men unconnected with her and almost strangers, this former slavewoman set an example which particularly shone when free men, Roman knights and senators, were betraying, before anybody had laid a hand on them, their nearest and dearest. For Lucan and Senecio and Quintianus gave away their fellow-conspirators wholesale.

Nero became increasingly frightened. His guard had been redoubled. Indeed, the whole of Rome was virtually put in custody – troops manned the walls, and blockaded the city by sea and river. Roman public squares and homes, and even neighbouring towns and country districts, were invaded by infantry and cavalry. Among them were Germans; being foreigners, the emperor trusted them particularly.

Line after line of chained men were dragged to their destination at the gates of Nero's Gardens. When they were brought in to be interrogated, guilt was deduced from affability to a conspirator, or a chance conversation or meeting, or entrance to a party or a show together. Fierce interrogation by Nero and Tigellinus was supplemented by savage attacks from Faenius Rufus. No informer had denounced him yet; so, to establish his independence of his fellow-conspirators, he bullied them. When Subrius Flavius, who was standing by, inquired by a sign – in the middle of an actual trial – if he should draw his sword and assassinate Nero, Faenius Rufus shook his head and checked Subrius' impulse as his hand was already moving to the hilt.

After the betrayal of the plot, while Milichus was talking and Scaevinus hesitating, Piso was urged to go to the Guards' camp and test the attitude of the troops, or mount the platform in the Forum and try the civilians. 'If your fellow-conspirators rally round you', it was argued, 'outsiders will follow. Once a move is made the publicity will be immense – a vitally important point in revolutions. Nero has taken no precautions against this. Unforeseen developments intimidate even courageous men, so how could forcible countermeasures be feared from this actor – with Tigellinus and Tigellinus' mistresses as his escort! Many things that look hard to timid people can be done by trying.

'It is useless to expect loyal silence when so many accomplices are involved, body and soul. Tortures and rewards find a way anywhere. You too will be visited and put in chains – and ultimately to a degrading death. How much finer to die for the good of your country, calling for men to defend its freedom! The army may fail you, the people abandon you. But you yourself – if you must die early – die in a way of which your ancestors and posterity could approve!'

But Piso was unimpressed. After a brief public appearance, he shut himself in his house and summoned up courage for his end, waiting for the Guardsmen. Nero, suspicious of old soldiers as likely supporters of Piso, had selected new or recent recruits as his assassins. But Piso died by opening the veins in his arms. He loaded his will with repulsive flattery of Nero. This was done because Piso loved his own wife Satria Galla, though she was low-born and her beauty her only asset. He had stolen her from her former husband, a friend of his called Domitius Silus, whose complaisance – like her misconduct – had increased Piso's notoriety.

The next to be killed by Nero was the consul-designate Plautius Lateranus. His removal was so hasty that he was not allowed to embrace his children or given the customary short respite to choose his own death. Hurried off to the place reserved for slaves' executions, Lateranus was dispatched by a Guard colonel, Statius Proxumus. He died in resolute silence – without denouncing the officer's equal guilt.

Seneca's death followed. It delighted the emperor. Nero had no proof of Seneca's complicity but was glad to use arms against him when poison had failed. The only evidence was a statement of Antonius Natalis that he had been sent to visit the ailing Seneca and complain because Seneca had refused to receive Piso. Natalis had conveyed the message that friends ought to have friendly meetings; and Seneca had answered that frequent meetings and conversations would benefit neither: but that his own welfare depended on Piso's.

A colonel of the Guard, Gavius Silvanus, was ordered to convey this report to Seneca and ask whether he admitted that those were the words of Natalis and himself. Fortuitously or intentionally, Seneca had returned that day from Campania and halted at a villa four miles from Rome. Towards evening the officer arrived. Surrounding the villa with pickets, he delivered the emperor's message to Seneca as he dined with his wife Pompeia Paulina and two friends. Seneca replied as follows: 'Natalis was sent to me to protest, on Piso's behalf, because I would not let him visit me. I answered excusing myself on grounds of health and love of quiet. I could have had no reason to value any private person's welfare above my own. Nor am I a flatterer. Nero knows this exceptionally well. He has had more frankness than servility from Seneca!'

The officer reported this to Nero in the presence of Poppaea and Tigellinus, intimate counsellors of the emperor's brutalities. Nero asked if Seneca was preparing for suicide. Gavius Silvanus replied that he had noticed no signs of fear or sadness in his words or features. So Silvanus was ordered to go back and notify the death-sentence. According to Fabius Rusticus, he did not return by the way he had come but made a detour to visit the commander of the Guard, Faenius Rufus; he showed Faenius the emperor's orders, asking if he should obey them; and Faenius, with that ineluctable weakness which they all revealed, told him to obey. For Silvanus was himself one of the conspirators – and now he was adding to the crimes which he had conspired to avenge. But he shirked communicating or witnessing the atrocity. Instead he sent in one of his staff-officers to tell Seneca he must die.

Unperturbed, Seneca asked for his will. But the officer refused. Then Seneca turned to his friends. 'Being forbidden', he said, 'to show gratitude for your services, I leave you my one remaining possession, and my best: the pattern of my life. If you remember it, your devoted friendship will be rewarded by a name for virtuous accomplishments.' As he talked – and sometimes in sterner and more imperative terms – he checked their tears and sought to revive their courage. Where had their philosophy gone, he asked, and that resolution against impending misfortunes which they had devised over so many years? 'Surely nobody was unaware that Nero was cruel!' he added. 'After murdering his mother and brother, it only remained for him to kill his teacher and tutor.'

These words were evidently intended for public hearing. Then Seneca embraced his wife and, with a tenderness very different from his philosophical imperturbability, entreated her to moderate and set a term to her grief, and take just consolation, in her bereavement, from contemplating his well-spent life. Nevertheless, she insisted on dying with him, and demanded the executioner's stroke. Seneca did not oppose her brave decision. Indeed, loving her wholeheartedly, he was reluctant to leave her behind to be persecuted. 'Solace in life was what I commended to you,' he said. 'But you prefer death and glory. I will not grudge your setting so fine an example. We can die with equal fortitude. But yours will be the nobler end.'

Then, each with one incision of the blade, he and his wife cut their arms. But Seneca's aged body, lean from austere living, released the blood too slowly. So he also severed the veins in his ankles and behind his knees. Exhausted by severe pain, he was afraid of weakening his wife's endurance by betraying his agony – or of losing his own self-possession at the sight of her sufferings. So he asked her to go into another bedroom. But even in his last moments his eloquence remained. Summoning secretaries, he dictated a dissertation. (It has been published in his own words, so I shall refrain from paraphrasing it.)

Nero did not dislike Paulina personally. In order, therefore, to avoid increasing his ill-repute for cruelty, he ordered her suicide to be averted. So, on instructions from the soldiers, slaves and ex-slaves bandaged her arms and stopped the bleeding. She may have been unconscious. But discreditable versions are always popular, and some took a different view – that as long as she feared there was no appeasing Nero, she coveted the distinction of dying with her husband, but when better prospects appeared life's attractions got the better of her. She lived on for a few years, honourably loyal to her husband's memory,

with pallid features and limbs which showed how much vital blood
she had lost.

Meanwhile Seneca's death was slow and lingering. Poison, such as
was formerly used to execute State criminals at Athens,[1] had long
been prepared; and Seneca now entreated his experienced doctor
Annaeus Statius, who was also an old friend, to supply it. But when it
came, Seneca drank it without effect. For his limbs were already cold
and numbed against the poison's action. Finally he was placed in a
bath of warm water. He sprinkled a little of it on the attendant slaves,
commenting that this was his libation to Jupiter. Then he was carried
into a vapour-bath, where he suffocated. His cremation was without
ceremony, in accordance with his own instructions about his death –
written at the height of his wealth and power.

It was rumoured that Subrius Flavus and certain company-commanders of the Guard had secretly plotted, with Seneca's knowledge,
that when Nero had been killed by Piso's agency Piso too should be
murdered, and the throne given to Seneca: it would look as though
men uninvolved in the plot had chosen Seneca for his moral qualities.
Flavus was widely quoted as saying that, in point of disgrace, it made
little difference to remove a lyre-player and replace him by a per-
former in tragedies. For Nero's singing to the lyre was paralleled by
Piso's singing of tragic parts.

But the respite of the army conspirators was at an end. Finding
Faenius Rufus' dual role as plotter and inquisitor intolerable, those
who had turned informers longed to betray him. So while he pressed
and threatened Scaevinus the latter retorted sneeringly that no one
was better informed than Faenius himself – he should demonstrate his
gratitude voluntarily to his excellent emperor. Words failed Faenius
in reply. So did silence; a stammering utterance betrayed his terror.
The remaining conspirators, especially the knight Cervarius Proculus,
pressed for his conviction. The emperor ordered a soldier named
Cassius, who was in attendance because of his great physical strength,
to seize Faenius and bind him.

The evidence of the same fellow-conspirators next destroyed the
Guard colonel Subrius Flavus. His first line of defence was difference
of character: a soldier like him would never have shared such an
enterprise with these effeminate civilians. But, when pressed, Flavus

1. The poison drunk by Seneca, as by Socrates, was hemlock.

admitted his guilt, and gloried in it. Asked by Nero why he had forgotten his military oath, he replied: 'Because I detested you! I was as
loyal as any of your soldiers as long as you deserved affection. I began
detesting you when you murdered your mother and wife and became
charioteer, actor, and incendiary!' I have given his actual words because they did not obtain the publicity of Seneca's; yet the soldier's
blunt, forceful utterance was equally worth recording. Nothing in
this conspiracy fell more shockingly on Nero's ears. For although
ready enough to commit crimes, he was unaccustomed to be told
about them.

A fellow-colonel, Veianius Niger, was detailed to execute Flavus.
But when he ordered a grave to be dug in a field nearby, Flavus
objected it was too shallow and narrow. 'More bad discipline,' he
remarked to the soldiers in attendance. Then, bidden to offer his neck
firmly, he replied: 'You strike equally firmly!' But the executioner,
trembling violently, only just severed the head with two blows.
However he boasted of his ferocity to Nero, saying he had killed
Flavus with 'a stroke and a half!'

Another officer of the Guard, the company-commander Sulpicius
Asper, was the next to show exemplary courage. For when Nero
asked why he had plotted to kill him, Asper replied that it was the
only way to rescue Nero from evil ways. He was convicted and executed. His equals likewise died without disgracing themselves. But
Faenius Rufus was less brave – and could not keep lamentations even
out of his will.

Nero was also expecting the incrimination of the consul Marcus
Julius Vestinus Atticus, whom he regarded as revolutionary and disaffected. But none of the conspirators had confided in Vestinus. Some
had longstanding feuds with him; others thought him impetuous and
independent. Nero hated him as a result of their intimate association.
For Vestinus knew and despised the emperor's worthlessness, while
Nero feared this outspoken friend, who made him the butt of crude
jokes; when they are based on truth, they rankle. Besides, Vestinus had
added a further motive by marrying Statilia Messalina, although he
knew her to be one of Nero's mistresses. Yet no accuser came forward, and there was no charge.

So Nero could not assume the judge's role. Accordingly, he behaved like an autocrat instead, and sent a battalion of the Guard. Its

commander, Gerellanus, was ordered to forestall the consul's designs, seize his 'citadel', and overpower his picked young followers. For the house where Vestinus lived overlooked the Forum, and he kept handsome slaves, all young. Vestinus had finished his consular duties for the day and was giving a dinner-party – unsuspecting, or pretending to be – when the soldiers entered and said the commander wanted him. He instantly rose and rapidly initiated all his arrangements. Shutting himself in his bedroom, he called his doctor and had his veins cut. Before the effects were felt, he was carried to a vapour-bath, and plunged into hot water. No word of self-pity escaped him. Meanwhile his dinner-companions were surrounded by Guardsmen and not released until late at night. It amused Nero to picture their expectation of death after dinner. But finally he ruled that they had been punished enough for their consular party.

Then he ordered Lucan to die. When he felt loss of blood numbing his feet and hands, and life gradually leaving his extremities (though his heart was still warm, and his brain clear), Lucan remembered verses he had written about a wounded soldier who had died a similar death. His last words were a recitation of this passage. Claudius Senecio, Afranius Quintianus, and Flavius Scaevinus were the next to die. Their deaths belied their effeminate lives. Then, without memorable words or actions, the remaining conspirators perished.

Executions now abounded in the city, and thank-offerings on the Capitol. Men who had lost their sons, or brothers, or other kinsmen, or friends, thanked the gods and decorated their houses with laurel, and fell before Nero, kissing his hand incessantly. Interpreting this as joy, he pardoned Antonius Natalis and Cervarius Proculus for their prompt information. Milichus was richly compensated, and adopted the Greek word for 'Saviour' as his name. One colonel of the Guard, Gavius Silvanus, was acquitted but killed himself, and another, Statius Proxumus, frustrated the imperial pardon by a melodramatic suicide. Four more, Pompeius, Cornelius Martialis, Flavius Nepos, and Statius Domitius, were deprived of their rank. They did not hate the·emperor: but it was believed that they did.

Three unimplicated men, Decimus Novius Priscus, Glitius Gallus and Annius Pollio, were disgraced and exiled – the first of them because he was Seneca's friend. Priscus and Gallus were accompanied by their wives, Artoria Flaccilla and Egnatia Maximilla respectively. Egnatia's departure was to her credit, because her wealth was not confiscated – and its later confiscation did her credit too. Rufrius Crispinus was banished. The ostensible reason was conspiracy, but it was really because Nero hated him as Poppaea's ex-husband. Two more, Verginius Flavus and Gaius Musonius Rufus, went because of their distinction as professors of rhetoric and philosophy. The massive list continues with five more: Cluvidienus Quietus, Julius Agrippa, Blitius Catulinus, Petronius Priscus, and Julius Altinus. They were permitted to live in the Aegean islands. Caesennius Maximus and Caedicia, the wife of Scaevinus, only learnt of their trial when they received their sentence: exclusion from Italy. Lucan's mother, Acilia, was ignored – unacquitted, but unpunished.

When this was all done, Nero addressed the Guard and presented each man with two thousand sesterces and free corn (they had hitherto paid the market price). Then, as though to announce a military victory, he summoned the senate and awarded honorary Triumphs to the former consul Publius Petronius Turpilianus, the praetor-designate Marcus Cocceius Nerva,[1] and the commander of the Guard Tigellinus. The two last were also awarded statues in the Palace, as well as triumphal effigies in the Forum. An honorary consulship was bestowed on Nymphidius Sabinus.[2] This is his first appearance, so I must dwell on him for a moment – for he was to be deeply involved in Rome's imminent calamities. His mother was an attractive ex-slave who had hawked her charms among the slaves and freed slaves of emperors. His father, he claimed, was Gaius. For Nymphidius happened to be tall and grim-faced. And it was certainly possible that his mother had taken part in the amusements of Gaius, whose tastes ran to prostitutes.

After his speech in the senate, Nero published an edict appending the statements of the informers and confessions of the convicted. For widespread popular attacks charged him with murdering even innocent men from jealousy or fear. However, the initiation, development, and suppression of the conspiracy are fully documented in reliable contemporary writings; and exiles who returned to Rome after Nero's death told the same story.

1. The future emperor Nerva (A.D. 96–8).
2. Parts of this passage about Nymphidius Sabinus are missing. He now became joint Guard commander with Tigellinus.

In the senate, there was abundant congratulation – especially from those with most to lament. Its manifestations included attacks on Lucius Annaeus Junius Gallio.[1] Terrified by his brother Seneca's death and appealing for his life, Gallio was denounced as a public enemy and parricide. But the prosecutor, Salienus Clemens, had to bow to the senate's unanimous refusal to let him utilize – as it seemed – national misfortunes for private animosities by reviving brutal measures concerning matters settled or dismissed by the clemency of the emperor.

Then thank-offerings were decreed to the gods for miraculously uncovering the conspiracy: and particularly to the Sun – who has an ancient temple in the Circus Maximus (where the crime was planned). The Circus Games of Ceres were to be enlarged by additional horse-races. The month of April was to take Nero's name. A Temple of Welfare was to be constructed, also a memorial in the temple from which Scaevinus had taken the dagger. Nero himself dedicated that weapon on the Capitol, to Jupiter 'Vindex' the Avenger. At the time this went unnoticed. But after the revolt of Gaius Julius Vindex[2] it was interpreted as a sign portending future retribution.

I find in the senate's minutes that the consul-designate Gaius Anicius Cerealis proposed that a temple should be erected, as a matter of urgency, to the Divine Nero. The proposer meant to indicate that the emperor had transcended humanity and earned its worship. But Nero himself vetoed this in case the malevolent twisted it into an omen of his death. For divine honours are paid to emperors only when they are no longer among men.

1. This is the Gallio of *Acts of the Apostles* xviii, 12–17.
2. It was Vindex whose Gallic rising in A.D. 68, though unsuccessful, precipitated Nero's downfall in favour of Galba (from Spain).

CHAPTER 16

Innocent Victims

*

B UT fortune was about to make a fool of Nero. For he credulously believed a lunatic Carthaginian named Caesellius Bassus. This man put faith in a dream, left for Rome, and bribed his way into the emperor's presence. Addressing Nero, he alleged the discovery on his estate of an immensely deep cave containing masses of gold, not in coin but in ancient, unworked bullion. There were ponderous ingots lying about and standing like columns, he said – all hidden centuries ago. His explanation of this windfall from antiquity was this: after her flight from Troy and foundation of Carthage, Phoenician Dido had hidden the treasure in case too much wealth might corrupt her young nation, or the already hostile Numidian kings, coveting the gold, might go to war.

Nero failed to check the man's credibility or to send investigators to confirm its truthfulness. Instead, his imagination exaggerated the report, and he dispatched men to fetch the spoils he believed were lying ready to hand. Warships were allocated, with picked rowers to accelerate their journey. This was the outstanding current subject of conversation. The public were optimistic, sensible people the reverse. It happened to be the year of the second five-yearly Neronian Games, and speakers, in their panegyrics of the emperor, made this a leading theme: 'Earth', they said, 'is now producing not only her accustomed crops, not only gold mixed with other substances – she is teeming with a new kind of fertility! Wealth unsought is sent by the gods!' – and every other invention which eloquent sycophants could devise. They were confident of their imperial listener's credulity.

These vain hopes increased Nero's extravagance. Existing resources were squandered as though the material for many more years of wastefulness were now accessible. Indeed, he already drew on this imaginary treasure for free distributions; his expectation of wealth actually contributed to the national impoverishment. Meanwhile Bassus dug up his ground – and a wide area round about – declaring that this or that was the location of the promised cave. The soldiers accompanied him, together with a horde of rustics engaged to undertake the work. Finally, however, he recovered from his delusion – expressing amazement that, after all his other hallucinations had come true, this one alone had deceived him. He sought escape from his shame and fright in suicide. (According to other sources, he was arrested but soon released, his property however being confiscated in compensation for the imaginary Royal Treasure.)

The five-yearly Games were now close. The senate tried to avert scandal by offering the emperor, in advance, the first prize for song, and also conferred on him a crown 'for eloquence' to gloss over the degradation attaching to the stage. But Nero declared that there was no need for favouritism or the senate's authority; he would compete on equal terms and rely on the conscience of the judges to award him the prize he deserved. First he recited a poem on the stage. Then, when the crowd shouted that he should 'display all his accomplishments' (those were their actual words), he made a second entrée as a musician.

Nero scrupulously observed harpists' etiquette. When tired, he remained standing. To wipe away perspiration, he used nothing but the robe he was wearing. He allowed no moisture from his mouth or nose to be visible. At the conclusion, he awaited the verdict of the judges in assumed trepidation, on bended knee, and with a gesture of deference to the public. And the public at least, used to applauding the poses even of professional actors, cheered in measured, rhythmical cadences. They sounded delighted. Indeed, since the national disgrace meant nothing to them, perhaps they were.

But people from remote country towns of austere, old-fashioned Italy, or visitors from distant provinces on official or private business, had no experience of outrageous behaviour; they found the spectacle intolerable. Their unpractised hands tired easily and proved unequal to the degrading task, thereby disorganizing the expert applauders and earning many cuffs from the Guardsmen who, to prevent any momentary disharmony or silence, were stationed along the benches. Numerous knights, it is recorded, were crushed to death forcing their way up through the narrow exits against the crowd. Others, as they sat day and night, collapsed and died. For absence was even more dangerous than attendance, since there were many spies unconcealedly (and more still secretly) noting who was there – and noting whether their expressions were pleased or dissatisfied. Humble offenders received instant punishment. Against important people the grudge was momentarily postponed, but paid later. Vespasian, the story went, nodded somnolently; he was reprimanded by an ex-slave called Phoebus, and only rescued by enlightened intercession. Nor was this the last time he was in peril. But his imperial destiny saved him.

Soon after the Games Poppaea died. She was pregnant, and her husband, in a chance fit of anger, kicked her. Some writers record that she was poisoned; but this sounds malevolent rather than truthful, and I do not believe it – for Nero wanted children and loved his wife. She was buried in the Mausoleum of Augustus. Her body was not cremated in the Roman fashion, but was stuffed with spices and embalmed in the manner of foreign potentates. At the State funeral, Nero mounted the platform to praise her looks, her parenthood of an infant now deified, and her other lucky assets which could be interpreted as virtues.

Publicly Poppaea's death was mourned. But those who remembered her immorality and cruelty welcomed it. However, Nero's action caused disgust, which was accentuated when he forbade Gaius Cassius Longinus to attend the funeral. This was the first sign of impending trouble: and it came quickly. Lucius Junius Silanus Torquatus (II) became involved. His only offence was to be a respectable young member of the highest nobility; those of Cassius were his remarkable ancestral wealth and outstanding character. Nero wrote to the senate requesting that both should be expelled from public life. He charged Cassius with revering, among the statues of his ancestors, a representation of Gaius Cassius, labelled 'Leader of the Cause'[1] – thus planting the seeds of civil war and treason to the house of the Caesars.

But (the emperor added) a hated name was not enough material for revolution, so Cassius had taken on the unbalanced young nobleman Lucius Silanus as the rebellion's figurehead. Then Nero attacked Silanus (as he had earlier attacked his uncle, Decimus Junius Silanus Torquatus) for already allocating imperial responsibilities by desig-

1. The inscribed bust was of Julius Caesar's assassin, whose full name was likewise Gaius Cassius Longinus.

nating his ex-slaves Financial Secretary, Petitions Secretary, and Secretary-General. The charge was fatuous. It was also untrue. For Silanus, besides feeling the effects of the prevalent terror, had been frightened by his uncle's death into extreme caution. Next, so-called informers fabricated against Cassius' wife, Junia Lepida, accusations of black magic and incest with her brother's son – Lucius Silanus. Two senators, Volcacius Tertullinus and Cornelius Marcellus, and a knight, Gaius Calpurnius Fabatus, were charged with complicity. But they avoided imminent condemnation by appealing to Nero. For he was preoccupied with important crimes, and they were eventually saved by their insignificance.

For Cassius and Silanus, the senate decreed banishment. Concerning Junia Lepida the emperor was to decide. Cassius was deported to Sardinia, where old age was left to do its work. Silanus was first removed to Ostia, with Naxos as his supposed destination; but he was instead confined in the Apulian country town of Barium. There, as he philosophically endured his thoroughly undeserved misfortune, a company-commander of the Guard was sent to kill him. Seized and told to open his veins, he answered that he was ready to die but would not excuse his assassin the glorious duty. The officer, however, noting that though unarmed he was very strong and far from intimidated, ordered his men to overpower him. Silanus did not fail to resist, hitting back as much as his bare hands allowed. Finally the commander's sword struck him down, and he fell, wounded in front, as in battle.

Lucius Antistius Vetus, and his mother-in-law Sextia and daughter Antistia Pollitta, died just as courageously. All three appeared detestable to the emperor as living reproaches for his murder of Vetus' son-in-law, Rubellius Plautus. A chance for Nero to display his brutality was afforded by a former slave of Vetus named Fortunatus. This person, after stealing his patron's money, turned accuser, mobilizing an individual named Claudius Demianus who had been imprisoned for criminal actions by Vetus during his governorship of Asia but subsequently released by Nero as a reward for this accusation. When Vetus heard this, and knew he had to face the ex-slave on equal terms, he withdrew to his estate at Formiae, under secret military surveillance.

With him was his daughter. Besides the imminent peril, she was

embittered by sorrow. This had lasted unceasingly ever since she had
seen her husband Rubellius Plautus assassinated. She had clasped his
bleeding neck, and kept his bloodstained clothes – an unkempt widow
grieving incessantly, eating barely enough to stay alive. Now, at her
father's plea, she went to Neapolis. Refused access to Nero, she lay
in wait for him at the door. When he came, she entreated him to hear
an innocent man, and not surrender his former fellow-consul to a
man who had been a slave. She cried like a woman. She also screamed
in unwomanly fury. But appeals and reproaches alike left the emperor
cold.

So she sent her father word to abandon hope and accept the inevitable. Simultaneously there came forewarning of a trial in the senate,
and a harsh verdict. Some advised Vetus to name the emperor as his
principal heir, thus securing the residue for his grandchildren. But he
scorned to spoil what had mostly been a life of freedom by servility at
its close. So he distributed his ready cash among his slaves, and bade
them remove everything portable for themselves, keeping only three
couches for the end.

Then, in one room, with a single weapon, all three of them – Vetus,
his mother-in-law, and his daughter – opened their veins. Wearing a
single garment each for decency's sake, they were hastily carried into
the bath. The young woman gazed long at her father and grandmother, and they at her. All three prayed to cease their feeble breathing speedily and be the first to die – but not be long outlived. Fate
observed the right order. First the two eldest perished, then the young
Antistia. After burial, they were denounced, and condemned
to punishment in the ancient fashion. Nero intervened, allowing
them to die unsupervised. But this farce was subsequent to their
deaths.

A knight called Publius Gallus was outlawed for being on good terms
with Vetus as well as a close friend of Faenius Rufus. The ex-slave who
had preferred the charge against Vetus was rewarded by a seat in the
theatre among the attendants of the tribunes. The names of the months
following 'Neroneus' – otherwise April – were changed. May became
'Claudius', June 'Germanicus'. According to the originator of the
proposal, Servius Cornelius Orfitus by name, the latter change was
necessary because the execution of two Junii Torquati had made the
name 'June' ill-omened.

Heaven, too, marked this crime-stained year with tempest and pestilence. Campania was ravaged by a hurricane which destroyed houses, orchards, and crops over a wide area and almost extended its fury to the city. At Rome, a plague devastated the entire population. No miasma was discernible in the air. Yet the houses were full of corpses, and the streets of funerals. Neither sex nor age conferred immunity. Slave or free, all succumbed just as suddenly. Their mourning wives and children were often cremated on the very pyres by which they had sat and lamented. Senators and knights were not spared. But their deaths seemed less tragic; for by dying like other men they merely seemed to be forestalling the emperor's bloodthirstiness.

In this year the Roman army in the Illyrian provinces, weakened by discharges due to age and unfitness, was replenished by recruiting in Narbonese Gaul, Africa, and Asia.

A disastrous fire at Lugdunum was alleviated by an imperial gift of four million sesterces to repair the town's damage – the same sum as its people had contributed to Rome's similar misfortunes.

When, in the following year, Gaius Suetonius Paulinus and Gaius Luccius Telesinus became consuls, Antistius Sosianus, who, as I have mentioned, was in exile for writing offensive poems about Nero, noted the rewards paid to informers and the emperor's readiness for bloodshed. A restless opportunist by nature, he utilized the similarity of their fortunes to make friends with a fellow-exile at the same place, called Pammenes. The latter's fame as an astrologer had won him many friends. Sosianus noted that messengers were continually arriving to consult him – and deduced that there must be a purpose behind their visits.

He also learnt that Pammenes received an annual subsidy from Publius Anteius. Nero hated Anteius (Sosianus knew) as a friend of Agrippina, and might well covet his wealth – a frequent cause of fatalities. Sosianus therefore intercepted a letter from Anteius. He also stole from Pammenes' secret files documents giving Anteius' horoscope and destiny. He likewise found there papers relating to the birth and life of Marcus Ostorius Scapula. Then he wrote to the emperor, intimating that, if he were granted a brief respite from his banishment, he would bring information vital to Nero's safety. For Anteius and Ostorius, he said, were studying their own and the emperor's destinies – and thus imperilling the empire.

Fast ships were immediately sent, and Sosianus was soon there. When his denunciation became known, Anteius and Ostorius were regarded less as defendants than as persons already condemned. Indeed, no one would witness Anteius' will until Tigellinus sanctioned this – after warning the testator to complete the formalities speedily. Anteius took poison, but impatient with its slowness obtained a quicker death by cutting his veins.

Ostorius was at the time at a remote estate on the Ligurian border. There a staff-officer of the Guard was dispatched to kill him rapidly. The reason for this haste was Nero's fear of a personal attack. Always cowardly, he was more terrified than ever since the recently discovered conspiracy. Besides, Ostorius was of huge physique and an expert with weapons – his distinguished military record included the oak-wreath for saving a citizen's life in Britain. The officer arrived; and closing every exit from the house, he told Ostorius of the emperor's orders. The courage he had often demonstrated against the enemy Ostorius turned upon himself. Because his veins, when opened, let the blood out too slowly, he ordered a slave to hold up his hand firmly with a dagger in it – nothing more. Then Ostorius pulled the slave's hand on to his own throat.

Even if I were describing foreign wars and patriotic deaths, this monotonous series of events would have become tedious both for me and for my readers. For I should expect them to feel as surfeited as myself by the tragic sequence of citizen deaths – even if they had been honourable deaths. But this slavish passivity, this torrent of wasted bloodshed far from active service, wearies, depresses, and paralyses the mind. The only indulgence I would ask the reader for the inglorious victims is that he should forbear to censure them. For the fault was not theirs. The cause was rather heaven's anger with Rome – and not an isolated burst of anger such as could be passed over with a single mention, as when armies are defeated or cities captured. And let us at least make this concession to the reputation of famous men: just as in the manner of their burial they are distinguished from the common herd, so when their deaths are mentioned let each receive his separate, permanent record.

Within a few days there fell, one after another, Annaeus Mela,

Gaius Anicius Cerealis, Rufrius Crispinus, and Petronius. Mela and Crispinus were Roman knights who enjoyed the status of senators[1]. The latter, formerly commander of the Guard – and an honorary consul – but recently exiled to Sardinia on a charge of conspiracy, received the order to die, and committed suicide. Mela, brother of Seneca and of Lucius Annaeus Junius Gallio, had refrained from seeking office owing to his perverse ambition to achieve a consul's influence while remaining a knight. He had also seen a shorter road to wealth in becoming an agent handling the emperor's business. The fact that he was Lucan's father greatly enhanced his reputation. But after his son's death Mela called in Lucan's debts so harshly that one of the latter's intimate friends, Fabius Romanus, denounced him, fabricating a charge that father and son had shared complicity in the plot. The evidence was a forged letter from Lucan, which Nero examined: then he sent it to Mela, whose wealth he coveted.

Mela died in the fashionable way, opening his veins. First, however, he recorded large bequests to Tigellinus and the latter's son-in-law Cossutianus Capito – hoping to save the residue. He added a postscript protesting against his unfair fate, and contrasting his undeserved death with the survival of Crispinus and Cerealis, the emperor's enemies. But the postscript was regarded as a fabrication, Crispinus figuring because capital punishment had already been inflicted on him, and Cerealis to ensure its infliction. Soon afterwards Cerealis duly committed suicide – less pitied than the rest, because he was remembered to have betrayed a conspiracy to Gaius.

Petronius[2] deserves a brief obituary. He spent his days sleeping, his nights working and enjoying himself. Others achieve fame by energy, Petronius by laziness. Yet he was not, like others who waste their resources, regarded as dissipated or extravagant, but as a refined voluptuary. People liked the apparent freshness of his unconventional and unselfconscious sayings and doings. Nevertheless, as governor

---

1. Annaeus Mela and Rufrius Crispinus were knights who though not senators ranked with members of the senate because they satisfied its property qualification.

2. This Petronius 'Arbiter' was very probably the author of the earliest surviving Latin novel, the *Satyricon*, which includes the *Dinner of Trimalchio*. He may well be identifiable with Titus Petronius Niger, who was *consul suffectus* (i.e. after the beginning of the year) in about A.D. 62.

of Bithynia and later as consul, he had displayed a capacity for business.

Then, reverting to a vicious or ostensibly vicious way of life, he had been admitted into the small circle of Nero's intimates, as Arbiter of Taste: to the blasé emperor nothing was smart and elegant unless Petronius had given it his approval. So Tigellinus, loathing him as a rival and a more expert hedonist, denounced him on the grounds of his friendship with Flavius Scaevinus. This appealed to the emperor's outstanding passion – his cruelty. A slave was bribed to incriminate Petronius. No defence was heard. Indeed, most of his household were under arrest.

The emperor happened to be in Campania. Petronius too had reached Cumae; and there he was arrested. Delay, with its hopes and fears, he refused to endure. He severed his own veins. Then, having them bound up again when the fancy took him, he talked with his friends – but not seriously, or so as to gain a name for fortitude. And he listened to them reciting, not discourses about the immortality of the soul or philosophy, but light lyrics and frivolous poems. Some slaves received presents – others beatings. He appeared at dinner, and dozed, so that his death, even if compulsory, might look natural.

Even his will deviated from the routine death-bed flatteries of Nero, Tigellinus, and other leaders. Petronius wrote out a list of Nero's sensualities – giving names of each male and female bed-fellow and details of every lubricious novelty – and sent it under seal to Nero. Then Petronius broke his signet-ring, to prevent its subsequent employment to incriminate others. Nero could not imagine how his nocturnal ingenuities were known. He suspected Silia, a woman of note (she was a senator's wife) who knew all his obscenities from personal experience – and was a close friend of Petronius. For breaking silence about what she had seen and known, she was exiled. Here the grievance was Nero's own. It was to Tigellinus' malevolence, however, that he sacrificed a former praetor, Minucius Thermus (II). A freed slave made criminal charges against this man; the ex-slave's penalty was torture, the patron's an undeserved death.

After the massacre of so many distinguished men, Nero finally coveted the destruction of Virtue herself by killing Thrasea and Marcius Barea Soranus. He had long hated them both. Against Thrasea there were additional motives. He had, as I mentioned, walked out of

the senate during the debate about Agrippina. He had also been incon-
spicuous at the Youth Games. This gave all the more offence because
during Games (the festival instituted by Antenor the Trojan) at his
birthplace, Patavium, he had participated by singing in tragic costume. Besides, on the day when the praetor Antistius Sosianus was
virtually condemned to death for writing offensive verses about
Nero, he had proposed and carried a more lenient sentence. Again,
after Poppaea's death, he had deliberately stayed away when divine
honours were voted to her, and was not present at her funeral.

Cossutianus Capito kept these memories fresh. For that criminal
bore Thrasea a grudge for helping a Cilician deputation to convict
him for extortion. So now Capito added further charges: 'At the New
Year, Thrasea evaded the regular oath. Though a member of the
Board of Fifteen for Religious Ceremonies, he absented himself from
the national vows. He has never sacrificed for the emperor's welfare or
his divine voice. Once an indefatigable and invariable participant in
the senate's discussions – taking sides on even the most trivial proposal
– now, for three years, he has not entered the senate. Only yesterday,
when there was universal competition to strike down Lucius Junius
Silanus Torquatus (II) and Lucius Antistius Vetus, he preferred to take
time off helping his dependants.

'This is party-warfare against the government. It is secession. If
many more have the same impudence, it is war. As this faction-loving
country once talked of Caesar versus Cato, so now, Nero, it talks of
you versus Thrasea. And he has his followers – or his courtiers rather.
They do not yet imitate his treasonable voting. But they copy his
grim and gloomy manner and expression: they rebuke your amusements. He is the one man to whom your safety is immaterial, your
talents unadmired. He dislikes the emperor to be happy. But even
your unhappiness, your bereavements, do not appease him. Disbelief
in Poppaea's divinity shows the same spirit as refusing allegiance to
the acts of the divine Augustus and divine Julius. Thrasea rejects religion, abrogates law.

'In every province and army the official Gazette is read with special
care – to see what Thrasea has refused to do. If his principles are better,
let us adopt them. Otherwise, let us deprive these revolutionaries of
their chief and champion. This is the school which produced men like
Quintus Aelius Tubero and Marcus Favonius – unpopular names even

in the old Republic.¹ They acclaim Liberty to destroy the imperial régime. Having destroyed it, they will strike at Liberty too. Your removal of a Cassius was pointless if you propose to allow emulators of the Brutuses to multiply and prosper. Finally – write no instructions about Thrasea yourself. Leave the senate to decide between us.' Nero whipped up Cossutianus' hot temper still further, and associated with him the bitingly eloquent Titus Clodius Eprius Marcellus.

The prosecution of Marcius Barea Soranus had been claimed by Ostorius Sabinus, a knight, on the grounds of alleged incidents during the defendant's governorship of Asia. The energy and fairness of Barea Soranus in that post had increased the emperor's malevolence. He had industriously cleared the harbour of Ephesus, and had refrained from punishing Pergamum for forcibly preventing an ex-slave of Nero called Acratus from removing its statues and pictures. However the charges against him were friendship with Rubellius Plautus and courting the provincials with revolutionary intentions. His conviction was timed just before Tiridates' arrival to receive the Armenian crown. This was to divert attention from domestic outrages to foreign affairs – or, perhaps, to display imperial grandeur to the visitor by a truly royal massacre of distinguished men.

All Rome turned out to welcome the emperor and inspect the king. Thrasea's presence, however, was forbidden. Undismayed, he wrote to Nero inquiring what the charges against him were and insisting that he would clear himself if he were told them and given an opportunity to dispose of them. Nero took the letter eagerly, hoping Thrasea had been frightened into some humiliating statement that would enhance the imperial prestige. But this was not so. Indeed, it was Nero who took fright, at the innocent Thrasea's spirited independence; so he convened the senate.

Thrasea consulted his friends whether he should attempt or disdain to defend himself. The advice he received was contradictory. Some said he should attend the senate. 'We know you will stand firm,' they said. 'Everything you say will enhance your renown! A secret end is for the feeble-spirited and timid. Let the people see a man who can face death. Let the senate hear inspired, superhuman utterances. Even

1. Tubero was a lawyer-politician of the second century B.C. who opposed the Gracchi. Favonius, a Republican opponent of Julius Caesar, was killed after Philippi (42 B.C.).

Nero might be miraculously moved. But if his brutality persists, at least posterity will distinguish a noble end from the silent, spiritless deaths we have been seeing.'

Other friends, while equally complimentary to himself, urged him to wait at home, forecasting jeers and insults if he attended the senate. 'Avert your ears from taunts and slanders,' they advised. 'Cossutianus and Eprius are not the only criminals. Others are savage enough not to stop at physical violence – and fear makes even decent men follow their lead. You have been the senate's glory. Spare them this degrading crime: leave their verdict on Thrasea uncertain. To make Nero ashamed of his misdeeds is a vain hope. Much more real is the danger of his cruelty to your wife and daughter and other dear ones. No – die untarnished, unpolluted, as gloriously as those in whose footsteps and precepts you have lived!'

One of those present, the fervent young Lucius Junius Arulenus Rusticus, sought glory by proposing, as tribune, to veto the senate's decree. Thrasea rejected his enthusiastic plan as futile – fatal to its author, and not even any help to the accused. 'My time is finished,' he said. 'I must not abandon my longstanding, unremitting way of life. But you are starting your official career. Your future is uncompromised, so you must consider carefully beforehand what political cause you intend to adopt in such times.' The advisability of his own presence or absence he reserved for personal decision.

Next morning, two battalions of the Guard, under arms, occupied the temple of Venus Genetrix.[1] The approach to the senate-house was guarded by guards in civilian clothes displaying their swords. Troops too were arrayed round the principal forums and the law-courts. Under their menacing glares, the senators entered the building. The emperor's address was read by his quaestor. Without mentioning any name he rebuked members for neglecting their official duties and setting the knights a slovenly example. What wonder, he said, if senators from distant provinces stayed away, when many ex-consuls and priests showed greater devotion to the embellishment of their gardens?

The accusers seized the weapon which this gave them. Cossutianus began the attack. Eprius Marcellus, following with even greater violence, claimed that the issue was one of prime national importance.

1. In the Forum of Julius Caesar.

The emperor's indulgence, he said, was hampered by the insubordination of those beneath him, and the senate had hitherto been overlenient. 'For you have allowed yourselves', he said, 'to be ridiculed with impunity – by the rebellious Thrasea, his equally infatuated son-in-law Helvidius Priscus (II), Gaius Paconius Agrippinus (heir to his father's hatred of emperors), and that scribbler of detestable verses Curtius Montanus. I insist that a former consul should attend the senate; a priest take the national vows; a citizen swear the oath of allegiance. Or has Thrasea renounced our ancestral customs and rites in favour of open treachery and hostility?

'In a word: let this model senator, this protector of the emperor's critics, appear and specify the reforms and changes that he wants. His detailed carpings would be more endurable than the universal censure of his silence. Does world-peace give him no satisfaction, or victories won without a Roman casualty? Do not gratify the perverted ambitions of a man who deplores national success, thinks of courts, theatres, and temples as deserts – and threatens to exile himself. Here is a man to whom senatorial decrees, public office, Rome itself, mean not a thing. Let him sever all connection with the place he has long since ceased to love, and has now ceased even to honour with his attendance!'

While Eprius Marcellus spoke in this vein, grim and blustering as ever, fanatical of eye, voice, and features, the senators did not feel any genuine sadness: repeated perils had made the whole business all too familiar. And yet as they saw the Guardsmen's hands on their weapons, they felt a new, sharper terror. They thought of Thrasea's venerable figure. Some also pitied Helvidius, to suffer for his guiltless marriage relationship. And what was there against Agrippinus except his father's downfall? – for he too, though as innocent as his son, had succumbed to imperial cruelty under Tiberius.[1] The worthy young Montanus, too, was no libellous poet. The cause of his banishment was his manifest talent.

Next Ostorius Sabinus, the accuser of Barea Soranus, entered and began to speak. He denounced the defendant's friendship with Rubellius Plautus, and claimed that Barea's governorship of Asia had been planned not to serve the public interest but to win popularity for him-

1. Presumably Tacitus had written, in the lost part of his work, of the arrest of Agrippinus' father Marcus Paconius under Tiberius.

self – by encouraging the cities to rebellion. That was stale. But there was also a new charge involving Barea's daughter, Servilia, in his ordeal. She was said to have given large sums to magicians. This was true; but the cause was filial affection. Young and imprudent, she had consulted the magicians out of love for her father – but only about the prospects of her family's survival, and of Nero's compassion, and of a happy outcome to the senate's investigation. So she too was summoned before the senate. There, at opposite ends of the consul's dais, stood the elderly father and his teenage daughter, unconsolable for the loss of her exiled husband Annius Pollio – and unable even to look at her father, whose perils she had clearly intensified.

The accuser demanded whether she had sold her *trousseau* and taken the necklace from her neck in order to raise money for magical rites. At first she collapsed on the ground, weeping incessantly and not answering. But then she grasped the altar and its steps, and cried: 'Never have I called upon forbidden gods or spells! My unhappy prayers have had a single aim: that you, Caesar, and you, senators, should spare my dear father. I gave my jewels and clothes – the things that a woman in my position owns – as I would have given my blood and my life if the magicians had wanted them! I did not know the men before. They must answer for their own reputations and methods; that is not for me to do. I never mentioned the emperor except as a god. And everything was done without my poor father's knowledge. If it was a crime, I alone am to blame!'

Soranus broke in with the plea that she had not gone with him to the province, was too young to have known Rubellius Plautus, and was unimplicated in the charges against her husband. 'Her only crime is too much family affection,' he urged. 'Take her case separately – for me any fate will be acceptable.' Then he moved towards his daughter to embrace her, and she towards him. But attendants intervened and kept them apart.

Evidence was then heard. The brutality of the prosecution aroused compassion – which was only equalled by the indignation felt against one of the witnesses, Publius Egnatius Celer. He was a dependant of Soranus bribed to ruin his friend. Though professing the Stoic creed, he was crafty and deceitful at heart, using a practised demeanour of rectitude as a cover for viciousness and greed. But money was capable of stripping off the mask. Egnatius became a standard warning that

men of notorious depravity or obvious deceit yield nothing in nastiness
to hypocritical pseudo-philosophers and treacherous friends. However, the same day provided a model of integrity – Cassius Asclepio-
dotus, the richest man in Bithynia. Having honoured Soranus when he
prospered, he would not desert him in his fall. So he was deprived of
his whole fortune and ordered into exile – thus affording a demonstration of heaven's impartiality between good and evil.

Thrasea, Soranus, and Servilia were allowed to choose their own
deaths. Helvidius and Paconius were banned from Italy. Montanus
was spared for his father's sake, with the stipulation that his official
career should be discontinued. The accusers Eprius and Cossutianus
received five million sesterces each, Ostorius twelve hundred thousand and an honorary quaestorship.

The consul's quaestor, sent to Thrasea, found him in the evening in
his garden. In his company were numerous distinguished men and
women. His attention, however, was concentrated on a Cynic[1] professor, Demetrius. To judge from Thrasea's earnest expression, and
audible snatches of their conversation, they were discussing the nature
of the soul and the dichotomy of spirit and body. A close friend,
Domitius Caecilianus, came and informed him of the senate's decision.
Thrasea urged the weeping and protesting company to leave rapidly
and avoid the perils of association with a doomed man. His wife
Arria, like Arria her mother,[2] sought to share his fate. But he told her
to stay alive and not deprive their daughter of her only protection.

Thrasea walked to the colonnade. There the quaestor found him,
happy rather than sorrowful, because he had heard that his son-in-law
Helvidius Priscus was merely banned from Italy. Then, taking the
copy of the senate's decree, he led Helvidius and Demetrius into his
bedroom, and offered the veins of both his arms. When the blood
began to flow, he sprinkled it on the ground, and called the quaetor
nearer. 'This is a libation', he said, 'to Jupiter the Liberator. Look,
young man! For you have been born (may heaven avert the omen!)
into an age when examples of fortitude may be a useful support.'

1. The Cynics, who rejected all monarchy (among other institutions), claimed
Diogenes of Sinope as their founder.
2. Arria's mother had committed suicide with her husband after the revolt of
Lucius Arruntius Camillus Scribonianus against Claudius in A.D. 42 had
collapsed.

Then, as his lingering death was very painful, he turned to Demetrius . . .

[*The manuscript breaks off here. The lost part of the work described the
visit of King Tiridates, the beginning of the Jewish revolt, Nero's visit to
Greece, the suppression of the revolt of Gaius Julius Vindex in Gaul, and
the final desertion of Nero by the senate in favour of Galba, imperial governor of Nearer Spain. Nero fled to a villa of his freed slave Phaon, four miles
outside Rome. There he died, his hand guided by another former slave
Epaphroditus.*]

LISTS OF SOME EASTERN MONARCHS

Note: The exact dates of many, or most, of the
Parthian and Armenian reigns are uncertain.

KINGS OF PARTHIA

Phraates IV	c. 38–2 B.C.
Tiridates II	31–25
Phraates V (Phraataces)	2 B.C.–A.D. 4 or 6
Orodes III	short reign round about A.D. 6 or 7
Vonones I (Roman nominee)	A.D. 8/9–11/12
Artabanus III	11/12–38
Phraates VI (Roman nominee)	35
Tiridates III (Roman nominee)	35–6
? Cinnamus	37
Gotarzes II	38–40
Vardanes I	38/40–45/6
Gotarzes II (restored)	45/6–51
Meherdates (Roman nominee)	49
Vonones II	51
Vologeses I	51–77
Son of Vardanes I	55–8

KINGS OF ARMENIA

Artavasdes I	56–34 B.C.
Artaxias II	33–20
Tigranes II (Roman nominee)	20–7
Tigranes III and Queen Erato	7 B.C.–A.D. 2
Artavasdes II (Roman nominee)	3–1 B.C.
Ariobarzanes (Roman nominee)	A.D. 2–4
Artavasdes III (Roman nominee)	? 4–6
Tigranes IV (Roman nominee)	short reign between A.D. 6 and 12
Queen Erato (restored)	short reign before or after Tigranes IV
Interregnum	A.D. ?–12

Vonones (from Parthian throne)	12–16
Orodes	16–18
Artaxias III (from Pontus) (Roman nominee)	18–34
'Arsaces'	34–5
Orodes (restored)	35
Mithridates (from Iberia) (Roman nominee)	35–7
Interregnum (Parthian satrap Demonax)	37–41
Mithridates (restored as Roman nominee)	41–early 50s
Radamistus (from Iberia)	two short reigns in early 50s
Tiridates	from early 50s to early 60s, with intermission
Tigranes V (from Judaea) (Roman nominee)	60–61
Interregnum (Roman occupation)	63–6
Tiridates (restored as Roman nominee)	66–?

KINGS OF THRACE

Rhoemetalces I	11 B.C.–A.D. 12

W. THRACE		E. THRACE	
Rhescuporis II A.D.	12–19	Cotys IV A.D.	12–19
Rhoemetalces II	19–40	[Trebellenus Rufus regent]	
		Rhoemetalces III 37/8–46	

LIST OF ROMAN EMPERORS

JULIO-CLAUDIAN DYNASTY

Augustus (assumed that name in 27 B.C.)	31 B.C.–A.D. 14
Tiberius	A.D. 14–37
Gaius (Caligula)	37–41
Claudius	41–54
Nero	54–68

CIVIL WARS

Galba	68–69
Otho	69–69
Vitellius	69–69

FLAVIAN DYNASTY

Vespasian	69–79
Titus	79–81
Domitian	81–96

'ADOPTIVE' EMPERORS

Nerva	96–98
Trajan	98–117
Hadrian	117–138

KEY TO TECHNICAL TERMS

AEDILES. Roman officials ranking above quaestors and below praetors (qq.vv.). There were two branches of the aedilate, 'curule' and 'plebeian', but by this time the functions of both mainly related to little more than the care of the city of Rome. Nero lessened their powers further.

AGENTS, IMPERIAL. This term is used here for the 'procurators' of the emperor (see KNIGHTS), whom he employed to staff certain departments under his control, to manage his property and to handle the national finances in the provinces and armies for which he was directly responsible (see GOVERNORS). They possessed certain juridical authority from the time of Claudius. Other 'procurators' served as governors of certain minor provinces. For the Treasury Agent see TREASURY.

ASSEMBLY. This ancient, democratic element in the State had lost its power. Its elective and judicial functions gradually lapsed under the first emperors. But throughout the first century A.D. it remained, formally, Rome's law-giving body.

ASSISTANT. See QUAESTOR.

AUGURS. The official Roman diviners – one of the four great Orders of Priesthood: believed to owe their lore to the Etruscans. Augural observations, which particularly related to the inspection of birds, still preceded every important public action. The Augury for the Welfare of Rome was a periodical religious inquiry from the gods (in time of peace only) whether it was permissible to pray for the national wellbeing.

AUGUSTA. The first 'Augusta' was Augustus' widow Livia, who became 'Julia Augusta' by adoption in his will – probably to the grave embarrassment of Tiberius. I have followed Tacitus in calling her the Augusta and not Livia, since certain of his effects demand this employment of the more solemn designation. Agrippina (II) was named 'Augusta' by Claudius, and Nero's wives received the same appellation.

AUGUSTUS. The name selected by or for the young Octavian (officially, by adoption, Gaius Julius Caesar) in 27 B.C. as the emperor's most distinctive title, and assumed by all his successors. Believed to be etymologically akin to 'augur' (q.v.) and 'augere' = to increase, it may mean the possessor of superhuman Increase, the 'augmented' and sanctified. The same term had of old been applied to temples and sacred objects.

AUXILIARIES. From the third century B.C. Rome had increasingly recruited certain cavalry and light infantry (in which she was weak) in Italy. Augustus established a permanent auxiliary army which probably numbered over 100,000 (cf. 150,000 regulars = legionaries). Units were named after the locality of their formation, but though they gradually lost their local character this did not, for the most part, happen during our period. The auxiliaries were not Roman citizens but were officered by citizens, sometimes of native origin. See also DIVISION.

BALLET. These were the highly popular, sophisticated dances of the 'pantomimi', who danced traditional themes in dumb-show, with music and chorus. These performances were first seen in Rome under Augustus.

BANISHMENT. This penalty, reserved for the upper class – for offences punished in their inferiors by forced labour or death – comprised various degrees of severity. 'Relegation' was often merely exclusion from certain territories, especially Rome or Italy. 'Deportation' (introduced by Tiberius) meant not only perpetual exile but loss of citizenship and the confiscation of all property.

BOARD OF FIFTEEN for Religious Ceremonies. One of the four great priestly Orders. Originally custodians of the Sibylline books (q.v.), they later supervised all foreign cults allowed at Rome, and directed the Secular Games (q.v.).

BOARD OF TWENTY (twenty-six until Augustus). A group of minor offices held by men intending to stand for the quaestorship (q.v.) and so enter the senate. Half these officials formed a special tribunal for lawsuits concerning free status. Three others were responsible to the State for issuing the coinage.

BRIGADE. See DIVISION.

CENSORS. Roman officials originally appointed every four (then, every five) years to draw up and maintain the list of citizens, and from the fourth century B.C. entrusted with the revision of the senate list as well. Practically defunct in the Principate. The last appointments outside the imperial family date from Augustus, who also assumed censorial powers himself. Claudius had himself made censor (later Domitian assumed the office for life).

CENTURION. See COMPANY-COMMANDER.

CITIZEN'S WREATH. An oak-wreath awarded to Romans for saving another citizen's life – the supreme military decoration. The State habitually awarded it to emperors (who showed it, as well as the laurel-wreath, on their coinage); but Tiberius refused it.

CLIENTS. See DEPENDANTS.

COMEDY, MUSICAL. The topical, farcical, coarse performances of the 'mimus', beloved by the Roman public and patronized by many emperors.

COMPANY-COMMANDER. This is the translation I have generally used for *centurio*, though the number of men under the command of the sixty-odd centurions in a legion varied between 100 and 1000. When a centurion (especially of the Guard) is on extra-regimental duties (as we should say), I have described him as a (junior) staff-officer.

CONSULS. Still the highest officials of the State and senate (the principate itself was not yet, legally, an office). Emperors usually took pains to show outward deference to the consulate. Tenure had normally been annual, but replacements during the year were nowadays frequent, so as to spread the honour as widely as possible. Emperors had means of securing the acceptance of their candidates. They themselves, too, accepted the office at intervals (Nero five times). Tacitus dates the years of his annalistically constructed work by the names of the consuls. The governorships of the most important provinces were reserved for ex-consuls (except Egypt; see KNIGHTS).

CORPS, ARMY. See DIVISION.

COUNCIL OF TEN 'to write laws'. It was traditionally believed that in 451–449 B.C. the Republican constitution was suspended in favour of two successive Councils of Ten to draw up the Twelve Tables of laws.

CURULE. See AEDILE.

DEPENDANTS. These are the 'clients' whose moral and legal relation to the Roman citizens who were their 'patrons', with its powerful and hereditary mutual obligations, formed a vital element in Roman social (and political) life. Freed slaves became automatically and permanently the 'clients' of their former masters, and the children of both parties inherited the relationship. The dependent and semi-dependent monarchies which bordered the frontiers of the empire were of 'client' status and their rulers regarded as clients of the Roman emperors. See also EX-SLAVE.

DIVISION. For purposes of translation the Roman 'legion' is regarded as a brigade when its regular (citizen) troops – 5,000 infantry and 120 cavalry – are alone concerned, and as a division when it is thought of in conjunction with the auxiliary (q.v.) troops which were often united under the same command during operations in the field. In the early imperial epoch the 'praefectus castrorum', or (to use an American term) divisional chief-of-staff, sometimes represented more than one division, in which case he is here described as corps chief-of-staff.

EX-SLAVE. The Roman *libertus* or *libertinus*, freedman. A freed slave still owed deference and service to his former master as patron (see also DEPENDANTS), but his son, although supposed to maintain the family tie, became a full citizen. When the households of the emperors gradually turned into state departments, freedmen – mostly Hellenised orientals – took charge of them, and became extremely rich and powerful, especially under Claudius. Tacitus often sneers at their servile origin.

FETIALS, an ancient order of Roman priestly officials who conducted ritual concerning international relationships, e.g. treaties and declarations of war.

FIELD OF MARS. A flat area immediately to the north of Rome containing monumental buildings of Augustus' reign, including his Mausoleum.

FORUM. The chief public square of a town, generally surrounded by important temples and halls. At Rome, this is the Forum Romanum, near which Julius Caesar, Augustus, and later emperors constructed supplementary Forums bearing their names.

FREEDMAN, FREED SLAVE. See EX-SLAVE.

GAMES. Formal sports and shows, usually annual (but see SECULAR GAMES) and religious in origin and purpose. At Rome they took place in the Circus (races, etc.), in Forums and amphitheatres (e.g. gladiatorial displays and wild-beast hunts), in temples and in theatres (dramatic and musical). There were also semi-military Games or manoeuvres (e.g. the 'Troy Pageant'). By the last decade B.C. each year included sixty-six days of Games (forty-eight theatrical). By the death of Tiberius twenty-one further days had been added. But neither Tiberius nor Nero (who made further additions) enjoyed blood-sports.

GOVERNORS were of two main kinds, the 'proconsul' who governed 'senatorial' provinces – still elected (ostensibly) by the senate, without imperial intervention – and the 'legatus' (here 'imperial governor') of an 'imperial' province, the emperor's direct subordinate – and commander of an army. Under Tiberius the governor of the 'senatorial' province of Africa also controlled an army (Gaius removed it from him in A.D. 37). Governors were ex-consuls or ex-praetors except for a few 'imperial' governors who were 'knights' (see KNIGHTS) (the prefect of Egypt was by far the most important).

GUARD. The 'Praetorians', imperial bodyguard organized by Augustus in nine battalions 1,000 strong. Sejanus concentrated them in a single camp under his own command in A.D. 23, thereby making them into a political factor of the first importance. Gaius added three battalions.

IMPERIAL GOVERNORS, PROVINCES. See GOVERNORS.

KNIGHTS (Order of). The Roman 'equites, equester ordo'. In the later

Republic this Order comprised a powerful class of financial interests (with a minimum property qualification of 400,000 sesterces) outside the senate and often opposed to it. Augustus reformed the Order, which henceforward, though it still remained outside the senate and its career (and included the families of ex-slaves), provided holders of many important new administrative posts, e.g. the governors of Egypt and elsewhere, and imperial AGENTS (q.v.). Members of this class were regarded as the patrons of young imperial princes, whom they named 'Princes of Youth' – the 'Youth' being knights under thirty-five (and senators' sons under twenty-five) who recalled the ancient cavalry origins of the Order by parading for the emperor's inspection. Company-commanders in the army became knights on retirement.

LATIN FESTIVAL. Held on the Alban Mount – usually, in historical times, in April – this was the successor of the ancient joint festival of the communities of Latium. It was attended by the chief Roman officials, who left behind a temporary and honorary mayor.

LATIN RIGHTS. 'Latin rights' were by this time a means of conferring on a provincial community Roman citizen status for its officials (though its remaining members were not citizens).

LEGION. See DIVISION.

MAYOR, HONORARY. See LATIN FESTIVAL.

MILITARY POLICEMEN. See POLICEMEN, MILITARY.

MILITARY TREASURY. See TREASURY, MILITARY.

MUSICAL COMEDY. See COMEDY, MUSICAL.

OVATION. A lesser form of Triumph, in which the victorious general wore a wreath of myrtle instead of laurel.

PATRONS. See DEPENDANTS.

POLICEMEN, MILITARY. One of the duties of the 'exploratores' and 'speculatores', scouts and dispatch-carriers attached to emperors, generals, and brigades, and particularly employed on frontier service.

PONTIFICAL ORDER. The 'Pontifices', one of the four great Orders of Priesthood, presided over the State Cult generally. The head of the Order, and of the entire State clergy, was the emperor (since 12 B.C.). He was the Supreme Pontiff or Chief Priest, a title subsequently adopted by the Popes.

PRAETORS. The State officials next in importance to the consuls. Usually, at this time, twelve in number (it was Tiberius' practice to nominate four of these). Though their administration of justice had declined in scope, emperors placed praetors in charge of important bureaux including (for a time) the Treasury. Most provincial governors (q.v.) were ex-praetors.

PREFECTS OF THE CITY. The post became permanent under Augustus.

Prefects were responsible for maintaining order in Rome, and commanded the three (later four) battalions of city-police.

PRIESTS. See AUGURS, BOARD OF FIFTEEN, FETIALS, PONTIFICAL ORDER.

PRINCIPATE. The imperial régime – the Empire as opposed to the Republic. 'Princeps' was the most general appellation of the emperor; from '*a* leader' it had come to mean '*the* leader'.

PROVINCES. See GOVERNORS.

QUAESTORS. The lowest office of State in the senator's official career, ranking below the aedilate and tribunate (q.v.). From Augustus onward there were twenty quaestors, many of them attached as finance officers and assistants to the governors of 'senatorial' provinces. See also SENATE.

REGULAR ARMY. See DIVISION.

RELEGATION. See BANISHMENT.

SALIAN HYMN. The ancient ritual hymn of the priestly Order of the Salii, connected with the worship of Mars. This hymn, of which fragments have survived, was already incomprehensible in the later Roman Republic.

SECULAR GAMES. A much venerated religious ceremony – administered by the Board of Fifteen (q.v.) with the emperor as chairman – to purify and 'renew' the city. These rites took place at irregular intervals, sometimes corresponding – as under Claudius – with multiple centenaries of the legendary foundation-date 753 B.C. Horace, however, in his *Secular Hymn*, refers to calculations based on a cycle of 110 years.

SENATE. Still the chief Council of the State, though severely limited in power by even the most ostensibly deferential emperors. Augustus fixed membership at 600 and imposed a minimum property qualification of 1,000,000 sesterces. Its automatic recruitment from new quaestors (q.v.), themselves only elected if the emperor approved of them, was supplemented by imperial nominees – otherwise membership was restricted to senators' sons. Like the emperor, it developed far-reaching judicial functions, which overshadowed the law-courts. Its decrees, often moved by the emperor, were valid though not legally binding until the second century A.D. Acknowledgement by the senate was in theory the precondition of an emperor's legitimacy, though in practice the approval of the army or Guard was decisive. Those here described as 'junior senators' (senatores pedarii) had held no important office, and their participation in debates was perhaps limited.

SESTERCE (*sestertius*), the denomination in which Tacitus usually quotes

Roman currency (it was represented by a token coin of brass = one-quarter of the silver *denarius*). It is virtually impossible to translate its value into modern terms. In 1914 1,000 sesterces were reckoned the equivalent of just under £9, but since then the purchasing power of the pound sterling has decreased very considerably. However, the value of the Roman currency, compared to ours, would be set eight times higher if we accept the alternative suggestion that to have an *as* ($\frac{1}{4}$ sesterce) in one's hand probably felt like having a 10p piece. A few ancient statistics may be helpful. For example, late in the first century A.D. the normal price of wheat in central Anatolia was $2\frac{1}{2}$ sesterces a peck (or a little less); in Egypt very poor people spent about 100 sesterces a year on food; and a Roman private soldier earned 900 sesterces a year, of which rather less than 600 were deducted for full board. Early in the second century a uniform cloak or tunic cost 96 sesterces.

SETTLEMENT, the word used here to render the Roman term 'a colony of Roman citizens' = a city in Italy or the provinces created, or augmented (in ancient or recent times) by drafts of demobilized soldiers, for whom no regular gratuity or pension system existed before Augustus (see TREASURY, MILITARY).

SIBYLLINE BOOKS. The Sibyls were prophetesses consulted as oracles at many centres. Their ecstatic trances have been compared with those of Tartar Shamans today. Their heyday had been quite early in the first millennium B.C., but their utterances were still written down in historical times, notably at Cumae in south-west Italy, and were filed by the Roman State for consultation, at the senate's request, by the Board of Fifteen (q.v.). The collection was destroyed by fire in 83 B.C. but replaced from various sources by new Books, which were honoured by Augustus.

SLAVE, FORMER, FREED. See EX-SLAVE.

STAFF-OFFICER (JUNIOR). See COMPANY-COMMANDER.

STOICS. The philosophical school, founded by Zeno of Cyprus (*c.* 300 B.C.), which laid the greatest emphasis on ethics and so appealed particularly to the ethically-minded Romans, whose education, directly and then through Cicero and Seneca, its doctrines profoundly affected. Both the imperial administration and Republican-minded opposition claimed to be motivated by Stoic principles. But the effect of the opposition under Gaius and Nero was to identify the Stoics with disapproval not only of bad monarchy but of monarchy in general – the original attitude of Cynics, not Stoics, who had favoured this form of government in the hope of a 'sage' or philosopher-king (or king guided by a philosopher) on the throne.

TARPEIAN ROCK. A cliff, identified at the south-west corner of the Capitoline Hill, from which traitors and murderers were thrown.

TREASURY. The State Treasury of Rome (the *aerarium*). Probably this credited the emperor, periodically, with the sums he needed to discharge his functions at home and in the provinces. However, it required extensive subsidization from the enormous private resources of the emperors (see AGENTS). There were several changes in the administration of the Treasury, culminating in the creation of a joint controllership by Nero. The Treasury Agent was a slave, or more probably an ex-slave, who administered public property.

TREASURY, MILITARY. Established by Augustus in A.D. 6 to provide pensions for discharged soldiers (for whom no such regular provision had hitherto existed, so that they and their generals had often endangered the peace). The Military Treasury was fed by the proceeds of the 5 per cent Estates Duty and 1 per cent Sales Tax, both very unpopular in the senate.

TRIBES. For certain, largely formal purposes the Assembly (q.v.) was organized in conformity with the ancient territorial 'tribes' into which the Roman people (including citizens abroad) was divided. The tribes were also the units for taxation, census, and recruiting. Tradition recorded that in 444–367 B.C. the commanders of their contingents had, at intervals, been given the authority of consuls.

TRIBUNE of the People. A step in the senatorial career (for plebeians) corresponding with the aedilate (q.v.). Nero further restricted the powers of both; but the ancient revered 'democratic' powers of the tribunes, empowering them to 'protect the people' by intercession, veto, and punitive action had already long vanished. However, these ancient associations induced Augustus, followed by his successors, to choose the 'tribunician power' (divorced from office) as the most distinctive prerogative of an emperor. The numeral marking his years of this power replaced the number of his consulships (q.v.) as the official reckoning of his regnal years. Rulers also found the power useful as an unassuming legal basis for the introduction of measures in the senate. They also arranged for it to be conferred on their principal collaborators and, before long, on heirs within the imperial family.

KEY TO PLACE-NAMES

Ancient Name	Modern Name (or description of district)	Map No.
Actium	on Gulf of Ambracia	4
Adiabeni	S.E. Turkey–N.E. Iraq	5
Aedui	round Autun	2
Aegeae	Ayas	4*
Aegium	Aighion	8
Aequi	N.E. of Rome	IA
Africa	Tunisia and W. Libya	6
Agrippina, colonia	Köln	3
Alba Longa	Castel Gandolfo	IA
Albani	Soviet Azerbaijan	5
Alesia	Alise Ste Reine	2
Alexandria	Alexandria	7
Aliso	? near R. Lippe	3
Amathus	old Limassol (Cyprus)	5
Amorgos	Amorgos	8
Ampsivarii	Vecht-Ems area	3
Amyclae, Gulf of	S.E. of Rome	1
Ancona	Ancona	1
Andecavi	round Angers	2
Anemurium	Anamur	4*
Angrivarii	Hunte-Weser area	3
Anthemusias	Turco-Syrian frontier	5
Antioch	Antakya	4*, 5
Antium	Anzio	1
Aorsi (Yen-ts'ai)	S.E. of Rostov	9
Apamea	Dinar	4
Aphrodisias	Kehre	4
Apollonis	Palamut	4
Aquitania	S.W. France	2
Arduenna Forest	Ardennes	2
Argos	Argos	8
Aria	Iran–Afghanistan frontier	–
Armenia, Lesser	N.E. Turkey	5
Arsamosata	E. of Harput (Nağaran?)	5
Arsania, R.	Murat R.	5
Artaxata	Artashat	5

* IA, IB, and, 4* are inset maps.

Ancient Name	*Modern Name (or description of district)*	*Map No.*
Artemita	near Baquba	5
Asia	W. Anatolia	4
Assyria, *see* Adiabeni		
Augustodunum	Autun	2
Auzea	Aumale?	6
Avernus, L.	Averno	IB
Bactria	middle Oxus	–
Baduhenna Grove	Germany	–
Baiae	Baia	IB
Barium	Bari	I
Bastarnae	W. Ukraine	9
Batavian I.	Rhine-Waal mouths	3
Belgica	N.E. France and Belgium	2
Beneventum	Benevento	I
Bithynia	N.W. Anatolia	4
Bononia	Bologna	I
Bosphorus, Cim-		
merian	Kerch Str.	9
Bosphorus, Thracian	Bosphorus (Boğaziçi)	4
Bovillae	near Frattochie	IA
Brigantes	N. Humber–Mersey	2
Bructeri	Lippe–Ems	3
Brundusium	Brindisi	I
Byzantium	Istanbul	4
Cadra	S.E. Anatolia	–
Caesian Forest	beyond Rhine	–
Calabria	S. Puglie	I
Cales	Calvi	I
Camerium	N.E. of Rome	–
Camulodunum	Colchester	2
Canninefates	W. Holland	3
Canopus	Aboukir	7
Cappadocia	E. Anatolia	5
Capreae	Capri	IB
Capua	Capua	I
Carana	Erzurum	5
Carmania	S. Iran	–
Carrhae	Haran	5
Caspian Road	Dariel Pass (Georgia)	5

Ancient Name	*Modern Name (or description of district)*	*Map No.*
Caudine Forks	Campania	–
Celenderis	Gilindire	4*
Cercina I.	Kerkenna	6
Chalcedon	Kadiköy	4
Chatti	Upper Weser	3
Chauci	Lower Weser-Elbe	3
Chauci, Lesser	Lower Ems-Weser	3
Cherusci	Middle Weser	3
Cibyra	Horzun	4
Cietae	Central Taurus (S. Anatolia)	–
Cinithii	Tunisia	6
Cirta	Constantine or El Kef	6
Clarus	near Ahmet Beyli	4
Coelaletae	Bulgaria	8
Colchi	W. Georgia	5
Colophon	Değirmendere	4
Commagene	E. Taurus- Euphrates	5
Corcyra	Kerkyra (Corfu)	8
Corinth	Korinthos	8
Corma, R.	? Adhaim, R.	5
Cos	Kos	4
Cosa	Ansedonia	1
Ctesiphon	S.E. of Baghdad	5
Cumae	Cuma	1B
Cyclades	Kyklades	8
Cyrrhus	Khoros	5
Cythnos	Kythnos	8
Cyzicus	Bal Kiz (near Bandirma)	4
Dahae	W. Turkmenistan	–
Dalmatia	Dalmatia	1
Dandaridae (Dandarii)	N. of Lower Kuban	9
Davara	S.E. Anatolia	–
Degeangli (Decangi)	N.E. Wales and Cheshire	2
Delos	Delos	8
Delphi	Delphi	8
Dii	S. Bulgaria	8
Donusa	Donousa	8
Ecbatana	Hamadan	5

Ancient Name	Modern Name (or description of district)	Map No.
Edessa	Urfa	5
Elephantine	Jeziret Assuan	7
Elymaei	S.W. Iran	5
Ephesus	Selçuk	4
Erindes, R. (? Charindas)	? Barferush, R. (N. Iran)	–
Eryx	Mt S. Giuliano	1
Etruria	Tuscany-Lazio	1
Euboea	Evvia	2
Ferentum	Ferento (near Viterbo)	1
Fidena(e)	Castel Giubileo	1A
Flevum	Schiermonnikoog	3
Florentia	Florence	1
Formiae	Formia	1
Forum Julii	Fréjus	2
Frisii	Friesland	3
Fucinus L.	Fucino (Celano)	1
Fundi	Fondi	1
Gabii	Castiglione	1A
Galatia	Central Anatolia	–
Galilaea	Galil	5
Gallia Comata, see Aquitania, Belgica, Lugdunensis		
Garamantes	Fezzan	6
Gaugamela	between Tigris and Great Zab (N. Iraq)	5
Getae	Rumania	–
Gorneae	Garnia (Soviet Armenia)	5
Gotones	N. Poland	3
Gyaros	Gyaros	8
Hadrumetum	Sousse	6
Halicarnassus	Bodrum	4
Halus	? near Qasr-i-Shirin (Iran-Iraq frontier)	5
Heliopolis	Heliopolis	7
Heniochi	round R. Çoruh	5
Hermunduri	Saxony-Thuringia	3
Hibernia	Ireland	2
Hierocaesarea	Saz Ova (near Kumkuyucak)	4

Ancient Name	Modern Name (or description of district)	Map No.
Massilia	Marseille	2
Mattiaci	round Wiesbaden	3
Mattium	S.W. of Kassel	3
Mauretania	Morocco and W. Algeria	6
Mauri	E. Atlas	6
Media	Ustan Yakum and Ustan Duwum (Iran)	5
Media Atropatene	Iranian Azerbaijan	5
Melitene	Malatya area	5
Mesopotamia	N. Iraq	5
Messene	Messini	9
Miletus	Yeniköy	4
Misenum	Miseno	IB
Moesia	N. Bulgaria and E. Yugoslavia	–
Mona	Anglesey	2
Mostene	S. of Manisa	4
Musulamii	Sahara	6
Nabataei	S. Jordan and N.W. Saudi Arabia	5
Narbonese Gaul	S. France	2
Narnia	Narni	1
Nauportus	Vrhnika	–
Neapolis	Naples	1, IB
Nemetes	W. of Karlsruhe	3
Nicephorium	Raqqa	5
Nicephorius, R.	Armenia	–
Nicopolis	Nikopolis	8
Ninus, Nineveh	Mespila	5
Nisibis	Nusaybin	5
Nola	Nola	IB
Noricum	E. Austria and N.W. Slovenia	–
Nuceria	Nocera	IB
Numantia	Castillejo-Peña Redonda	2
Numidia	E. Algeria and W. Tunisia	6
Odrysae	S. Bulgaria	8
Ordovices	N. Wales	2
Ostia	Ostia-Scavi	IA
Pagyda, R.	Algeria	–
Pamphylia	S. Anatolia	4
Panda, R.	Kuban area	–

Ancient Name	Modern Name (or description of district) Map No.	
Pandateria I.	Pantellaria	IB
Pannonia	W. Hungary and N. Yugoslavia	–
Paphos	Paphos (W. Cyprus)	–
Patavium	Padua	I
Pelusium	near Tell Faramâ	7
Pergamum	Bergama	4
Perinthus	Ereğli	4
Perusia	Perugia	I
Pharsalus	Palaiopharsalos	8
Philadelphia	Alaşehir	4
Philippi	near Dhoxaton	8
Philippopolis	Plovdiv	8
Picenum	Marche and Abruzzi	I
Piraeus	Peiraiefs	8
Placentia	Piacenza	I
Planasia I.	Pianosa I.	I
Pompeiopolis (Soli)	near Mezitli	4*
Pontia	Ponza	IB
Pontine Marshes	Sabaudia-Latina area	I
Pontus	N. Anatolia	5
Praeneste	Palestrina	IA
Propontis	Sea of Marmora	4
Puteoli	Pozzuoli	IB
Quadi	Bohemia and Moravia	3
Raetia	S. of Upper Danube	–
Ravenna	Ravenna	I
Reate	Rieti	I
Rhegium	Reggio Calabria	I
Rome	Rome	I, IA
Roxolani	N. Dobrogea	–
Sabini	N. Lazio	I
Salamis	Famagusta	5
Samnites	S. Apennines	I
Samos	Samos	4, 8
Samothrace	Samothrake	8
Sanbulus, M.	? Sunbula, M.	5
Santones	Saintonge	2
Sardis	Sert	4

Ancient Name	Modern Name (or description of district)	Map No.
Thebes (Egypt)	Karnak-Luxor	7
Thebes (Greece)	Thive	8
Thermae, Gulf of	Thermai, Gulf of	8
Thubuscum (Thubursicum Numidarum)	Khamissa	6
Thurii	near Thuria	1
Tibur	Tivoli	1A
Ticinum	Pavia	1
Tigranocerta	? Meyafarkin	5
Tmolus	? near Ödemiş	4
Torone, Gulf of	Torone, Gulf of	8
Tralles	Aydin	4
Transpadani	N. Italy	1
Trimerum Is.	Tremiti	1
Trinobantes	Essex	2
Troy (Ilium)	Hisarlik	4
Tubantes	Ijssel-Vecht area	3
Turones	round Tours	2
Tusculum	near Frascati	1A
Tyre	es-Sur	5
Ubii	round Köln (Cologne)	3
Umbria	Umbria	1
Unsingis, R.	? Hunte, R.	3
Usipetes	Ijssel-Ruhr area	3
Uspe, see Siraci		
Vangiones	S. of Mainz	3
Veneti	Venezia	1
Verulamium	St Albans	2
Vienna	Vienne	2
Volandum	? Iğdir	5
Vulsci	S. Lazio	1
Vulsinii	Orvieto	1
Zeugma	Balkis	5

Note: For Rivers Murat, Adhaim, Barferush, Menderes, Tedzhen, Hunte see Arsania, Corma, Erindes, Maeander, Sindes, Unsingis respectively.

MAP 1   419

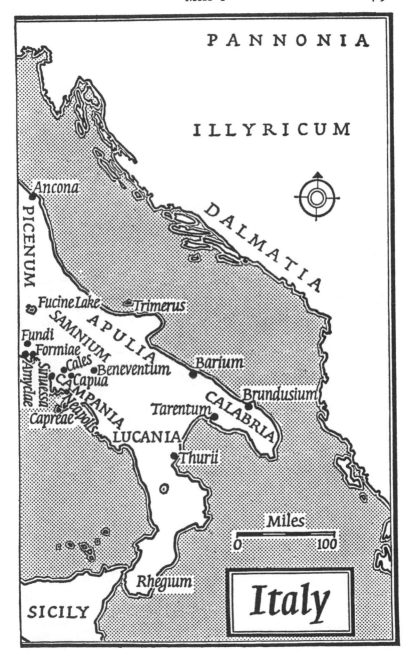

PANNONIA

ILLYRICUM

DALMATIA

Ancona

PICENUM

Fucine Lake • Trimerus

APULIA

SAMNIUM

Fundi

Formiae

Cales

Amyclae

Sinuessa

Caleae

Capua

Beneventum

Barium

Brundusium

CAMPANIA

Neapolis

CALABRIA

Capreae

Tarentum

LUCANIA

Thurii

Miles

0   100

Rhegium

SICILY

Italy

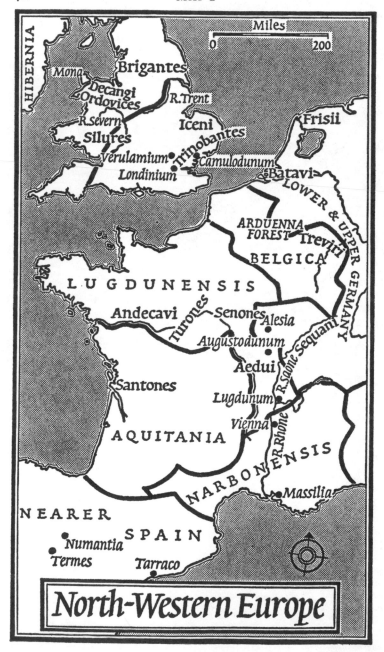

North-Western Europe

MAP 3   421

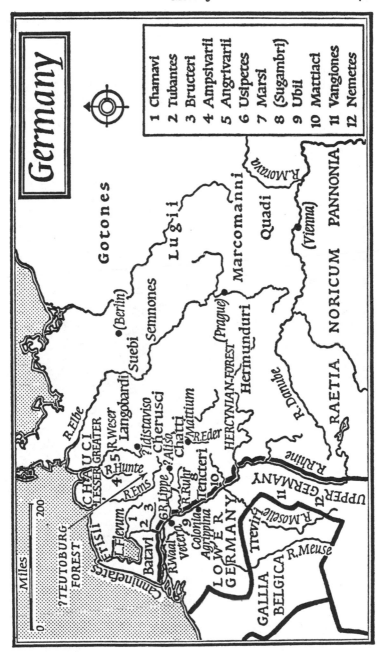

Germany

1 Chamavi
2 Tubantes
3 Bructeri
4 Ampsivarii
5 Angrivarii
6 Usipetes
7 Marsi
8 (Sugambri)
9 Ubii
10 Mattiaci
11 Vangiones
12 Nemetes

Gotones

Lugii

Semnones

Suebi

(Berlin)

Langobardi

R.Elbe

GREATER
CHAUCI
LESSER

R.Weser

?Idistaviso
Cherusci

5

R.Hunte

4

R.Ems

Marcomanni

Quadi

(Vienna)

R.Morava

PANNONIA

NORICUM

RAETIA

R.Danube

HERCYNIAN-FOREST

(Prague)

Hermunduri

Chatti

Mattium
R.Eder

?Aliso

6 R.Lippe

R.Ruhr

Tencteri

8

10

R.Rhine

Colonia
vetera

Agrippina

9

R.Waal

1 2 3

Batavi

L.Flevum

Cananefates

FRISII

?TEUTOBURG
FOREST

Miles

0   200

LOWER
GERMANY

UPPER GERMANY

11

12

R.Moselle

Treviri

GALLIA
BELGICA

R.Meuse

MAP 4

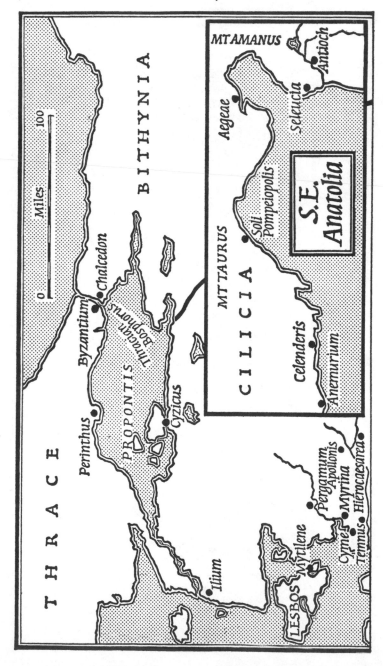

MAP 4   423

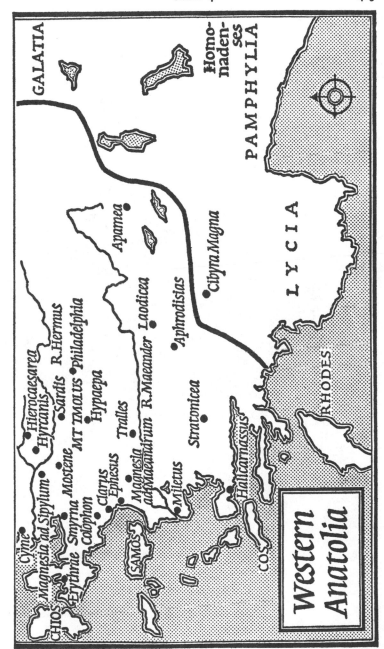

GALATIA

Homo-
naden-
ses

PAMPHYLIA

LYCIA

RHODES

Apamea

CibyraMagna

Hierocaesarea
Hyrcanis
Sardis R.Hermus
MT TMOLUS •Philadelphia
Hypaepa

Laodicea
R.Maeander
•Aphrodisias

Tralles
Magnesia
ad Maeandrum

Stratonicea

Cyme
Magnesia ad Sipylum
Smyrna
Erythrae   mostene
Colophon
Clarus
Ephesus
•Miletus

CHIOS

SAMOS

COS

•Halicarnassus

*Western
Anatolia*

The Middle East

MAP 5   425

CAUCASUS MTS
Pass
IBERIA
R.Kura ALBANIA
CASPIAN SEA
•Gorneae?
•Artaxata
Volandum?
Mt.Ararat
ARMENIA
R.Aras
MEDIA
ATROPATENE
MARDI
Gaugamela
ADIABENE
Ninus
Gt.Zab R.
R.Adhaim
R.Tigris
MEDIA
PARTHIAN
•Ecbatana
N. •Halus?
EMPIRE
Artemita
Ctesiphon
Seleucia ad Tigrim
Sunbula Mt
ELYMAEI
200
PERSIAN GULF

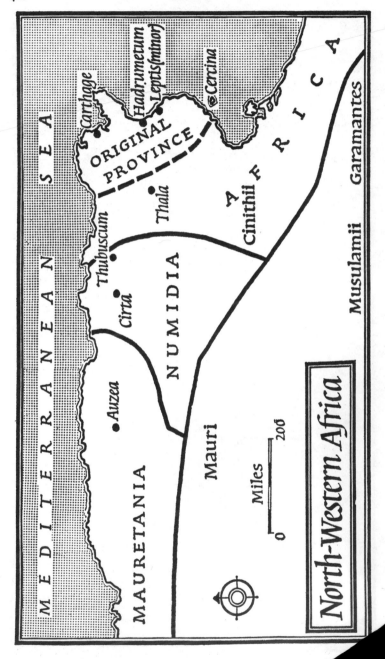

MEDITERRANEAN SEA

Carthage

Hadrumetum
Leptis (minor)

Cercina

ORIGINAL PROVINCE

AFRICA

Thala

Thubuscum

Cinithii

Cirta

NUMIDIA

Auzea

Musulamii

Garamantes

MAURETANIA

Mauri

Miles

0   200

North-Western Africa

MAP 7   427

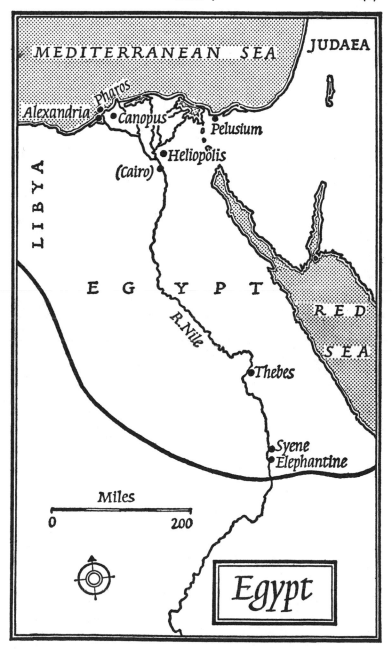

MEDITERRANEAN SEA

JUDAEA

Alexandria *Pharos*
Canopus
Pelusium
Heliopolis
(Cairo)

LIBYA

E G Y P T

R. Nile

RED

SEA

Thebes

Syene
Elephantine

Miles
0   200

Egypt

MAP 8

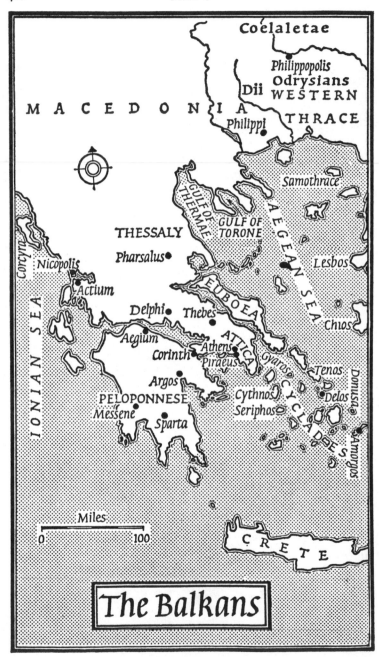

Coelaletae

Philippopolis
**Odrysians
WESTERN**
Dii

M A C E D O N I A
THRACE
Philippi

Samothrace

GULF OF
THERMAE
THESSALY
GULF OF
TORONE

AEGEAN SEA

Pharsalus

Lesbos

Corcyra
IONIAN SEA
Nicopolis
Actium

EUBOEA

Delphi • Thebes

Chios

Aegium
ATTICA
Athens
Corinth
Piraeus

Gyaros

Tenos

Donusa

Argos
PELOPONNESE
Cythnos
Delos
Seriphos

C Y C L A D E S

Messene
Sparta

Amorgos

Miles
0   100

C R E T E

The Balkans

MAP 9   429

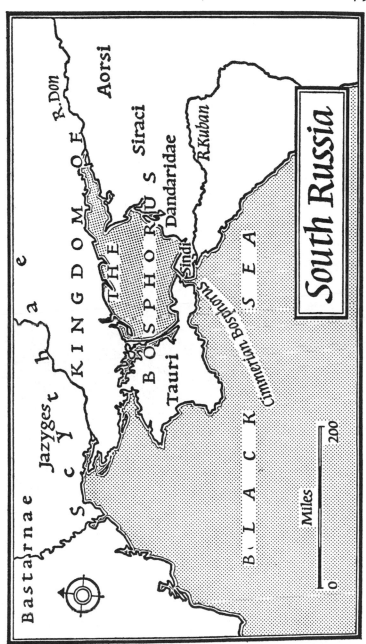

South Russia

Bastarnae

Jazyges

S c y t h a e

R. Don

Aorsi

Siraci

KINGDOM OF

THE BOSPHORUS

Dandaridae

Sindi

R. Kuban

Cimmerian Bosphorus

Tauri

BLACK SEA

Miles
0   200

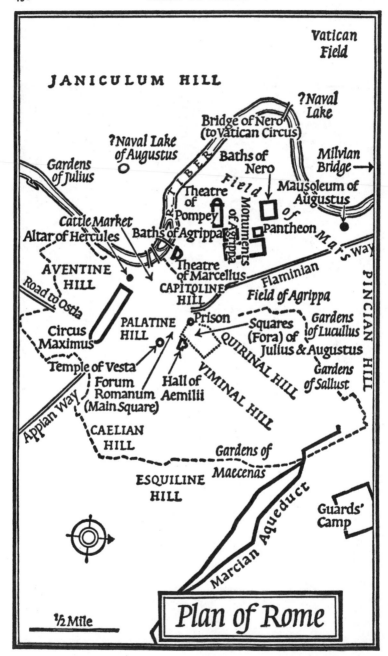

Plan of Rome

GENEALOGICAL TABLES

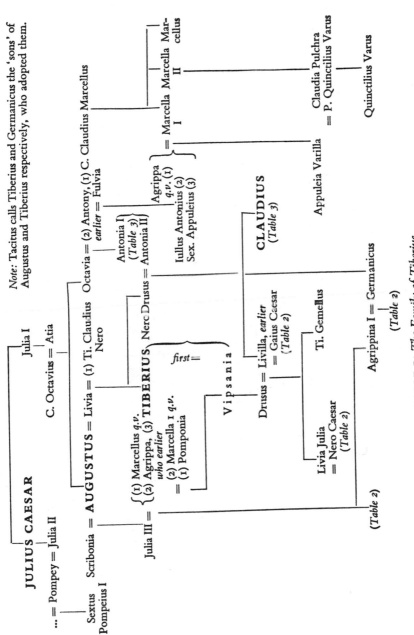

Note: Tacitus calls Tiberius and Germanicus the 'sons' of Augustus and Tiberius respectively, who adopted them.

TABLE 1: *The Family of Tiberius*

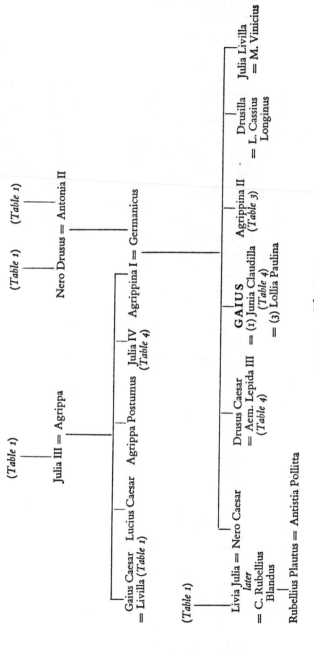

TABLE 2: *The Heirs*

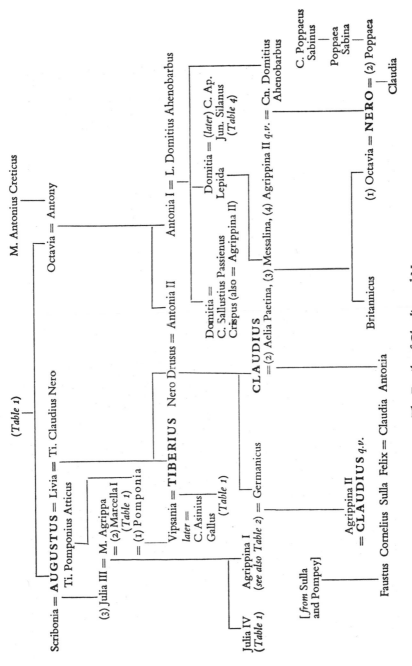

TABLE 3: *The Family of Claudius and Nero*

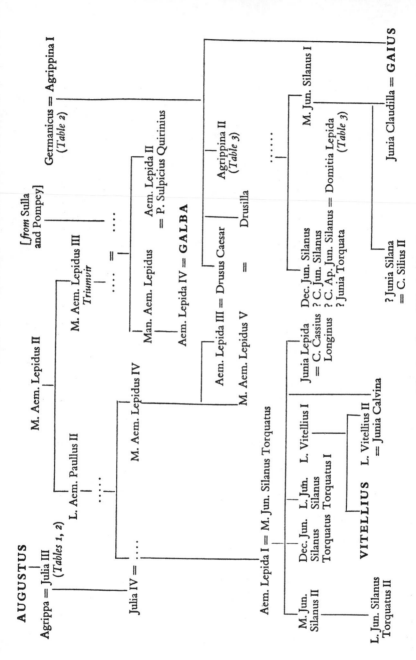

TABLE 4: *The Aemilian and Junian Families*

FURTHER READING

TACITUS

Tacitus, *Agricola* (ed. R. M. Ogilvie and I. Richmond), Oxford, 1967.
Tacitus, *The Agricola and the Germania* (translated by H. Mattingly, rev.
ed. S. A. Handford), Penguin, 1970.
Tacitus, *Histories* (trans. by K. Wellesley), Penguin, 1965; rev. ed. 1968.
D. R. Dudley, *The World of Tacitus*, Secker & Warburg, 1968.
R. Syme, *Tacitus*, Oxford, 1958.
B. Walker, *The Annals of Tacitus*, Manchester, 1952; rev. ed. 1961.
F. R. D. Goodyear, *Tacitus* ('Greece and Rome'), Oxford, 1970.

OTHER ROMAN HISTORIANS

F. E. Adcock, *Caesar as Man of Letters*, Cambridge, 1956.
T. A. Dorey (ed.), *Latin Historians*, Routledge & Kegan Paul, 1966.
M. Grant, *The Ancient Historians*, Weidenfeld & Nicolson, 1970.
M. L. W. Laistner, *The Great Roman Historians*, University of Cali-
fornia, 1947; rev. ed. 1963.
R. Syme, *Sallust*, Cambridge, 1964.
S. Usher, *The Historians of Greece and Rome*, Hamish Hamilton, 1969.
P. G. Walsh, *Livy*, Cambridge, 1961.
There are also translations in the Penguin Classics of Caesar, *Civil War*
(Jane F. Mitchell) and *The Conquest of Gaul* (S. A. Handford); Livy,
The Early History of Rome and *The War with Hannibal* (A. de Sélin-
court), and Sallust, *The Jugurthine War* and *The Conspiracy of Catiline*
(S. A. Handford).
Greek historians of the period include Josephus (G. A. Williamson,
Jewish War).

CONTEMPORARIES OF TACITUS

There are translations in the Penguin Classics of Juvenal, *The Sixteen
Satires* (P. Green), Pliny the Younger, *Letters* (B. Radice), and Sue-
tonius, *The Twelve Caesars* (R. Graves); also of the Greek biographer
Plutarch (three volumes translated by I. Scott-Kilvert and one by
R. Warner).

INDEX

INDEX OF PERSONAL NAMES

*Except for members of the imperial family, whose best-known name is generally given, Romans are mostly designated here by the name of their family (gens).**

*The following (ancient) abbreviations are used for Roman first names
(*praenomina*): A: Aulus; Ap.: Appius; C: Gaius; Cn: Gnaeus; Dec: Decimus;
L: Lucius; M: Marcus; Man: Manius; P: Publius; Q: Quintus; Ser: Servius;
Sex: Sextus; Sp: Spurius; T: Titus; Ti: Tiberius.